Wine Label Language

Wine Label Language

Peter Saunders

FIREFLY BOOKS

A FIREFLY BOOK

Published by Firefly Books Ltd. 2004

First published in 2004 in New Zealand by David Bateman Ltd.,
30 Tarndale Grove, Albany, Auckland, New Zealand

First printing

Publisher Cataloging-in-Publication Data (U.S.)
Saunders, Peter, 1948-
  Wine label language / Peter Saunders.
Revised and updated edition.
[368] p. : col. photos. ; cm.
Originally published: Auckland, New Zealand : Wineglass Publishing Ltd, 1976.
Includes bibliographical references.
Summary: An explanation of the information contained on wine labels from major wine
producing countries including France, Italy, Spain, Portugal, Germany, USA, Canada,
South Africa, Australia, New Zealand, Chile and Argentina.
ISBN 1-55297-720-X (pbk.)
1. Wine and wine label making. 2. Wine Labels. I. Title.
641.2/ 2 21   TP548.S36   2004

National Library of Canada Cataloguing in Publication
Saunders, Peter Lionel, 1948-
        Wine label language / Peter Saunders.
Includes bibliographical references.
ISBN 1-55297-720-X
        1. Wine labels. 2. Wine and wine making--Terminology. I. Title.
TP548.S29 2004   641.2'2'014   C2002-903151-6

Published in the United States in 2004 by
Firefly Books (U.S.) Inc.
P.O. Box 1338, Ellicott Station
Buffalo, New York 14205

Published in Canada in 2004 by
Firefly Books Ltd.
66 Leek Crescent
Richmond Hill, Ontario L4B 1H1

Cover design: Ingrid Paulson
Cover photo: © Johner/Photonica

Printed in China through Colorcraft Ltd., HK

Contents

Preface

The rising interest in the world's wine by an increasingly wider audience indicates that those who sip regularly wish to know more about what they are buying and tasting. Wine fanciers now want to understand more than the distinction between a Chambertin and a Pauillac; they also wish to grasp the more subtle differences between the fine names of the world and find out where each fits into the international spectrum.

Knowing whether to look up the Santenay appellation in a regionalized wine book under Bordeaux, Burgundy, Loire or Rhône can be a challenge to the wine student. So why not produce a book in which all the appellations are listed in alphabetical order for easy reference?

This book began life 25 years ago from my own longing to sort out the information on labels, to understand terms – such as *grand cru* and what it meant in different areas – and to know more about factors that were then considered only of interest to "wine geeks." The book, an amateurish effort, was published and fell on unfertile ground. Now the time seems right, with expanding wine markets all over the world and the changing face of Europe in particular, to publish a single volume reference containing basic information for wine enthusiasts and wine students.

Do "minimum alcohol" and "maximum yield" figures make compelling reading? Perhaps not all the time, but they are relevant when comparing one appellation with another. Such details enable comparison of like with like and show the relative standings of each. They also help clarify an international picture, where figures such as tonnes per hectare provide a useful comparative barometer, although these figures do need to be taken with a grain of salt from region to region.

The grape varieties allowed or required to be grown in an appellation may be of much more interest than yield or alcohol figures, although in many instances these are complex formulae. If appellations were first considered useful for traditional character, or "typicity," many of them today have lost that thrust, with one of several grape varieties able to dominate. Who can find typicity, for example, in an appellation that allows Mourvèdre, Tempranillo or Grenache to be the predominant variety?

The New World has also developed its own set of requirements for labels, varying from the American Viticultural Areas (AVAs) of North America to the debates about soil type and entitlement to names like "Coonawarra" in Australia. Finding meaning and substance requires involvement and lots of investigation. The rising South American picture tells us more about the European system than North America, a reflection on that continent's heritage and history. It's a colorful fabric.

This book has required enormous research in several languages. The sheer volume of so much detail may carry with it the odd slip; indeed it would be remarkable if it didn't, given the variable nature of communications in our everchanging world. I've done my best, despite being occasionally hampered by "official bodies" that don't consider communication with a Kiwi important and also by websites that were years out of date! I ask for your patience and welcome any corrections and updates for later editions, which you can send to my e-mail address at winecast@xtra.co.nz.

My sincere thanks and appreciation to my family for allowing me time off home duties to complete this work. Also to Barbara McDonald who made a magnificent contribution, and to Alan Young of the International Wine Academy for his support and assistance. Bob Campbell's input was part of the initial book 28 years ago, and he has been helpful with contacts and material for this edition as well. There are others who have lent a book, read through sections, offered an e-mail address, and volunteered their help with interest and enthusiasm. My thanks to the network.

To you as readers, thank you for giving this a try. I hope the background and detail, much of it never presented like this before, will enhance your understanding and enjoyment of wine.

Peter Saunders
Auckland, New Zealand
2004

Traditional bottle shapes and colors from the famous regions of Europe are often "borrowed" around the world for similar grape varieties. Here, working clockwise from above, the green Mosel bottle from the Mosel-Saar-Ruwer district of Germany contrasts with the similarly shaped, but distinctly brown bottle of the Rhine River region. The traditional Alsace bottle is widely used in the New World for Rieslings, in particular. The long-necked Bordeaux bottle is often used elsewhere for Cabernet and Merlot based wines, while the sloping shoulders of the traditional Burgundy bottle is often used around the world for the Burgundian varieties of Pinot Noir and Chardonnay.

Joseph Drouhin®

LAFORET

BOURGOGNE
CHARDONNAY

APPELLATION BOURGOGNE CONTROLÉE

MIS EN BOUTEILLE PAR JOSEPH DROUHIN NÉGOCIANT
ÉLEVEUR A BEAUNE, CÔTE - D'OR, FRANCE, AUX CELLIERS
DES ROIS DE FRANCE ET DES DUCS DE BOURGOGNE

www.drouhin.com

13% vol.   FRANCE   75 cl

MISE DU DOMAINE   ESTATE BOTTLED

MEURSAULT
LA BARRE

APPELLATION MEURSAULT CONTROLÉE

—— JEAN MONNIER & SON FILS ——
PROPRIÉTAIRES-RÉCOLTANTS A MEURSAULT, COTE-D'OR

750 ml

The Joseph Drouhin Laforet label shows a popular change on lower price wines from the Bourgogne appellation by showing the name of the grape. This was controversial when it first occurred some 15 years ago but it does help consumers from New World countries who are far more used to buying wines by grape variety than by appellation. The AOC appears as well. Red Burgundy in these cases would state Pinot Noir.

The Meursault wine shows the name of the vineyard site, or *climat*. Because this is not a *premier cru* site, the size of the lettering of the vineyard name must be no more than half the size of the name of the appellation. A *premier cru* wine by contrast can show its name in the same size type – like MEURSAULT CHARMES for example.

Chateau Doisy-Védrines shows not only its appellation but also that it was classified *grand cru* in 1855, a classification used less today but still runs basically true to the ratings made nearly 150 years ago. Sauternes appellation can be used by chateaux in the adjacent Barsac commune – they have the choice of Barsac or Sauternes AOC, in this case choosing Sauternes. The requirements are identical in terms of grapes, alcohol, yield, etc.

The German Zellerschwarze Katz (black cat) is a straight forward example of an area wine. There is Zell (the "er" on the end is like the "er" in New Zealander), the defined area of Schwarze Katz, the classification "Qualitätswein," the iden-tification of A.P. Number and the name of the producer. More specific detail appears in the German section.

The Rheinhessen wine similarly shows the region, "Westhofen" with an "er" on the end and the vineyard name Riechspiel. Because this is a *mit Prädikat* wine, it must also show the classification, in this case *Auslese*, which the wine fits into this year. Under the German system, the classification needs to be earnt each year; unlike the French system which classifies the vineyards regardless of vintage conditions. The grape variety is very specific and must make up at least 95% by volume.

The Pegasus Bay label from New Zealand is only used for wines from their home vineyards in Canterbury and thus no regional name is shown. Most other producers would identify the vineyard region although at this stage there is no regional requirements in New Zealand except that where a region is mentioned, 85% of the wine must come from that region. This can be seen in the Goldwater label from Waiheke Island. Their Zell vineyard is the source of their grapes.

PEIRANO ESTATE

VINEYARDS

1997

OLD VINE

ZINFANDEL

LODI

ALC. 14.4% BY VOL.

ESTATE BOTTLED

Wm. Harrison

Cabernet Sauvignon

1998

NAPA VALLEY
RUTHERFORD DISTRICT

From California, Peirano Estate shows its home in the Lodi American Viticultural Area, but these last words don't have to be written under the AVA as Appellation Contrôlée would in Europe. However, by using the name Lodi, the AVA rules need to be adhered to.

The Wm Harrison Cabernet Sauvignon, however, uses Rutherford District AVA and thus under local rules needs to also specify the Napa Valley AVA in which Rutherford lies.

Spain and Portugal both follow the French and Italian system with the DO (Spain) and the DOC (Portugal) appearing in full immediately under the defined regional (appellation) name. The Portugese label adds the English "Red Wine" beside the Portugese "Vinho Tinto" but not all labels do this. On the Spanish label, because five varieties are allowed in this DO, the name of the grape is identified clearly. Centenaria indicates 100 year old vines.

Part One

The European Way:

Wine of the Land

The European Way:

Wine of the Land

The legacy of European winemakers, whose vineyards have frequently been owned by their families for many generations, is rooted in the land. "This is the wine of my land," they will tell you with pride, "wine like my forefathers made here, in the same way." Not for them the purchase of grapes from regions hundreds, even thousands of miles away to blend into one wine – like Penfolds Grange Shiraz in Australia, for example. In times past, a Rhône red used to be shipped up to Bordeaux to "strengthen" the claret of the day. This is no more.

To be sure, there are multi-regional or even multi-country wines produced in Europe, but such wine tends to be *ordinaire*, classified as *Vin de Table*. The French give their recognition of "quality wine" (a term with significance under the European Union) to specifically denoted areas. *Appellation d'Origine Contrôlée* (AOC) recognizes several hundred named vineyard areas, and producers have the right to use that name on their labels only if the grapes are grown within specific geographical confines and conform to the rules of each area. These rules set down specific grape varieties; pruning and viticultural practices; a maximum yield per hectare of vineyard; required winemaking practices; a minimum alcohol percentage (sometimes allowed to be adjusted by the addition of sugar); and a few other idiosyncratic requirements depending on the area.

The Italian system has both similarities and differences; their classification is *Denominazione di Origine Controllata* (DOC), with the word *garantita* appended in special cases (DOCG). The Spanish have a *Denominación de Origen* (DO) and Portugal has *Denominação de Origem Controlada* (DOC). The aim of each of these is first to define the region, the boundaries of which may be political or natural – like rivers, mountains or roads – specifying the allowable vineyard sites that can use the name of the defined region, and then establish other rules based on history, quality and consistency. Grape varieties are also specified in the regulations of appellations; Italy's DOC regulations even specify what proportion of each variety must be contained in some blends.

Terroir

Only relatively recently have European winemakers given overt recognition to the grapes they grow. Of course they knew their universal names, though they often used local jargon instead. But they had a firm belief that it was the land that gave the wine its character, not the grape. The grape was inherited from generations before and replanted when necessary. It was but a part of the statement of the land, the soil, the drainage, the weather, humidity or lack of it, water supply, the angle of the vineyard towards the sun – in short, the whole natural environment.

The French have a word for this concept: *terroir*, which doesn't translate directly into English. In its holistic use the term includes the people, customs, traditions, even the local food of an area. More commonly, however, *terroir* relates to the land, nearby lakes, rivers and seas, and the climate as it affects the working vineyard. In a new wine region the *terroir* is examined before suitable grapes are chosen. In Europe the grape varieties are there because they have always been. The forefathers had decided what to plant based on *terroir*.

The Italians have been prepared to be flexible about the introduction of new grapes, especially in Tuscany, and there have been some changes to DOCs in response. This has also occurred in Spain. But wine is a long-term business, and passionate, loyal people do not quickly change the heritage of their land.

So even today the grape in European wine is scarcely mentioned on the label unless several grapes are allowed in the appellation, as in some DOCs of Italy, or in Alsace, for example, when customers clearly need to know whether they are buying Hugel Alsace Gewürztraminer or Hugel Alsace Riesling. In situations like this, the grape then becomes important.

Indicating the name of the grape variety that predominates or is entirely used to make up the wine has also been useful as a marketing tool. Now that markets in the U.K., for example, are exposed to Californian Cabernet Sauvignon and Australian Chardonnay, some French producers have also introduced varietal labeling. This is especially so in wines from the Languedoc, but some of the AOC Bourgogne producers also began showing "Chardonnay" and "Pinot Noir" on their labels in the late 1980s.

Yet if we buy a French wine carrying the Chablis or Meursault AOC, we are not told on the label that the wine is made from Chardonnay. We should be drinking "the land" rather than "the grape." That's fine, but with growing interest in wine, and new wine countries using varietal names, more and more wine drinkers want to know what grape is used for each appellation.

Part of this interest has come from the newer wine countries, which have not restricted grape varieties in viticultural areas. Lacking a long wine history like Europe, new countries have experimented widely, and it is not uncommon to find a New World region growing Alsace varieties next to Rhône, Burgundian and Bordeaux grapes. As knowledge and experience increases, some may be withdrawn over time, but currently no New World region limits or restricts which grapes may be grown, even though the boundaries of a viticultural region may be established. Thus the inclusion of varietal names on labels has created interest in varieties rather than geographical areas, the grape rather than the land.

In Los Angeles we hear "I love a good Merlot," while in Paris (and even London until recently) wine drinkers are more inclined to say "I love a good Bordeaux." The first prefers, or thinks of, a grape; the second an area. Both may love their wine equally, but the difference in wine cultures means we consider our wines in different ways.

Of course when we look at regions like Burgundy with its one red and one white grape, the terminology seems so simple compared with five red grapes used in Bordeaux and even more in Southern Rhône. It's so much easier to refer to "Pauillac" or "Gigondas" rather than the varietal mix.

Indeed, the EU won't allow wine labeled with more than two varietals to be imported. So the many wines from around the world that carry a blend of Cabernet Sauvignon, Cabernet Franc, Merlot, perhaps Malbec and Petit Verdot as well, cannot carry a varietal label and instead are given names like Declaration, Quintology, Talisman or Coleraine, to use a few examples from New Zealand.

The European system is of course under criticism in the changing world, especially as new wine countries enter old wine markets. France is now experiencing serious competition in the English market. Italy has pulled out more hectares of vineyards in the last 25 years than most of the new countries collectively have planted. There have been riots and protests in the south of France over subsidies for wine, including the blocking of highways with trucks and attempts to blow up the warehouse of a wine merchant (*négociant*) who bought grapes from across the border rather than local product.

Subsidies in agriculture are an issue not just because of world trade agreements and pressures to cut subsidies, but because traditional European markets are shrinking. Wine consumption per capita in Western Europe is sharply down from 25 years ago, and export growth is more difficult as new countries enter the market and gain publicity, a status and a following.

All these things put pressure on the appellation system; there are no guarantees that what's in place today will hold for 20 more years. Already the Languedoc has started to market a lot of its simple wines (*Vins de Pays*) by the grape variety, purely to compete in markets that know Cabernet and Chardonnay better than European regions.

The orientation towards the land is also a big part of German labels. Germany's wine rule book is focused on a 1971 set of laws that is not always friendly to producer or consumer, yet this too is evolving in a time of change.

Wine law seems timeless, and much of the regulatory detail in this book has remained unchanged for 70 years. But as the market evolves, the new wine countries take on more supply and Europe reduces its vineyard, no system is set in stone. Change in something so historic, however, will be long debated in romantic countries like France and Italy. The 1855 Classification of the wines of Médoc, where châteaux were graded between one and five or "unlisted," has had only one change in the list despite huge changes in the factors surrounding the châteaux themselves.

Perhaps this is why "the land" persists as a vital, driving force. Winemakers come and go, owners change and management styles may differ, but the 1855 Classification shows that almost 150 years later the land, the *terroir*, still gives us a second-growth wine from this vineyard and a fifth-growth from that one, just as it did back then!

VQPRD

Vin de Qualité Produit dans une Région Déterminée (VQPRD) is a European Union definition for "quality wine" and the term, or initials, sometimes appear almost alone (with a brand) on labels, especially from Spain and Portugal. However, under this EU rule "quality wine" covers wine from EU member countries under the appellation system of each *"région déterminée"* (determined region); thus the AOC wines of France, DOC and DOCG wines of Italy, DO wines of Spain, DOC and IPR wines of Portugal, and the *Qualitätswein* and *Qualitätswein mit Prädikat* of Germany are all "quality wines" under EU law.

According to this European law, if wine is not "quality wine," it is "table wine." In France this is called *Vin de Table* or *Vin de Pays*; in Italy the terms used are *Vino da Tavola* and more recently *Indicazione Geografica Tipica* (IGT); in Spain *Vino de Mesa* and *Vino de la Tierra* are table wines; and in Germany *Tafelwein* also has the same status. This is not to say all such wines are poor, indeed many are exceptionally good, but they are wines that have not, or cannot for some reason conform to "quality wine" status.

In striving to achieve consistency, the European Union is encouraging new member countries to develop their own system with some similarities to the European way. Joining the EU required Spain to modernize its labeling system, for example, and other countries with wine industries hoping to join the EU are reviewing their own systems.

Some Future Issues

The issues facing Europe's wine industry today are the same issues facing the wine industry in the New World. For now the appellation system rules, based on area with support from related factors of yield, minimum sugar-alcohol levels and defined grapes proven over time, along with techniques in the vineyard and the winery. Such a system has many advantages. In opening its markets to newer wine countries, the EU likes to see systems in place that require a wine labeled Sonoma to have come from Sonoma-grown grapes, just as a wine from Chablis comes from Chablis and is not adulterated by including it in a blend of anything from California.

In some ways, however, perhaps the system has let itself down by not allowing new varieties to come to the surface, especially in the more staunch parts of Europe. Is it not time to try new clones of Pinot Noir in Bordeaux? Tuscany and Spain have been trying and accepting new varieties, and are being more liberal in order to bring the best to the table. Germany has crossed some pedigree grapes with others that have desirable qualities (like earlier picking, for example) to create new hybrid crosses of all-*vinifera* varieties, which can add new tones to the taste of wine as well as provide economic benefits for growers in difficult, cool and hilly growing conditions.

Another recent and contentious issue in the world of wine is the advent of screw caps. This is a move away from the traditional cork bark, which frequently results in 10 percent of wines being tainted and another 10 percent with less overt taint but a flatness to the wine. In fact, the only real advantage of a cork seems to be the satisfying pop when it is extracted. This is an emotional issue, and reluctance to change seems to be based around public acceptance rather than the quality of the wine so there will be much water to pass under this bridge over the next decade.

Indeed, the long-term acceptance of many of these things must always be slow and elusive. Some drinkers may reject a variety like Kerner, just as many drinkers may resist wines with a screw cap. For others, the grape or the cap doesn't matter – the taste of the wine, sometimes related to price and perceived value, is much more important.

Meanwhile more people the world over are enjoying wine – markets are expanding in the United States and all over Asia, and consumption is edging up in the new wine-producing countries, including consumption of imported wine in countries like the United States, Australia and New Zealand. The wine drinker varies from a budget-conscious university student to a fashion-conscious person keen to be seen with in-vogue wines to the true enthusiast, not always wealthy but with enormous interest in wine and what is behind each bottle.

Such a resurgence of interest in wine means every producing region gains. The demand for classy wines is certainly expanding; some of the most respected labels are becoming exceptionally expensive, and their prestige has awakened an interest in Asian countries, where ownership of a prestige wine can sometimes be of greater importance than its enjoyment.

It is a changing world, a changing market. As wine drinkers, wine writers, wine educators, speciality retailers and marketers for retail chains all become more aware of the finer points of wine, value and prestige will become all-important. With this comes the need to be informed, to understand and appreciate what we are buying, promoting, writing about – and drinking.

CHAPTER 1

France

Appellation d'Origine Contrôlée (AOC)
Vin Doux Naturel (VDN)
Vin Délimité de Qualité Supérieure (VDQS)
Vin de Pays (VdP)
Vin de Table (VdT)

As noted in the introduction to this section, the French have a strong affection for the history and traditions of winemaking. This affection is based on the land and has given rise to the term *terroir* – the collection of natural environmental factors that affect each vineyard and region. One could say that the French labeling system is *terroir*-based, and recognizes each area with a style, a regional typicity – at least in theory.

Appellation d'Origine Contrôlée (AOC)

In a system administered by the *Institut National des Appellations d'Origine* (INAO), some 350 AOCs or defined areas cover the best vineyards of France. For the statistically minded, the number of AOCs could be considerably increased if the reds, whites, rosés and sparklings of some regions, the *premiers crus* of others were separately included. Because they have differing requirements, mostly in grape varieties, yield and alcohol, they could technically be regarded as separate AOCs. But in counting 350 AOCs, we are speaking of the defined areas of land with their own name.

The requirements for each AOC first define the area in which its supplying vineyards must be found – for example, between this road, that river and those mountains. They then state which grape varieties can be grown and sometimes even their proportions, though this is less often stated in France than in Italy. The maximum yield – the greatest quantity of wine that can be produced from each hectare of vineyard – is also specified, as well as the minimum percentage of alcohol of such wines, and certain factors such as the vineyard density, the way the vines are trained and pruned, and the method of vinification permitted. These vary with each AOC and the *usages locaux* – the local traditions of viticulture and winemaking.

To allow an audit trail of the source and progress of each wine, adequate records must be kept in each winery to show the movements of all grapes from the vineyard through the tanks and barrels until final bottling. Conformity is vital to the authenticity of the system. Some allowable grape varieties are no longer used, but they are preserved in the historic nature of the AOC. There is currently very little Malbec used in most Bordeaux AOCs, for example, yet that grape is held up internationally as having its spiritual home there. The AOC concept is based on the land, and what grows on it has traditionally been secondary – not of less importance, but considered to have been sorted out by the forefathers and set down in AOC rules.

AOC wine represents 35 percent to 40 percent of French production, depending on vintage, as crop weight can vary markedly from region to region and from year to year. The production level in viticulture is not established before vintage by a marketing manager talking to a production manager; Mother Nature can wipe out huge proportions of crop with an unkind frost, just when the export orders are flooding in.

AOC wines can be recognized on the label by the use of the words "Appellation Contrôlée" usually split by the insertion of the name of the specific appellation, for example "Appellation Bordeaux Contrôlée." Where this does not occur, the words "Appellation Contrôlée" must appear directly underneath the name of the AOC. Champagne is the only AOC that does not require the words "Appellation Contrôlée" on the label, but the word "CHAMPAGNE" in capitals must be in a strong, bold typeface.

The appearance of an AOC on a label indicates that the wine conforms to the rules; it is not an assurance of quality. Even in terms of consistency of style, there can be variations among wines from vineyards in the same AOC region and the same vintage. The blending of two neighboring estates, for example, may be quite different. In Margaux, one château may have a 55 percent Cabernet Sauvignon content this year while literally across the road, a neighboring château may have 75 percent Cabernet Sauvignon. In Châteauneuf-du-Pape, Grenache may rule in more than 60 percent of AOC wines, but Syrah, Mourvèdre or another allowed variety might be the predominant in the others. So the "typicity" of a region needs to be regarded as flexible.

The creativity of the winemaker is not limited by the AOC, even if some methods (like destemming rather than whole-bunch pressing the grapes, for example) may be standardized in the rule book.

Quality Indications

In some areas, the AOC system exists quite separately from any recognition of quality. In other areas, a quality recognition overlaps the AOC. This can be confusing, so it is worth addressing here. "Grand Cru Burgundy," for example, is a status that recognizes what should be among the best sites of Burgundy. However, rather than using an AOC and adding the words "Grand Cru," in Burgundy these higher status vineyards are given their own AOC. Chambertin and Montrachet are two examples; these are *grand cru* status vineyards yet have no mention of such words on their label – just their own AOC. The next level down, "Premier Cru Burgundy," either has the name of the recognized vineyard hyphenated to the village name (Meursault-Charmes, for example) or the words "Premier Cru" hyphenated to the village name (Meursault-Premier Cru).

If the Burgundy is a single-vineyard wine from a site not classified as *premier cru*, the vineyard name may still be on the label but in a typeface that is half the size. The important issue here is that in Burgundy *grand cru* status is given to the *vineyard* – in other words, the *land*, as noted earlier. This does not mean, however, that every vintage is a top one! Burgundy is a marginal wine site anyway, and not every year will be great. One of the ongoing arguments about classification in the AOC system is simply that the land has the status, not the wine. In Germany's prestige vineyards, a classification system is applied each year to the wine which defines whether it is sold as *Qualitätswein* or as *Auslese*, *Spätlese* or *Beerenauslese*; this starts with the ripeness of the grapes, which must reach a required level for each classification (*refer* page 263).

In St-Émilion in Bordeaux, *grand cru* status is administered to a number of vineyards differently than it is in Burgundy, but still as part of the AOC system. AOC St-Émilion Premier Grand Cru Classé is at the top and (confoundingly, as life is never easy) that particular AOC is divided into two divisions referred to as "A" and "B" – the A-group being the châteaux Ausone and Cheval Blanc, the B-group a further 11 châteaux. The next quality group uses AOC St-Émilion Grand Cru Classé (note in this class the word "Premier" has been dropped). Then there is AOC St-Émilion Grand Cru, which is the third group (or fourth if we allow for "A" and "B" in the top group) despite its use of the term *grand cru*, which in Burgundy means the best. After this there is AOC St-Émilion for those châteaux or vineyards not making it to the higher groups.

Across the river, the Médoc is different again; here the 1855 Classification reigns, grading châteaux into *crus* or "growths." However, this classification, significant and important though it may be, is entirely independent of the AOC system. The AOCs of the area are what appears on the label (Pauillac, Margaux, St-Julien, etc.) while the standing of the château under the classification (first growth, third growth, etc.) requires reference to a completely separate and unrelated list.

To understand the Médoc system, picture a crossroads, with a château and its vineyard on each corner. They all use the same AOC and thus the same grapes and winemaking rules. But one may be a first growth, another a third growth, another a fifth, and one may not make it into the classification at all. It may be that when the classification was made in 1855, different soils were analyzed, or one site may have been a bit more exposed than another, or one may have had a better slope to the south, facing the sun. And from the quality of the wine in the years building up to 1855, each was given a different classification even though they share the same number of sunshine hours.

Although this example is hypothetical, it is common for entirely different classifications to be found on châteaux neighboring each other, or separated by nothing more than a road.

AOCs Within AOCs

The important point to keep in mind about France's 350 named AOCs is that each is an area of land. This simplifies things when various other factors get involved. For example, an AOC may be a very large area like Bordeaux, within which 38 other AOCs make up some of the territory. These are AOCs within an AOC. The Haut-Médoc AOC is within Bordeaux, and within Haut-Médoc there are six more AOCs covering the best areas of the Haut-Médoc.

Burgundy (Bourgogne) is one AOC, but within its boundaries over 120 separate AOCs are recognized for their status, from *grand cru* to *premier cru* to village or commune wines, down to broader area AOCs like Côte de Beaune-Villages, for example. AOC Côtes du Rhône has about 20 AOCs within its borders, and similarly some Loire AOCs also have AOCs within others.

Broader catchall AOCs such as Bordeaux, Bourgogne or Côtes du Rhône will have lower requirements (a higher allowed yield, lower minimum alcohol) than the AOCs within it. AOC Bordeaux has lower standards than AOC Haut-Médoc, while AOC Pauillac (inside Haut-Médoc) has higher standards than AOC Haut-Médoc.

This is especially significant when considering the yield; because the yield is lower in the better quality "inside" AOCs, a higher yield can lead to wine being declassified and sold to the surrounding AOC, as we will see later.

The AOCs of Bordeaux

Bordeaux is a major industrial city and port in the southwest of France. The city is formed at the junction of two rivers, the Garonne and the Dordogne, which becomes the Gironde where they meet and flow out to sea. The vineyard area around the city is known to wine drinkers as Bordeaux, but in French geographical terms it is the Department of Gironde.

AOC Bordeaux covers the wider region, and within it are 38 other AOCs highlighting some of the better areas and different styles. The AOC count rises if white wine is included as a separate AOC when red uses the same name, as in Graves, for example. This is a little misleading to those of us who want simplicity, but the whites do have a different set of rules so in theory they could be considered as a separate AOC.

To qualify for any of the Bordeaux appellations, the red wines must be made from the grower's choice of Cabernet Sauvignon, Cabernet Franc, Merlot, Malbec and Petit Verdot. Almost all Bordeaux reds are blends of two or more of these varieties. Although Cabernet Sauvignon is best known as *the* Bordeaux variety, it is Merlot that dominates the plantings, covering considerably more vineyard area than Cabernet Sauvignon.

White Bordeaux AOCs, including the sweet ones, are made from the grower's choice of Sauvignon Blanc, Sémillon and Muscadelle.

Inside the Haut-Médoc lie some of the big name châteaux of Bordeaux. As quality châteaux, they tend to be in clusters, reflecting specific *terroir*. Six of the AOCs in the Haut-Médoc renowned for the quality of their *terroir* are Margaux, St-Julien, Pauillac, St-Estèphe, Moulis and Listrac. All these AOCs, including Médoc and Haut-Médoc, only have red wine able to qualify for AOC status. Any white wine made in the area can only be sold as Bordeaux AOC.

The 1855 Haut-Médoc Classification

Nearly 150 years ago, the local chamber of commerce in Bordeaux decided to classify the many châteaux of the Haut-Médoc. The process had begun years before, but had become bogged down in discussion and politics. However, the end result has held remarkably true to this day. Only one change has been made – the 1973 elevation of Château Mouton-Rothschild from second growth to first growth (a matter the château has always maintained was an error back in 1855).

Of course some adjustments might be made based on current history if the full list was redone now. At any time, some châteaux may be doing better, or worse, than during the build-up to 1855. New names might also be added to the top listings. But the old list has been remarkably stable as a guide for the wine buyer and drinker. It does not, of course, address variations in vintage. A first growth wine in a poor vintage might be thrown out. But those following the château will know that this was what that vineyard produced that year – and expect to pay less for it if it was not a good year!

What has happened is that sometimes various owners or winemakers, reviewed over a number of vintages in their control, have seen quality rise above or fall below the status of 1855 for some periods. Château Margaux (a château in the Margaux AOC) would almost certainly have not been rated a first growth for a period in the 1970s and early 1980s, before new owners brought in an immediate revamp. It may well be the territory where the grapes are grown that sets the quality, but owners and workers are needed to uphold that quality.

There is a school of thought that says that Graves (including AOC Pessac-Léognan, as it has now become known) was included in the 1855 Classification, which was essentially a grading of all the châteaux down the left bank of the Gironde, running further down the Médoc. Yet only Château Haut-Brion (outside the Médoc, in Graves) was ultimately included because of its outstanding record. The other Graves châteaux were not considered worthy even of fifth-growth status. It's much debated, and the fact that Sauternes and Barsac sweet wines had a classification that year gives weight to the thought that Graves was considered, but only one château made it!

There are 60 top mainly Médoc châteaux given the status of *grand cru* or "classed growth" (the word "growth" being a rather limited interpretation of the French word *cru*) although this term conflicts with its use in St-Émilion, Burgundy and elsewhere.

These 60 top châteaux, which now form an elite group, were divided into five further groups according to quality, starting with *premiers crus* or as we know them, first growths, then *deuxièmes crus* (second growths), down to fifth growths.

Below the top 60 châteaux, there have been attempts to classify some of the balance. *Bourgeoise Supérieure* recognizes the best of the rest, the "superior middle class." Of these, 13 châteaux have been singled out as *cru exceptionnel*, an evolved and unofficial classification.

The AOCs of Burgundy (Bourgogne)

The name burgundy (like chablis and champagne) has often been borrowed and applied to wines by regions around the world, but it is now gradually being phased out from countries that wish to export into Europe. The EU won't recognize burgundy other than from Burgundy, chablis other than from Chablis and champagne other than from Champagne.

Burgundy is a region with a lot of appellations but very small holdings. The division of vineyards under old French law here has meant that many people and companies have ended up owning very small parts of a vineyard, often no more than an acre (less than half a hectare) and sometimes just part of a row. This also means the wine is made in small quantities (compared with an average château in Bordeaux, which would have about 100 acres [40 ha] of vineyard under one owner). Often an extended family may combine their grapes from the same appellation and the resulting wine may be largely sold to a wine merchant (*négociant*) who may blend various parcels of wine, including those from his own vineyard holdings, to sell in larger, more economic quantities. Although substantially smaller than Bordeaux, Burgundy has far more AOCs, partly because of historic inheritance laws introduced by Napoleon in the early 1800s that stated property must be equally divided among all heirs. One vineyard of 148 acres (60 ha) may have as many as 120 owners.

The Burgundy wine region comprises a "strip" that runs south from Dijon to Lyon in central France, plus Chablis – a separate area to the northwest of Dijon. In French geographical terms the province of Burgundy (le Bourgogne) covers several *Départements*; but in wine region terms Chablis, Côte d'Or, the hills of Mâcon and Chalon (Mâconnais, Chalonnais) and Beaujolais just north of Lyon all come under the general name "Burgundy" in a generous sweep that includes many ranges of quality and styles but remarkably few grapes. Most white AOC wine in this area is from Chardonnay grapes, with a couple of minor AOCs allowing Aligoté, while reds are from Pinot Noir – apart from Beaujolais, which is based around the Gamay Noir.

The Côte d'Or ("slope of gold") is the most prestigious part of Burgundy in terms of attention and discussion. It begins at Dijon and runs south. The northern half of the Côte d'Or is called the Côte de Nuits (*nuits* means nights) and the emphasis here is on Pinot Noir grapes. The southern half is the Côte de Beaune (Beaune being the name of the main city and center of the Burgundy trade) and its wines are based around Chardonnay. Red and white wines are made in both Côte de Beaune and Côte de Nuits, but it is notable that the *grand cru* of the north (Nuits) is related to Pinot Noir and the *grand cru* of the south (Beaune) to Chardonnay. There is one exception, right on the border: Corton is a red wine *grand cru* from just inside the Côte de Beaune.

After *grand cru,* each with its own AOC, the next classification level is *premier cru,* sometimes written as 1er Cru. This is a division of the village AOC – like Meursault Premier Cru, for example – recognizing the special qualities of those vineyards within AOC Meursault. Often the vineyard name is used instead of the words "Premier Cru" but blends of two or three *premier cru* sites within the AOC can also hold the classification. Next are village appellations, like Meursault, Gevrey-Chambertin and Vosne-Romanée. Sometimes these village names are linked (hyphenated) to the name of a *grand cru* (like Gevrey-Chambertin) but are quite separate AOCs.

South of the Côte d'Or are hills known as the Mâconnais (around the town of Mâcon) and Chalonnais (around the town of Chalon). This region, also using Chardonnay and Pinot Noir, produces some less-highly regarded whites and reds; but these hilly sites have improved enormously and some fine wines can be found under AOCs like Pouilly-Fuissé, St-Veran and Mâcon-Villages. Such wines can be especially good value, because their prices are usually much lower than wines from the Côte d'Or.

South of these hills is AOC Beaujolais based on the Gamay grape, this includes AOC Beaujolais-Villages, which recognizes the better sites, and, at the top of the tree, 10 Beaujolais *crus* with their own AOCs, usually based around a hill or elevated site. The fresh new wine released early each year in November is Beaujolais Nouveau, which comes under either the Beaujolais or Beaujolais-Villages AOCs.

The AOCs of the Rhône

The valley south of Lyon down to the Mediterranean Sea is much easier to understand than the Bordeaux region or the complexities of Burgundy. Draw a line across the middle of the Rhône Valley just north of Montélimar and label the halves north and south. The north is based around the Syrah grape and has mainly red wine AOCs. A little Viognier (white grape) is allowed to be blended with AOC Côte Rôtie. There is also a tiny AOC in Château-Grillet that uses Viognier. Some other white grapes, Marsanne and Rousanne, provide a little white wine for AOC Hermitage. But most of the wine from the northern Rhône is Syrah-based red, under the AOCs of Hermitage, Crozes-Hermitage, St-Joseph and Côte Rôtie.

The southern half of the Rhône gives us blends, predominantly red. Grenache is the most predominant variety, blended with Syrah, Cinsault, Mourvèdre and others, as considered appropriate, in AOCs like Châteauneuf-du-Pape, Gigondas and Vacqueyras and in lighter styles in AOCs like Tavel. Wine writer Jancis Robinson suggests Syrah gives longevity to Grenache, a comment meant lightheartedly no doubt, but which probably contains a grain of truth – the long history of winemaking in the Rhône Valley has allowed plenty of time to figure out what works well where, and with what.

Yields

The maximum yield factor in France is expressed in hectoliters of wine per hectare of vineyard (hl/ha). A hectoliter (100 liters) is 26.42 gallons; a hectare is 2.47 acres. A maximum yield is set for each of the 350 AOCs. In Sauternes and Barsac where *Botrytis cinerea* (the noble rot) reduces the quantity, the allowable yield is the lowest in France at 25 hl/ha, while in Alsace the plain "Alsace" AOC is at the other extreme – 100 hl/ha of some varieties is allowed.

Control of the yield has a two-fold purpose. When the AOC concept was emerging in the late 1920s, the control of supply was important. It was not desirable for winemakers to produce a whole stack of wine and flood or manipulate the market. Secondly, over-production was becoming an aim in itself; this was done through the use of fertilizers but greed was also encouraging growers to use special pruning techniques, water the vines close to picking and employ other methods to enhance volume at the cost of reducing quality. Hence yield has since been policed as part of AOC limits.

Under the historic "cascade" system, the extra yield is transferable in some instances, should nature produce a big-yielding vintage. As an example, let's say a property in St-Julien produced 55 hl/ha of wine in a given year. It could use 43 hl/ha for its home label and "declassify" 3 hl/ha into AOC Haut-Médoc, a further 7 hl/ha into Bordeaux AOC, and 2 hl/ha would have to become *Vin de Table*. Of course the property name or top DOC cannot be used on any declassified wine. And there's a further weakness in that the better AOC, whose quality a low yield was designed to protect, has still produced 55 hl/ha and is thus lighter and potentially dilute, even though only part of the production carries that AOC.

An alternative to this flawed system was introduced in the 1970s. On to the base maximum yield or *tenement de base* (as shown in the pages ahead for each AOC), local grower committees review each vintage and seek a higher (or lower in theory) yield from the INAO to suit the specific vintage conditions. Up to a 20 percent increase is available on application by specific growers, who must submit their wine to a tasting panel for approval; if rejected, the whole lot must be distilled. The moral of the story here is don't apply for a higher yield unless you're sure the extra production is good enough.

What this new system does allow is that wine from a vintage that has given a larger yield without reducing quality – and such years do occur throughout the world – can be sold under its home label, rather than having to be cascaded and declassified into other AOCs.

In Burgundy, where technology in the vineyard and winery is a considerably better than in the early days, the maximum yields have been under close scrutiny recently. Growers have been telling authorities that they can produce more of equal quality than the official limits, especially in the *grand cru* AOCs. As a result, allowable maximum yields have been raised by 10 to 20 percent. In Bordeaux, AOCs like Pauillac and Margaux have also been lifted from 40 to 45 hl/ha in the 1990s.

Vin Doux Naturel (VDN)

A handful of areas in the Languedoc, the Rhône and Roussillon use this appellation look-alike for one type of wine. Strictly speaking, a VDN is not an AOC, but the production of the wine is monitored in the same way to ensure it conforms to the style. Production methods vary slightly among the VDNs, but essentially very ripe grapes with the potential for 14 percent alcohol are crushed, partly fermented and then fortified with pure grape spirit to retain natural grape sugar and acidity at about 15 percent alcohol. This style of wine can generally be enjoyed young, while fresh, aromatic and fruity.

Vin Délimité de Qualité Supérieure (VDQS)

Vin Délimité de Qualité Supérieure (VDQS) is an appellation similar to an AOC in that it has a defined area and a similar set of regulations in line with local varieties and traditions. VDQS does qualify as "quality wine" under the EU system, but VDQS does not have the status of AOC, and the difference is noticeable in lower alcohol requirements and higher yields. VDQS rates higher than *Vin de Pays* in the pecking order of quality, and in many instances VDQS status has been accorded a few years prior to an area becoming an AOC as a form of apprenticeship. VDQS status can be a proving ground before higher status is bestowed.

VDQS wine must have the words (in full) shown on the label underneath the specific VDQS area in the same way as an AOC. As of today, VDQS wines have not reached more than about 1 percent of French wine volume.

Wine Terms

Alcool	Alcohol.
Blanc	White.
Brut	Dry, for sparkling wine.
Cave	Cellars where wine is made.
Climat	Single-vineyard site, sometimes a specific part of a vineyard.
Clos	Enclosed vineyard, usually surrounded by a wall or sometimes a hedge. Mostly used in Burgundy.
Côte	Slope.
Domaine	A vineyard estate.
Doux	Sweet.
Récolte	Harvest or vintage.
Rouge	Red.
Sec	Dry, for still wine.
Vendange	Grape harvest, sometimes the year of the vintage.
Vigne	Vine.
Vignoble	Vineyard.
Vin	Wine.
Vin de Garde	Wine which will improve with age.
Vin de Pays	Table wine.
Vin de Table	Table wine.
Viticulteur	Grape grower.

Appellations of France

Ajaccio   **Region: Corsica**
Appellation Contrôlée
Refer **Coteaux d'Ajaccio**

Aloxe-Corton   **Region: Burgundy**
Appellation Contrôlée
Red, min alc 10.5%, Premier Cru 11%; max yield 40 hl/ha. White, min alc 11%, Premier Cru 11.5%; max yield 45 hl/ha.
Grapes: Red, Pinot Noir. White, Chardonnay.

AOC to the north of the Côte de Beaune, just over the "border" from Côte de Nuits, making mostly red. Bordering some of the great Corton *grand cru* AOCs, Aloxe-Corton is generally highly regarded. The *premiers crus* of the adjacent villages of Ladoix and Pernand-Vergelesses may also use the Aloxe-Corton appellation.

Alsace   **Region: East border,**
Appellation Contrôlée   **on the banks of the Rhine**
Red, min alc 9%. White and rosé 8%. Max yield 100 hl/ha.
Grapes: (named varietally on label) Riesling, Gewürztraminer, Muscat, Pinot Gris, Pinot Blanc, Pinot Noir, Sylvaner, Chasselas, Auxerrois, Klevner. Note that wine labeled Pinot Blanc may come from white Pinot Noir, Pinot Gris or Auxerrois. Auxerrois is not widely used on labels and it can be blended with wines labeled as Pinot Blanc and Klevner.
Sélection de Grains Nobles: wine made from botrytis-affected grapes.
Alsace Edelzwicker ("noble mixture") usually represents a light and easy blend of the white grapes.
Vendange Tardive ("late picked") since 1983 can only be made from the four "premium" grapes (Riesling, Gewürztraminer, Muscat and Pinot Gris) without any enrichment and with a minimum sugar content of 220 g/L for Riesling and Muscat and 243 g/L for Gewürztraminer and Pinot Gris. Not all are botrytis-affected. The German regulatory system is in place, where growers must advise in advance that they wish to make Vendange Tardive wine, and picking is restricted until a specific date, with sugar levels (*oechsle*, refer page 269) checked before harvest. Despite all the extra sugar at harvest, not all wines are very sweet, because some producers allow the higher sugar to ferment out into alcohol.

The Alsace wine area is some 68 miles (110 km) long by an average 2 miles (3 km) wide, across the Rhine River from Germany. AOC wine can come from some 94 villages within the area, although the better wines are generally thought to come from the area to the south, between Ribeauvillé and Guebwiller. One AOC covered the region for many years but the Alsace Grand Cru appellation was introduced in 1983 to highlight better sites

for four grapes. The region has been part of France and part of Germany alternately over the centuries and this is reflected in the mixed cultures, the names of towns and people, and the mix of grape varieties, some of which are not seen elsewhere in France.
Refer **Alsace Grand Cru** and **Crémant d'Alsace.**

Alsace Grand Cru   Region: East border,
Appellation Contrôlée   on the banks of the Rhine

White only, min alc 10% for Riesling and Muscat, 12% for Pinot Gris and Gewürztraminer. Max yield 70 hl/ha.

Grapes: Must be 100% from one of four grape varieties – Riesling, Muscat, Gewürztraminer or Pinot Gris. The variety must be named on the label.

The best Alsace vineyards were recognized in a 1983 allocation of *grand cru* status, but only for these four grape varieties. Thus wines made from grapes grown on these vineyards can claim this appellation, which has a higher minimum alcohol content and a noticeably lower maximum yield requirement than for the larger Alsace AOC. A taste test to prove quality and typicity is also required. Note that wines labeled "Appellation Alsace Contrôlée Grand Cru" – i.e., with the words "Grand Cru" outside the appellation – are only applicants for *grand cru* status and are under review. There is some controversy over this appellation, and not all are regarded as highly as they might be, while some with the status choose not to use it for various reasons, including the requirement to reduce yield. There has also been consideration given to an Alsace *premier cru* level to sit in the middle, but while *grand cru* has its problems in recognized quality status, any further status will be opposed by many.

Anjou   Region: Loire
Appellation Contrôlée

Red, min alc 10%, max yield 40 hl/ha. White, min alc 9.5%, max yield 45 hl/ha.

Grapes: Red, Cabernet Sauvignon and Franc, Gamay, Pineau d'Aunis. White, Chenin Blanc, Chardonnay, Sauvignon Blanc.

AOC from both sides of the Loire River, to the south of the town of Angers. The better areas within have their own appellations. This leaves Anjou with fairly plain wine, but it can also be good value.
Refer **Rosé d'Anjou.**

Anjou-Coteaux de la Loire   Region: Loire
Appellation Contrôlée

White only, min alc 11%, max yield 40 hl/ha.

Grape: Chenin Blanc.

AOC on the Loire to the west of the town of Angers. Grapes are picked late, resulting in sweet wines of good repute.

Anjou-Gamay   Region: Loire
Appellation Contrôlée
Red only, min alc 10%, max yield 40 hl/ha.
Grape: Gamay.

Gamay, the Beaujolais grape, offers an easy-drinking, dry red quaffing wine.

Anjou Mousseux   Region: Loire
Appellation Contrôlée
Sparkling white and rosé, min alc 9.5%, max yield 65 hl/ha.
Grapes: Red, Cabernet Sauvignon and Franc, Gamay, Groslot, Pineau
d'Aunis. Rosé, same grapes as red, but does not include Gamay. White,
Chenin Blanc, Chardonnay, Sauvignon Blanc.

Predominantly *méthode traditionnelle* (the method must be stated on the
label) from an AOC on both sides of the Loire near the town of Angers.
Usually lightly sweet.

Anjou-Villages   Region: Loire
Appellation Contrôlée
Red only, min alc 9.5%, max yield 50 hl/ha.
Grapes: Cabernet Sauvignon and Franc.

Relatively new and well-spread AOC. This is considered a more serious red
from the winery, using more classical techniques.

Anjou-Villages-Brissac   Region: Loire
Appellation Contrôlée
Red only, min alc 9.5%, max yield 50 hl/ha.
Grapes: Cabernet Sauvignon and Franc.

A recent AOC (1996) respecting the vineyards of Brissac, which claim individual style and recognition.

Arbois   Region: Jura
Appellation Contrôlée
Red and rosé, min alc 10%, max yield 55 hl/ha. White, min alc 12%, max
yield 60 hl/ha.
Grapes: Red and rosé, Poulsard, Trousseau, Pinot Noir. White, Chardonnay,
Savagnin.
Vin jaune: Wine made from the Savagnin grape and aged in casks for six
years, in which time a *flor* film grows across the top of the wine, leaving it
similar to an unfortified sherry, with min alc of 11.5%. Bottled in a stubby
traditional bottle. Château-Chalon nearby is an AOC with a similar style.
Vin de paille: Savagnin grapes only are picked when very ripe and laid
out on straw wine mats (*paille* means "straw") to assist evaporation of the
water, leaving a rich, luscious high-alcohol wine. Min alc 14.5%, max yield
25 hl/ha.

Pupillin: Made from grapes grown in this village.

This unusual mix of red varieties thrives on the limestone and sandy soil of the area, producing robust red as well as the *vin jaune* and *vin de paille* for which the area is best known in some markets.

Arbois Mousseux   *Region: Jura*
Appellation Contrôlée
Sparkling red and white, min alc 10%, max yield 60 hl/ha.
Grapes: Chardonnay and Savagnin.

Sparkling wine from an area in the north of the Jura, to the east of Burgundy. Made by the champagne method, although not claiming to be half that standard.

Arbois Pupillin   *Region: Jura*
Appellation Contrôlée
Refer **Arbois.** (Pupillin is a subregion of Arbois.)

Auxey-Duresses   *Region: Burgundy*
Appellation Contrôlée
Red, min alc 10.5%, Premier Cru 11%; max yield 40 hl/ha. White, min alc 11%, Premier Cru 11.5%; max yield 45 hl/ha.
Grapes: Red, Pinot Noir. White, Chardonnay.

AOC in central Côte de Beaune, adjacent to Meursault and Volnay. Mostly red wine. Not a prestige or sought-after burgundy but its nine *premiers crus* are spoken of highly and represent about a quarter of Auxey-Duresses AOC vineyards.

Bandol   *Region: Southeast France*
Appellation Contrôlée
Red, white and rosé, min alc 11%, max yield 40 hl/ha.
Grapes: Red and rosé, Grenache, Cinsault, Mourvèdre, Syrah, Carignan. White, Trebbiano, Bourboulenc, Clairette, Sauvignon Blanc.

AOC on the Mediterranean Coast in the district of Provence some 25 miles (40 km) from Marseille. This was not always a fashionable AOC but it has developed a much stronger image through the 1990s. Its best red is rated as highly as any in Provence, and is well-priced. Rosé is spicy and vibrant. Little white is made.

Banyuls   *Region: Roussillon*
Appellation Contrôlée
Red and white, min alc 15%, max yield 30 hl/ha.
Grapes: Grenache Noir min 50%, Grenache Blanc and Gris, Maccabeo, Tourbat, Muscat à Petits Grains, Muscat d'Alexandrie, Carignan, Syrah, Cinsault.

Vin Doux Naturel of lightly-fortified wine, made from red grapes as part of the blend and aged in wood; some is left to develop mellow oxidized and *rancio* characters, like sherry.

Banyuls Grand Cru   **Region: Roussillon**
Appellation Contrôlée
Red and white, min alc 15%, max yield 30 hl/ha, min wood-age
30 months.
Grapes: Red, Grenache Noir min 75%, Carignan, Syrah, Cinsault, Maccabeo, Tourbat, Muscat à Petits Grains, Muscat d'Alexandrie, Grenache Blanc and Gris.

With its minimum wood-aging requirement, this is supposedly a step up from "plain" Banyuls *Vin Doux Naturel.*

Barsac   **Region: Bordeaux**
Appellation Contrôlée
Sweet white only, min alc 13%, max yield 25 hl/ha.
Grapes: Sauvignon Blanc, Sémillon, Muscadelle.

AOC adjacent to Sauternes, 25 miles (40 km) southeast of Bordeaux city. Châteaux within Barsac are permitted to use AOC Sauternes but most prefer to use Barsac. Barsac has some obvious similarities to Sauternes in its sweet, luscious, botrytis-affected white, but is generally less heavy (although "lighter" would convey the wrong impression). This is usually a reflection of Barsac having less gravelly soil but a little more clay. Certainly delicious, luscious sweet wines.

Bâtard-Montrachet   **Region: Burgundy**
Appellation Contrôlée
White only, min alc 11.5%, max yield 40 hl/ha.
Grape: Chardonnay.

Grand Cru AOC of 30 acres (12 ha), partly in Puligny-Montrachet and partly Chassagne-Montrachet. This vineyard borders the great Montrachet vineyard and although seldom priced as highly, is still highly respected as a fine white burgundy.

Béarn   **Region: Southwest France**
Appellation Contrôlée
Red, white and rosé, min alc 10.5%, max yield 50 hl/ha.
Grapes: Red and rosé, Tannat min 60% (usually blended with Cabernet Sauvignon and Franc), Fer. White, Petit Manseng, Gros Manseng, Roussette, Camaralet, Sauvignon Blanc.

AOC in the lower western corner of France, near the Spanish border. Best known for hearty red; very little white.

Béarn-Bellocq   **Region: Southwest France**
Appellation Contrôlée
Mainly red, min alc 10.5%, max yield 50 hl/ha.
Grapes: Red and rosé, Tannat min 60% (usually blended with Cabernet
Sauvignon and Franc), Fer. White, Petit Manseng, Gros Manseng,
Roussette, Sauvignon Blanc.

A northern Bellocq subdivision within AOC Béarn. A similar hearty style to
Béarn with a slightly elevated reputation.

Beaujolais   **Region: Beaujolais**
Appellation Contrôlée
Red and rosé, min alc 10%, max yield 55 hl/ha. White, min alc 10%, max
yield 60 hl/ha.
Grapes: Red, Gamay. White, Chardonnay, Aligoté.

Beaujolais is an area south of the Côte d'Or, a few kilometers north of Lyon.
It runs some 43 miles (70 km) in length and averages 3 miles (5 km) wide.
In the greater Beaujolais AOC, there are some 100 villages of which 10 are
designated *cru* status. Each of these villages has its own AOC, which are
listed separately – Brouilly, Chénas, Chiroubles, Côte de Brouilly, Fleurie,
Julienas, Morgon, Moulin-à-Vent, Régnié, St-Amour. Thirty-five villages are
entitled to the AOC Beaujolais-Villages appellation. These supposedly have
a higher standard than AOC Beaujolais yet not as high as the 10 *cru*. AOC
Beaujolais Supérieur is given to a small number of vineyards; it requires a
higher minimum alcohol content. Some Beaujolais and Beaujolais Supérieur
is also produced from declassified wine from the Beaujolais-Villages appellation and the 10 *cru*. Only 1% of Beaujolais is white wine.

Beaujolais Nouveau is an early-released style of wine, not with its own
AOC but using that of Beaujolais, Beaujolais Supérieur or Beaujolais-Villages.
Released on the third Thursday of November, its popularity worldwide has
diminished since the 1980s and early 1990s but remains a celebration of early wine from the season's harvest. This is helped by the Beaujolais fermenting
practice of partial carbonic maceration, which aids young, fruity styles.

Jancis Robinson says in her *Oxford Concise Wine Companion* (2001):
"Beaujolais at its best provides the yardstick for all the world's attempts to
put red refreshment into a bottle, a wine which is flirtatious, with a juicy
aroma..."

Beaujolais Supérieur   **Region: Beaujolais**
Appellation Contrôlée
Red and white, min alc 10.5%, max yield 55 hl/ha.
Grape: Red, Gamay.

A small number of vineyards are assigned this AOC when their alcohol is at
a higher level than AOC Beaujolais.

Beaujolais-Villages   **Region: Beaujolais**
Appellation Contrôlée
Red, min alc 10.5%, max yield 50 hl/ha.
Grapes: Red, Gamay and rarely Pinot Noir.

AOC that recognizes designated "better" villages, generally to the north of
the Beaujolais area.

Beaune   **Region: Burgundy**
Appellation Contrôlée
Red, min alc 10.5%, Premier Cru 11%; max yield 40 hl/ha. White, min alc
11%, Premier Cru 11.5%; max yield 45 hl/ha.
Grapes: Red, Pinot Noir. White, Chardonnay.

Wine from an area surrounding the north of the city of Beaune extending up a slope away from Beaune, of which the best vineyards lie between
755–1050 feet (230–320 m). A strip 2.5 miles (4 km) long by an average of
half a mile (less than 1 km) wide carries a large number of *premiers crus*. The
wine of Beaune is predominantly red and contains no *grands crus* despite its
long list of *premiers crus*. It is looked on highly, however, as consistently fine
burgundy, able to age well over five to seven years.

Bellet   **Region: Provence**
Appellation Contrôlée
Red and rosé, min alc 10.5%, max yield 40 hl/ha. White, min alc 11%, max
yield 40 hl/ha.
Grapes: Red, Braquet, Folle Noire, Grenache, Cinsault. White, Rolle,
Chardonnay.

AOC on the Mediterranean Coast, just outside Nice, in Provence. Not an
area of great repute, but the rosé is very popular with visitors to the Riviera.
Little is exported.

Bergerac   **Region: East of Bordeaux**
Appellation Contrôlée
Red, min alc 10%, max yield 55 hl/ha. Rosé, min alc 11%, max yield
55 hl/ha. White, min alc 10.5%, max yield 60 hl/ha.
Grapes: Red, Cabernet Franc, Sauvignon, Merlot. White, Sauvignon Blanc,
Sémillon, Muscadelle.

An area of no great distinction on the Dordogne River inland from Bordeaux.
Heady reds are the most voluminous, but dry and botrytis-affected sweet
whites are also popular.

Bienvenues-Bâtard-Montrachet   **Region: Burgundy**
Appellation Contrôlée
White only, min alc 11.5%, max yield 40 hl/ha.
Grape: Chardonnay.

Highly regarded, 10-acre (4-ha) single-vineyard Grand Cru AOC in the village of Puligny-Montrachet in the Côte de Beaune, neighboring the great Le Montrachet vineyard.

Blagny   **Region: Burgundy**
Appellation Contrôlée
Red, min alc 10.5%, max yield 40 hl/ha.
Grape: Pinot Noir

A tiny AOC of less than 25 acres (10 ha). Some vineyards spill over the border into Meursault and Puligny-Montrachet. The quality is regarded generally as high, although only small quantities are produced. Only red wine uses the Blagny AOC; white wine made in the region (from Chardonnay) uses either AOCs Meursault or Puligny-Montrachet, depending where the vineyard is.

Blanc-Fumé-de-Pouilly   **Region: Loire**
Appellation Contrôlée
An alternative name for AOC Pouilly-Fumé.

Blanquette de Limoux   **Region: Languedoc**
Appellation Contrôlée
Sparkling white only, min alc 10%, max yield 50 hl/ha.
Grapes: Mauzac (known locally as Blanquette) min 70%, Chardonnay and Chenin Blanc up to 30%.

AOC around the town of Limoux, south of Carcassonne. Hilly area has some variability in elevation, and soils and wines can vary accordingly. Mostly champagne techniques (*méthode traditionnelle*) are used and almost all wine is dry to dryish.

AOC Limoux covers the non-sparklings, AOC Crémant de Limoux covers sparklings with more Chardonnay in the blend and AOC Blanquette Méthode Ancestrale (*below*) covers those bottled just before fermentation is finished to provide a little *pétillance*.

Blanquette Méthode Ancestrale   **Region: Languedoc**
Appellation Contrôlée
Lightly fizzy white only, min alc 10%, max yield 50 hl/ha.
Grape: Mauzac.

AOC around the town of Limoux, south of Carcassonne, retaining the traditional *ancestrale* sparkling method. This involves bottling wine from Mauzac grapes just before fermentation is finished, allowing some *pétillance* in the wine; it is sold without disgorgement, so is a little cloudy. Style varies from being like a good sweet cider to dry and appetizing. The AOC Blanquette de Limoux (*above*) is a partner; but allows Chardonnay and Chenin to be added, and disgorgement to be carried out.

Blayais   Region: Bordeaux
Appellation Contrôlée
Alternative spelling for **Blaye**.

Blaye (also known as Blayais)   Region: Bordeaux
Appellation Contrôlée
Red, min alc 10%, max yield 50 hl/ha. White, min alc 10%, max yield
45 hl/ha.
Grapes: Red, Cabernet Sauvignon and Franc, Merlot, Malbec, Petit Verdot.
White, Sauvignon Blanc, Sémillon, Muscadelle.

AOC on the right bank of the Gironde River in upper Bordeaux. It is adjacent
to Bourg, with which some similarity in wine style is apparent. There are
three AOCs within this AOC: Premières Côtes de Blaye (mostly red), Côtes
de Blaye (white only) and Blaye (mostly white). Generally an area thought of
as sound and good value.

Bonnes Mares   Region: Burgundy
Appellation Contrôlée
Red only, min alc 11.5%, max yield 35 hl/ha.
Grape: Pinot Noir.

Côte de Nuits Grand Cru AOC of 37 acres (15 ha) mostly within Chambolle-
Musigny village but a tiny part within Morey-St-Denis. Highly regarded for
sturdy, long-life wines, but missing a little of the respect given to some other
grands crus.

Bonnezeaux   Region: Loire
Appellation Contrôlée
White only, min alc 12%, max yield 25 hl/ha.
Grape: Chenin Blanc (known locally as Pineau de la Loire).

AOC on the Layon River (a tributary of the Loire) in the Anjou district. Well
regarded (but not quite famous) for sweet white. A low-yielding wine com-
bining late-picked and botrytis-affected grapes.

Bordeaux   Region: Bordeaux
Appellation Contrôlée
Red and rosé, min alc 9.5%, max yield 55 hl/ha. White, min alc 11%, max
yield 60 hl/ha.
Grapes: Red, Cabernet Franc and Sauvignon, Merlot, Malbec, Petit Verdot,
Carmenère. White, Sémillon min 70%, Sauvignon Blanc, Muscadelle,
Merlot Blanc up to 30%, Colombard, Mauzac, Ondenc, Trebbiano.

The broadest AOC of Bordeaux; the big catchall regional appellation within
which AOCs with specific styles, *terroir* and qualities stake their claim. AOC
Bordeaux has the lesser vineyards of the region – those that don't fall into
any other AOC within the province. This doesn't mean all wine is of inferior

quality; in fact the 2000 vintage, for example, has produced a good range of well-fruited reds at very affordable prices.

Bordeaux Côtes de Castillon   **Region: Bordeaux**
Appellation Contrôlée
Refer **Côtes de Castillon.**

Bordeaux Côtes de Francs   **Region: Bordeaux**
Appellation Contrôlée
Red and white, min alc 11%, max yield 50 hl/ha.
Grapes: Red, Merlot, Cabernet Sauvignon and Franc, Malbec. White, Sémillon, Sauvignon Blanc, Trebbiano, Colombard, Muscadelle.

AOC north of Côtes de Castillon, east of St-Émilion; in fact until their own AOC status, wines here were sold under AOC St-Émilion. Now the reds are making a claim to fame with a growing reputation. A little white is made.

Bordeaux-Haut-Benauge   **Region: Bordeaux**
Appellation Contrôlée
White only, min alc 11.5%, max yield 50 hl/ha.
Grapes: Sémillon, Sauvignon Blanc, Muscadelle, Merlot Blanc, Columbard, Trebbiano, Mauzac.

AOC on the south of Entre-Deux-Mers producing dry and slightly sweet white quaffing wine. Some producers sell their wine under the AOC Bordeaux.

Bordeaux Mousseux   **Region: Bordeaux**
Appellation Contrôlée
Sparkling white only, min alc 10%, max yield 50 hl/ha.
Grapes: Sauvignon Blanc, Sémillon, Trebbiano, Muscadelle, Colombard.

Sparklings made within the Bordeaux area by various methods, including the traditional method and the *charmat* process.

Bordeaux Supérieur   **Region: Bordeaux**
Appellation Contrôlée
Red and rosé, min alc 10%, max yield 50 hl/ha. White, min alc 12%, max yield 50 hl/ha.
Grapes: Red, Cabernet Sauvignon and Franc, Merlot, Malbec, Carmenère, Petit Verdot. White, Sémillon, Sauvignon Blanc, Muscadelle.

Note lower yields and higher minimum alcohol than Bordeaux AOC. This AOC is permitted only in some specified areas.

Bourg   **Region: Bordeaux**
Appellation Contrôlée
Refer **Côtes de Bourg.**

Bourgeais   **Region: Bordeaux**
Appellation Contrôlée
Refer **Côtes de Bourg.**

Bourgogne   **Region: Burgundy**
Appellation Contrôlée
Red and rosé, min alc 10%, max yield 50 hl/ha. White, min alc 10.5%, max yield 60 hl/ha.
Grapes: Pinot Noir (red) and Chardonnay (white) are the foundation of the region. Gamay may be used if declassified from one of the 10 Beaujolais *crus*. However, there are others like Pinot Liebault, Pinot Blanc, Pinot Gris and others that may be significant in a small number of wines but not overall. Aligoté is a recognized grape that has its own AOC – Bourgogne Aligoté.

Known in English as Burgundy, Bourgogne is the large catchall AOC, extending from Dijon to Lyon, although most Beaujolais is sold under its own collection of AOCs. Inside the large Bourgogne AOC are more than 100 smaller AOCs, each with their own style and quality. The main thrust of AOC Bourgogne is the sound, clean wines from the lower slopes of the Côte d'Or and vineyards not considered to be quite at village appellation status. Some declassified wine from "higher" AOCs also used to be important, but these are less relevant today. Excellent value for the low prices can certainly be found; Bourgogne is a large AOC and has many surprises. AOC Bourgogne is an appellation above AOC Bourgogne Grand Ordinaire, AOC Bourgogne Ordinaire and AOC Bourgogne Passetoutgrains.

Bourgogne Aligoté   **Region: Burgundy**
Appellation Contrôlée
White only, min alc 9.5%, max yield 60 hl/ha.
Grapes: Aligoté (85–100%) and Chardonnay (up to 15%).

Minor and cheaper AOC, using Aligoté grapes instead of the Chardonnay that dominates mainstream Burgundy AOC white. Little is exported. Nevertheless, it can be a clean quaffing wine, the white equivalent of the red AOC Bourgogne Passetoutgrains.

Bourgogne Grand Ordinaire   **Region: Burgundy**
Appellation Contrôlée
Red and rosé, min alc 9%, max yield 55 hl/ha. White, min alc 9.5%, max yield 60 hl/ha.
Grapes: Red, Pinot Noir, Gamay, César, Tréssot. White, Aligoté, Chardonnay and Melon de Bourgogne.

Catchall AOC for blended wines, not highly regarded. Below AOC Bourgogne in status, and just above AOC Bourgogne Passetoutgrains.

Bourgogne Hautes-Côtes de Beaune   **Region: Burgundy**
Appellation Contrôlée
Red and rosé, min alc 10%, max yield 50 hl/ha. White, min alc 10.5%, max yield 55 hl/ha.
Grapes: Pinot Noir (red), Chardonnay (white) are the significant varieties. Others allowed are minor in their usage.

Relatively low-rated AOC in the Burgundy hierarchy, used for wine from selected villages in the Côte de Beaune after approval by a tasting panel each year.

Bourgogne Hautes-Côtes de Nuits   **Region: Burgundy**
Appellation Contrôlée
Red and rosé, min alc 10%, max yield 50 hl/ha. White, min alc 10.5%, max yield 55 hl/ha.
Grapes: Pinot Noir (red) and Chardonnay (white) are the significant varieties. Others are allowed but are relatively minor in their usage.

Relatively low-rated AOC in the Burgundy hierarchy, used for wine from selected villages in the Côte de Nuits after approval by a tasting panel each year.

Bourgogne Mousseux   **Region: Burgundy**
Appellation Contrôlée
Sparkling red and rosé, min alc 8.5%, max yield 55 hl/ha. Sparkling white, min alc 9.5%, max yield 40 hl/ha.
Grapes: Pinot Noir, Chardonnay.

AOC for Burgundy sparkling, though it is mostly the red that uses this AOC; white sparkling has moved to AOC Crémant de Bourgogne.

Bourgogne Ordinaire   **Region: Burgundy**
Appellation Contrôlée
Refer **Bourgogne Grand Ordinaire.**

Bourgogne Passetoutgrains   **Region: Burgundy**
Appellation Contrôlée
Red only, min alc 9.5%, max yield 55 hl/ha.
Grapes: Gamay up to 66%, Pinot Noir min 33%.

Another catchall AOC for blended reds containing at least one-third Pinot Noir, the balance Gamay. The wine is not highly regarded and is seldom exported.

Bourgueil   **Region: Loire**
Appellation Contrôlée
Red and rosé, min alc 9.5%, max yield 55 hl/ha.
Grapes: Cabernet Sauvignon and Franc.

AOC on the northern banks of the Loire River in the Touraine province, some 18 miles (30 km) west of the city of Tours. The wine tends to be light, well regarded as a minor red of France, and one of the better reds in the Loire. Two or three years bottle age is recommended. The best wine of Bourgueil comes from an area to the north with its own AOC, St-Nicolas-de-Bourgueil.

Bouzeron   Region: Burgundy
Appellation Contrôlée
White only, min alc 10%, max yield 55 hl/ha.
Grape: Aligoté.

New AOC as of 1997 (previously Bourgogne Aligoté de Bouzeron) in the Côte Chalonnaise, a cheerful drink-young aperitif or quaffer.

Brouilly   Region: Beaujolais
Appellation Contrôlée
Red only, min alc 10.5%, single vineyard 10.5%; max yield 48 hl/ha.
Grape: Gamay.

A Beaujolais *cru* producing better quality wine and therefore entitled to its own AOC. There are 10 such *crus* in Beaujolais, Brouilly being the largest and generally offering a robust style. Adjacent and higher up the slopes is the Côte de Brouilly AOC. Better vineyards in the village may add their name to the village name (a classification that carries a higher alcohol requirement) but "Appellation Brouilly Contrôlée" will appear underneath.

Buzet   Region: Southwest France near Bordeaux
Appellation Contrôlée
Red and rosé, min alc 10%. White, min alc 9.5%. Max yield 55 hl/ha.
Grapes: Red, Merlot, Cabernet Sauvignon and Franc, Malbec. White, Sauvignon Blanc, Sémillon, Muscadelle.

On the left bank of the Garonne River, this is quite a large area AOC (almost 30 villages) producing mostly reds. Surprisingly good quality for low prices. Some viticultural growth and development is going on in the area.

Cabardés   Region: Southwest France
Appellation Contrôlée
Red and rosé, min alc 11%, max yield 50 hl/ha.
Grapes: Cabernet Sauvignon and Franc, Merlot, Malbec, Syrah, Grenache, Cinsault, Fer, Carignan.

Delightful historic region. Wines are unsophisticated, but have interesting and long-life styles, mixing Bordeaux and Rhône grapes.

Cabernet d'Anjou   Region: Loire
Appellation Contrôlée
Rosé only, min alc 10%, max yield 40 hl/ha.

Grapes: Cabernet Franc and/or Cabernet Sauvignon.

Rosé (some lightly sweet) from an area on both sides of the Loire around the town of Angers.

Cabernet de Saumur   Region: Loire
Appellation Contrôlée
Rosé only, min alc 11%, max yield 40 hl/ha.
Grapes: Cabernet Sauvignon and Franc.

AOC south of the town of Saumur, on the southern banks of the Loire. Wines tend to be quite pale for rosé but generally respected.

Cadillac   Region: Bordeaux
Appellation Contrôlée
Sweet white, min alc 12%, max yield 40 hl/ha.
Grapes: Sémillon, Sauvignon Blanc, Muscadelle.

An AOC adjacent to Entre-Deux-Mers, making mainly sweet, botrytis-affected white. Not very highly regarded but there are some success stories. Reds and dry whites from the same area use AOC Premières Côtes de Bordeaux-Cadillac.

Cahors   Region: East of Bordeaux
Appellation Contrôlée
Red only, min alc 10.5%, max yield 50 hl/ha.
Grapes: Malbec min 70%, Merlot, Tannat max 20%, Folle Noire max 10%.

AOC of some size, about 46 miles (75 km) east of Bordeaux around the town of Cahors on the Lot River. A respected wine, able to develop well with age. The only red wine AOC in the whole of the Southwest that doesn't allow the two Cabernets.

Canon-Fronsac   Region: Bordeaux
Appellation Contrôlée
Red only, min alc 11%, max yield 42 hl/ha.
Grapes: Cabernet Sauvignon and Franc, Merlot, Malbec.

AOC beginning just over a mile (2 km) west of Libourne where the river Isle meets the Dordogne. This AOC is on the more elevated vineyards. These big, fruity and long-lived reds, with more of the Cabernets than St-Émilion, are a rising star on the horizon. Also from the north is AOC Fronsac, arguably inferior but like Canon-Fronsac buoyed by investment from people keen to see the potential unleashed.

Cassis   Region: Provence
Appellation Contrôlée
Red, white and rosé, min alc 11%, max yield 45 hl/ha.

Grapes: Red and rosé, Mourvèdre, Cinsault, Grenache. White, Clairette, Marsanne, Trebbiano, Sauvignon Blanc, Bourboulenc.

Predominantly white AOC on the Mediterranean Coast, 9 miles (15 km) from Marseille. Whites are regarded quite highly; rosé is popular with Riviera tourists. Little wine is exported.

Cerons   Region: Bordeaux
Appellation Contrôlée
White only, min alc 12.5%, max yield 40 hl/ha.
Grapes: Sémillon, Sauvignon Blanc, Muscadelle.

Small sweet white AOC (dry white and red from this area use AOC Graves) adjacent to Barsac, 20 miles (32 km) southeast of the city of Bordeaux on the Garonne River. Not regarded as highly as Barsac and Sauternes, and much smaller in volume. Note that the allowed yield is much higher also. *Botrytis cinerea* affects the style, but there are fewer pickings and the intensity is thus not as great as its neighbors.

Chablis   Region: Northwest of Burgundy
Appellation Contrôlée
White only, min alc 10%, max yield 50 hl/ha.
Grape: Chardonnay.

An AOC in the Department of Yonne between Champagne and the Côte de Beaune, and separated from the latter by the Morvan hills, Chablis is always considered part of Burgundy (just as Beaujolais is, though Chablis at least uses the Burgundy variety). Chablis is in effect the third of four AOC levels, below AOC Chablis Grand Cru and AOC Chablis Premier Cru and above AOC Petit Chablis. Yet Chablis is the biggest appellation, with about 5,000 acres (2,000 ha) of Chardonnay vineyards, almost three times the size of the Grand and Premier Cru AOCs. The style of Chablis has been one of fresh, crisp white, developing a nicely mealy tone with age. However, attitudes to oak are important and evolving: Some producers are using none, or using old oak purely for storage, while others are using a regular rotation of new, one, two and three year-old barrels, with a resultant impact on the wine. There are many owners, many attitudes and many choices, and as such, "Chablis" as a style and quality varies widely.

Chablis Grand Cru   Region: Northwest of Burgundy
Appellation Contrôlée
White only, min alc 11%, max yield 45 hl/ha.
Grape: Chardonnay.

An AOC that recognizes the top seven vineyards in the Chablis catchment area, the highest classification of Chablis wine. The Grand Cru vineyards are Blanchots, Bougros, Clos (or Les Clos), Grenouilles, Preuses, Valmur and Vaudésir. Each may have several owners, so accordingly there are many labels.

Chablis Premier Cru   **Region: Northwest of Burgundy**
Appellation Contrôlée
White only, min alc 10.5%, max yield 50 hl/ha.
Grape: Chardonnay.

AOC of some 24 vineyards in the villages of Chablis, Milly and Poinchy. Some use the abbreviation "1er Cru" for Premier Cru. This is the second class (but still a very respected class) of Chablis after AOC Chablis Grand Cru. As in AOC Chablis, attitudes to oak vary between producers.

Chambertin   **Region: Burgundy**
Appellation Contrôlée
Red only, min alc 11.5%, max yield 35 hl/ha.
Grape: Pinot Noir.

A Grand Cru AOC of 32 acres (13 ha) in the village of Gevrey-Chambertin in the Côte de Nuits. Le Chambertin is very highly regarded; one of the best Burgundys and priced accordingly.

Chambertin-Clos de Bèze   **Region: Burgundy**
Appellation Contrôlée
Red only, min alc 11.5%, max yield 35 hl/ha.
Grape: Pinot Noir.

A single-vineyard Grand Cru AOC of 37 acres (15 ha) in the village of Gevrey-Chambertin in the Côte de Nuits. Highly respected.

Chambolle-Musigny   **Region: Burgundy**
Appellation Contrôlée
Red only, min alc 10.5%, max yield 40 hl/ha.
Grape: Pinot Noir.

A serious and respected AOC in the southern half of the Côte de Nuits enclosing the famous *grands crus* of Le Musigny and Bonnes Mares. Chambolle-Musigny has a number of fine *premiers crus* as well.

Champagne   **Region: East of Paris**
Appellation Contrôlée
Sparkling white and rosé, min alc 11% after secondary fermentation, max yield 65 hl/ha. Although AOC criteria still apply, the words "Appellation d'Origine Contrôlée" are not required on the label as long as the word "Champagne" is given due importance.
Grapes: Pinot Noir, Pinot Meunier, Chardonnay, Pinot Blanc, Petit Meslier, Arbane.

A strictly defined area to the east of Paris, Champagne also has strictly defined methods. While these are sometimes duplicated elsewhere, "champagne," the French insist, can only come from Champagne. Most is blended from two, three or four vintages to provide balance and consistency. Sometimes older wine collected in magnums is added to give a final touch to a blend. A small proportion of champagne is made using only the black grapes (this is called *Blanc de Noir*, or "white from black"); some is made from Chardonnay only (and is called *Blanc de Blanc* Chardonnay, or "white from white").

"Vintage" champagne is made when a particularly fine year allows a crop to be bought that has all the attributes needed for a top quality wine. This will then be labeled with the vintage year shown. A small amount of "balancing" from other years is allowed. Vintage champagne must be submitted to and approved by a tasting committee of experts, and none may be sold at less than three years of age.

Each area of vineyard in Champagne has been graded for its quality, though vineyard ratings are more implicit than explicit on labels. Top areas are rated 100% *cru*, where the growers get the full established price for their grapes, a price that varies from year to year; lesser-quality areas are rated as low as 70%, where the growers get 70% of the price established for that year. This does not affect premium champagne producers, as they own much of their own supplying vineyards anyway. These have been established on the best sites, and produce top labels like Moët & Chandon's Dom Pérignon or Veuve Clicquot's La Grande Dame.

"Brut" (very dry) champagne has less than 15 g/L of residual sugar, while "extra brut" has no more than 6 g/L, although a higher amount of sweetness in extra brut was allowed in the past. "Sec" (dry) champagne allows up to 30 g/L, "demi-sec" up to 45 g/L, and "doux" (sweet) up to 100 g/L.

Chapelle-Chambertin   *Region: Burgundy*
Appellation Contrôlée
Red only, min alc 11.5%, max yield 37 hl/ha.
Grape: Pinot Noir.

Single-vineyard Grand Cru of 13.5 acres (5.5 ha) in the village of Gevrey-Chambertin in the Côte de Nuits. Not widely seen, this is a small AOC that is excellent in the right years.

Charlemagne   *Region: Burgundy*
Appellation Contrôlée
Refer **Corton-Charlemagne.**

Charmes-Chambertin   *Region: Burgundy*
Appellation Contrôlée
Red only, min alc 11.5%, max yield 37 hl/ha.
Grape: Pinot Noir.

Single-vineyard Grand Cru AOC of 91 acres (37 ha), in the village of Gevrey-Chambertin in the Côte de Nuits, adjacent to the great vineyard of Chambertin. Very highly respected.

Chassagne-Montrachet   **Region: Burgundy**
Appellation Contrôlée
Red, min alc 10.5%, Premier Cru 11%; max yield 40 hl/ha. White, min alc
11%, Premier Cru 11.5%; max yield 45 hl/ha.
Grapes: Red, Pinot Noir. White, Chardonnay.

Village AOC on the southern section of the Côte de Beaune. The village has
sections of several *grands crus* (each with their own, separate AOC), which
enhances the image and reputation of Chassagne-Montrachet. An area of
good pedigree for whites; reds are well-regarded also.

Château-Chalon   **Region: Jura**
Appellation Contrôlée
Vin jaune, min alc 12%, max yield 30 hl/ha.
Grape: Savagnin.

Not a château in the traditional sense of the word, but an area in the Jura
east of Burgundy. Château-Chalon produces a wine called *vin jaune* from the
Savagnin grape, by aging the wine in casks for six years and allowing a *flor*
film to grow across the top of the wine in the manner of sherry. The result
is like an unfortified sherry and is bottled in a squat unit called a *clavelin*.
Reasonably sought after if not particularly highly respected. In lesser years
the local committee may decide not to produce any.

Château-Grillet   **Region: Rhône**
Appellation Contrôlée
White only, min alc 11%, max yield 37 hl/ha.
Grape: Viognier.

Famous AOC from a 7.5 acre (3 ha) vineyard with one owner, situated within
the Condrieu AOC on the Rhône River south of Lyon. With its south-facing
slope (lots of sun) and its poor granite soil, this AOC can offer a robust, full-
bodied wine that has attracted lots of attention. It sometimes produces the
world's best Viognier, with its own tight power and strength, but in some
vintages it produces just a simple dry white.

Châteaumeillant   **Region: Loire**
VDQS
Red and rosé, min alc 9%, max yield 45 hl/ha.
Grapes: Gamay predominates; some Pinot Noir and Pinot Gris.

An area 45 miles (75 km) south of Bourges making a light, easy style of red
and rosé.

Châteauneuf-du-Pape   **Region: Rhône**
Appellation Contrôlée
Red, min alc 12.5%, max yield 35 hl/ha.
Grapes: Grenache, Cinsault, Syrah, Carignan, Mourvèdre, Gamay, Terret

Noir, Counoise, Vaccarese, Muscardin, Roussanne, Bourboulenc, Marsanne, Clairette, Picardin.

Important, well-respected AOC from an area on the Rhône River 9 miles (15 km) north of Avignon. Although 13 varieties are allowed historically (eight red, five white), most Châteauneuf is made from Grenache, Syrah, Mourvèdre and Cinsault, although a little of the white may be used to "tone" a blend in the right year. The style is generally lighter than Hermitage to the north, and enjoyable at three to five years. An AOC of amazing history, of strong vinous evolution and still containing some of the best French wine values, as well as a few shockers.

Châtillon-en-Diois   Region: Rhône
Appellation Contrôlée
Red and rosé, min alc 10%. White, min alc 10.5%. Max yield 50 hl/ha.
Grapes: Red, Gamay, Syrah, Pinot Noir. White, Aligoté, Chardonnay.

AOC on the east of the Rhône River near the town of Die. Mostly sparkling. The still wines not highly regarded.

Chénas   Region: Beaujolais
Appellation Contrôlée
Red only, min alc 10%, single vineyard 10.5%, max yield 48 hl/ha.
Grape: Gamay.

A Beaujolais *cru* producing better quality wine and therefore entitled to its own AOC. There are 10 such *crus* in Beaujolais. Better vineyards may hyphenate their name to the village name (a classification that carries a higher alcohol requirement) but "Appellation Chénas Contrôlée" will appear underneath.

Chevalier-Montrachet   Region: Burgundy
Appellation Contrôlée
White only, min alc 12%, max yield 40 hl/ha.
Grape: Chardonnay.

Famous 18.3-acre (7.4-ha), single-vineyard Grand Cru AOC partly in Puligny-Montrachet village and partly in Chassagne-Montrachet, in the Côte de Beaune. With Le Montrachet, it is rated as one of the top dry white wines of the world.

Cheverny   Region: Loire
Appellation Contrôlée
Red, rosé and white, min alc 9.5%. Red, max yield 55 hl/ha. White, max yield 60 hl/ha.
Grapes: Red, Gamay, Pinot Noir, Cabernet Sauvignon and Franc, Malbec. White, Sauvignon Blanc, Chardonnay, Arbois, Chenin Blanc, Romorantin.

AOC south of the Loire River in northeast Touraine, near the town of Blois. A wide range of styles, generally regarded as cheerful. A specific AOC from within, Cour Cheverny, uses only Romorantin.

Chinon   Region: Loire
Appellation Contrôlée
Red, rosé and white, min alc 9.5%, max yield 55 hl/ha.
Grapes: Red and rosé, Cabernet Sauvignon and Franc. White, Chenin Blanc.

AOC on the southern banks of the Loire River in the province of Touraine, some 18 miles (30 km) downstream, west of the city of Tours. Some AOC Chinon wines are recommended less than a year after vintage. The largest proportion is consumed within Touraine. Rosé is also made from Cabernet Franc; white is declining in quantity in recent years. Although previously better grapes were grown and some still remain, Chinon, with Bourgueil and St-Nicolas-de-Bourgueil, is looked on as being the best of Loire's red appellations.

Chiroubles   Region: Beaujolais
Appellation Contrôlée
Red only, min alc 10%, single vineyard 10.5%; max yield 48 hl/ha.
Grape: Gamay.

A Beaujolais *cru* regarded as producing better quality wine and therefore entitled to its own AOC. There are 10 such *crus* in Beaujolais. Better vineyards may hyphenate their name to the village name (a classification with a higher alcohol requirement) but "Appellation Chiroubles Contrôlée" will appear underneath.

Chorey-lès-Beaune   Region: Burgundy
Appellation Contrôlée
Red, min alc 10.5%, Premier Cru 11%; max yield 40 hl/ha. White, min alc 11%, Premier Cru 11.5%; max yield 45 hl/ha.
Grapes: Red, Pinot Noir. White, Chardonnay.

Wine from a small AOC directly north of Beaune city. No *grands crus* or *premiers crus* are produced in this village. Generally regarded as a minor appellation.

Clairette de Bellegarde   Region: Languedoc
Appellation Contrôlée
White only, min alc 11%, max yield 60 hl/ha.
Grape: Clairette.

AOC 27 miles (45 km) off the Mediterranean Coast, south of Avignon. Simple wine, best enjoyed young and fresh.

Clairette de Die   Region: Southeast France
Appellation Contrôlée
White only, including sparkling, min alc 9%, max yield 50 hl/ha.
Grapes: Clairette up to 30%, Muscat à Petits Grains.

Sparkling wine from an area north of Avignon, to the east of the Rhône, on the banks of a tributary, the Drôme. Wine generally sweet, enjoying recent popularity.

Clairette du Languedoc   Region: Languedoc
Appellation Contrôlée
White only, min alc 12%, max yield 50 hl/ha.
Grape: Clairette.

AOC some 12 miles (20 km) off the Mediterranean Coast, east of Montpellier. Clairette du Languedoc sits within the bounds of Coteaux du Languedoc, and reds in the area carry that AOC, but Clairette du Languedoc offers a single-variety white, usually dry, sometimes sweet, or even oak-matured and *rancio,* sherry-like with a nutty, tangy flavor.

Clos de Lambrays   Region: Burgundy
Appellation Contrôlée
Red only, min alc 11.5%, max yield 35 hl/ha.
Grape: Pinot Noir.

Lifted from Premier Cru Morey-St-Denis to a Grand Cru AOC in 1979; a lot of work is still going on to develop the potential of this 20-acre (8-ha) AOC.

Clos de la Roche   Region: Burgundy
Appellation Contrôlée
Red only, min alc 11.5%, max yield 35 hl/ha.
Grape: Pinot Noir.

Single-vineyard Grand Cru AOC of 42 acres (17 ha) in the village of Morey-St-Denis in the center of the Côte de Nuits. One of the bigger Grand Cru vineyards in Burgundy and well-regarded, especially in the best vintages.

Clos de Tart   Region: Burgundy
Appellation Contrôlée
Red only, min alc 11.5%, max yield 35 hl/ha.
Grape: Pinot Noir.

Single-vineyard Grand Cru AOC of 17 acres (7 ha), partly in the village of Morey-St-Denis but partly also in Chambolle-Musigny. There is currently only one owner of this vineyard (*négociant* Mommessin) and therefore only one label carries this appellation. Perhaps less highly regarded than it was in the 1980s, yet offering a slightly different style to the other *grands crus* around it.

Clos de Vougeot
Appellation Contrôlée
Region: Burgundy

Red only, min alc 11.5%, max yield 35 hl/ha.
Grape: Pinot Noir.

In the southern half of the Côte de Nuits, this Grand Cru vineyard in the village of Vougeot has 55 owners. Clos de Vougeot is on a hill, and the higher vineyards are considered slightly superior; but unfortunately elevation is not shown on the label!

Clos de Vougeot is renowned for its bouquet and finesse rather than as a big powerful burgundy. With many owners and labels some wines will inevitably be better than others, but Clos de Vougeot is held in enormous esteem.

Clos St-Denis
Appellation Contrôlée
Region: Burgundy

Red only, min alc 11.5%, max yield 35 hl/ha.
Grape: Pinot Noir.

A 16.3-acre (6.6-ha) Grand Cru AOC in the village of Morey-St-Denis in the center of the Côte de Nuits. Very highly regarded, especially in good years.

Collioure
Appellation Contrôlée
Region: Roussillon

Red and rosé, red min alc 12%, rosé 11.5%; max yield 40 hl/ha.
Grapes: Red, Grenache, Syrah and Mourvèdre min 60%, with Carignan and Cinsault. Rosé, same as red but also contains Grenache Gris.

The table wine AOC (not the *Vin Doux Naturel*) of the Banyuls area, tucked in the lower-right corner of France near the Spanish border, on the Mediterranean coast. Mostly red wine; rising in popularity.

Condrieu
Appellation Contrôlée
Region: Rhône

White only, min alc 11%, max yield 37 hl/ha.
Grape: Viognier.

A growing AOC, Condrieu covered just 17 acres (7 ha) in 1976 and extends to more than 250 acres (100 ha) today. During that time the style has changed considerably and Condrieu's new plantings battle with those in the New World in the handling of Viognier, malolactic fermentation and the use of oak.

Within the bounds of Condrieu is the tiny AOC of Château-Grillet with its own identity. Mostly enjoyed young, Condrieu continues its evolution and competes with its devoted followers who, seeking an alternative to Chardonnay, have planted Viognier in California and other places in the New World.

Corbières
Region: Languedoc, south of France
Appellation Contrôlée
Red and rosé, min alc 11.5%, white, min alc 11%; max yield 50 hl/ha.
Grapes: Red, Carignan min 50%, Syrah, Mourvèdre, Cinsault, Terret Noir, Picpoul. White, Bourboulenc, Maccabeo, Grenache Blanc, Malvoisie, Clairette, Muscat, Terret Blanc, Marsanne, Roussanne, Muscat d'Alexandrie, Muscat à Petits Grains, Picpoul Blanc.

AOC in the Midi towards the Spanish-French border, to the west of the Mediterranean. Essentially a red speciality area, the wine is varied (the AOC is quite large) and some is dark and intense. It has smaller quantities of pretty good white and a rosé that demand attention.

Cornas
Region: Rhône
Appellation Contrôlée
Red only, min alc 10.5%, max yield 40 hl/ha.
Grape: Syrah.

AOC just outside Valence on the west bank of the northern part of the Rhône. Wines of similar robustness to Hermitage but often without the finesse. Some age very well. The land has granite soils, slopes south for maximum sun and seems to have huge potential. In some years Cornas may almost be too much of a good thing, but the best are very highly regarded.

Corton
Region: Burgundy
Appellation Contrôlée
Red, min alc 11.5%, max yield 35 hl/ha. White, min alc 12%, max yield 40 hl/ha.
Grape: Pinot Noir.

Single-vineyard Grand Cru AOC in the village of Aloxe-Corton in the northern Côte de Beaune. The vineyards run around a hill. The wine of this AOC is regarded very highly. Mainly red wine, the only red *grand cru* of the Côte de Beaune. Louis Latour is one renowned owner; his wine is labeled Corton Grancey.

Corton-Charlemagne
Region: Burgundy
Appellation Contrôlée
White only, min alc 12%, max yield 40 hl/ha.
Grape: Chardonnay.

Grand Cru AOC in the village of Aloxe-Corton (and extends into one or two others) in the northern Côte de Beaune. Very highly respected white wine.

Costières de Nîmes
Region: Languedoc
Appellation Contrôlée
Red, rosé and white, min alc 11%, max yield 60 hl/ha.
Grapes: Red, Grenache, Syrah, Mourvèdre, Counoise, Terret Noir, Carignan

and Cinsault up to 50%. White, Clairette min 50%, Grenache Blanc, Trebbiano, Marsanne, Roussanne, Maccabeo and Rolle up to 50%.

AOC south of the town of Nîmes, just to the west of the Rhône. Predominantly red wines.

Côte de Beaune   Region: Burgundy
Appellation Contrôlée
Red only, min alc 10.5%, max yield 45 hl/ha.
Grape: Pinot Noir.

Fairly rare AOC referring to wine from the Beaune village plus a further 25 acres (10 ha). Wine not generally regarded highly. Note this appellation should not be confused with the term "Côte de Beaune" meaning the whole of the southern half of the Côte d'Or.

Côte de Beaune-Villages   Region: Burgundy
Appellation Contrôlée
Red only, min alc 10.5%, max yield 42 hl/ha.
Grapes: Red, Pinot Noir. White, Chardonnay.

An AOC that allows a *négociant* to blend wine from two or more of 16 speci- fied villages in the Côte de Beaune, in order to lift the combined standard above that of the individual wines, or to make volume more economic. Not generally regarded highly, but can be good value for money.

Côte de Brouilly   Region: Beaujolais
Appellation Contrôlée
Red only, min alc 10.5%, max yield 48 hl/ha.
Grape: Gamay.

A Beaujolais *cru* producing better quality wine and therefore entitled to its own AOC. There are 10 such *cru* in Beaujolais. Côte de Brouilly is higher up the slopes than the adjacent Brouilly AOC and is highly regarded for intense Beaujolais with some longevity. Better vineyards in the village may add their name to the village name (a classification that requires a higher alcohol percentage) but "Appellation Côte de Brouilly Contrôlée" will ap- pear underneath.

Côte de Nuits-Villages   Region: Burgundy
Appellation Contrôlée
Red, min alc 10.5%, max yield 42 hl/ha. White, min alc 11%, max yield 45 hl/ha.
Grapes: Red, Pinot Noir. White, Chardonnay.

An AOC that absorbs the minor villages of the Côte de Nuits; rated above Hautes Côtes de Nuits. Very little white. Lower-priced wine, can be very good value.

Côte Rôtie
Region: Rhône
Appellation Contrôlée
Red only, min alc 10%, max yield 40 hl/ha.
Grapes: Syrah min 80%, Viognier up to 20%.

Côte Rôtie (literally "roasted slopes") is an AOC to the north of the Rhône Valley, about 19 miles (30 km) south of Lyon. It is situated on an elevated site sloping quite steeply in places towards the south (and the sun). The best slopes of the area are in two sections: the "Blonde," producing lighter, more delicate wines, and the "Brune," whose soil is darker, producing a more full-bodied, heavier style that needs bottle age. A few wines mention their origin from either or both Blonde or Brune on the label but there is only one AOC.

Côte Rôtie is a strong AOC, the wines usually comfortably exceeding the minimum alcohol limit, and some premium estates get prices in line with Bordeaux first-growths. A relatively recent discovery as a special area. Much may yet evolve in Côte Rôtie, including possibly its labeling, which may divide it into as many as four AOCs instead of the one at present.

Coteaux d'Aix-en-Provence
Region: Provence
Appellation Contrôlée
Red, rosé and white, min alc 11%, max yield 60 hl/ha.
Grapes: Red and rosé, Carignan, Cinsault, Grenache, Counoise, Syrah, Mourvèdre, Cabernet Sauvignon. White, Clairette, Trebbiano, Sauvignon Blanc, Sémillon, Grenache Blanc, Bourboulenc.

AOC of some 8,000 acres (3,200 ha) around the town of Aix-en-Provence in the southeastern corner of France. Quite a large physical area yet without a strong wine reputation. Wines are popular with visitors and most are sold locally. Syrah is on the rise and able to age well.

Coteaux d'Ajaccio
Region: Corsica
Appellation Contrôlée
Red, rosé and white, min alc 12%, max yield 45 hl/ha.
Grapes: Red, Sciacarello, Nielluccio, Barbarossa, Rolle, Grenache, Cinsault, Carignan. White, Vermentino (locally known as Roll), Trebbiano.

AOC on the central west coast of the island of Corsica.

Coteaux d'Ancenis
Region: Loire
VDQS
Red, rosé and white, min alc 9%, max yield 40 hl/ha.
Grapes: Red and rosé, Gamay, Cabernet Sauvignon and Franc. White, Chenin Blanc, Pinot Gris (locally known as Malvoisie).

Area on the north banks of the Loire northeast of the town of Nantes. Lots of light red, some semi-sweet white. Wines labeled varietally.

Coteaux de l'Aubance
Region: Loire
Appellation Contrôlée
White only, min alc 10.5%, max yield 30 hl/ha.
Grape: Chenin Blanc.

AOC south of the town of Angers, on the south side of the Loire. Style is generally lightly sweet white. Some producers grow red, sold as Anjou.

Coteaux Champenois
Region: Champagne
Appellation Contrôlée
Red, rosé and white, min alc 10%, max yield 87 hl/ha.
Grapes: Red, Pinot Noir, Pinot Meunier. White, Chardonnay.

Still wine from Champagne, a debatable mix of mostly light red and often thin whites. Quite expensive beside Burgundy, for example, yet a little novel. Interesting, something different from Champagne.

Coteaux du Giennois
Region: Loire
Appellation Contrôlée
Red and white, min alc 10.5%, max yield 50 hl/ha.
Grapes: Red, Gamay, Pinot Noir. White, Sauvignon Blanc.

Previously known as Côtes de Gien this AOC was promoted from VDQS status in 1999. Mostly light reds from Gamay.

Coteaux du Languedoc
Region: Languedoc
Appellation Contrôlée
Red, rosé and white, min alc 11% (*cru*, 11.5%), max yield 50 hl/ha.
Grapes: Red, Carignan max 50%, Syrah, Mourvèdre, Grenache, Lladoner Pelut, Cinsault (these five max 50% also), with Counoise and Terret, a rather difficult formula but one that requires Grenache, Syrah and Mourvèdre to be at least 50% of the blend. White, Bourboulenc, Clairette, Grenache Blanc, Trebbiano, Maccabeo, Picpoul, Roussanne, Marsanne, Terret Blanc, Rolle, Viognier.

The following "best" vineyards are given *cru* status, the right to hyphenate their name to the AOC (note that a higher minimum alcohol is required for this status):

Cabrières: North of Pezenas, a *cru* that has AOC Clairette du Languedoc within it.
Coteaux de la Mejanelle: A *cru* around the town of this name, east of Montpellier, known for robust red wines.
Coteaux de St-Christol: Another small and minor *cru*, east of the AOC.
Coteaux de Vérargues: Northeast of Montpellier, a tiny *cru* with little recognition, the territory overlapping with Muscat de Lunel AOC.
La Clape: Named after an extinct volcano between Narbonne and the sea, this *cru* uses more Carignan than the more northern vineyards.

Montpeyrous: *Cru* west of Montpellier, mostly above the Herault River. Wines are considered to age well.

Picpoul de Pinet: *Cru* near the town of Pinet on the Mediterranean coast. This does not have the prestige of some of the other *cru* in this area, partly because of the bracing sharpness (or freshness) of its wines. This is a varietal wine, from the grape Picpoul (also known as Piquepoul, which means lip-stinger).

Pic St-Loup: Named after a peak of jagged rock about 15 miles (25 km) north of Montpellier, this *cru* for red and rosé only is considered high on the list for full AOC status. Bulky reds that age well.

Quatourze: South of Narbonne, a small *cru* with robust reds.

St-Drézéry: North east of Montpellier, a tiny *cru* with little recognition.

St-Georges d'Orques: A small *cru* on the on the southwestern suburbs of Montpellier, an area being squeezed out over the decades by city growth.

St-Saturnin: *Cru* around the town of this name and St-Felix-de-Lodez, well known in the region for a dark rosé.

This AOC is spread widely and is made up of what seems to be a hundred "patches" of vineyard overlooking the coast from Herault to Gard. There are some hilly areas, some flatter areas and a mix of soils and climates, and thus many styles of wine. A big area producing a lot of wine, this is also a popular tourist destination, as it is quite near the coast. This is not an AOC of wall-to-wall vines, however, as other horticultural produce (and quite a lot of *Vins du Pays*) is also produced here. As is evident from the list of *cru* above, there are lots of individual sites of varying size and image.

Coteaux du Layon   Region: Loire
Appellation Contrôlée
Sweet white only, min alc 11%, max yield 30 hl/ha.
Grape: Chenin Blanc.

AOC on the banks of the Layon River, a small tributary to the Loire. Only the Chenin Blanc grape may be used. Some rosé is produced, but it is sold under AOC Rosé d'Anjou. Some dry white is also produced in some years under AOC Anjou. Coteaux du Layon AOC is able to attract *Botrytis cinerea* in most years, and the final product is regarded generally as an important and respected wine.

Coteaux du Layon-Villages   Region: Loire
Appellation Contrôlée
Sweet white only, min alc 12%, max yield 30 hl/ha.
Grape: Chenin Blanc.

Seven better villages on the north side of the Coteaux du Layon form this AOC, often hyphenating the specific village name, rather than "Villages" to the AOC.

Coteaux du Loir   Region: Loire
Appellation Contrôlée
Red and rosé, min alc 9%, max yield 55 hl/ha. White, min alc 9.5%, max yield 55 hl/ha.
Grapes: Red, Cabernet Franc, Pineau d'Aunis, Malbec. Rosé, same grapes as for red, but includes Groslot. White, Chenin Blanc.

The Loir is a river, a tributary to the Loire. AOC Loir is some 24 miles (40 km) north of the city of Tours, producing wine considered highly enjoyable in a good year. The best Loir wine is thought to come from the village of Jasnières, which has its own AOC.

Coteaux du Lyonnais   Region: Rhône
VDQS
Refer **Vin du Lyonnais.**

Coteaux de Pierrevert   Region: Provence
Appellation Contrôlée
Red, rosé and white, min alc 11%, max yield 50 hl/ha.
Grapes: Red, Carignan, Cinsault, Grenache, Mourvèdre, Petite Syrah, Terret Noir. White, Clairette, Grenache Blanc, Marsanne, Roussanne, Rolle, Picpoul, Trebbiano.

AOC quite high on the hill in the southeastern corner of France, where the Verdon and Durance rivers meet. A fairly normal rosé seems to be the most popular style here, and is not widely seen outside the immediate area.

Coteaux de Quercy   Region: Southwest France
VDQS
Red and rosé, min alc 11%, max yield 50 hl/ha.
Grapes: Auxerrois, Tannat, Cabernet Sauvignon and Franc, Merlot, Jurançon, Gamay.

Between the Aveyron and Lot rivers, in a big catchment that includes Cahors. Given VDQS status in 1999, the style is regarded as having plenty of interest, and is cheerful and enjoyable without long cellaring.

Coteaux de Saumur   Region: Loire
Appellation Contrôlée
White only, min alc 11%, max yield 35 hl/ha.
Grape: Chenin Blanc.

AOC on the southern banks of the Loire southeast of the town of Saumur, and including the smaller village of Saumur-Champigny, which has its own AOC for red wines.

Coteaux du Tricastin   Region: Rhône
Appellation Contrôlée
Red, white and rosé, min alc 11%, max yield 52 hl/ha.
Grapes: Red, Grenache, Cinsault, Mourvèdre, Syrah, Picpoul, Carignan,
and up to 20% white grapes. White, Grenache Blanc, Clairette, Picpoul
Blanc, Bourboulenc, plus Trebbiano, Marsanne, Roussanne and Viognier up
to 30%.

A high altitude AOC on the Ardèche side of the Rhône Valley but still mostly
east of the Rhône. Generally regarded as simple wine. Mainly red; only the
best is given oak maturation up to 20%.

Coteaux Varois   Region: Provence
Appellation Contrôlée
Red, rosé and white, min alc 11%, max yield 55 hl/ha.
Grapes: Red and rosé, Grenache, Syrah, Mourvèdre min 80% with
Cabernet Sauvignon, Cinsault. White, Rolle, Trebbiano, Clairette,
Sauvignon Blanc.

Quite a widely spread AOC in the middle of the Côtes de Provence. Rosé
predominates. Some grapes for heavier wines struggle to ripen, yet a lot
of effort seems to have gone into developing better quality reds after AOC
status was granted in 1993.

Coteaux du Vendômois   Region: Loire
VDQS
Red and rosé, min alc 9%, max yield 60 hl/ha. White, min alc 9.5%, max
yield 65 hl/ha.
Grape: Pineau d'Aunis.

Wine from a 346-acre (140-ha) area around the town of Vendôme, some
28 miles (45 km) north of the Loire, and 31 miles (50 km) northeast of Tours.
Simple wine from fairly extreme conditions.

Coteaux de Vérargues   Region: Languedoc
VDQS
Red and rosé, min alc 11%, max yield 50 hl/ha.
Grapes: Aramon, Cinsault, Carignan, Grenache.

Wine from an area to the west of the town of Nîmes and south of St-
Christol.

Côtes d'Auvergne   Region: Loire
VDQS
Red, white and rosé, min alc 9%, max yield 45 hl/ha.
Grapes: Red and rosé, Gamay, Pinot Noir. White, Chardonnay.

A 988-acre (400-ha) AOC, almost closer to the Rhône than the Loire. Wines are considered tidy and low priced. Most are consumed in the region. Villages may hyphenate their name to the VDQS.

Côtes de Bergerac   **Region: Southwest France**
Appellation Contrôlée
Red and white, min alc 11%, max yield 50 hl/ha.
Grapes: Red, Cabernet Franc and Sauvignon, Merlot. White, Sauvignon Blanc, Sémillon, Muscadelle.

AOC offering more consistent wine than the straight Bergerac appellation, usually oak-matured and with a rising image through the 1990s. Whites are generally sweetish, made by late-picking the grapes. Reds are oak aged, serious and quite long-lived.

Côtes de Blaye   **Region: Bordeaux**
Appellation Contrôlée
White only, min alc 11%, max yield 50 hl/ha.
Grapes: Sémillon, Sauvignon Blanc, Muscadelle, Trebbiano, Colombard.

AOC over the Gironde River from Margaux.

Côtes de Bordeaux-St-Macaire   **Region: Bordeaux**
Appellation Contrôlée
White only, min alc 11.5%, max yield 50 hl/ha.
Grapes: Sauvignon Blanc, Sémillon, Muscadelle.

Area borders the end of Premières Côtes de Bordeaux and borders Entre-Deux-Mers. Fairly sweet and considered generally undistinguished.

Côtes de Bourg   **Region: Bordeaux**
Appellation Contrôlée
Red, min alc 10.5%, max yield 50 hl/ha. White, min alc 11%, max yield 60 hl/ha.
Grapes: Merlot, Cabernet Sauvignon and Franc, Malbec. White, Sémillon, Sauvignon Blanc, Muscadelle, Trebbiano, Merlot Blanc, Colombard.

AOC opposite Margaux over the Gironde, growing in image as a producer of sound, well-priced wines, mostly red. In earlier years, white wine was sold as AOC Bourgeais, red as AOC Côtes de Bourg.

Côtes du Brulhois   **Region: Southwest France**
VDQS
Red and rosé, min alc 10%, max yield 50 hl/ha.
Grapes: Cabernet Sauvignon and Franc, Merlot, Malbec, Tannat, Fer.

AOC on the south side of the Garonne River, near the town of Agen. Mostly wine from cooperatives, not thought of as special.

Côtes du Cabardés et de l'Orbiel   Region: Languedoc
Appellation Contrôlée
Red and rosé only, min alc 11%, max yield 50 hl/ha.
Grapes: Merlot, Cabernet Sauvignon and Franc 40% min, Grenache and Syrah also 40% min, Malbec, Cinsault, Fer.

Light style of red in an AOC towards the west of the Languedoc, recently promoted to AOC status. An unusual mix of Bordeaux and Rhône varieties. Wines are not regarded as special or unique, but continued efforts are being made to improve quality.

Côtes de Castillon   Region: Bordeaux
Appellation Contrôlée
Red only, min alc 11%, max yield 50 hl/ha.
Grapes: (Predominantly) Merlot, Cabernet Franc and Sauvignon, Malbec.

Previously "Bordeaux Côtes de Castillon." AOC from nine villages in and surrounding the town of Castillon on the Dordogne River, east of St-Émilion with Côtes de Francs adjacent to the north. Soil largely clay or lime, with alluvial deposits from the river; good Merlot and Cabernet Franc territory.

Côtes de Duras   Region: Southwest France
Appellation Contrôlée
Red, min alc 10%, max yield 55 hl/ha. Rosé, min alc 10.5%, max yield 55 hl/ha. White, min alc 10.5%, max yield 60 hl/ha, except for sweet white, max yield 50 hl/ha.
Grapes: Red, Cabernet Sauvignon and Franc, Malbec, Merlot. White, Sauvignon Blanc, Sémillon, Muscadelle.

AOC further up the Garonne River, east of Entre-Deux-Mers beyond Bordeaux boundaries. Mostly dry white. A sweet, fairly rich character aligns Côtes de Duras with Sauternes and Barsac. While missing the glamor and excitement of great Bordeaux, Côtes de Duras can be of surprisingly good value.

Côtes du Forez   Region: Loire
Appellation Contrôlée
Red and rosé, min alc 9%, max yield 55 hl/ha.
Grape: Gamay.

A hilly 500-acre (200-ha) AOC near the source of the Loire in Central France. Although given AOC status in 1999, the enthusiasm of the wine trade is minimal, as carbonic maceration is not quite working for the territory.

Côtes du Frontonnais   Region: Southwest France
Appellation Contrôlée
Red and rosé, min alc 10.5%, max yield 50 hl/ha.
Grapes: Négrette 50–70%, with Cabernet Sauvignon and/or Franc 30–50%, plus Syrah, Gamay and Tannat up to 20%.

North of Toulouse, an AOC linking Villaudric and Fronton, both previously VDQS and both hyphenating their name to the AOC as appropriate. The reputation here is for a lighter, easy style of red, generally enjoyed young.

Côtes de Gien   **Region: Loire**
Appellation Contrôlée
Refer **Coteaux du Giennois.**

Côtes du Jura   **Region: Jura, east of Burgundy**
Appellation Contrôlée:
White wine is made from Chardonnay and Savagnin grapes. Dry in character. Min alc 10%, max yield 60 hl/ha.
Red, rosé and gray wine (that is, very pale rosé) are made from Poulsard, Trousseau, Pinot Noir. Min alc 10%, max yield 55 hl/ha.
Vin jaune is a wine for which the area has a reputation. Made from Savagnin grapes, the wine is aged for six years in casks, allowing a *flor* to form on top as in the sherry tradition. The resultant wine is similar to an unfortified sherry. Min alc 11%.
Vin de paille (straw wine) is also produced. Savagnin grapes are left to overripen on the vines, then allowed to lie on straw mats in the sun to further evaporate water from the juice. The resultant wine is sweet, rich and high in alcohol (min 14.5% but can be 18%). Max yield 20 hl/ha.
Sparkling wine is also produced. *Refer* **Côte de Jura Mousseux.**

Three superior AOCs in the area: Arbois (and Arbois Mousseux), L'Étoile (and L'Étoile Mousseux) and Château-Chalon. These are listed separately.

Côtes du Jura Mousseux   **Region: Jura, east of Burgundy**
Appellation Contrôlée
Sparkling white and rosé, min alc 10%, max yield 65 hl/ha.
Grapes: White, Chardonnay, Savagnin. Rosé, Pinot Noir, Trousseau, Poulsard.

Wines from the area of Jura. Sparkling wine is made by the traditional method from Chardonnay and Savagnin grapes. Not considered in the Champagne class, but good value.

Côtes du Lubéron   **Region: Provence (officially Rhône)**
Appellation Contrôlée
Red, rosé and white, min alc 11%, max yield 55 hl/ha.
Grapes: Red and rosé, Syrah and/or Grenache, Mourvèdre, Cinsault, Carignan up to 20%. White, Grenache Blanc, Clairette, Trebbiano, Bourboulenc, Marsanne, Roussanne.

Near Provence, east of the Rhône River, this AOC with Côte du Ventoux running along its northern border produces a mix of wines and styles, with even Chardonnay (sold as *Vins du Pays*) becoming popular.

Côtes de la Malepère
Region: Languedoc
Appellation Contrôlée
Red and rosé, min alc 11%, max yield 50 hl/ha.
Grapes: Malbec, Cinsault and Merlot at least 60%, plus Cabernet Sauvignon and Franc, Grenache and Syrah up to 30%.

AOC in the greater Limoux area, on the far-west side of the Languedoc. Regarded with interest, this elevated area between 1,300 and 1,500 feet (400–450 m) has recently been promoted to AOC status. Cooperative oriented, with mainly light, fresh, simple reds.

Côtes du Marmandais
Region: Southwest France
Appellation Contrôlée
Red, min alc 10%, max yield 56 hl/ha. White, min alc 10%, max yield 66 hl/ha.
Grapes: Red, Cabernet Sauvignon and Franc, Malbec, Merlot, Fer, Abouriou, Syrah. White, Sauvignon Blanc, Sémillon, Muscadelle.

Wine from an area on both banks of the Garonne River, immediately east of Bordeaux. Mostly reds, this is a little different to Bordeaux (it uses some extra varieties, including Syrah) and does not have a big reputation. Two cooperatives control most of the winemaking.

Côtes de Millau
Region: Southwest France
VDQS
Red and rosé, min alc 11%, max yield 60 hl/ha. White, min alc 10.5%, max yield 60 hl/ha.
Grapes: Red, Gamay and Syrah min 30%, Cabernet Sauvignon up to 20%, Fer. White, Chenin Blanc, Mauzac.

A tiny region around the town of Millau on hilly territory suitable for growing cool-climate grapes. Work is going on to develop quality and changes to the VDQS are anticipated.

Côtes de Montravel
Region: Southwest France
Appellation Contrôlée
White only, min alc 12%, max yield 50 hl/ha.
Grapes: Sémillon, Sauvignon, Muscadelle.

AOC from a defined section of Montravel considered superior to the plain AOC.

Côtes de Provence
Region: Southeast France
Appellation Contrôlée
Red, rosé and white, min alc 11%, max yield 55 hl/ha.
Grapes: Red and rosé, Grenache, Syrah, Cinsault, Mourvèdre, Tibouren, Carignan, Cabernet Sauvignon. White, Rolle, Sémillon, Trebbiano, Clairette.

Accounting for three-quarters of Provence wine, this is a large AOC between Nice and Marseille along the Mediterranean coast. It is not a wall-to-wall area, as there are a few pockets separated from the rest. This is a warm, sunny AOC, tempered by the mistral. The wines are influenced by tourist demand for large quantities of light, easy-drinking rosé. Not always cheap for what they offer, but the shapely "skittle" bottle helps it to sell. There are more serious wines, red particularly, and an evolution has been spotted by most commentators.

Côtes du Rhône
Appellation Contrôlée
Region: Rhône

Red, rosé and white, min alc 11%, max yield 52 hl/ha.
Grapes: Red, Grenache, Syrah, Mourvèdre, Carignan, Cinsault, Muscardin, Camarese, Picpoul Noir, Terret Noir, Grenache Gris, Clairette Rosé. White, Grenache Blanc, Clairette, Marsanne, Roussanne, Bourboulenc, Viognier, Trebbiano, Picpoul Blanc.

AOC catchment area some 120 miles (190 km) long between Vienne, south of Lyon, and Avignon, in which there are a number of quality subregions with their own AOCs (Châteauneuf-du-Pape, Vacqueyras, Hermitage).

A further classification, AOC Côtes du Rhône-Villages, allows recognition of what can be a higher quality level. This leaves the Côtes du Rhône AOC (which is about 85% red) to represent a large quantity of varied wine, much of it very good value, some a little thin and plain, some excellent. The large number of grapes and the large size of the catchment area for Côtes du Rhône AOC (or "CDR" as it is affectionately known) offers lower priced wine generally, often available at places like railway stations in France, where the expectation is one of refreshment and stimulation rather than elegance and class. But it is a big AOC with a big mix of characters and quality.

Côtes du Rhône-Villages
Appellation Contrôlée
Region: Rhône

Red and rosé, min alc 12.5%, max yield 42 hl/ha. White, min alc 12%, max yield 42 hl/ha.
Grapes: Red, Grenache up to 65%, with Syrah, Cinsault and Mourvèdre at least 25% collectively, the balance (if any) from the Côtes du Rhône list above, up to 10%. White, Clairette, Roussanne, Marsanne, Bourboulenc, Grenache Blanc.

There are about 16 villages in this AOC and they are allowed to hyphenate their name to the AOC name, which makes something of a mouthful! Some villages drop the word "Villages" from the AOC and insert the name of their own village instead. The villages in this AOC are Vinsobres, Rochegude, St-Maurice-sur-Eygues, Rousset-les-Vignes, St-Pantaléon-les-Vignes, Cairanne, Courthezon, Rasteau, Roaix, Seguret, Valréas, Visan, Sablet, Chusclan, Laudun, St-Gervais, and Beaumes-de-Venise.

This AOC is a step up from AOC Côtes du Rhône. The better villages in the 120-mile (190-km) long Côtes du Rhône catchment area between Vienne and Avignon are mostly towards the south. However, there is a higher alcohol requirement and fewer allowable grapes in this AOC, and the higher restrictions on yield than AOC Côtes du Rhône mean this "Villages" AOC represents good quality and value. Whites are made, but mainly a sound, alive, hearty red can be expected.

Côtes Roannaise   Region: Loire
Appellation Contrôlée
Red and rosé, min alc 9%, max yield 55 hl/ha.
Grape: Gamay.

Small, 420-acre (170-ha) AOC based near the source of the Loire River, on the hills around Roanne. This is just over the hills from Beaujolais and shares the same grape variety.

Côtes du Roussillon   Region: Roussillon
Appellation Contrôlée
Red, rosé and white, min alc 11.5% (red and rosé), 10.5% (white), max yield 50 hl/ha.
Grapes: Red, Carignan max 60%, Syrah and/or Mourvèdre min 20%, Grenache, Lladoner Pelut, Cinsault. White, Maccabeo, Grenache Blanc, Malvoisie du Roussillon, Roussanne, Marsanne, Rolle.

A large AOC in the bottom-right corner of France, on the coast of the Mediterranean with the Spanish border to the south. A region with a mix of *terroir*, and wines generally for drinking young. Mostly red, although some white which don't qualify for the AOC (including Chardonnay, Viognier and Sauvignon Blanc), are sold as *Vins de Pays*. Some red is given carbonic maceration, some is given traditional fermentation and oak, and some wines are a blend of both. A mixed bag. Better wines to the north use the Côtes du Roussillon-Villages AOC.

Côtes du Roussillon-Villages   Region: Roussillon
Appellation Contrôlée
Red only, min alc 12%, max yield 45 hl/ha.
Grapes: Carignan max 60%, Syrah and/or Mourvèdre min 20%, Grenache, Lladoner Pelut, Cinsault. White, Maccabeo up to 10%.

AOC in northern Roussillon, up in the hills, with a smaller yield than the overall AOC. Generally thought to be a little higher in standards, though perhaps without great excitement.

Côtes de St-Mont   Region: Southwest France
VDQS
Red, rosé and white, min alc 10%, max yield 60 hl/ha.

Grapes: Red, Cabernet Sauvignon and Franc, Tannat, Fer. White, Courbu, Petit and Gros Manseng, Arrufiac.

Area around Armagnac, north of Madiran. This AOC does not have a strong image.

Côtes de Toul
Region: Northeast France, east of Champagne
VDQS
Red, rosé and white, min alc 8.5%, max yield 60 hl/ha.
Grapes: Red and rosé, Gamay, Pinot Meunier, Pinot Noir. White, Aligoté, Aubin, Auxerrois.

Area in the province of Lorraine, 62 miles (100 km) east of Champagne. Not a big following outside the region.

Côtes du Ventoux
Region: Rhône
Appellation Contrôlée
Red, rosé and white, min alc 11%, max yield 50 hl/ha.
Grapes: Red, Carignan, Grenache, Mourvèdre, Syrah, Cinsault, Picpoul, Counoise. (White grapes allowed also.) White, Clairette, Bourboulenc.

Large AOC, a big chunk of the southern Rhône Valley with a varied topography. A spread of quality, but a light, easy red dominates. Some wines show carbonic maceration characters. Very little white.

Côtes du Vivarais
Region: Rhône
Appellation Contrôlée
Red, rosé and white, min alc 10.5%, max yield 50 hl/ha.
Grapes: Red, Grenache and Syrah min 90%, Cinsault, Carignan. White, Clairette, Marsanne, Grenache Blanc, Trebbiano.

Wine from an area on the western banks of the Rhône in the district of Ardèche.

Cour Cheverny
Region: Loire
Appellation Contrôlée
White only, min alc 9.5%, max yield 60 hl/ha.
Grape: Romorantin.

A small (less than 124 acres/50 ha) AOC near the town of Blois near the AOC Cheverny. The nearby town of Romorantin gives its name to the local grape variety for Cour Cheverny, producing a fairly tart white; nevertheless drink-youngest is available. The grape is losing favor.

Crémant d'Alsace
Region: Northeast France
Appellation Contrôlée
Sparkling, min alc 8%, max yield, 100 hl/ha.
Grapes: Pinot Blanc, Pinot Noir, Riesling, Pinot Gris.

Big production AOC making a bubbly that can be wonderful but is not regarded too seriously internationally.

Crémant de Bourgogne   **Region: Burgundy**
Appellation Contrôlée
Sparkling white or rosé, min alc 10%, max yield 55 hl/ha.
Grapes: Chardonnay, Pinot Noir.
For sparkling red, *refer* **Bourgogne Mousseux**.

An overlooked AOC which has quality controls in place to lift quality. The traditional method is used, minimum age is nine months, and wine must pass a taste test before release.

Crémant du Jura   **Region: Jura**
Appellation Contrôllée
Rosé and white, min alc 10%, max yield 65 hl/ha.
Grapes: Rosé, Pinot Noir, Trousseau, Poulsard. White, Chardonnay, Savignon.

Not highly regarded but can surprise.

Crémant de Loire   **Region: Loire**
Appellation Contrôlée
Sparkling rosé and white, min alc 9.5%, max yield 50 hl/ha.
Grapes: Chenin Blanc, Cabernet Franc, Pineau d'Aunis, Pinot Noir, Chardonnay, Arbois, Groslot max 30%.

Lower yielding AOC than some of the Loire sparklings, with a little longer lees-aging required before disgorgement.

Crépy   **Region: Swiss border**
Appellation Contrôlée
White only, min alc 9.5%, max yield 55 hl/ha.
Grape: Chasselas (known locally as fondant).

AOC of a small village in the Savoie district close to the shores of Lake Geneva on the eastern boundaries of France. Wines regarded as pleasant and usually the best of Savoie.

Criots-Bâtard-Montrachet   **Region: Burgundy**
Appellation Contrôlée
White only, min alc 11.5%, max yield 40 hl/ha.
Grape: Chardonnay.

A tiny Grand Cru AOC of less than 5 acres (2 ha) in the village of Chassagne-Montrachet in central Côte de Beaune. This vineyard is adjacent to the famous Le Montrachet vineyard and is regarded very highly, although the size means its wines are seldom seen.

Crozes-Hermitage
Region: Rhône
Appellation Contrôlée
Red and white, min alc 10%, max yield 45 hl/ha.
Grapes: Syrah, Marsanne, Roussanne. The latter two are white varieties but may also be (rarely) blended in the red.

Mainly red AOC from extensive vineyards below the famous hill of AOC Hermitage on the Rhône. The wines have some similarity to AOC Hermitage but are lighter generally, without the distinction of the overlooking hill. Nonetheless they can be excellent, spicy and alive, and are enjoyable young. They are usually much cheaper than AOC Hermitage (AOC Crozes-Hermitage is available in much greater volume). This is quite a large AOC, and styles and quality vary.

Échezeaux
Region: Burgundy
Appellation Contrôlée
Red only, min alc 11.5%, max yield 35 hl/ha.
Grape: Pinot Noir.

Grand Cru Burgundy AOC in the Côte de Nuits. Highly respected, but has perhaps dropped a little from favor over the past 20 years.

Entraygues et du Fel
Region: Southwest France
VDQS
Red, rosé and white, min alc 9%, max yield 45 hl/ha.
Grapes: Red, Cabernet Sauvignon and Franc, Gamay, Négrette, Fer. White, Chenin Blanc, Mauzac.

Situated 108 miles (175 km) east of Bordeaux (past Cahors) on the banks of the Lot River, this is a tiny region without a big following.

Entre-Deux-Mers
Region: Bordeaux
Appellation Contrôlée
White only, min alc 10%, max yield 60 hl/ha.
Grapes: Sauvignon Blanc, Sémillon, Muscadelle, Trebbiano, Colombard, Merlot Blanc, Mauzac.

Entre-Deux-Mers ("between two seas") actually lies between the Dordogne and Garonne rivers, before they meet to become the Gironde. A big volume AOC that consists of many growers linked by cooperatives, producing some cheerful low-priced wines. In an AOC this large clearly some will be better than others, but generally the region provides good quaffing white.

Faugères
Region: Languedoc
Appellation Contrôlée
Red only, min alc 11.5%, max yield 50 hl/ha.
Grapes: Carignan max 40%, Syrah, Mourvèdre, Grenache and Lladoner Pelut min 20%, Cinsault max 60%.

Carbonic maceration used to rule this small AOC, but as time passes this method is being used less. A complex AOC Faugères holds no special reputation, its wines being a mix of evolution and development related to market requirements. Red can be bold and cheerful. Whites are sold as AOC Coteaux du Languedoc.

Fiefs Vendéens   Region: Loire
VDQS
Red, rosé and white, min alc 9%, max yield 50 hl/ha.
Grapes: Red and rosé, Pinot Noir, Gamay, Cabernet Sauvignon and Franc, Grolleau Gris. White, Chenin Blanc, Sauvignon Blanc, Chardonnay, Colombard.

The Vendée region is south of the Muscadet AOCs, towards the Atlantic end of the Loire. These are considered country wines; not much is exported.

Fitou   Region: Languedoc
Appellation Contrôlée
Red only, min alc 12%, max yield 45 hl/ha.
Grapes: Carignan and Grenache at least 90% but Carignan must have max 75%, Syrah, Mourvèdre, Cinsault collectively up to 10%. Changes are occurring in blends here, which will carry on through to 2007, in particular easing back on Carignan and lifting Syrah.

AOC Fitou, from *fita*, a local word meaning the limit or boundary (here between France and Spain), is a large area with a variation in climate and wine style. From light to solid red, there are some quaffers and some better wines, each priced accordingly. AOC Rivesaltes can also be made in this region.

Fixin   Region: Burgundy
Appellation Contrôlée
Red, min alc 10.5%, Premier Cru 11%; max yield 40 hl/ha. White, min alc 11%, Premier Cru 11.5%; max yield 45 hl/ha.
Grapes: Red, Pinot Noir. White, Chardonnay.

Wine from the most northern village in the Côte de Nuits, a few miles south of Dijon. It has eight *premiers crus* vineyards. Although not enjoying the top reputation of Burgundian villages, Fixin can be depended on for good burgundy at lower prices than some of the big names.

Fleurie   Region: Beaujolais
Appellation Contrôlée
Red only, min alc 10%, single vineyard 10.5%; max yield 48 hl/ha.
Grape: Gamay.

A Beaujolais *cru* producing better quality wine than those using simply AOC Beaujolais, and therefore entitled to its own AOC. There are 10 such *cru* in Beaujolais. Better vineyards in the village may add their name to the village name (a classification that has a higher alcohol requirement) but "Appellation Fleurie Contrôlée" will appear underneath.

Fronsac   **Region: Bordeaux**
Appellation Contrôlée
Red only, min alc 11%, max yield 42 hl/ha.
Grapes: Cabernet Sauvignon and Franc, Merlot, Malbec.

Region close to Libourne and linked to the Canon-Fronsac AOC. Considered a generous, well-spined style (Cabernet Sauvignon plays its part here) that can be exceptional value.

Gaillac   **Region: Southwest France**
Appellation Contrôlée
Red and rosé, min alc 10.5%, max yield 55 hl/ha. White and sparkling, min alc 10%, max yield 60 hl/ha. Sweet white, min alc 11%, max yield 45 hl/ha.
Gaillac Premières Côtes, min alc 11%, max yield 45 hl/ha.
Wine from 11 communes on slopes.
Grapes: Red, Duras, Fer and Gamay (from 2000 vintage onwards, at least 60% of these is required), with Syrah (included up to 1999), Cabernet Sauvignon and Franc. White, Merlot, Mauzac, Len de l'El, Muscadelle, Sémillon, Ondenc and Sauvignon Blanc.

As seen in the list of grape varieties, this is a diverse, multi-cultured AOC that produces some wonderful sweet whites from oak-aged Mauzac; Gaillac Perlé, which has a hint of sparkling; and a regional style of red with a big mix of grapes. The Premières Côtes (literally "best slopes") AOC, an appellation for wine from 11 villages in the center of the Gaillac region, has extra requirements.

Gevrey-Chambertin   **Region: Burgundy**
Appellation Contrôlée
Red only, min alc 10.5%, Premier Cru 11%; max yield 40 hl/ha.
Grape: Pinot Noir.

Something of a special AOC towards the north of the Côte de Nuits. Gevrey-Chambertin is the village and within it lie eight *grands crus* (each with their own AOC and using "Chambertin" as part of their name) and almost 30 *premiers crus* (which use AOC Gevrey-Chambertin). This is a village surrounded by highly regarded vineyards and containing its own complex, sometimes rich, sometimes vibrant style. For this we pay a little more!

Gigondas   **Region: Rhône**
Appellation Contrôlée
Red and rosé only, min alc 12.5%, max yield 35 hl/ha.
Grapes: Grenache, Syrah, Mourvèdre, Cinsault, Carignan.

Wine from a village 12 miles (20 km) northeast of Avignon, not far from Châteauneuf-du-Pape and sharing a border with Vacqueyras, with which the wine is most often compared. Gigondas offers very tasty reds, nicely spicy, sometimes full-bodied. Generally very well-respected, though the rosé is less so, and not for keeping.

Givry   Region: Southern Burgundy
Appellation Contrôlée
Red, min alc 10.5%, Premier Cru 11%; max yield 45 hl/ha. White, min alc 11%, Premier Cru 11.5%; max yield 50 hl/ha.
Grapes: Red, Pinot Noir. White, Chardonnay.

Producing mostly red wine, Givry AOC, in the Chalonnaise (the hills of Chalon), attracts a little more interest and has a slight lift in quality compared to the more ordinary wines from other AOCs of the Chalonnaise. Givry has 22 *premiers crus* vineyards, but the AOC covers just 90 acres (36 ha).

Grand Roussillon   Region: Roussillon
Vin Doux Naturel
White only, min alc 15%, max yield 30 hl/ha.
Grapes: Grenache Noir, Gris and Blanc, Muscat à Petits Grains, Muscat d'Alexandrie, Maccabeo, Tourbut, and Carignan, Cinsault and Syrah up to 10%.

The exact reason for Grand Roussillon seems uncertain; it is essentially a variation on VDN Rivesaltes, a classification preferred by most producers for this style.

Grands Échezeaux   Region: Burgundy
Appellation Contrôlée
Red only, min alc 11.5%, max yield 35 hl/ha.
Grape: Pinot Noir.

Single-vineyard Grand Cru AOC in the Côte de Nuits with several owners. Well respected.

Graves   Region: Bordeaux
Appellation Contrôlée
Red, min alc 10%, max yield 50 hl/ha. White, min alc 11%, max yield 50 hl/ha.
Grapes: Red, Cabernet Sauvignon and Franc, Malbec, Merlot, Petit Verdot. White, Sauvignon Blanc, Sémillon, Muscadelle.

On the left bank of the Garonne River, Graves is a shrinking AOC for two reasons: the ongoing urban spread of housing and an airport have taken historic vineyard land; and the introduction of a new AOC, Pessac-Léognan in 1987. The new AOC took some significant châteaux out of Graves but the region with the sandy and gravelly soil that gave the AOC its name, still houses some interesting and varied châteaux and vineyards making dry white and red. The southern end of Graves is "interrupted" by the sweet white AOCs of Cerons, Barsac and Sauternes, where the humidity in the river valley allows botrytis. Indeed, some botrytis-affected Graves wines are represented by the AOC Graves Supérieur.

The soil is gravelly and sandy and appears to reflect itself in an "earthy" taste in Graves wines. Roughly three times more white wine (both sweet and dry) is produced than red, although the red wines are generally more respected than the white, with the odd notable fine white exception.

Graves Supérieur   Region: Bordeaux
Appellation Contrôlée
White only, min alc 12%, max yield 50 hl/ha.
Grapes: Sémillon, Sauvignon Blanc, Muscadelle.

Sweet white AOC for vineyards around Graves that produce botrytis-affected white.

Graves de Vayres   Region: Bordeaux
Appellation Contrôlée
Red and white, min alc 10.5%, max yield 50 hl/ha.
Grapes: Red, Cabernet Sauvignon and Franc, Merlot, Malbec, Petit Verdot. White, Sauvignon Blanc, Sémillon, Muscadelle.

No connection with Graves, but soil gravelly. Area adjoins Entre-Deux-Mers on the northeast, 5 miles (8 km) from St-Émilion and Pomerol across the Dordogne River. Light, delicate reds, mellow whites, both dry and lightly sweet.

Griottes-Chambertin   Region: Burgundy
Appellation Contrôlée
Red only, min alc 11.5%, max yield 37 hl/ha.
Grape: Pinot Noir.

Single vineyard Grand Cru AOC adjacent to the great vineyard of Chambertin. Covers some 6.7 acres (2.7 ha) in the village of Gevrey-Chambertin in the Côte de Nuits. Highly respected wine from a tiny site.

Gros Plant du Pays Nantais   Region: Loire
VDQS
White only, min alc 8.5%, max yield 50 hl/ha.
Grape: Gros Plant (locally known as Picpoul and Folle Blanche).

Wine made from an area around Nantes near the Atlantic mouth of the Loire River. This area generally produces Muscadet grapes for the AOCs of that region; but this VDQS wine is made from the Gros Plant grape (a local synonym for Folle Blanche, one of the grapes used to make cognac). Wine is ideally fresh, light and slightly tart.

Haut-Médoc
Appellation Contrôlée   **Region: Bordeaux**
Red only, min alc 10%, max yield 48 hl/ha.
Grapes: Cabernet Sauvignon and Franc, Merlot, Malbec, Petit Verdot.

The AOC begins near the city of Bordeaux and runs up the left bank of the Gironde River for nearly 18 miles (30 km) to just north of the village of St-Éstèphe. The northern border of AOC Haut-Médoc is shared with the southern border of the area known as AOC Médoc, also known as the Bas-Médoc. The general term "Médoc" is taken frequently to refer to both the Haut-Médoc and Bas-Médoc. In AOC terms, however, the two should be identified separately.

There are 26 villages within the Haut-Médoc. The most highly-regarded six of these have their own AOCs: St-Éstèphe, Pauillac, St-Julien, Listrac, Moulis, Margaux, although AOC Margaux includes Soussans, Cantenac and the better parts of Arsac and Labarde. The other villages use AOC Haut-Médoc. Some fine château wine comes under this AOC, and previously some declassified wine from the six prestigious AOCs, but this is now less relevant. AOC Haut-Médoc may also include some *négociant* wine purchased from growers and châteaux throughout the defined AOC area.

Haut-Montravel
Appellation Contrôlée   **Region: Southwest France**
Sweet white, min alc 12%, max yield 50 hl/ha.
Grapes: Semillon, Sauvignon Blanc, Muscadelle.

Liqueur-like AOC from within the Montravel AOC on the north banks of the Dordogne River, near Bergerac. Fruity and sweet, often botrytis-affected.

Hermitage
Appellation Contrôlée   **Region: Rhône**
Red and white, min alc 10%, max yield 45 hl/ha. *Vin de Paille*, min alc 14%, max yield 15 hl/ha.
Grapes: Red, Syrah. White, Marsanne, Roussanne. Sometimes a little white is added to the red.

AOC including about 320 acres (130 ha) of vineyards on the slopes of the "hill" of Hermitage in the northern Rhône Valley, surrounded by the much larger AOC of Crozes-Hermitage. AOC Hermitage is famous and is respected for its full-bodied, strong red, some of the most delicious of its style in the world. Up to 15% of the two white grapes is permitted with the red; producers from Hermitage don't discuss their blends, but even if white *has* been blended in, it does not seem noticeable.

In the minority of Hermitage, the white can be pretty solid also, a little oxidative as a style. Perhaps not a great traveler or keeper, but some believe there is a long development phase for well-made wine, and this can be seen in white Hermitage very well after six to 10 years in the bottle. A small quantity of low-yielding *Vin de Paille* is made also in some years. For this, white grapes are allowed to overripen, then left on straw mats to dry out further in the sun; this results in high sugar-content and concentrated juice, which produces a high-alcohol, rich-flavored sweet wine.

Irouléguy   Region: Southwest France
Appellation Contrôlée
Red, min alc 10%. White and rosé, min alc 10.5%. Max yield 55 hl/ha.
Grapes: Red, Tannat, Cabernet Sauvignon and Franc. White, Gros Manseng, Petit Courbu, Petit Manseng.

AOC near the Spanish border; some vineyards are "built" into the southern slopes of the Pyrénées. Not big (about 296 acres/120 ha of vineyards) with the cooperative playing a big part in production. This is a region of well-drained soil, although not without some clay. Mostly producing reds, this is an area attracting interest in its best wines.

Jasnières   Region: Loire
Appellation Contrôlée
White only, min alc 10%, max yield 52 hl/ha.
Grape: Chenin Blanc.

Small AOC of Coteaux du Loir (not Loire), which produces the best white wine of the area. Being fairly high in acid, it needs bottle maturity to show its best; when young it would be described as "steely" or "austere." Some sweet, botrytis-affected wines can come from the right years.

Julienas   Region: Beaujolais
Appellation Contrôlée
Red only, min alc 10%, max yield 48 hl/ha.
Grape: Gamay.

A Beaujolais *cru* producing better quality wine than those using simply AOC Beaujolais and therefore entitled to its own AOC. There are 10 such *crus* in Beaujolais. Better vineyards in the village may add their name to the village name (a classification that has a higher alcohol requirement) but "Appellation Julienas Contrôlée" will appear underneath. Some white wine can be sold as AOC St-Véran.

Jurançon   Region: Southwest France
Appellation Contrôlée
White only. Dry white (*sec*), min alc 11%, max yield 60 hl/ha. Sweet white (*moelleux*), min alc 12%, max yield 40 hl/ha.
Grapes: Petit Manseng, Gros Manseng, Courbu and others.

AOC from a hilly area in the foothills of the Pyrénées, once very good for sweet white, and comparable to Sauternes and sweet Loire wines. The risk of leaving the grapes as late as December turned growers to dry wines, but now the trend is back to sweet, still with risk, but with some fine results.

Ladoix   **Region: Burgundy**
Appellation Contrôlée
Red, min alc 10.5%, Premier Cru 11%; max yield 40 hl/ha. White, min alc
11%, max yield 45 hl/ha.
Grapes: Red, Pinot Noir. White, Chardonnay.

AOC in the village of Ladoix-Serrigny, adjacent to Aloxe-Corton in the northern Côte de Beaune. A logical person may wonder why this AOC exists, since
much of the area is sold as Corton-Charlemagne, Côte de Beaune-Villages,
Aloxe-Corton and other AOCs. But some well-respected wines carry the
Ladoix AOC. Some from Serrigny are less respected.

La Grande Rue   **Region: Burgundy**
Appellation Contrôlée
Red only, min alc 11.5%, max yield 35 hl/ha.
Grape: Pinot Noir.

One vineyard, one owner. This controversial elevation of a 4-acre (1.7-ha)
Premier Cru Vosne-Romanée vineyard to Grand Cru status in the early 1990s
continues to be debated on its merits, but is a well-regarded *domaine* nevertheless.

Lalande-de-Pomerol   **Region: Bordeaux**
Appellation Contrôlée
Red only, min alc 10.5%, max yield 42 hl/ha.
Grapes: Merlot predominates, Cabernet Sauvignon and Franc, Malbec.

A sizeable AOC adjacent to Pomerol, including the village of Néac. Lots of
wine; some average, but the best châteaux have established a very strong
reputation.

La Romanée   **Region: Burgundy**
Appellation Contrôlée
Red only, min alc 11.5%, max yield 30 hl/ha.
Grape: Pinot Noir.

Tiny but highly-respected Grand Cru AOC from a single vineyard of less than
2.5 acres (1 ha) in the village of Vosne-Romanée in the southern half of the
Côte de Nuits.

La Tache   **Region: Burgundy**
Appellation Contrôlée
Red only, min alc 11.5%, max yield 35 hl/ha.
Grape: Pinot Noir.

Single-vineyard Grand Cru AOC of 14.8 acres (6 ha) in the village of Vosne-
Romanée in the southern half of the Côte de Nuits, enjoying a very high
reputation.

Latricières-Chambertin
Region: Burgundy
Appellation Contrôlée
Red only, min alc 11.5%, max yield 37 hl/ha.
Grapes: Pinot Noir.

Single-vineyard Grand Cru AOC of 18.5 acres (7.5 ha) adjacent to the great vineyard of Chambertin in the village of Gevrey-Chambertin in the Côte de Nuits. Highly respected.

Lavilledieu
Region: Rhône
VDQS
Red and rosé, min alc 10.5%, max yield 45 hl/ha.
Grapes: Gamay, Syrah and Cabernet Franc 25% each, Négrette 10%, Tannat 15%.

Area west of the Rhône, 90 miles (145 km) north of Avignon around the town of La Ville Dieu. Some say this VDQS is "obscure," others say it is "diminishing." Not a "hot" area at this time.

Les Baux-en-Provence
Region: Southeast France
Appellation Contrôlée
Red and rosé, min alc 11.5%, max yield 50 hl/ha.
Grapes: Red, Syrah, Cinsault and Grenache min 60%, Cabernet Sauvignon max 30%. White, Trebbiano, Rolle, Sauvignon Blanc, Grenache Blanc, Clairette.

AOC on a small hilltop area in the west of Provence with an average reputation. The most respected estate in this area, Domaine de Travallon, is excluded from using the AOC because its Cabernet proportion is too high.

L'Étoile
Region: Jura
Appellation Contrôlée
White only, min alc 10.5%, max yield 60 hl/ha.
Grapes: Chardonnay, Savagnin, Poulsard.
Vin jaune: This is made by aging wine from Savagnin grapes for six years in oak casks and allowing a *flor* growth to form in the sherry tradition. The resultant wine is similar in style to unfortified sherry. Min alc 11.5%.
Vin de paille (straw wine): A rich, golden sweet wine, this is made by picking the grapes very ripe, then laying them out on straw mats for a few days to further evaporate the water. This leaves a very concentrated juice with high sugar, resulting in sweet wine with a high alcohol content. Min alc 14.5%, max yield 20 hl/ha.

AOC in the south of the Jura, east of Burgundy.

L'Étoile Mousseux
Region: Jura
Appellation Contrôlée
Sparking white, min alc 10.5%, max yield 60 hl/ha.

Grapes: Chardonnay, Savagnin, Poulsard.

Wine from an area in the south of the Jura, to the east of Burgundy. The wine is made from Savagnin (better known elsewhere as Traminer) and Chardonnay grapes, using the champagne method.

Limoux   Region: Languedoc
Appellation Contrôlée
White only, min alc 10%, max yield 50 hl/ha.
Grapes: Chardonnay, Chenin Blanc, Mauzac.

AOC around Limoux township south of the town of Carcassonne. Area has some variability in elevation, and soils and wines can vary accordingly. This non-sparkling white has evolved from Mauzac grape to Chenin Blanc and Chardonnay, and now Mauzac must be only 15% (to retain typicity and heritage). AOC Limoux covers the non-sparklings, while AOC Crémant de Limoux covers sparklings with more Chardonnay in the blend and AOC Blanquette Méthode Ancestrale covers those bottled just before fermentation is finished to provide a little *pétillance*. Some red was also made under *Vin de Pays* until the new Rouge AOC was established in 2003.

Limoux Rouge   Region: Languedoc
Appellation Contrôlée
Red only, min alc 11%, max yield 50 hl/ha.
Grapes: Merlot min 50%, Malbec, Syrah and Carignan up to 30%, Cabernet Sauvignon and Franc up to 20%.

An AOC introduced in 2003 replacing Vin de Pays de la Haute Vallée de l'Aude. Limoux Rouge produces a blended red, light and fruity in style. Its potential is being developed.

Lirac   Region: Southern Rhône
Appellation Contrôlée
Red and rosé, min alc 12%, max yield 42 hl/ha. White, min alc 11.5%, max yield 42 hl/ha.
Grapes: Grenache, Mourvèdre, Syrah, Cinsault, Carignan. White, Clairette, Trebbiano, Bourboulenc, Marsanne, Roussanne.

AOC adjacent to Tavel with quite a sandy soil and, like Tavel, making plenty of rosé. Growing in popularity, this AOC is attracting investment interest from those winemakers who see its potential. Here decent red is respected, white can be idiosyncratic, and the best of this AOC is not exported widely. The reputation of Lirac is generally pretty good.

Listrac   Region: Bordeaux
Appellation Contrôlée
Red only, min alc 10.5%, max yield 45 hl/ha.
Grapes: Cabernet Sauvignon and Franc, Merlot, Malbec, Petit Verdot.

AOC in the Haut-Médoc, about 5.5 miles (9 km) northwest of Margaux, an area of clay and gravel soil with a little sand. The village has no classed growths from 1855. Good wine can be found here, if often a little hard and in need of aging.

Loupiac   Region: Bordeaux
Appellation Contrôlée
White only, min alc 13%, max yield 40 hl/ha.
Grapes: Sémillon, Sauvignon, Muscadelle.

Sweet white AOC from a hilly little area on the Garonne River opposite Barsac, surrounded by Premières Côtes de Bordeaux. Good solid sweet white, if not quite as distinguished as Sauternes and Barsac across the river. It is, of course, a lot cheaper. Some red wine is made here, which must use AOC Bordeaux.

Lussac-St-Émilion   Region: Bordeaux
Appellation Contrôlée
Red only, min alc 11%, max yield 45 hl/ha.
Grapes: Merlot, Cabernet Sauvignon and Franc, Malbec.

AOC northeast of St-Émilion, regarded as a "satellite" AOC. Some châteaux better than others, some regarded as good or better than St-Émilion. New vineyard land buyers have recently brought an increase in quality. Overlooked vineyards producing quality wine have been asking relatively low prices, which has increased investor interest and standards.

Mâcon   Region: Southern Burgundy
Appellation Contrôlée
Red and rosé, min alc 10%, max yield 55 hl/ha. White, min alc 11%, max yield 60 hl/ha.
Grapes: Red, Gamay, Pinot Noir. White, Chardonnay.

AOC in the Mâconnais, south of the Côte d'Or, producing large quantities of mainly red wine from the Gamay grape. Wines can be sound and lively. Not as respected (or as expensive) as the Côte d'Or but good opportunities for interesting, clean, decent wine at the right price. Better wines from the area use AOC Mâcon Supérieur and AOC Mâcon-Villages.

Mâcon-Blanc-Villages   Region: Southern Burgundy
Appellation Contrôlée
White only, min alc 11%, max yield 50 hl/ha.
Grape: Chardonnay.

Wine from selected villages in the Mâconnais. The selected areas are not of tremendous merit, and the quality is reputably better only in name than Mâcon Supérieur.

Mâcon Supérieur   **Region: Southern Burgundy**
Appellation Contrôlée
Red, min alc 10.5%, max yield 50 hl/ha. White, min alc 11.5%, max yield
55 hl/ha.
Grapes: Red, Gamay, Pinot Noir. White, Chardonnay.

Wine from a defined area in the Mâconnais producing nearly 3 million gallons (13 million L) or more in a high-yielding year. White generally regarded
as good palatable wine from Chardonnay grapes.

Mâcon-Villages (or village name)   **Region: Southern Burgundy**
Appellation Contrôlée
Red, min alc 10.5%, max yield 50 hl/ha. White, min alc 11.5%, max yield
55 hl/ha.
Grapes: Red, Gamay, Pinot Noir. White, Chardonnay.

Wine from a named village within the Mâconnais.

Madiran   **Region: Southwest France**
Appellation Contrôlée
Red only, 11% alc, max yield 55 hl/ha.
Grapes: Annat 40–60%, Cabernet Sauvignon and Franc, Fer.

AOC near Nearn with gutsy red wines that can age well, although they do
not have a big reputation. White from the area is sold under AOC Pacherenc
du Vic Bilh.

Maranges   **Region: Burgundy**
Appellation Contrôlée
Red, min alc 10.5%, Premier Cru 11%; max yield 40 hl/ha. White, min alc
11%, Premier Cru 11.5%; max yield 45 hl/ha.
Grapes: Red, Pinot Noir. White, Chardonnay.

Replacement AOC (1989) for Cheilly-les-Maranges, Dezize-les-Maranges
and Sampigny-les-Maranges. Area in the south of the Côte de Beaune making mostly red, which seems to be best enjoyed young and fresh.

Marcillac   **Region: Southwest France**
Appellation Contrôlée
Red and rosé, min alc 10%, max yield 50 hl/ha.
Grapes: Fer (known locally as Mansoi), Cabernet Sauvignon and Franc,
Merlot.

Wine from a very small area in the southwest of France in the district of
Aveyron centered on the town of Rodez. Fer is the grape in the majority
here. This remote AOC is struggling to find its feet.

Margaux
Region: Bordeaux
Appellation Contrôlée
Red only, min alc 10.5%, max yield 45 hl/ha.
Grapes: Cabernet Sauvignon and Franc, Merlot, Petit Verdot.

Highly respected AOC in the Haut-Médoc on the Gironde River, south of St-Julien. Wine from the surrounding villages of Cantenac and Soussans plus part of Arsac and Labarde are entitled to use the Margaux AOC instead of AOC Haut-Médoc (but this reduces their allowable maximum yield). The Margaux soil is the lightest of the Haut-Médoc region and contains the most gravel. The wine is generally lighter than Pauillac and St-Éstèphe and frequently matures earlier, depending on vintage and individual châteaux. Margaux has some famous châteaux (including Château Margaux), most with Cabernet Sauvignon making up 50% or more of the blend.

Marsannay
Region: Burgundy
Appellation Contrôlée
Red, min alc 10.5%, max yield 40 hl/ha. Rosé, min alc 10.5%, max yield 45 hl/ha. White, min alc 11%, max yield 45 hl/ha.
Grapes: Red, Pinot Noir. White, Chardonnay.

AOC to the north of the Côte de Nuits between Fixin and Dijon, including the villages of Marsannay, Couchey and Chenove. The rosé in particular has gained a fine reputation.

Maury
Region: Roussillon
Appellation Contrôlée
Sweet red only, min alc 15%, max yield 30 hl/ha.
Grapes: Grenache min 75%, Carignan, Macabeu.

Sweetish red, not quite like port but deliciously rich and smooth. Lightly fermented, it is oxidized to help the style, but bottled when young and fresh.

Mazis-Chambertin
Region: Burgundy
Appellation Contrôlée
Red only, min alc 11.5%, max yield 37 hl/ha.
Grape: Pinot Noir.

Single vineyard Grand Cru AOC of 22 acres (9 ha), close to the great estate of Le Chambertin in the village of Gevrey-Chambertin. Being a Burgundy Grand Cru, this is a highly respected wine. Not available in big quantities.

Mazoyères-Chambertin
Region: Burgundy
Appellation Contrôlée
Refer **Charmes-Chambertin.**

Médoc   Region: Bordeaux
Appellation Contrôlée
Red only, min alc 10%, max yield 50 hl/ha.
Grapes: Cabernet Sauvignon and Franc, Merlot, Petit Verdot.

Wine from an area formerly known as the Bas-Médoc; that is, the seaward part of the Médoc, not the Haut-Médoc. The name Médoc can be misunderstood as it is also used as a collective term to refer to both. As far as the AOC is concerned, however, Médoc wine comes from the area beginning just north of St-Éstèphe and extending 24 miles (40 km) down the Gironde River to its mouth. The area is always considered less favorably than the Haut-Médoc and has fewer top-rated châteaux. Yet the wines are cheaper, and are often very worthwhile and excellent value.

Menetou-Salon   Region: Loire
Appellation Contrôlée
Red, white and rosé, min alc 10.5%, max yield 60 hl/ha.
Grapes: Red and rosé, Pinot Noir. White, Sauvignon Blanc.

Smallish, 272-acre (110-ha) Loire AOC between the cities of Bourges and Sancerre, on the river north of Nevers. A little overlooked but quite able to produce excellent Sauvignon.

Mercurey   Region: Burgundy
Appellation Contrôlée
Red, min alc 10.5%, Premier Cru 11%; max yield 40 hl/ha. White, min alc 11%, Premier Cru 11.5%; max yield 45 hl/ha.
Grapes: Red, Pinot Noir. White, Chardonnay.

A large AOC by Burgundy standards, 1,325 acres (530 ha), in the Côte Chalonnaise south of the Côte de Beaune. Barely 5% is white. The area is respected for producing a fine second-level burgundy, soft in character; wine produced from good years matures well. Prices are typically well below Côte d'Or prices. Production of this size will, of course, bring strong variations in quality.

Meursault   Region: Burgundy
Appellation Contrôlée
Red, min alc 10.5%, Premier Cru 11%; max yield 40 hl/ha. White, min alc 11%, Premier Cru 11.5%; max yield 45 hl/ha.
Grapes: Red, Pinot Noir. White, Chardonnay.

Wine from an important village in the central Côte de Beaune. More than 95% is white wine. Red can use the Volnay AOC. Meursault has no *grands crus* but nevertheless is highly regarded for consistently good white burgundy, dry and soft. Some *premiers crus* are thought to be magnificent.

Minervois
Region: Languedoc
Appellation Contrôlée
Red and rosé, min alc 11.5%, max yield 50 hl/ha. White, min alc 11%, max yield 50 hl/ha.
Grapes: Red and rosé, up to at least 60% of Syrah, Mourvèdre, Lladoner Pelut and Grenache (Syrah must be at least 10%), plus Carignan, Cinsault, Picpoul, Terret Noir and Aspiran Noir max 40%. White, Bourboulenc and Maccabeo min 50%; plus Marsanne, Picpoul, Clairette, Grenache Blanc, Terret Blanc, Listan Blanc, Muscat à Petits Grains, Muscat d'Alexandrie.

Big AOC in the Midi, towards the Spanish border, with many variables throughout in topography, soil and climate. One "heartland" subregion, Minervois la Livinière, has its own AOC (*refer* below). The reputation of AOC Minervois is one of sound, sometimes very good, wines amidst such a variable catchment area.

Minervois la Livinière
Region: Languedoc
Appellation Contrôlée
Red and rosé, min alc 11.5%, max yield 45 hl/ha. White, min alc 11%, max yield 45 hl/ha.
Grapes: Red and rosé, up to at least 60% of Syrah, Mourvèdre, Lladoner Pelut and Grenache (Syrah must be at least 10%), plus Carignan, Cinsault, Picpoul, Terret Noir and Aspiran Noir max 40%. White, Bourboulenc and Maccabeo min 50%; plus Marsanne, Picpoul, Clairette, Grenache Blanc, Terret Blanc, Listan Blanc, Muscat à Petits Grains, Muscat d'Alexandrie.

From within the heartland of Minervois, this AOC has been selected as showing quality to the point of being granted its own appellation, with a reduced allowable yield.

Monbazillac
Region: Southwest France
Appellation Contrôlée
White only, min alc 12.5%, max yield 40 hl/ha.
Grapes: Sauvignon Blanc, Sémillon, Muscadelle.

This was once considered the "poor man's Sauternes," with noble rot (botrytis) and the same grape varieties as Sauternes downriver. Considered best at two or three years, it has a different character to Sauternes and a higher allowable yield. Some good wines, particularly in good years, and priced well below their downriver cousins.

Montagne-St-Émilion
Region: Bordeaux
Appellation Contrôlée
Red only, min alc 11%, max yield 45 hl/ha.
Grapes: Cabernet Sauvignon and Franc, Malbec, Merlot.

AOC to the north of, and adjacent to, St-Émilion, and a little higher in elevation. The largest of the "satellite" AOCs of St-Émilion, this is regarded well enough, if without the status of St-Émilion. However, in recent years, the lower priced vineyards have been given enthusiastic new life by investors and winemakers from outside the region, and there are some châteaux and sites now doing much better than previously. This AOC now incorporates two others, St-Georges-St-Émilion and Parsac-St-Émilion.

Montagny   Region: Southern Burgundy
Appellation Contrôlée
White only, min alc 11%, Premier Cru 11.5%; max yield 50 hl/ha.
Grape: Chardonnay.

Wine from an area in the Côte Chalonnaise south of Mercurey. Generally considered good quality and can be very good value.

Monthelie   Region: Burgundy
Appellation Contrôlée
Red, min alc 10.5%, Premier Cru 11%; max yield 40 hl/ha. White, min alc 11%, Premier Cru 11.5%; max yield 45 hl/ha.
Grapes: Red, Pinot Noir. White, Chardonnay.

A small AOC, with almost entirely red wine from Monthelie, a village in the northern half of the Côte de Beaune, adjoining Volnay and Meursault. Similar in style to Volnay and perhaps underrated.

Montlouis   Region: Loire
Appellation Contrôlée
White only, min alc 10.5%, max yield 52 hl/ha.
Grape: Chenin Blanc.

AOC on the south side of the Loire, across the river from Vouvray. Montlouis can be a little softer than Vouvray, but it is often difficult to tell them apart.

Montlouis Mousseux   Region: Loire
Appellation Contrôlée
Sparking white only, min alc 9.5%, max yield 65 hl/ha.
Grape: Chenin Blanc.

AOC on the south side of the Loire, across the river from Vouvray. These sparkling wines are similar to Vouvray, and better known. Well regarded.

Montrachet   Region: Burgundy
Appellation Contrôlée
White only, min alc 12%, max yield 40 hl/ha.
Grape: Chardonnay.

Very famous 20-acre (8-ha) single-vineyard Grand Cru AOC partly in Puligny-Montrachet village and partly in Chassagne-Montrachet, in the Côte de Beaune. Rated as one of the top dry white wines of the world.

Montravel   **Region: Southwest France**
Appellation Contrôlée
White only, min alc 10%, max yield 50 hl/ha.
Grapes: Sémillon predominates, with Sauvignon Blanc and Muscadelle.

AOC on the edge of Bergerac on the north bank of the Dordogne River, but out of Bordeaux. The wines tend to be dry but fruity. The better wines use the appellations Côtes de Montravel and Haut-Montravel.

Montravel Rouge   **Region: Southwest France**
Appellation Contrôlée
Red only, min alc 11.5%, max yield 45 hl/ha.
Grapes: Merlot min 50%, Cabernet Sauvignon and Franc, Malbec.

A new (2003) AOC almost adjacent to St-Émilion and Pomerol with which the wine has often been compared, although it is much cheaper. Montravel Rouge is the first AOC to award a wine AOC status only after the wine is bottled and tested as a finished wine – this includes the requirement that it have an "aptitude for aging".

Morey-St-Denis   **Region: Burgundy**
Appellation Contrôlée
Red, min alc 10.5%, Premier Cru 11%; max yield 40 hl/ha. White, min alc 11%, Premier Cru 11.5%; max yield 45 hl/ha.
Grapes: Red, Pinot Noir. White, Chardonnay.

AOC in the central part of the Côte de Nuits. This village carries four famous *grands crus* (with their own AOCs) and 26 *premiers crus*, which indicates the high overall strength of the area.

Morgon   **Region: Beaujolais**
Appellation Contrôlée
Red only, min alc 10.5%, max yield 48 hl/ha.
Grape: Gamay.

A Beaujolais *cru* producing better quality wine than those using simply AOC Beaujolais and therefore entitled to its own AOC. There are 10 such *crus* in Beaujolais. Morgon offers a little more color and depth than some *crus*, leading to longer bottle age. Better vineyards in the village may add their name to the village name (a classification with a higher alcohol requirement) but "Appellation Morgon Contrôlée" will appear underneath.

Moulin-à-Vent   **Region: Beaujolais**
Appellation Contrôlée
Red only, min alc 10.5%, max yield 48 hl/ha.
Grape: Gamay.

A Beaujolais *cru* producing better quality wine than those using simply AOC

Beaujolais and therefore entitled to its own AOC. There are 10 such *crus* in Beaujolais. Moulin-à-Vent tends to be concentrated and matures well in the bottle, perhaps more than the other *crus*. Better vineyards in the village may add their name to the village name (a classification with a higher alcohol requirement) but "Appellation Moulin-à-Vent Contrôlée" will appear underneath.

Moulis   Region: Bordeaux
Appellation Contrôlée
Red only, min alc 10.5%, max yield 45 hl/ha.
Grapes: Cabernet Sauvignon and Franc, Merlot, Petit Verdot.

The smallest appellation in the Haut-Médoc, about 4 miles (7 km) northwest of Margaux township. The area boasts no classed growths and has only a moderate reputation. Several labels include "Poujeaux" as part of the wine title; this refers to a gravelly part of Moulis generally regarded as superior. The wines are looked on as being hard in character and requiring bottle age.

Mousseux de Savoie   Region: East of Burgundy
Appellation Contrôlée
Refer **Vin de Savoie Mousseux** or **Pétillant**.

Muscadet   Region: Loire
Appellation Contrôlée
White only, min alc 9%, max yield 65 hl/ha.
Grape: Muscadet locally known as Melon de Bourgogne. Not to be confused with either Muscat or Muscadelle, which are grown elsewhere.

Large AOC 60 miles (100 km) from the mouth of the Loire, south and southwest of the town of Nantes. Wine from an area some 695 square miles (1,800 square km). Two other AOCs (Muscadet de Sèvre-et-Maine and Muscadet des Coteaux de la Loire) are adjacent to this area and also use Muscadet grapes. Within the three areas, Gros Plant grapes may be planted but wine made from this qualifies only as Gros Plant du Pays Nantais VDQS. Wine with the Muscadet appellation is regarded quite highly as light, fresh wine, ready when young.

This is not a wine for aging. Much is sold as *sur lie* – these words on the label mean it has had some lees contact, which may add a little more richness and complexity to what can otherwise be a simple white style.

Muscadet des Coteaux de la Loire   Region: Loire
Appellation Contrôlée
White only, min alc 9%, max yield 55 hl/ha.
Grape: Muscadet locally known as Melon de Bourgogne. Not to be confused with either Muscat or Muscadelle, which are grown elsewhere.

AOC to the east of the town of Nantes, near the mouth of the Loire, on both sides of the river around the towns of Ancenis, Varades and Bouzille, with Ligne on the northern boundary. Well regarded for light fruity wine to be enjoyed young. *Sur lie* (some lees contact) is sometimes used to give the yeast cells the chance to impose a little richness and complexity.

Muscadet Côtes de Grand Lieu   Region: Loire
Appellation Contrôlée
White only, min alc 9%, max yield 55 hl/ha.
Grape: Muscadet locally known as Melon de Bourgogne. Not to be confused with either Muscat or Muscadelle, which are grown elsewhere.

Fairly new AOC (1994) around Bouaye and Lege, southwest of Nantes, surrounding the Grand Lieu Lake. Different soil (less clay, more sand) than AOC Muscadet de Sèvre-et-Maine and a slightly different style (though still light) emerges.

Muscadet de Sèvre-et-Maine   Region: Loire
Appellation Contrôlée
White only, min alc 9%, max yield 55 hl/ha.
Grape: Muscadet locally known as Melon de Bourgogne. Not to be confused with either Muscat or Muscadelle, which are grown elsewhere.

AOC defined as "vineyards between the rivers Sèvre and Maine," both tributaries of the Loire, on the eastern side of the town of Nantes, at the Atlantic end of the Loire River, barely 60 miles (100 km) from the river mouth. AOC well regarded for light, dry whites. Plenty of volume. Much is sold as *sur lie* – these words on the label mean it has had some lees contact, which may add some richness and complexity.

Muscat de Beaumes-de-Venise   Region: Rhône
Appellation Contrôlée
Sweet white, min alc 15%, max yield 30 hl/ha.
Grape: Muscat à Petits Grains.

Sweetish white AOC wine that most of the time has a little alcohol added, although the style is referred to as *Vin Doux Naturel*. A nice grapey white wine, which can be delicious. Red can use the AOC Rhône Villages with Beaumes-de-Venise hyphenated as the village.

Muscat de Frontignan   Region: Languedoc
Vin Doux Naturel
White only. No min alc or max yield, but min sugar at picking 14° Baumé.
Grape: Muscat à Petits Grains.

At its best, a nicely grapey, fruity style, made by lightly fortifying the Muscat partway through fermentation. One of four such VDNs in the Languedoc; often compared to Muscat de Beaumes-de-Venise, which has AOC status.

Muscat de Lunel
Region: Languedoc
Vin Doux Naturel
White only. No min alc or max yield, but min sugar at picking 14° Baumé.
Grape: Muscat à Petits Grains.

At its best, a nicely grapey, fruity style, made by lightly fortifying the Muscat partway through fermentation. One of four such VDNs in the Languedoc; often compared to Muscat de Beaumes-de-Venise, which has AOC status.

Muscat de Mireval
Region: Languedoc
Vin Doux Naturel
White only. No min alc or max yield, but min sugar at picking 14° Baumé.
Grape: Muscat à Petits Grains.

At its best, a nicely grapey, fruity style, made by lightly fortifying the Muscat partway through fermentation. One of four such VDNs in the Languedoc; often compared to Muscat de Beaumes-de-Venise, which has AOC status.

Muscat de Rivesaltes
Region: Roussillon
Vin Doux Naturel
White only, min alc 15%, max yield 30 hl/ha.
Grapes: Muscat d'Alexandrie, Muscat à Petits Grains.

Sweet wine that can be made from Muscat grapes grown throughout the Roussillon and adjacent regions (including AOC Fiteau). Something of a catchall appellation for its style and location but with some sound, enjoyable white of varying sweetness levels. (Note that both Muscat grape varieties are allowed here, while only one is allowed in Muscat de Beaumes-de-Venise).

Muscat de St-Jean-de-Minervois
Region: Languedoc
Vin Doux Naturel
White only. No min alc or max yield, but min sugar at picking 14° Baumé.
Grape: Muscat à Petits Grains.

At its best, a nicely grapey, fruity style made by lightly fortifying the Muscat partway through fermentation. One of four such VDNs in the Languedoc; often compared to Muscat de Beaumes-de-Venise, which has AOC status.

Musigny
Region: Burgundy
Appellation Contrôlée
Red, min alc 11.5%, max yield 35 hl/ha. White, min alc 12%, max yield 40 hl/ha.
Grapes: Red, Pinot Noir. White, Chardonnay.

Grand Cru vineyard in the village of Chambolle-Musigny, on the southern half of the Côte de Nuits. This vineyard is very highly regarded for its red, mentioned in the same company as some of the very best *grand cru* reds, such as Clos de Vougeot and Romanée Conti. (All *grands crus* are fantastic, but some are more fantastic than others!) The white is the only *grand cru* white in the whole of the Côte de Nuits, but only a very small proportion of production here.

Nuits-St-Georges
Appellation Contrôlée   **Region: Burgundy**

Red, min alc 10.5%, Premier Cru 11%; max yield 40 hl/ha. White, min alc 11%, Premier Cru 11.5%; max yield 45 hl/ha.
Grapes: Red, Pinot Noir. White, Chardonnay.

AOC from around the town of Nuits-St-Georges in the central Côte de Nuits. The area includes Premeaux, a village adjacent to Nuits-St-Georges that produces fine wine. Collectively, however, the area produces no *grand crus*, but the wine style is often generalized as being "typically burgundy."

The appellation can be regarded as of generally good quality; the name having become a household word in wine circles perhaps puts the price up slightly.

Orléanais
VDQS   **Region: Loire**
Refer **Vins de l'Orléanais.**

Pacherenc du Vic Bilh
Appellation Contrôlée   **Region: South of Bordeaux**

White only, min alc 12%, max yield 40 hl/ha.
Grapes: Arrufiac, Courbu and Petit Manseng min 60%, with Gros Manseng and Sauvignon Blanc.

AOC of about 500 acres (200 ha) from within the Madiran area, the dry and dry-medium style seen as similar to whites of the Jurançon further south.

Palette
Appellation Contrôlée   **Region: Provence**

Red, rosé and white, min alc 11%, max yield 40 hl/ha.
Grapes: Red and rosé, Grenache, Mourvèdre and Cinsault min 80%; with Syrah, Carignan, Castet, Manosquin, Muscat Noir and Cabernet Sauvignon up to 20%. White, Clairette min 80%, with Bourboulenc, Trebbiano, Grenache Blanc, Muscat.

AOC 12 miles (20 km) northeast of Marseille. This is a small area of barely 62 acres (25 ha), but produces some distinctive wines in the right years. Its reputation is limited by availablility.

Patrimonio
Appellation Contrôlée   **Region: Corsica**

Red, min alc 12%, max yield 50 hl/ha. Rosé and white, min alc 11.5%, max yield 50 hl/ha.

Grapes: Red, Nielluccio, Grenache, Sciacarello, Rolle. White, Vermentino.

Wine from the northwest of the island. Only small quantities leave the area, generally bound for restaurants in Paris and Marseille.

Pauillac   Region: Bordeaux
Appellation Contrôlée
Red only, min alc 10.5%, max yield 45 hl/ha.
Grapes: Cabernet Sauvignon and Franc, Merlot, Malbec, Petit Verdot.

AOC in the Haut-Médoc on the Gironde River. Highly-respected village and châteaux. Soil is quite heavy and gravelly with a stony subsoil. As a result the wines, with a slightly higher proportion of Cabernet Sauvignon, can be big, round and firm, and need more time to age than those of Margaux and St-Julien, which are generally softer and ready for drinking a little earlier.

Pécharmant   Region: Southwest France
Appellation Contrôlée
Red only, min alc 11%, max yield 45 hl/ha.
Grapes: Cabernet Sauvignon and Franc, Merlot, Malbec.

Wine from an area just outside Bergerac town, selling Bordeaux blends that can carry very good bottle development. Not much exported.

Pernand-Vergelesses   Region: Burgundy
Appellation Contrôlée
Red, min alc 10.5%, Premier Cru 11%; max yield 40 hl/ha. White, min alc 11%, Premier Cru 11.5%; max yield 45 hl/ha.
Grapes: Red, Pinot Noir. White, Chardonnay.

Wine from a village adjacent to Aloxe-Corton in the northern Côte de Beaune. Part of the famous vineyard areas of Corton and Corton-Charlemagne are actually in this village, but are always referred to as being in Aloxe-Corton. The *premiers crus* of this village are also entitled to use the Aloxe-Corton appellation. Other village wine is not highly regarded, but the area is in good company. (The Vergelesses vineyards extend into the village of Savigny-lès Beaune.) However, wine transported by a particular shipper must be regarded in the light of that shipper's reputation and integrity.

Pessac-Léognan   Region: Bordeaux
Appellation Contrôlée
Red, min alc 10%, max yield 45 hl/ha. White, min alc 11%, max yield 48 hl/ha.
Grapes: Red, Cabernet Sauvignon and Franc, Merlot, Malbec, Petit Verdot. White, Sauvignon Blanc, Sauvignon Gris, Sémillon, Muscadelle.

A new AOC, essentially splitting Graves into two pieces, in the late 1980s. Pessac-Léognan was the part closest to the city of Bordeaux and with high-reputation châteaux. This AOC requires a smaller yield than AOC Graves, in line with the main AOCs of the Haut-Médoc. As with the prestige of Chateau Haut Brion and others, Pessac-Léognan has a high image and commands respect. Most châteaux make both red and white wines; for the red, Cabernet Sauvignon is almost always the highest percentage in the blend.

Petit Chablis   **Region: Northwest of Burgundy**
Appellation Contrôlée
White only, min alc 9.5%, max yield 50 hl/ha.
Grape: Chardonnay.

The fourth of four AOC in Chablis, a junior sister to AOC Chablis. This appellation does not carry a lot of respect, and with its low minimum alcohol does not always travel well. The influence of the climate is strong in Chablis, which further reduces the consistency in quality of this AOC. Petit Chablis, although with surprises, should be considered as a low-cost quaffing wine.

Pomerol   **Region: Bordeaux**
Appellation Contrôlée
Red only, min alc 10.5%, max yield 42 hl/ha.
Grapes: Mainly Merlot and Cabernet Franc (known locally as Bouchet), with Malbec and Cabernet Sauvignon.

AOC around the town of Libourne on the Dordogne River. The area shares a boundary with St-Émilion, with whose wine the much smaller appellation of Pomerol is often compared. The style is soft and generally early-maturing, although there are long-life exceptions in the prestige châteaux. Pomerol has its own "unofficial" classification of its châteaux, over which Château Petrus reigns, but unlike St-Émilion, classification is not part of the AOC.

Pommard   **Region: Burgundy**
Appellation Contrôlée
Red only, min alc 10.5%, Premier Cru 11%; max yield 40 hl/ha.
Grape: Pinot Noir.

AOC from a famous village southwest of the city of Beaune. The village produces several *premiers crus*, some 40% of the AOC's production. Pommard has achieved a reputation for quality red, somewhat light in body but deep in color and usually with plenty of flavor.

Pouilly-Blanc-Fumé   **Region: Loire**
Appellation Contrôlée
Refer Pouilly-Fumé.

Pouilly-Fuissé   **Region: Southern Burgundy**
Appellation Contrôlée
White only, min alc 11%, single vineyard 12%; max yield 45 hl/ha.

Grape: Chardonnay.

Famous AOC in the Mâconnais, surrounded by Beaujolais. For Burgundy, this is quite a large AOC (2,100 acres/850 ha). Variable quality, but there are continued efforts to perform well and some excellent wines are produced. The wine must come from around the villages of Solutré, Pouilly, Fuissé, Chaintré and Vergisson. Single-vineyard wine (note its higher minimum alcohol requirement) can hyphenate the vineyard name onto the AOC.

Pouilly-Fumé   **Region: Loire**
Appellation Contrôlée
White only, min alc 10.5%, max yield 60 hl/ha.
Grape: Sauvignon Blanc.

Not to be confused with Pouilly-Fuissé (made from Chardonnay grapes) or Pouilly-sur-Loire (from Chasselas). Pouilly-Fumé is from the right bank of the Loire, towards its source and across the river from Sancerre, which also produces Sauvignon Blanc. Usually a sound, alive, slightly fruity wine drunk best as an accompaniment to food.

Pouilly-Loché   **Region: Southern Burgundy**
Appellation Contrôlée
White only, min alc 11%, single vineyard 12%; max yield 45 hl/ha.
Grape: Chardonnay.

AOC of barely 99 acres (40 ha) around the village of Loché, adjacent to AOC Pouilly-Fuissé in the Mâconnais, and may be sold as AOC Pouilly-Vinzelles. Lesser known and much smaller than Pouilly-Fuissé, but on average just as good. Single-vineyard wine (note its higher minimum alcohol) can hyphenate the vineyard name onto the AOC.

Pouilly-sur-Loire   **Region: Loire**
Appellation Contrôlée
White only, min alc 9%, max yield 60 hl/ha.
Grape: Chasselas.

AOC on the eastern bank of the Loire, before it curves to run through Touraine and Anjou and on to the sea. No connection with AOC Pouilly-Fuissé, nor should it be confused with the interrelated AOC Pouilly-Fumé (which uses only Sauvignon Blanc). Pouilly-sur-Loire is Chasselas territory across the river from Sancerre. Pouilly-sur-Loire carries little prestige, yet the wine is generally well-made and is enjoyed as a sensibly-priced quaffer.

Pouilly-Vinzelles   **Region: Burgundy**
Appellation Contrôlée
White only, min alc 11%, single vineyard 12%; max yield 45 hl/ha.
Grape: Chardonnay.

AOC from the village of Vinzelles, 259 acres (105 ha) adjacent to AOC Pouilly-Fuissé in the Mâconnais and AOC Beaujolais. Wine from this AOC is often as good as most Pouilly-Fuissé, but without the famous name of the latter it generally sells for much less and thus offers good value. AOC Pouilly-Loché is included within this AOC.

Premières Côtes de Blaye   **Region: Bordeaux**
Appellation Contrôlée
Red, min alc 10.5%, max yield 50 hl/ha. White, min alc 11%, max yield 60 hl/ha.
Grapes: Red, Cabernet Sauvignon and Franc, Merlot, Malbec, Petit Verdot. White, Sémillon, Sauvignon Blanc, Muscadelle, Trebbiano, Colombard.

Predominantly red AOC facing the right bank of the Gironde River. Most whites sold as Blaye or Côtes de Blaye.

Premières Côtes de Bordeaux   **Region: Bordeaux**
Appellation Contrôlée
Red, min alc 10.5%, max yield 50 hl/ha. White, min alc 12%, max yield 55 hl/ha.
Grapes: Red, Cabernet Sauvignon and Franc, Merlot, Malbec, Petit Verdot. White, Sémillon, Sauvignon Blanc, Sauvignon Gris, Muscadelle.

Area some 45 miles (75 km) long and 3.5 miles (6 km) wide running down the Garonne River opposite Graves and, at the lower end, opposite Sauternes. The other boundary is Entre-Deux-Mers. Red wines generally come from the top half of the area and sweet whites from the lower part, closer to Sauternes and Barsac (across the river). The quality generally is regarded as fair, and often good value. Red wine volume is by far the greatest; whites are often lightly sweet, as they are at least partially affected by botrytis.

Premières Côtes de Bordeaux-Cadillac   **Region: Bordeaux**
Appellation Contrôlée
Red, min alc 10.5%, max yield 50 hl/ha. White, min alc 12%, max yield 55 hl/ha.
Grapes: Cabernet Sauvignon and Franc, Merlot, Malbec, Petit Verdot.

AOC surrounded by Entre-Deux-Mers and Premières Côtes de Bordeaux but given the recognition of its own name hyphenated as a suffix. Mostly red and some dry white regarded as decent, good-value wine to be enjoyed at two to three years of age. Some sweet wine is also made in the area; this uses the straight Cadillac AOC.

Puisseguin-St-Émilion   **Region: Bordeaux**
Appellation Contrôlée
Red only, min alc 11%, max yield 45 hl/ha.
Grapes: Merlot, Cabernet Sauvignon and Franc, Malbec, Petit Verdot.

Wine from a village east of St-Émilion. Not generally regarded as highly as St-Émilion itself, but some châteaux will surpass minor St-Émilion châteaux.

Puligny-Montrachet   **Region: Burgundy**
Appellation Contrôlée
Red, min alc 10.5%, Premier Cru 11%; max yield 40 hl/ha. White, min alc 11%, Premier Cru 11.5%; max yield 45 hl/ha.
Grapes: Red, Pinot Noir. White, Chardonnay.

Wines from a village in the southern half of the Côte de Beaune, with part of Montrachet and three other *grand cru* vineyards extending into it. The remaining vineyards are in the adjoining village of Chassagne-Montrachet. The area, therefore, is highly regarded for quality, and the *premiers crus* and village wines of Puligny-Montrachet are sought after as top quality white burgundy. Normally less than 15% of production is red wine.

Quarts de Chaume   **Region: Anjou, Loire**
Appellation Contrôlée
White only, min alc 12%, max yield 25 hl/ha.
Grape: Chenin Blanc.

Small AOC of 100 acres (40 ha) on the banks of the Layon River, a tributary of the Loire. Well-regarded AOC for botrytis-affected sweet white. The maximum yield is as low as Sauternes.

Quincy   **Region: Loire**
Appellation Contrôlée
White only, min alc 10.5%, max yield 60 hl/ha.
Grape: Sauvignon Blanc (known locally as Pinot de la Loire).

AOC some 10 miles (16 km) west of Bourges on the Cher River, a tributary of the Loire. A dry white is produced from Sauvignon Blanc grapes, similar in style to Sancerre and Pouilly-Fumé. Regarded as a pleasant, spicy dry white, without a big reputation.

Rasteau   **Region: Rhône**
Vin Doux Natural
Red (known as *tuile*) and white (*ambre*), min alc 15%, max yield 30 hl/ha.
Grapes: Grenache min 90%, plus up to 10% Syrah, Cinsault and Carignan.

A *Vin Doux Naturel* made around the Rasteau village, which produces small quantities of oak-aged and often oxidated wine (*rancio*). Dry red can use the AOC Rhône Villages and hyphenate the Rasteau name as the village.

Régnié   **Region: Beaujolais**
Appellation Contrôlée
Red only, min alc 10.5%, max yield 48 hl/ha.
Grape: Gamay.

A relatively recent (1988) Beaujolais *cru* producing better quality wine than those using simply AOC Beaujolais and therefore entitled to its own AOC. There are 10 such *crus* in Beaujolais. Some vineyards in the village may add their name to the village name (a classification with a higher alcohol requirement) but "Appellation Régnié Contrôlée" will appear underneath.

Reuilly   Region: Loire
Appellation Contrôlée
Red and rosé, min alc 10%, max yield 55 hl/ha. White, min alc 10.5%, max yield 60 hl/ha.
Grapes: Red and rosé, Pinot Noir, Pinot Gris. White, Sauvignon Blanc.

AOC from an area near Quincy, 14 miles (24 km) west of Bourges. Wine is mostly dry white – there is some decent rosé, but little red volume. Frost damage can be hard, which means a difficult living for an AOC struggling to be noticed internationally.

Richebourg   Region: Burgundy
Appellation Contrôlée
Red only, min alc 11.5%, max yield 35 hl/ha.
Grape: Pinot Noir.

Single-vineyard Grand Cru AOC in the village of Vosne-Romanée in the southern half of the Côte de Nuits. This Grand Cru borders onto the other famous vineyards of Romaneé-Conti, La Romanée and Romanée St-Vivant. It is a very respected vineyard in a highly regarded top Burgundy red-wine village.

Rivesaltes   Region: Roussillon
Vin Doux Naturel
Red (known as *tuile*) and white (*ambre*), min alc 15%, max yield 30 hl/ha.
Grapes: Grenache, Muscat à Petits Grains, Muscat d'Alexandrie, Maccabeo and Tourbat, with Carignan, Cinsault and Syrah up to 10%.

Spread through the entire Roussillon area except for AOC Banyuls and AOC Collioure, this is a *Vin Doux Naturel*. A mixed bag; it comes in white, sometimes amber with oxidation, sometimes fresh with a grapey muscat tone. A large appellation for this style of wine, from varied *terroir*.

Romanée-Conti   Region: Burgundy
Appellation Contrôlée
Red only, min alc 11.5%, max yield 35 hl/ha.
Grape: Pinot Noir.

Tiny 4.5-acre (1.8-ha) single-vineyard Grand Cru in the village of Vosne-Romanée, in the southern half of the Côte de Nuits. Produces just 1,319 gallons (6,000 L) per year. This scarcity, together with the fact that Romanée-Conti is regarded by many who have tried it as the greatest wine in the world (except in bad years) ensures it one of the highest prices of the world's wine.

Romanée-St-Vivant   Region: Burgundy
Appellation Contrôlée
Red only, min alc 11.5%, max yield 35 hl/ha.
Grape: Pinot Noir.

Single-vineyard Grand Cru in the village of Vosne-Romanée. The 23-acre (9.4-ha) vineyard with several owners adjoins Romanée-Conti, and is regarded extremely highly. The wine of this vineyard could be as costly as Romanée-Conti if the latter were not so scarce, although Romanée-St-Vivant itself only produces some 1,500 cases in a good year.

Rosé d'Anjou   Region: Loire
Appellation Contrôlée
Rosé only, min alc 10%, max yield 50 hl/ha.
Grape: Groslot.

Fairly voluminous rosé AOC on both sides of the Loire, around the town of Angers. The local rosé made from Cabernet grapes has its own AOC, Cabernet d'Anjou, which is considered superior.

Rosé des Riceys   Region: Champagne
Appellation Contrôlée
Rosé, min alc 10%, max yield 87 hl/ha.
Grape: Pinot Noir.

A Champagne influence exists here, but this AOC is for non-sparkling, still light red. Rosé can be appealing, but generally it is undistinguished.

Rosette   Region: Southwest France
Appellation Contrôlée
White only, min alc 12%, max yield 40 hl/ha.
Grapes: Sémillon, Sauvignon, Muscadelle.

Mostly slightly sweet white, from an area north of the town of Bergerac; including part of the area that produces red wine under AOC Pécharmant.

Roussette du Bugey   Region: East of Burgundy
VDQS
White only, min alc 10.5% (when village name included, 11%), max yield 50 hl/ha.
Grape: Roussanne (known locally as Roussette).

Wine from an area east of the city of Lyon. Better villages may add their name to the label, but this classification has a higher alcohol requirement.

Roussette de Savoie   **Region: East of Burgundy**
VDQS
White only, min alc 10.5% (with village name, 11%), max yield 50 hl/ha.
Grape: Roussanne (known locally as Roussette).

Wine from an area east of the city of Lyon. Better villages may add their name to the label, but this classification has a higher alcohol requirement.

Ruchottes-Chambertin   **Region: Burgundy**
Appellation Contrôlée
Red only, min alc 11.5%, max yield 37 hl/ha.
Grape: Pinot Noir.

A single-vineyard Grand Cru of some 8.6 acres (3.5 ha) very close to the great vineyard of Chambertin, in the village of Gevrey-Chambertin in the Côte de Nuits. Highly respected.

Rully   **Region: Southern Burgundy**
Appellation Contrôlée
Red, min alc 10.5%, Premier Cru 11%; max yield 40 hl/ha. White, min alc 11%, Premier Cru 11.5%; max yield 50 hl/ha.
Grapes: Red, Pinot Noir. White, Chardonnay.

AOC surrounding the town of this name, just south of the Côte de Beaune, in the Côte Chalonnaise. Well-respected white wines, but 65% of production is a sound fruity red. In addition, quite a volume of sparkling wine is made here using the Bourgogne Mousseux and Crémant AOCs.

St-Amour   **Region: Beaujolais**
Appellation Contrôlée
Red only, min alc 10.5%, max yield 48 hl/ha.
Grape: Gamay.

A small Beaujolais *cru* producing better quality wine than those using simply AOC Beaujolais and is therefore entitled to its own AOC. There are 10 such *crus* in Beaujolais. Better vineyards in the village may add their names to the village name (a classification that has a higher alcohol requirement) but "Appellation St-Amour Contrôlée" will appear underneath. Some white wine can be sold as AOC St-Véran.

St-Aubin   **Region: Burgundy**
Appellation Contrôlée
Red, min alc 10.5%, Premier Cru 11%; max yield 40 hl/ha. White, min alc 11%, Premier Cru 11.5%; max yield 45 hl/ha.
Grapes: Red, Pinot Noir. White, Chardonnay.

Smallest AOC of Chassagne-Montrachet and Puligny-Montrachet. About two-thirds of the output is red wine. Not regarded as a premium AOC, although it does have *premiers crus*. Can be good value and can surprise.

St-Chinian   Region: Languedoc
Appellation Contrôlée
Red and rosé only, min alc 11.5%, max yield 50 hl/ha.
Grapes: Grenache, Lladoner Pelut, Syrah and Mourvèdre min 60%; Carignan up to 40% and Cinsault up to 30%. Thus can be made from up to 100% of any of the first four varieties if desired.

AOC northwest of Narbonne, between the AOCs of Minervois and Faugères. St-Chinian is about 6,700 acres (2,700 ha), with some vineyards on elevated, hilly land and some on flatter terrain. The style is not expensive, can be enjoyed young and is considered to be on the rise in terms of quality.

Ste-Croix-du-Mont   Region: Bordeaux
Appellation Contrôlée
White only, min alc 13%, max yield 40 hl/ha.
Grapes: Sémillon, Sauvignon, Muscadelle.

Sweet wine AOC, across the Garonne River from Sauternes and Barsac. Quality considered generally as fair. Not as highly regarded as those across the river, although it shares the same humid, botrytis-producing climate. Adjacent AOC is Loupiac, which makes similar wines.

St-Émilion   Region: Bordeaux
Appellation Contrôlée
Red only, min alc 11%, max yield 45 hl/ha.
Grapes: Merlot, Cabernet Sauvignon and Franc, Malbec.

AOC around Libourne, near but not quite bordering on the Dordogne River, with Pomerol on its northwestern border. St-Émilion produces wines with a high percentage of Merlot (compared with Cabernet Sauvignon, the dominant grape in the Haut-Médoc) and many St-Émilion châteaux use no Cabernet Sauvignon. However, Cabernet Franc (known here as Bouchet) does play a part. Malbec (known here as Pressac) is a minor grape.

St-Émilion is highly regarded for its softer, Merlot-based wines, although there are a large number of châteaux, and quality and style does vary. It is generally said that, unless the vintage is poor, St-Émilion wines mature faster than those from the Médoc, say within five or six years. Top growths may sometimes need more maturation.

There are, in effect, four AOCs within this general AOC, incorporating classifications for quality. The best châteaux are in the Premier Grand Cru Classé, and this group is split into an "A" group of two (Châteaux Ausone and Cheval Blanc) and a "B" group of 11 further châteaux. Then follows the Grand Cru Classé, a large group – currently about 55 châteaux – reassessed every 10 years (last time was in 1996) to ensure all are still worthy of the status. The third level is St-Émilion Grand Cru (a misleading name in French wine jargon, as it is well below the usual *grands crus* in terms of quality); this term also encompasses a long list of châteaux, and they can vary in style and quality significantly. Finally, the AOC St-Émilion offers the also-rans, yet once again it is important to remember that there are surprises out there among the masses, wines of good quality at fair prices, just needing some bottle age.

I should mention here the "garagites," a new word deriving from the suggestion that these wines are made in the garage. Garagites are small quantities of expensive wines that have been given lots of tender loving care then left to be "discovered," preferably by a major wine commentator. Garagites seem to have flourished from about 1995 onwards in both St-Émilion and Pomerol.

St-Émilion Grand Cru   Region: Bordeaux
Appellation Contrôlée
Red only, min alc 11.5%, max yield 40 hl/ha.
Grapes: Merlot, Cabernet Sauvignon and Franc, Malbec.

"Grand Cru" is really the AOC for the third level châteaux of the St-Émilion region, and although they are supposedly reassessed every 10 years, in the 1996 review there was more "Grand Cru" wine than the straight St-Émilion AOC! Sound wine, and there are bargains to be had, but the prestige châteaux are in the two grades above Grand Cru.
Refer **St-Émilion.**

St-Émilion Grand Cru Classé   Region: Bordeaux
Appellation Contrôlée
Red only, min alc 11.5%, max yield 40 hl/ha.
Grapes: Merlot, Cabernet Sauvignon and Franc, Malbec.

Fifty-five châteaux are recognized in this second class of St-Émilion.
Refer **St-Émilion.**

St-Émilion Premier Grand Cru Classé   Region: Bordeaux
Appellation Contrôlée
Red only, min alc 11.5%, max yield 40 hl/ha.
Grapes: Merlot, Cabernet Sauvignon and Franc, Malbec.

This is the top echelon of St-Émilion, recognizing 13 châteaux from the 1996 assessment. (The St-Émilion classification is normally reviewed every 10 years.) The 13 are split into an "A" grade (Châteaux Ausone and Cheval Blanc) and a "B" grade covering the other 11 chateaux; the latter are still highly respected and expensive wines.
Refer **St-Émilion.**

St-Éstèphe
Region: Bordeaux

Appellation Contrôlée

Red only, min alc 10.5%, max yield 45 hl/ha.

Grapes: Cabernet Sauvignon (predominant in most châteaux), Cabernet Franc, Merlot, Malbec, Petit Verdot.

Important and highly regarded AOC in Haut-Médoc on the Gironde River, adjacent to Pauillac on the south side and close to the Bas-Médoc to the north. Some highly rated châteaux are located here, although there are no "first growth" châteaux from the 1855 Classification. The soil is heavy, even more so than Pauillac, with clay and a lime subsoil. The wines tend to be robust and develop very well with cellar time.

Ste-Foy-Bordeaux
Region: Bordeaux

Appellation Contrôlée

Red, min alc 10.5%, max yield 48 hl/ha. White, min alc 12%, max yield 45 hl/ha.

Grapes: Red, Merlot, Cabernet Sauvignon and Franc, Malbec, Petit Verdot. White, Sémillon, Sauvignon Blanc, Muscadelle.

AOC situated on the eastern border of Bordeaux, adjacent to Entre-Deux-Mers. White wines in AOC Ste-Foy-Bordeaux are regarded more highly than the red.

St-Joseph
Region: Rhône

Appellation Contrôlée

Red only, min alc 12%, max yield 40 hl/ha.

Grapes: Red, Syrah. White, Marsanne, Roussanne.

AOC situated on the west bank of the Rhône, roughly opposite the hill of Hermitage and AOC Crozes-Hermitage, 12 miles (20 km) north of Valence. An area of good basic wine, often without distinction, but at its best sound, well-priced and enjoyable. White St-Joseph is rare and not highly sought-after.

St-Julien
Region: Bordeaux

Appellation Contrôlée

Red only, min alc 10.5%, max yield 45 hl/ha.

Grapes: Cabernet Sauvignon and Franc, Merlot, Malbec, Petit Verdot.

Wine from a small Haut-Médoc village on the Gironde River, on the south side of Pauillac. Soil contains gravel from the river, but the extent of the gravel reduces as the distance from the river increases. Reputation is generally very good; despite the smallness of the village, it holds 11 classed châteaux. Often referred to as a "typical" claret, the St-Julien style is said to be between the strength and robustness of a Pauillac or a St-Éstèphe and the softness of Margaux.

St-Nicolas-de-Bourgueil   Region: Loire
Appellation Contrôlée
Red and rosé, min alc 9.5%, max yield 55 hl/ha.
Grapes: Cabernet Sauvignon and Franc.

Considered one of the best Loire reds, this is an AOC on the northern banks
of the Loire in the province of Touraine, some 19 miles (30 km) west of the
city of Tours.

St-Peray   Region: Rhône
Appellation Contrôlée
White only, min alc 9.5%, max yield 45 hl/ha.
Grapes: Marsanne, Roussanne.

AOC from an area opposite Valence on the right bank of the Rhône, known
best for an unlikley sparkling wine from these two solid grapes! Occasionally
noble rot (*Botrytis cinerea*) is allowed and a sweeter wine is made, with the
assistance of further evaporation by lying the grapes on mats in the sun. This
white has its followers. A small amount of still white is also made.

St-Peray Mousseux   Region: Rhône
Appellation Contrôlée
Sparkling white only, min alc 10.5%, max yield 50 hl/ha.
Grapes: Marsanne, Roussanne.

Wine from a small area on the west side of the Rhône, opposite the town of
Valence. The Champagne process is generally used, producing a sparkling
that is a little more bodied than champagne. Regarded only as fair quality by
French sparkling standards.

St-Romain   Region: Burgundy
Appellation Contrôlée
Red, min alc 10.5%, Premier Cru 11%; max yield 40 hl/ha. White, min alc
11%, Premier Cru 11.5%; max yield 45 hl/ha.
Grapes: Red, Pinot Noir. White, Chardonnay.

Wines from a village behind Meursault in the Côte de Beaune. Although provided for in this AOC, there are no *premiers crus*, and a large part of the small
quantity of wine made is sold under a Bourgogne AOC. AOC St-Romain is
only available in small quantities and is not keenly sought after, which means
it can be good value. Lesser vintages produce light, often thin reds.

St-Véran   Region: Southern Burgundy
Appellation Contrôlée
White only, min alc 11%, single vineyard 12%; max yield 45 hl/ha.
Grape: Chardonnay.

AOC from the village of Verand (note different spelling) in the Mâconnaise.

Sancerre   Region: Loire
Appellation Contrôlée
Red and rosé, min alc 10%, max yield 55 hl/ha. White, min alc 10.5%, max yield 60 hl/ha.
Grapes: Red and rosé, Pinot Noir. White, Sauvignon Blanc.

AOC on the west bank of the Loire (opposite Pouilly-Fumé) before it curves into the straight run to the sea through Touraine and Anjou. The area is some 22 miles (35 km) northeast of Bourges, and to the north of Nevers. A lot of its Sauvignon Blanc is made here, in a style competitive with New Zealand's use of the same grape. Some evolution is occurring, but the style survives when available at a good price. Some Pinot Noir is grown here, but it is only highly regarded in top vintages.

Santenay   Region: Burgundy
Appellation Contrôlée
Red, min alc 10.5%, Premier Cru 11%; max yield 40 hl/ha. White, min alc 11%, Premier Cru 11.5%; max yield 45 hl/ha.
Grapes: Red, Pinot Noir. White, Chardonnay.

Wine from an AOC at the southern end of the Côte de Beaune, mostly producing red. A producer of good red burgundy, though sometimes lacking the distinction and finesse of many areas further north. There are wines of excellent value among the range available.

Saumur   Region: Loire
Appellation Contrôlée
Red and rosé, min alc 10%, max yield 40 hl/ha. White, min alc 10%, max yield 45 hl/ha.
Grapes: Red, Cabernet Sauvignon and Franc, Pineau d'Aunis, Grolleau. White, Chenin Blanc min 80%, Sauvignon Blanc, Chardonnay.

AOC from an area south of the town of Saumur on the southern banks of the Loire, in the westernmost part of the Anjou. Whites are generally dryer than other Anjou whites. Reds of a good vintage can be fine wine, but are regarded in general as somewhat inconsistent. The better whites of the area come from a section of Saumur, the Coteaux de Saumur, that has its own appellation. The better reds come from Saumur-Champigny to the north of Saumur (nearer the river) and also have their own appellation.

Saumur-Champigny   Region: Loire
Appellation Contrôlée
Red only, min alc 10%, max yield 40 hl/ha.
Grapes: Cabernet Sauvignon and Franc, Pineau d'Aunis.

Well-regarded AOC from the southern banks of the Loire, southeast of the town of Saumur, surrounded by the white wine AOC Coteaux de Saumur. A warmer AOC but the reds are lower in tannin and enjoyed younger.

Saumur d'Origine   Region: Loire
Appellation Contrôlée

Sparkling red, white and rosé, min alc 9.5%, max yield 60 hl/ha.

Grapes: Red, Cabernet Sauvignon and Franc, Malbec, Grolleau, Gamay, Pineau d'Aunis, Pinot Noir. White, Chenin Blanc, Chardonnay, Sauvignon Blanc and the red grapes excluding Gamay.

Previously called Saumur Mousseux, this is an AOC on the southern banks of the Loire, southeast of the town of Saumur. Its reputation is pretty good, and ownership by some champagne houses is helping the image. Varied quality and style, the best is very good.

Saussignac   Region: Southwest France
Appellation Contrôlée

Sweet white only, min alc 11.5%, max yield 50 hl/ha.

Grapes: Sémillon, Sauvignan Blanc, Muscadelle.

AOC of 173 acres (70 ha) adjacent to St-Foy-Bordeaux, centered around the town of Saussignac near Bergerac. Sweet wine, well appreciated, some using botrytis-affected grapes. The best is more consistent and is highly regarded.

Sauternes   Region: Bordeaux
Appellation Contrôlée

Sweet white only, min alc 13%, max yield 25 hl/ha.

Grapes: Sauvignon Blanc, Sémillon and a small amount of Muscadelle.

AOC in southern Graves, 25 miles (40 km) southeast of the city of Bordeaux, on the Garonne River. Includes Barsac on the northern border, a village with a lighter style, which may use the Sauternes AOC, though most Barsac châteaux use their own AOC these days. Sauternes produces sweet, luscious wines of high repute. Soil type is chalk and stony gravel with clay subsoil. In the best of the vineyards, grapes are picked one by one (not as bunches) in as many as 12 or more pickings over a two-month period. Grapes become wrinkled with the "noble rot" (*Botrytis cinerea*) and through this and the very late picking, much water is evaporated, leaving a strong concentrated juice with enough sugar to give full 13% alcohol and retain high residual sweetness in the wine.

Sauvignon de St-Bris   Region: Between Chablis and Loire River
Appellation Contrôlée

White only, min alc 9.5%, max yield 60 hl/ha.

Grape: Sauvignon Blanc.

This AOC sits west of Chablis and is technically a burgundy, but with a Loire grape variety. A popular dry white, lifted to AOC from VDQS in the mid-1990s. Sauvignon from nearby villages is also included.

Savennières
Appellation Contrôlée
Region: Anjou, Loire

White only, min alc 10%, max yield 50 hl/ha.
Grape: Chenin Blanc.

Wine from an AOC 10 miles (16 km) southwest of Angers, on the Loire. A respected village, regarded as "making an effort" and offering serious wine that can age well.

Savennières-Coulée-de-Serrant
Appellation Contrôlée
Region: Anjou, Loire

White only, min alc 10%, max yield 50 hl/ha.
Grape: Chenin Blanc.

AOC of a respected single 4-acre (1.6-ha) vineyard in the village of Savennières, in the area of the Anjou-Coteaux de la Loire AOC. Two or three years bottle age is recommended.

Savennières-La Roche-aux-Moines
Appellation Contrôlée
Region: Anjou, Loire

White only, min alc 10%, max yield 50 hl/ha.
Grape: Chenin Blanc.

AOC in Savennières village in the area of the Anjou-Coteaux de la Loire AOC. Two to three years bottle age is considered a minimum. Delicious, semi-sweet wine in the right years.

Savigny-lès-Beaune
Appellation Contrôlée
Region: Burgundy

Red, min alc 10.5%, Premier Cru 11%; max yield 40 hl/ha. White, min alc 11%, Premier Cru 11.5%; max yield 45 hl/ha.
Grapes: Red, Pinot Noir. White, Chardonnay.

Large (for Burgundy) 519-acre (210-ha) AOC to the north of the Côte de Beaune, just north of the city of Beaune, producing mostly red wine. Savigny-lès-Beaune produces a respected light-red burgundy. It has more than 20 *premiers crus* making up more than 40% of the AOC. Overlooked at times, but some wines are outstanding.

Seyssel
Appellation Contrôlée
Region: Savoie, near the Italian border

White only, min alc 10%, max yield 45 hl/ha.
Grape: Roussette.

Wine from a tiny AOC surrounding the town of the same name near the eastern border of France, in the Savoie district. Wines are light and fresh, and best enjoyed when young. Sparkling wine uses Seyssel Mousseux AOC.

Seyssel Mousseux　　　　　　*Region: Savoie, near the Italian border*
Appellation Contrôlée
Sparkling white only, min alc 8.5%, max yield 65 hl/ha.
Grapes: Roussette, Molette, Chasselas.

A tiny area surrounding the town of the same name near the eastern border of France, in the Savoie district. Sparkling wine (traditional method) is rated very highly; one of the best outside Champagne. AOC requires the wine to be bottled and fermented in the region.

Tavel　　　　　　　　　　　　　　*Region: Rhône*
Appellation Contrôlée
Rosé only, min alc 11%, max yield 48 hl/ha.
Grapes: Grenache predominates (up to 60%), with Cinsault min 15%, plus Carignan, Syrah, Bourboulenc, Calitor, Mourvèdre, Picpoul.

AOC 3 miles (5 km) northwest of Avignon on the Rhône in the south of France. More than half the production is from a winemakers' cooperative. Tavel has an unusual claim to fame as a speciality rosé in France, considered best when fresh and young.

Thouarsais　　　　　　　　　　　*Region: Loire*
VDQS
Refer **Vins du Thouarsais.**

Touraine　　　　　　　　　　　　*Region: Loire*
Appellation Contrôlée
Red and rosé, min alc 9%, max yield 55 hl/ha. White, min alc 9.5%, max yield 55 hl/ha.
Grapes: Red and rosé, Gamay, Cabernet Sauvignon and Franc, Malbec, Pinot Noir, Pinot Gris, Pineau d'Aunis (and Groslot for rosé). White, Chenin Blanc.

Wine from a large AOC centered on the city of Tours on the Loire. The better villages and estates within the area have their own AOCs, leaving the plainer wine for the catchall "Touraine" appellation. Quality is constantly being worked on, however, and amidst a large volume, many wines are worthwhile and good value.

Touraine-Amboise　　　　　　　*Region: Loire*
Appellation Contrôlée
Red and rosé, min alc 9.5%, max yield 55 hl/ha. White, min alc 10%, max yield 60 hl/ha.
Grapes: Red, Gamay, Cabernet Sauvignon and Franc, Malbec. White, Chenin Blanc.

A small AOC of 519 acres (210 ha) lying 12 miles (20 km) east of Tours on the Loire. The village is just outside Vouvray, to which the wine is similar.

Touraine Azay-le-Rideau
Appellation Contrôlée
Region: Loire

Rosé, min alc 9%, max yield 55 hl/ha. White, min alc 10%, max yield 55 hl/ha.
Grapes: Red, Groslot, Malbec, Gamay, Cabernet Franc. White, Chenin Blanc.

Tiny AOC of just 123 acres (50 ha) southeast of Tours. White is similar to Vouvray but not as well known. The rosé is fresh and pleasant.

Touraine-Mesland
Appellation Contrôlée
Region: Loire

Red and rosé, min alc 9.5%, max yield 55 hl/ha. White, min alc 10%, max yield 60 hl/ha.
Grapes: Red, Gamay, Cabernet Franc, Malbec. White, Chenin Blanc, Sauvignon Blanc, Chardonnay.

Wine from a village between Blois and Tours in the greater area of Touraine. Most wine tends to be red and rosé, made from Gamay.

Touraine Mousseux
Appellation Contrôlée
Region: Loire

Sparkling red, white and rosé, min alc 9.5%, max yield 65 hl/ha.
Grapes: Red, Cabernet Franc, Malbec, Groslot, Gamay, Pineau d'Aunis, Pinot Noir. White, Chenin Blanc, Arbois, Sauvignon Blanc, Chardonnay max 20%.

Sparkling AOC on the Loire, a fairly large region centered on the city of Tours. The better areas within Touraine have their own AOC, leaving this general one for sparkling and *pétillant* (slightly sparkling) wines, wines from lesser areas and those that do not qualify for the more specific area appellations. Sparkling wines from the area are pretty well regarded.

Tursan
VDQS
Region: Southwest France

Red and rosé, min alc 10.5%. White, min alc 11%. Max yield 50 hl/ha.
Grapes: Red, Tannat, Cabernet Sauvignon and Franc. White, White Barroque, Sauvignon Blanc, Gros Manseng, Petit Manseng, Sémillon.

Light red and tasty white from a region near Madiran.

Vacqueyras
Appellation Contrôlée
Region: Rhône

Red, min alc 12.5%, max yield 35 hl/ha. Rosé and white, min alc 12%, max yield 35 hl/ha.
Grapes: Red, Grenache, Syrah, Mourvèdre, Cinsault, Carignan. White, Grenache Blanc, Clairette, Bourboulenc, Marsanne, Roussanne, Viognier.

AOC northeast of Avignon, adjacent to Gigondas and not far from Châteauneuf-du-Pape, to which the style is similar. Mostly red, despite the range of white grapes allowed. The main attraction is a hearty red, sometimes fresher than Gigondas, but often (yet not always) as spicy.

Valencay   Region: Loire
Appellation Contrôlée
Red and rosé, min alc 9%, max yield 45 hl/ha. White, min alc 9%, max yield 50 hl/ha.
Grapes: Red, Cabernet Sauvignon and Franc, Gamay, Malbec, Pineau d'Aunis. White, Arbois, Chenin Blanc, Sauvignon Blanc, Chardonnay.

A VDQS until late 2003 when AOC status was approved. Less than 370 acres (150 ha), Valencay is an area in the southeast of Touraine, south of the Cher River. Regarded as a fresh, light local style, predominantly producing red.

Vin de Béarn   Region: Southwest France
VDQS
Refer **Béarn.**

Vin du Bugey   Region: East of Burgundy
VDQS
Red, rosé and white, min alc 9%, max yield 45 hl/ha. When village name is hyphenated, min alc 9.5%, max yield 40 hl/ha.
Grapes: Red, Gamay, Pinot Noir. White, Roussette, Roussanne, Chardonnay, Jacquère, Molette.

Wine from a U-shaped area to the east of the city of Lyon on the banks of the Ain and Rhône rivers. Better villages add their name to the label, but this has a higher alcohol requirement. Whites from Roussette and Roussanne are the most respected when young.

Vin de Corse   Region: Corsica
Appellation Contrôlée
Red and white, min alc 11.5%, max yield 50 hl/ha.
Grapes: Red, Sciacarello, Nielluccio, Grenache, Syrah, Cinsault, Carignan, Barbarossa. White, Rolle, Trebbiano.

One of three AOCs on the island of Corsica; the other two being AOC Patrimonio and AOC Ajaccio. This one is the broad catchall with five subregions: Coteaux du Cap Corse, Calvi, Sartène, Figar and Porto Vecchio which may hyphenate their name to Vin de Corse on the label.

Vin du Lyonnias   Region: Rhône
VDQS
Red and rosé, min alc 9%, max yield 50 hl/ha. White, min alc 9.5%, max yield 50 hl/ha.

Grapes: Red, Mornen Noir, Syrah, Gamay. White, Gamay Blanc, Chardonnay, Chenin Blanc (known locally as Pineau de la Loire).

Wine from an area around the city of Lyon, south of Burgundy.

Vin de la Moselle   Region: East of Champagne
VDQS
Red and white, min alc 8.5%, max yield 60 hl/ha.
Grapes: Red, Gamay, Pinot Meunier, Pinot Noir. White, Auxerrois, Gewürztraminer, Müller-Thurgau, Pinot Blanc, Pinot Gris.

Tiny AOC near the Moselle River in northeastern France. The Moselle (its spelling changes to "Mosel" when it crosses the border into Germany) flows into the Rhine.

Vin de Savoie   Region: East of Burgundy
Appellation Contrôlée
Red, rosé and white, min alc 9.5% (10% for *cru*, when village name included). Red and rosé, max yield 60 hl/ha (*cru* 55 hl/ha). White, max yield 65 hl/ha (*cru* 60 hl/ha).
Grapes: Red, Gamay, Pinot Noir, Mondeuse. White, Chasselas, Aligoté, Roussanne.

Wine from a few small areas totaling about 3,705 acres (1,500 ha), northeast of Lyon near the Swiss border. Better villages can show their name on the label, but this classification requires a higher alcohol content. Style is considered light and grapes often find it difficult to ripen fully, but visiting skiiers are said to enjoy the wine. Little is exported.

Vin de Savoie Mousseux or Pétillant   Region: East of Burgundy
Appellation Contrôlée
Sparkling and *pétillant* (slightly sparkling) white only, min alc 9.5%, max yield 65 hl/ha.
Grapes: In addition to those given under AOC Vin de Savoie, a grape called Molette may be used.
Refer **Vin de Savoie**

Vins d'Estaing   Region: Southwest France
VDQS
Red, rosé and white, min alc 9%, max yield 45 hl/ha.
Grapes: Red, Cabernet Sauvignon and Franc, Gamay, Fer. White, Chenin Blanc and Mauzac.

Barely 49 acres (20 ha) of vineyards midway between Bordeaux and the Rhône, in the province of Areyron near the Lot River.

Vins Fins de la Côte de Nuits   Region: Burgundy
Appellation Contrôlée
Red, min alc 11%, max yield 45 hl/ha. White, min alc 11.5%, max yield 45 hl/ha.
Grapes: Red, Pinot Noir. White, Chardonnay.

Wine made in the villages of Brochon, Prissey, Comblanchien and Corgoloin plus part of Fixin may use this appellation (the rest of Fixin has its own appellation). Fixin and Brochon are at the north of the Côte de Nuits, while the other three villages are at the south end.

The wines are ranked under the village labels of other more noted areas. However, because this AOC is not well-known, prices are low; so individual wines and especially those distributed through reputable *négociants* can sometimes be good value.

Vins du Haut-Poitou   Region: Loire
VDQS
Red, rosé and white, min alc 9%, max yield 50 hl/ha.
Grapes: Red and rosé, Gamay, Pinot Noir, Cabernet Franc, Merlot, Malbec, Grolleau (the latter variety permitted only in rosé). White, Sauvignon Blanc, Chenin Blanc, Chardonnay, Pinot Blanc.

Region south of Saumur producing a range of wines from a wide range of grapes, most wines being labeled varietally. Fresh and racy summarizes the style.

Vins de l'Orléanais   Region: Loire
VDQS
Red, min alc 9%, max yield 45 hl/ha. White and rosé, min alc 10%, max yield 45 hl/ha.
Grapes: Red, Pinot Noir, Pinot Meunier, Cabernet Franc. White, Chardonnay, Pinot Blanc, Pinot Gris.

Small volume AOC – though one with a larger potential – around the town of Orléans, on both sides of the river. There are worthwhile wines here; the rosé, mostly from Pinot Meunier grapes, has become more popular recently but the area generally has lost both popularity and winemakers. Perhaps it is ready for a new beginning.

Vins de St-Pourçain-sur-Sioule   Region: Loire
VDQS
Red, white and rosé, min alc 9.5%, max yield 50 hl/ha.
Grapes: Red, Gamay, Pinot Noir. White, Tressalier, St Pierre Doré, Aligoté, Chardonnay, Sauvignon Blanc.

AOC of more than 1,235 acres (500 ha) of vineyards along the Sioule and Allier rivers (both tributaries of the Loire). Not highly regarded, but efforts to rise to AOC standard are seen as positive by the wine trade.

Vins du Thouarsais   Region: Loire
VDQS
Red, white and rosé, min alc 9%, max yield 50 hl/ha.
Grapes: Red, Cabernet Sauvignon and Franc, Gamay. White, Chenin Blanc, Chardonnay.

AOC some 25 miles (40 km) south of the Loire and Saumur, around the town of Thouars, which lies towards the mouth of the river on the Atlantic coast. Mainly a crisp white; also some light red.

Viré-Clessé   Region: Southern Burgundy
Appellation Contrôlée
White only, min alc 11%, max yield 50 hl/ha.
Grapes: Chardonnay, Pinot Blanc.

As of 1998, a new AOC in the Mâconnaise making fairly strong-flavored white. Considered best when young and fresh.

Volnay   Region: Burgundy
Appellation Contrôlée
Red only, min alc 10.5%, Premier Cru 11%; max yield 40 hl/ha.
Grape: Pinot Noir.

AOC in the northern half of the Côte de Beaune between Pommard and Meursault. The village has no *grands crus* but lots of *premiers crus,* and the vineyards and village wines are spoken of with high regard for their finesse. The white wines use AOC Meursault.

Volnay-Santenots   Region: Burgundy
Appellation Contrôlée
Red only, min alc 10.5%, Premier Cru 11%; max yield 40 hl/ha.
Grape: Pinot Noir.

A premium vineyard within the Volnay AOC in the northern half of the Côte de Beaune between Pommard and Meursault. The village has no *grands crus* but lots of *premiers crus,* and the vineyards and village wines are spoken of with high regard for their finesse.

Vosne-Romanée   Region: Burgundy
Appellation Contrôlée
Red only, min alc 10.5%, Premier Cru 11%; max yield 40 hl/ha.
Grape: Pinot Noir.

Famous village, which has some of the great *grands crus* within it. The AOC of this name, covering the village and a good number of *premiers crus* has a strong following. Wine from the adjacent village of Flagey-Échezeaux – which has two *grands crus* and one *premier cru* – also use this appellation. The range of vineyards within the AOC vary in quality and style with the usual variables of slope, soil and winemaking practices.

Vougeot   **Region: Burgundy**
Appellation Contrôlée
Red, min alc 10.5%, Premier Cru 11%; max yield 40 hl/ha. White, min alc 11%, Premier Cru 11.5%; max yield 45 hl/ha.
Grapes: Red, Pinot Noir. White, Chardonnay.

Wine from the 40 acres (16 ha) of vineyards – more than half of which are *premiers crus* – surrounding the Grand Cru vineyard of Clos de Vougeot on the east and part of the south.

Vougeot is on the same slopes that made Clos de Vougeot famous, but being on the lower part of the slopes somewhat reduces the respect. Nevertheless there are some fine wines under this AOC and they are often available at very fair prices for their quality.

Vouvray   **Region: Loire**
Appellation Contrôlée
White only, min alc 11%, max yield 52 hl/ha.
Grape: Chenin Blanc.

Major Loire AOC to the northeast and east of the city of Tours within the larger AOC area of Touraine. On the north side of the Loire. Wines are generally well thought of, yet they can be variable in an AOC producing some 1,320,000 gallons (five million L) of wine each year. Style can be from light and dry to fruity, to thick and sweet like a Sauternes. In a good year, this is one of the longest-lived white wines in the world.

Vouvray Mousseux   **Region: Loire**
Appellation Contrôlée
Sparkling white only, min alc 9.5%, max yield 65 hl/ha.
Grape: Chenin Blanc.

AOC in the area to the northeast and east of the city of Tours within the larger appellation of Touraine. The sparkling wine can be of various styles, from a slight sparkle (*pétillant*) in a light wine to a full sparkling; the latter is sometimes referred to as one of the best sparkling wines outside Champagne.

CHAPTER 2

Italy

Denominazione di Origine Controllata (DOC)
Denominazione di Origine Controllata e Garantita (DOCG)
Indicazione Geographica Tipica (IGT)
Vino da Tavola (VdT)

The grape is at the very soul of Italian culture, and, like Europe, Italy's long wine history has endured much change and evolution over the years. During the past couple of decades, domestic consumption has dropped from 31 gallons (120 L) per capita to less than 14 gallons (53 L), and about a million acres (400,000 ha) of Italian vineyard have been ripped out. The entire industry in Tuscany has been turned around as new varieties have taken much of the support role in blends like Chianti, even to the point of revolutionizing a labeling system that was only put in place as recently as the 1960s.

Yet wine remains a defining part of Italy. A carafe of wine is as natural on an Italian table as knives and forks. The country produces 1.6 billion gallons (6 billion L) of wine annually, and vineyards occupy three percent of the country, a percentage exceeded only by Portugal. Consumption of wine per capita, although down, is almost four times that of England. Wine exports remain a huge revenue earner for the country.

At the time of writing, 26 areas have evolved from *Denominazione di Origine Controllata* (DOC) class to become *Denominazione di Origine Controllata e Garantita* (DOCG). Meanwhile, high prices have been sought for wines that don't conform to the rules; hence a new labeling tier, *Indicazione Geographica Tipica* (IGT), has been introduced to avoid the embarrassment of some *Vino da Tavola* (VdT) wines bringing three and four times the price of wines that do conform to DOC.

Unlike the French, the Italians have been willing to change their attitude to traditional grape content, allowing new varieties to be experimented with and sometimes even adapted into DOC and DOCG classifications; the French, however, still loyally cling to their heritage of Grenache and Syrah in the Rhône, Merlot and Cabernet in Bordeaux and Pinot Noir and Chardonnay in Burgundy, despite dwindling market attention for some styles in traditional markets.

Almost 340 specific districts in Italy are registered as DOC and DOCG, and these are similar in some ways to the AOC districts of France. Each is a defined area of land with specified grape varieties and often rules on the proportions of each, minimum alcohol levels, maximum yields and specific methods of viticulture and winemaking. Each DOC has its own name, which appears on the label with *Denominazione di Origine Controllata* (written in full) directly underneath.

Sometimes the grape forms part of the DOC name: Barbera d'Alba, for example, which uses the Barbera grape from the Alba region. This is often because there are other grapes used in the same DOC that need their own identification, like Dolcetto d'Alba, for example. The obvious comparison in France (almost the only one, in fact) is in AOC Alsace, where a number of grapes can be used on their own and these, of course, need to be identified on the label – Alsace Riesling, Alsace Gewürztraminer, and so on.

The DOCGs are defined in a similar way to the DOCs, defined areas each with their own name and set of rules and grapes. The "Garantita" (guarantee) in this classification is a recognition of an area that was previously a DOC and that has proven itself able to provide consistent style wines of quality and standing in their region. Each wine must pass a taste test and a chemical analysis each year, and those that pass have a ribbon showing the approval number running around (or sometimes down) the capsule of each bottle. The DOCG is given to the whole area, not just the best wines. However, if a winemaker in the region does not attain the DOCG quality level required, his wine becomes not DOC, but simply *Vino da Tavola* in that year.

The DOCs and DOCGs listed in this chapter are part of a system set up in the 1960s and revised in the early 1990s. The first promotion to DOCG was made in 1986; others have been added since. Many more DOCs have also been added and there will be more. This is not because the system is too liberal, although some critics and commentators have suggested this. The reason for such a large number of DOCs is the desire to categorize the wines from a very large winemaking country, which has DOCs as small as a few hectares and others that cover several thousand.

A growing proportion of wine produced under the specific controls of DOC and DOCG does not necessarily mean that the country produces a high proportion of *better* wine; but it is an advance for a country like Italy, where people are not particularly fond of bureaucracy and regulations, and the industry must work hard to turn this mistrust around.

Italy's best wines are perhaps those in the northern half, from Rome upwards. To the south, plenty of wine is made and enjoyed locally, but many wines do not travel long distances well. The hot climate over the Mediterranean Sea encourages lower acids and simpler wines. Interestingly, this is the part of Italy where much effort is being made to lift the quality. The island of Sicily, for example, and Apulia in the heel of Italy's boot, are trying hard to produce sound bottled product and a gradual movement away from the big-volume quaffers of the past.

Even though a wine area may have a history of mediocrity it does not mean that it will not improve in the future under more knowledgeable winemakers. Indeed, there is no better place to make quality wine than where the land is cheap and the vineyards well established. There, by applying sound viticultural and winemaking procedures, the wine quality can be lifted to make a statement about the warm, sunny *terroir* provided in the region. Just as in the satellite appellations of St-Émilion, wine-wise investors are taking advantage of historically lower land prices, and much of Italy is moving away from mediocrity towards better things.

Italy is a complex country, and this is reflected in its wines. There are some remarkably straightforward wines, most ready for drinking when bottled and released, and some carrying DYA ("drink youngest available") recommendations from critics, writers and commentators; yet these often carry an appeal, a tangy statement, a drinkability that lifts food. The pure volume of Italian wine necessitates that much of it must be low-priced. Yet there are also complex Italian wines, rich, tannic and intensely fruited styles that can be as good as anything the rest of world can provide.

Wine Terms

Abboccato   Lightly sweet.

Alcole   Alcohol.

Amabile   Medium sweet, between *abboccato* and *dolce*.

Bianco   White.

Classico   Wine from the heartland of the DOC region, usually the original planted zone. This is often, but not necessarily, better than the general DOC quality, and sometimes carries a higher alcohol and yield requirement. But "Classico" on the label is a regional statement denoting wine from a specific area, not a quality statement, despite the inference.

Dolce   Sweet.

Frizzante	Like *spritzig*, a light sparkle (not as much as *spumante* or sparkling).
Incrocio	Hybrid grapes resulting from crossing of varieties.
Invecchiato	Aged, matured, some additional time required before release.
Liquoroso	Liqueur-like, with higher alcohol content. Wine is often made by drying the grapes to concentrate sugar and flavor (like Amarone in Veneto).
Novello	As in the French *nouveau* style, wines made for drinking young and fresh; often an add-on classification for a more-serious DOC.
Passito	"Dried fruit wine" made from grapes dried after picking; usually sweet but sometimes the extra sugar goes into alcohol rather than residual sweetness.
Riserva	Extra time is needed before this wine can be released, very often with a specified length of time in wood. Thus Chianti can be released after one year but Chianti Riserva not until three years have passed.
Rosato	Rosé.
Rosso	Red.
Secco	Dry.
Spumante	Sparkling.
Superiore	Higher quality wine, usually associated with a specific sub-district of the DOC, and may carry stricter requirements on yield and/or alcohol.
Tranquillo	Still, not sparkling or *spritzig*.
Vendemmia	Harvest, sometimes year of vintage.
Vendemmia Tardiva	Late-picked grapes, sometimes giving a lightly-sweet wine.
Vigna	Vineyard.
Vita	Vine.
Vitigno	Grape variety.
Vin Santo	Dried fruit wine, like *passito*, barrel aged (in oak or chestnut) and left to oxidize and develop a golden color. Finished wine can be sweet, medium or dry; traditionally used as a dessert style.

Appellations of Italy, DOC and DOCG

Acqui   *Region: Piedmont*
DOCG
Refer **Brachetto d'Acqui.**

Aglianico del Taburno   *Region: Campania*
DOC
Red only, min alc 11.5%, max yield 13 tonnes/ha.
Grapes: Aglianico min 85%, Piedirosso, Sciascinoso and Sangiovese up to
15%. Min age two years before release.
Riserva: min age three years before release.

Aglianico vines have adapted to some very cold winter conditions up in
the hills of Campania and succeed well in providing a sought-after style of
wine.
For other styles in this area, *refer* **Taburno.**

Aglianico del Vulture   *Region: Basilicata*
DOC
Red only, min alc 11.5%, max yield 10 tonnes/ha.
Grape: Aglianico
Vecchio: min age three years before release, at least two of these in wood;
min alc 12.5%.
Riserva: min age five years before release, at least two of these in wood;
min alc 12.5%.

A hearty cheerful wine, named after the Aglianico grape, of Greek origin,
which is grown in hilly vineyards. A little sweetness is allowed (up to 10 g/L)
but essentially this is a DOC of robust dry red. Note the low yield.

Albana di Romagna   *Region: Emilia-Romagna*
DOCG
White only, max yield 14 tonnes/ha.
Grape: Albana
Secco: dry, min alc 11.5%.
Amabile: slightly sweet, min alc 12%.
Dolce: sweet, min alc 12%.
Passito: some drying of grapes; min alc 15.5%, min sugar level 15 g/L.

The Albana grape is considered a little neutral when dry-medium, so the
DOCG status of this area caused some surprise. However, with the full treat-
ment of botrytis and oak, these wines are sometimes considered excellent.
There is a move to reduce yield to a maximum of 11 tonnes/ha.
A sparkling wine is made also, *refer* **Romagna Albana Spumante.**

Albugnano   Region: Piedmonte
DOC
Red and rosé, min alc 11%, max yield 8.5 tonnes/ha.
Grapes: Nebbiolo min 85%, with Freisa, Barbera and Bonarda up to 15%.
Superiore: min alc 11.5%.

High-altitude DOC north of Asti, giving a dryish red that does not receive wide acclaim, partly because of its tiny quantity.

Alcamo   Region: Sicily
DOC
White only, min alc 11.5%, max yield 12 tonnes/ha.
Grapes: Catarratto Bianco min 80%; Damaschino, Grecanico and Trebbiano up to 20%.

Sometimes called Bianco Alcamo, this important, 8-acre (3.3-ha) DOC on the island of Sicily, is dominated by Catarratto Bianco and a Lucido clone. Catarratto Bianco is the second most planted variety in Italy, but it is allowed in only three DOCs. The style is soft and light.

Aleatico di Gradoli   Region: Latium
DOC
Red only, min alc 12%, max yield 9 tonnes/ha.
Grape: Aleatico.
Liquoroso: grapes lightly dried to lift sugar and wine aged for six months; min alc 17.5%.

Tiny DOC of just 62 acres (25 ha) because hilltops and valleys are precluded from DOC status. Aromatic, fruity, soft red.

Aleatico di Puglia   Region: Apulia
DOC
Red only, min alc 15%, max yield 8 tonnes/ha.
Grapes: Aleatico min 85%; Negro Amaro, Malvasia Nera and Primitivo up to 15%.
Riserva: min age three years.
Liquoroso: moderate drying of grapes; min alc 18.5%.

Tiny DOC of less than 25 acres (10 ha) and only six producers, most making a sweet, alcoholic red; sometimes a full liqueur. A little grapey, like muscat.

Alezio   Region: Apulia
DOC
Red and rosé, min alc 12%, max yield 14 tonnes/ha.
Grapes: Negro Amaro up to 20%; plus Sangiovese, Malvasia, Montepulciano.
Riserva: red aged for two years; min alc 12.5%.

About equal amounts of red and rosé are produced from this 150-acre (60-ha) DOC in the Apulia region; the red wine can develop well with bottle age.

Alghero   Region: Sardinia
DOC

Red and rosé, min alc 10%, max yield 12 tonnes/ha. White, min alc 11%, max yield 10 tonnes/ha.
Grapes: Red, Cabernet Sauvignon and Franc, Cagnulari and Carmenère; other varieties up to 15%. White, Chardonnay.

DOC to the northwest of Sardinia, producing a large part (nearly half) of the island's DOC wine.

Alta Langa   Region: Piedmont
DOC

Sparkling red, rosé, white, min alc 12%, max yield 8 tonnes/ha.
Grapes: Chardonnay and Pinot Noir min 90%; other local grapes up to 10%.
Millesimato: vintage wine with min 30 months' age before release.

A recent (2002) DOC at 1,600 feet (500 m) on terraces among cheese-producing sheep farms, Alta Langa DOC is producing dry, bottle-fermented sparkling (*spumante*), developed after experimentation on the beautifully rough landscape in this part of Langhe province. A quite different style to the Asti Moscato sparkling for which Piedmont is known. Alta Langa is a new name, and the DOC is being established on the belief that the land is suited to these varieties of sparkling wine.

Alto Adige   Region: Trentino-Alto Adige
DOC

Varietal wines must contain a minimum of 95% of the grape variety named on the label. Other requirements are as follows:
Cabernet: min alc 11.5%, max yield 11 tonnes/ha.
Chardonnay: min alc 11%, max yield 13 tonnes/ha.
Lagrein Rosato: min alc 11.5%, max yield 14 tonnes/ha.
Lagrein Scuro: min alc 11.5%, max yield 14 tonnes/ha.
Malvasia: min alc 11.5%, max yield 11 tonnes/ha.
Merlot: min alc 11%, max yield 13 tonnes/ha.
Moscato Giallo: min alc 11%, max yield 8 tonnes/ha.
Moscato Rosa: min alc 12.5%, max yield 6 tonnes/ha.
Pinot Bianco: min alc 11%, max yield 13 tonnes/ha.
Pinot Grigio: min alc 11.5%, max yield 12 tonnes/ha.
Riesling Italico: min alc 11%, max yield 13 tonnes/ha.
Riesling x Sylvaner (Müller Thurgau): min alc 11%, max yield 13 tonnes/ha.

Riesling Renano: min alc 11%, max yield 12 tonnes/ha.
Sauvignon: min alc 11.5%, max yield 12 tonnes/ha.
Schiava: min alc 10.5%, max yield 14 tonnes/ha.
Spumante: (Sparkling) Pinot Blanc and/or Chardonnay min 70%, Pinot Noir and/or Pinot Gris up to 30%; min alc 11%, max yield 13 tonnes/ha.
Sylvaner: min alc 11%, max yield 13 tonnes/ha.
Traminer Aromatico: min alc 11.5%, max yield 12 tonnes/ha.

This is an important DOC of about 6,200 acres (2,500 ha) spread over a wide range of vines, as the above list shows. The highest volume of wine is Moscato Giallo.

The defined area permits qualifying vineyards only on suitable slopes, no reds higher than 2,300 feet (700 m), no white above 3,000 feet (900 m). The locals guard quality carefully and a lot of wine that might qualify for the DOC is not sold under that name because it does not pass their quality assessment.

Amarone della Valpolicella   **Region: Veneto**
DOC
Red only, min alc 14%, max yield 8 tonnes/ha, min age two years before release.
Grapes: Corvina Veronese 40–70%, Rondinella 20–40%, Molinara 5–25% plus Barbera, Negrara and Rossignola Sangiovese up to 15%, and other local approved varieties up to 5%.
Classico: from grapes grown in the Classico part of Valpolicella.

This DOC covers the same grapes and region as Valpolicella DOC. Amarone is made by drying the grapes after picking. Drying is carried out in a variety of ways; some producers use mats, some hangers and some air-dried rooms. The grapes shrivel, losing some water from the juice by this process and leaving a more intense amount of juice with a high skin-to-juice ratio. A slow fermentation and aging follows. The style is thus raisiny, spicy and quite heavy, but styles can vary among producers and in different seasons.

Ansonica Costa dell'Argentario   **Region: Tuscany**
DOC
White only, min alc 11.5%, max yield 10 tonnes/ha.
Grapes: Ansonica min 85%, with other local varieties up to 15%.

New DOC on the coast. The grape is considered to taste quite different here compared to the other parts of Italy where it is used.

Aprilia   **Region: Latium**
DOC
Varietal wines must contain a minimum of 95% of the grape variety named on the label. Other requirements as follows:
Merlot: min alc 11%, max yield 15 tonnes/ha.

Sangiovese: min alc 11.5%, max yield 14 tonnes/ha.
Trebbiano: min alc 11%, max yield 15 tonnes/ha.

Large, 9,000-acre (3,700-ha) DOC with about 75% Trebbiano grapes. Planted to give large quantities of good to average wine for almost immediate drinking, the region has had to evolve with the changing market and smaller demand. A lot of vineyards have been pulled out; others have been replanted with more innovative trellising, and new varieties are being experimented with.

Aquileia   Region: Friuli-Venezia Giulia
DOC

Varietal wines must contain a minimum of 85% of the variety named on the label. Also rosé.

Rosato: Merlot 70–80%; Cabernet Franc and Sauvignon, Refosco Nostrano and Refosco dal Peduncolo Rosso 20–30%; min alc 10.5%, max yield 13 tonnes/ha.
Merlot: min alc 10.5%, max yield 13 tonnes/ha.
Cabernet, Cabernet Franc and Cabernet Sauvignon: min alc 11%, max yield 12 tonnes/ha.
Refosco dal Peduncolo Rosso: min alc 10.5%, max yield 13 tonnes/ha.
Tocai Friulano: min alc 10.5%, max yield 13 tonnes/ha.
Pinot Bianco: min alc 11%, max yield 12 tonnes/ha.
Pinot Grigio: min alc 10.5%, max yield 13 tonnes/ha.
Riesling Renano: min alc 10.5%, max yield 13 tonnes/ha.
Sauvignon: min alc 11%, max yield 12 tonnes/ha.
Traminer Aromatico: min alc 11%, max yield 10 tonnes/ha.
Verduzzo Friulano: min alc 11%, max yield 12 tonnes/ha.
Chardonnay: min alc 11%, max yield 12 tonnes/ha.

DOC providing light wines to be enjoyed young but considered variable in quality. Most wine consumed within Italy.

Arborea   Region: Sardinia
DOC

Red and rosé, min alc 11%, max yield 18 tonnes/ha. White, min alc 10.5%, max yield 18 tonnes/ha.

Sangiovese Rosso or **Rosato:** Sangiovese min 85%, other local varieties up to 15%.
Trebbiano: Trebbiano Romagnolo and/or Trebbiano Toscano min 85%, other local varieties up to 15%.
Frizzante: a naturally spritzy type is also produced from Trebbiano as above, in *amabile* (lightly sweet) and *secco* (dry).

Considered with affection rather than for its quality, a DOC producing light, easy wines to be enjoyed young.

Arcole
Region: Veneto
DOC
Red, min alc 11%, max yield 14 tonnes/ha. White, min alc 10.5%, max yield 14 tonnes/ha.
Grapes: Red, Merlot min 50% plus other non-aromatic red varieties. White and sparkling, Garganega 50–100%, Chardonnay, Pinot Blanc, Pinot Gris up to 50%. Varietal wines (red and white) must contain a minimum 85% of the grape variety named on the label.

A DOC with a silty, sandy soil thought to establish the character of the wine. Some red Novello is also made.

Assisi
Region: Umbria
DOC
Red, min alc 12%, rosé, min alc 11%; max yield 12 tonnes/ha. White, min alc 10.5%, max yield 12 tonnes/ha.
Grapes: Red, Sangiovese 50–70%, Merlot 10–30%, other local varieties up to 40%. White, Trebbiano 50–70%, Grechetto 10–30%, other local varieties up to 40%. If the wine is labeled as Grechetto, it must contain a minimum of 85% Grechetto grapes.

Light and delicate wines from around the famous old town of Assisi, where St Francis is entombed in the Basilica.

Asti
Region: Piedmont
DOCG
Sparkling, lightly sweet white, min alc 7–9.5%; max yield 10 tonnes/ha.
Grape: Moscato Bianco.

Previously known as Asti Spumante, Asti is Italy's largest producing appellation by far. In 1993, to help identify the wine properly, DOCG Asti and DOCG Moscato d'Asti (lower in alcohol and less fizz pressure) were given separate status. A very popular, light (low alcohol), sweet white.

Atina
Region: Latium
DOC
Red only, min alc 12%, max yield 12 tonnes/ha.
Grapes: Cabernet Sauvignon 50–70%, Syrah 10–30%, Merlot 10–30%, Cabernet Franc 10–30%, other local red varieties up to 15%.
Cabernet: Cabernet Sauvignon and/or Franc min 85%, other local red varieties max 15%.
Riserva: min age two years before release; min alc 12.5%.

Named after the old city of Atina, southeast of Rome. Grapes planted in the alluvial marls around the city are relatively recent. This DOC is still establishing a reputation and image.

Aversa Region: Campania
DOC
Dry white and sparkling, min alc 10.5%, max yield 14 tonnes/ha.
Grapes: Asprinio min 85%; other approved varieties up to 15%.
Spumante: min alc 11%; mostly dry sparkling.

The Asprinio grape is only grown commercially in this DOC and it spreads by growing over poplar trees, often at great height and requiring some effort to pick! A light, fresh, crisp, dry white, the sparkling even crisper.

Bagnolo di Sopra (or Bagnoli) Region: Veneto
DOC
Red and rosé, min alc 11%. White, min alc 10.5%. Max yield 12 tonnes/ha.
Grapes: Red, Cabernet Sauvignon and Franc, and Carmenère (min 15% total), Raboso min 15%, Merlot 15–60%, other varieties max 10%. Rosé, Raboso min 50%, Merlot max 40%, other approved varieties max 10%. White, Chardonnay 30–70%, Sauvignon Blanc and/or Tocai Friulano 20–60%, other local grapes max 10%. Sparkling red and white, Raboso min 40%, Chardonnay min 20%, other local non-aromatic varieties max 10%.
Varietal wine: (the grape is named on label) must be 85% of that variety.
Friularo: Raboso min 90%, other varieties max 10%.
Passito: Raboso min 70%, other varieties max 30%.

Recent (1995) DOC which has helped the region to compete better in wider markets. Friularo is a special and idiosyncratic wine from an indigenous variety of two clones called Raboso. The Friularo Vendemmia Tardiva (late harvest), where the grapes are picked as they start to wither on the vine, is regarded as a great treat.

Barbaresco Region: Piedmont
DOCG
Red only, min alc 12.5%, max yield 8 tonnes/ha.
Grape: Nebbiolo.
Riserva: min age four years before release.

A well regarded Nebbiolo DOC of almost 1,300 acres (500 ha), much smaller than Barolo nearby. The style is usually a touch lighter than Barolo, often showing a more tawny hue while young, although it ages well. Barbaresco has its own distinctiveness and comes close to showing elegance for such a powerful wine.

Barbera d'Alba Region: Piedmont
DOC
Red only, min alc 12%, max yield 10 tonnes/ha.
Grape: Barbera.
Superiore: one year aging in wood; min alc 12.5%.

Hilly DOC around Alba, some 6,175 acres (2,500 ha), a well-regarded style in a region that competes with Barolo, which is twice the price. Ages well.

Barbera d'Asti
DOC
Region: Piedmont

Red only, min alc 12%, max yield 9 tonnes/ha.
Grape: Barbera.
Superiore: min age three years before release, at least one year in wood; min alc 13%.

DOC of more than 22,200 acres (9,000 ha) providing a fresh and invigorating red wine to be enjoyed young.

Barbera del Monferrato
DOC
Region: Piedmont

Red only, min alc 12%, max yield 10 tonnes/ha.
Grapes: Barbera, min 85–90%, Grignolino, Dolcetto and Freisa, alone or together, 10–15%.
Superiore: min age two years before release; min alc 12.5%.

Large DOC of almost 10,000 acres (4,000 ha) around the town of Monferrato.

Bardolino
DOC
Region: Veneto

Red only, min alc 10.5%, max yield 13 tonnes/ha.
Grapes: Corvina 35–65%, Rondinella 10–40%, Molinara 10–20%, Negrara 10%, plus Rossignola, Barbera, Sangiovese and Garganega up to 15%.
Classico: grapes are grown in defined heartland area (non-Classico Bardolino has a much wider catchment).

Bardolino makes a light, tangy style of red wine. While not simple, these are no-fuss wines that work very well with pasta or medium-flavored food. The region near Lake Garda has a very long winemaking tradition. The grapes are similar to Valpolicella, with a slightly different blend. Selected vineyards have their own DOCG.

Bardolino Superiore
DOCG
Region: Veneto

Red only, min alc 11.5%, max yield 8 tonnes/ha. One year aging before release.
Grapes: Corvina 35–65%, Rondinella 10–40%, with Molinara, Rossignola, Barbera, Sangiovese, Marzemino, Merlot, Cabernet Franc and Cabernet Sauvignon up to 20% and with no single variety more than 10%.

A recent addition (2001) to the DOCG list, Bardolino Superiore represents carefully selected prime Bardolino vineyards, which have had their vine density increased and their yield cut from 13 tonnes/ha to 8 tonnes/ha.

Barolo   **Region: Piedmont**
DOCG
Red only, min alc 13%, max yield 8 tonnes/ha; min age three years, at least
two in wood.
Grape: Nebbiolo.
Riserva: min age five years before release.

DOC of about 3,000 acres (1,200 ha) named after the town, Barolo is a big,
bold red. Usually needing age to soften tannin, it is not always made for long
keeping, as the region has now realized the world is not waiting for tannic
reds to mature. A modern style has evolved, a little more fruity and less tannic but still mouth-filling and alive.

Some villages within the DOCG have their own sub-identity and their
names – La Morra, Rocche, Cannubi – are sometimes used on single-vineyard wines from their district.

Bianchello del Metauro   **Region: Marche**
DOC
White only, min alc 11.5%, max yield 14 tonnes/ha.
Grapes: Bianchello (known locally as Biancame) min 95%, Malvasia
Toscana up to 5%.

Simple white from a little-known DOC of 1,500 acres (600 ha). Honest
quaffing wine.

Bianco Alcamo   **Region: Sicily**
DOC
Refer **Alcamo.**

Bianco Capena   **Region: Latium**
DOC
White only, min alc 11%, max yield 16 tonnes/ha.
Grapes: Malvasia di Candia, Malvasia del Lazio and Malvasia Toscana, up
to 55%, Trebbiano Toscano, Romagnolo and Giallo, min 25%, Bellone and
Bombino up to 20%.
Superiore: min alc 12%.
Asciutto: dry.
Abboccato: lightly sweet.

A smallish DOC of 395 acres (160 ha), 18.5 miles (30 km) north of Rome,
Bianco Capena has lifted its quality through the 1990s (still with a high yield)
to offer a safe white wine, well suited to food.

Bianco dei Colli Maceratesi   **Region: Marche**
DOC
Historic name for what is now **Colli Maceratesi.**

Bianco di Custoza   **Region: Veneto**
DOC
White only, min alc 11%, max yield 15 tonnes/ha.
Grapes: Trebbiano Toscano 20–45%, Garganega 20–40%, Tocai Friulano
(known locally as Trebbianello) 5–30%, Cortese, Malvasia Toscana, Riesling
Italico and Chardonnay, 20–30%. A sparkling (*spumante*) style is also made.

A DOC of some 210 acres (85 ha) on the southern side of Lake Garda. Only
specified vineyards are included in this DOC – those with the right soil and a
south-facing incline. The Trebbiano-based wine is not very highly regarded
and has a slight bitterness; good wine is considered to be soft and pleasant.

Bianco dell'Empolese   **Region: Tuscany**
DOC
White only, min alc 11%, max yield 14 tonnes/ha.
Grapes: Trebbiano at least 80%, other local white varieties up to 20%.
Vin Santo: min age three years before release.

A group of vineyards along the Arno River. DOC name comes from the village of Empoli.

Bianco di Pitigliano   **Region: Tuscany**
DOC
White only, min alc 11.5%, max yield 12.5 tonnes/ha.
Grapes: Trebbiano Toscano 65–70%, Greco, Malvasia Bianca, Toscana and
Verdello 30–35% altogether, with max of 15% of any one.

Southern Tuscan DOC, Trebbiano-based, with almost 2,470 acres (1,000 ha)
under vine. Regarded as average.

Bianco Pisano di San Torpe   **Region: Tuscany**
DOC
White only, min alc 11%, max yield 12 tonnes/ha.
Grapes: Trebbiano Toscano min 75%, other local varieties up to 25%.
Vin Santo: aged for at least four years in wood; min alc 16%.

This covers 1,062 acres (430 ha) of vineyard in Pisa province, located outside
the damp valleys.

Bianco della Valdinievole   **Region: Tuscany**
DOC
White only, min alc 11%, max yield 13 tonnes/ha.
Grapes: Trebbiano min 70%, Malvasia del Chianti, Canaiolo Bianco and
Vermentino, up to 25%, other authorized white up to 5%.
Vin Santo: aged for at least three years in wood; min alc 17%.
Dolce: min alc 12%.
Semi-secco: min alc 13%.
Secco: min alc 14%.

DOC of about 150 acres (60 ha) between Montecatini and Pescia. Attracting growing interest and has rising exports.

Bianco Vergine Valdichiana   Region: Tuscany
DOC
White only, min alc 11%, max yield 13 tonnes/ha.
Grapes: Trebbiano Toscano 70–85%, Malvasia del Chianti 10–20%, other non-aromatic white grape varieties 5–10%.

Valdichiana (Valley of Chiana), a DOC of more than 2,470 acres (1,000 ha). This white has a history of being used as a medicinal wine to treat liver ailments.

Biferno   Region: Molise
DOC
Red and rosé, min alc 11.5%, max yield 12 tonnes/ha. White, min alc 10.5%, max yield 12 tonnes/ha.
Grapes: Red and rosé, Montepulciano 60–70%, Trebbiano Toscano 15–20%, Aglianico 15–20%; other recommended grapes can be added up to a maximum of 5%. White, Trebbiano Toscano 65–70%, Bombino Bianco 25–30%, Malvasia Bianco 5–10%.

Named after the Biferno River, a DOC of 333 acres (135 ha) with a max height of 1,640 feet (500 m) for red and rosé, 2,000 feet (600 m) for white.

Bivongi   Region: Calabria
DOC
Red and rosé, min alc 12%, max yield 8 tonnes/ha. White, min alc 10.5%, max yield 12 tonnes/ha.
Grapes: Red and rosé, Gaglioppo and/or Greco Nero 30–50%, Nocera and/or Calabrese (Nero d'Avola) and/or Castiglione 30–50%, other local varieties, red up to 10% and white up to 15%. White, Greco Bianco and/or Guardavalle and/or Montonico 30–50%, Malvasia Bianca and/or Ansonica 30–50%, other local white varieties up to 30%.
Riserva: min age two years before release.

DOC on the slopes of Mount Consolino, with the Stilaro River running below.

Boca   Region: Piedmont
DOC
Red only, min alc 12%, max yield 9 tonnes/ha; aged for at least two years in wood, one year in the bottle.
Grapes: Nebbiolo 45–70%, Vespolina 20–40%, Bonarda Novarese max 20%.

Tiny 37-acre (15-ha) DOC with a long wine history. Situated in the Navara hills to the north of Piedmont. Provokes lots of interest, but does not produce much wine.

Bolgheri
Region: Tuscany
DOC
Red, white and rosé, min alc 10.5%, max yield 10 tonnes/ha.
Grapes: Red and rosé, Sangiovese 80–95%, Canaiolo 5–20%, other red varieties max 15% (Cabernet Sauvignon and Merlot generally make up a large part of these additional varieties). White, Trebbiano Toscano 10%–70%, Vermentino 10–70%, Sauvignon 10–70%, other recommended varieties max 15%.

Fairly new (1996) DOC towards the coast of Tuscany, famous for Sassicaia (now with its own DOC hyphenated to Bolgheri) and Ornellaia; less known for straightforward whites.

Bolgheri-Sassicaia
Region: Tuscany
DOC
Red only, min alc 10.5%, max yield 10 tonnes/ha.
Grapes: Cabernet Sauvignon 80%, other local red varieties 20% (traditionally this has been Sangiovese).

By obtaining single-vineyard DOC status, Sassicaia has earned recognition for the fact that it has something special (as reflected in price and demand) and has etched itself higher than the VdT classification it had to use for years. A highly-rated wine which has inspired many more wines blending Cabernet with Sangiovese.

Bosco Eliceo
Region: Emilia-Romagna
DOC
Red and white, min alc 10.5%, max yield 15 tonnes/ha.
Fortana: Fortana min 85%, min alc 10.5%. Frizzante (gassy), Amabile (sweet) and Abboccato (lightly sweet) versions also made.
Merlot: Merlot min 85%, min alc 10.5%.
Sauvignon: Sauvignon min 85%, Trebbiano Romagnolo max 15%; min alc 11%. Frizzante (gassy), Amabile (sweet) and Abboccato (lightly sweet) also made.
Bianco: Trebbiano Romagnolo 70%, Sauvignon and Malvasia Bianca di Candia max 30%, other white grapes max 5%. Frizzante (gassy), Amabile (sweet) and Abboccato (lightly sweet) versions also made.

A relatively new DOC still establishing an identity and image. A high-yielding region producing aromatic whites which can surprise.

Botticino
Region: Lombardy
DOC
Red only, min alc 12%, max yield 12 tonnes/ha.

Grapes: Barbera 30–40%, Schiava Gentile 20–30%, Marzemino 15–25%, Sangiovese 10–20%. Min age 10 months before release.

Small 82-acre (33-ha) DOC carrying some prestige. Fairly elevated, yet with lowlands as well as slopes, a combination of *terroir* factors that work well and make for a sought-after wine.

Brachetto d'Acqui   Region: Piedmont
DOCG

Red *frizzante*, min alc 5% (*spumante* 6%), max yield 8 tonnes/ha. Potential alcohol at picking 11.5% (*spumante* 12%).
Grape: Brachetto 100%. (Prior to receiving DOCG status in 1996, other varieties were allowed to be blended with Brachetto.)

Bubbly, frothy, strawberry-colored red made in a small 148-acre (60-ha) DOCG. *Spumante* (full sparkling) is also produced. Regarded as good drinking wine. Can be rather high in alcohol and low in yield. Part of this DOCG is in the Asti area.

Bramaterra   Region: Piedmont
DOCG

Red only, min alc 12%, max yield 7.5 tonnes/ha. Min 18 months aging in wood, six months in the bottle.
Grapes: Nebbiolo 50–70%, Croatina 20–30%, Bonarda and Vespolina alone or together up to 20%.
Riserva: two years aging in wood, one year in the bottle.

Another tiny region, a 54-acre (22-ha) DOC with a lighter red than other Nebbiolo-based wines in Piedmont. A low-yield region, potentially with lots to say.

Breganze   Region: Veneto
DOC

Red and white, min alc 11%, max yield 14 tonnes/ha.
Grapes: Red, Merlot min 85%, Marzemino, Cabernet Franc and Sauvignon, Grapello Gentile, Pinot Noir and Freisa up to 15%. White, Tocai min 85%, Pinot Blanc, Pinot Gris, Riesling Italico, Sauvignon and Vespaiolo up to 15%.
Rosso Superiore: min alc 12%.
Cabernet: Cabernet Sauvignon and Franc; min alc 11.5%, max yield 13 tonnes/ha.
Pinot Nero: Pinot Noir only; min alc 11.5% (Superiore 12%), max yield 13 tonnes/ha.
Pinot Grigio: Pinot Gris only; min alc 10.5% (Superiore 12%), max yield 13 tonnes/ha.
Pinot Bianco: Pinot Blanc only; min alc 11.5% (Superiore 12%), max yield 13 tonnes/ha.

Vespaiolo: Vespaiolo only; min alc 11.5% (Superiore 12%), max yield 13 tonnes/ha.

A DOC of 1,500 acres (600 ha) with largely varietal wines. Vineyards are on the foothills of the Alps and in the gravel soils on the plain to the south.

Brindisi   *Region: Apulia*
DOC
Red and rosé, min alc 12%, max yield 15 tonnes/ha.
Grapes: mainly Negro Amaro. Malvasia Nera di Brindisi and/or Montepulciano and/or Sangiovese permitted up to 30% (but only a max of 10% Sangiovese allowed).
Riserva: min age two years before release; min alc 12.5%.

DOC on the Adriatic coast producing a pleasant, robust red.

Brunello di Montalcino   *Region: Tuscany*
DOCG
Red only, min alc 12.5%, max yield 8 tonnes/ha. Min age five years before release, two of these in oak.
Grape: Brunello di Montalcino, also known as Sangiovese Grosso.
Riserva: min age six years before release, three of these in oak.

Very highly regarded DOCG of about 3,200 acres (1,300 ha), south of Chianti (almost two hours drive south of Florence) using a clone of Sangiovese known as Sangiovese Grosso. Wines are known for long life, and for robust flavors with finesse and good balance when well made. A DOCG that has climbed substantially since the 1980s. This is a prestige wine of Italy. The area also produces Rosso di Montalcino under a separate DOC.

Cacc'e mmitte di Lucera   *Region: Apulia*
DOC
Red only, min alc 11.5%, max yield 14 tonnes/ha.
Grapes: Uva di Troia (known locally as Sumarello) 35–60%, Montepulciano and/or Sangiovese and/or Malvasia Nera di Brindisi 25–35%, Trebbiano and/or Bombino Bianco and/or Malvasia del Chianti 15–30%.

An unusual term forms the name of the wine, related to a local dialectal reference to the wine being poured from the cask to the goblet, enjoyed and refilled. A 198-acre (80-ha) DOC with neither a strong nor a weak image.

Cagnina di Romagna   *Region: Emilia-Romagna*
DOC
Red only, min alc 11%, max yield 13 tonnes/ha.
Grapes: Refosco (known locally as Cagnina or Terrano) min 85%, other local varieties up to 15%.

Tiny DOC of barely 40.5 acres (16 ha) making a slightly sweetish red.

Caldaro or Lago di Caldaro   **Region: Trentino-Alto Adige**
DOC
Red only, min alc 10.5%, max yield 14 tonnes/ha.
Grapes: Schiava. Pinot Noir and Lagrein permitted up to max of 15%.
Classico: must be produced in the area of Caldaro, Appiano, Termeno, Cortaccia, Vadena, Egna, Montagna, Ora and Bronzolo.
Classico Superiore: Classico with min alc 10.5%.
Scelto or Selezionato: Classico with min alc 11%.

A large DOC of some 5,700 acres (2,300 ha). The high yield is helped by a sunny climate for the vine, usually leading to light, pleasant red.

Caluso   **Region: Piedmont**
DOC
Refer **Erbaluce di Caluso**.

Campi Flegrei   **Region: Campania**
DOC
Red, min alc 11.5%, max yield 12 tonnes/ha. White, min alc 10.5%, max yield 13 tonnes/ha. Varietal wines, min 90% of named grape and extra 0.5% min alc.
Grapes: Red, Piedirosso 50–70%, Aglianico and/or Sciascinoso 10–30%, other local varieties up to 10%. White, Falanghina 50–70%, Biancolella and/or Coda di Volpe 10–30%, other local white varieties up to 30%.

Seaside DOC around Naples, an idiosyncratic mix of old vines and new techniques. This is a name with a rising reputation.

Campidano di Terralba   **Region: Sardinia**
DOC
Red only, min alc 11.5%, max yield 15 tonnes/ha.
Grapes: Bovale di Spagna and Bovale Sardo min 80%. Pascale di Cagliari, Greco and Monica are also permitted to a max 20%. Five months aging required.

DOC of little more than 250 acres (100 ha) in the plain of Campidano on Sardinia's west coast, producing a hearty, popular style of red.

Canavese   **Region: Piedmont**
DOC
Red and rosé, min alc 10.5%, max yield 12 tonnes/ha. White, min alc 10%, max yield 12 tonnes/ha.
Grapes: Red, Nebbiolo, Barbera, Bonarda, Freisa or Neretto min 60% (min 85% if labeled by variety). White, Erbaluce 100%.

A relatively new (1996) DOC, a sister to DOC Erbaluce di Caluso, which was established 30 years earlier. Most wines labeled varietally.

Candia dei Colli Apuani
Region: Tuscany
DOC
White only, min alc 11.5%, max yield 8 tonnes/ha.
Grapes: Vermentino Bianco 70–80%, Albarola 10–20%, Trebbiano Toscano and Malvasia del Chianti varieties also permitted, with Malvasia max 5%.

Tiny DOC in the Apuan Hills.

Cannonau di Sardegna
Region: Sardinia
DOC
Red and rosé, min alc 12.5%, max yield 13.2 tonnes/ha.
Grapes: Mainly Grenache (known locally as Cannonau). Bovale Grande, Bovale Sardo, Carignan, Pascale di Cagliari, Monica and Vernaccia di San Gimignano to a total of 10% is permitted. Oliena, Nepentedi Oliena, Jerzu and Capo Ferrato indicate specific subareas as the general DOC may be produced from throughout Sardinia.
Riserva: min age two years; min alc 13%.
Liquorose Dolce: sweet; min alc 16%.
Secco: dry; min alc 18%.
Superiore: min age two years; min alc 15%.

A cheerful, hearty dinner wine which, like many Grenache wines, pales to an orange color after several years. Some vineyards are withdrawing the variety, but others see the vines as part of the island's heritage.

Capalbio
Region: Tuscany
DOC
Red, min alc 11%, max yield 10 tonnes/ha. Rosé and white, min alc 10.5%, max yield 12 tonnes/ha.
Grapes: Red and rosé, Sangiovese min 50%, other local varieties max 50%. White and Vin Santo, Trebbiano min 50%, other local varieties max 50%. Red and white varietally named wine must be 85% of the variety named.
Cabernet Sauvignon: Cabernet Sauvignon min 85%; min alc 12%.
Sangiovese: Sangiovese min 85%; min alc 12%.
Vin Santo: dry or sweet; min age three years before release.

DOC in the hilly parts to the south of Grosseto province; Cabernet Sauvignon doing well as a varietal, and as a blender with Sangiovese in the red.

Capri
Region: Campania
DOC
Red and white, min alc 11%, max yield 12 tonnes/ha.
Grapes: Red, Piedirosso min 80%. White, Falanghina, Greco (Greco limited to 50%), and Biancolella 20%.

Small DOC of about 62 acres (25 ha) on the island of Capri off the coast of Campania. Light-bodied, fruity wines, regarded as pleasant rather than special.

Capriano del Colle
DOC
Region: Lombardy

Red and white, min alc 11%, max yield 12.5 tonnes/ha.
Grapes: Sangiovese 40–50%, Marzemino 35–45%, Barbera 3–10%; Merlot and *incrocio* (hybrid) Terzi No. 1 can be used up to max of 15%.
Trebbiano: Trebbiano di Soave (Trebbiano Veronese or di Lugana) and Trebbiano Toscano; min alc 11%.

Small DOC in the hills of less than 100 acres (40 ha), Capriano del Colle offers a lively red and a simple but cheerful white.

Carema
DOC
Region: Piedmont

Red only, min alc 12%, max yield 8 tonnes/ha. Min age four years, at least two of these in wood
Grape: Nebbiolo.

Small DOC of about 100 acres (40 ha) near Turin. Nicely aromatic red with a round, velvety style.

Carignan del Sulcis
DOC
Region: Sardinia

Red and rosé, min alc 11.5%, max yield 16 tonnes/ha; min age five months.
Grapes: Carignan min 85%, plus Monica, Pascale and Alicante Bouschet to a total of 15%.
Invecchiato: min age 11 months.
Riserva: min age two years, at least one of these in wood and six months in the bottle; min alc 12.5%.
Superiore: min age two years, at least one of these in wood and six months in the bottle; min alc 13%.

The DOC region of Sulcis is in the southwest of Sardinia between Capo Teulada and Sant'Antioco and includes the island of Carloforte. A high-yielding DOC, considered to be improving with its light-medium bodied style.

Carmignano
DOCG
Region: Tuscany

Red, min alc 12.5%, max yield 8 tonnes/ha. Min age two years, at least one of these in wood.
Grapes: Red and rosé, Sangiovese min 50%, Canaiolo Nero max 20%, Cabernet Sauvignon and Franc 10–20%, Trebbiano Toscano, Canaiolo Bianco and Malvasia del Chianti, alone or together, max 10%. Other varieties permitted up to 10%.
Vin Santo: Trebbiano Toscano 65–75%, Canaiolo Bianco and/or Malvasia del Chianti 15–35%. Other authorized white varieties permitted up to 10%. Min alc 17%, max yield 11 tonnes/ha. Grapes must be subjected to

natural drying. Min age three years in wood.
Dolce: min alc 11%.
Semisecco: min alc 13%.
Secco: min alc 14%.
Riserva: Red only; min age three years, at least two of these in wood.

Once part of Chianti, this DOCG covers about 300 acres (120 ha) in the hills near Florence. The traditional Chianti varieties prevail, including the move to include Cabernet. The low hills (the DOCG qualification stops at 1,300 feet/ 400 m) allow Sangiovese to ripen nicely for softer wine.

Carso   *Region: Friuli-Venezia Giulia*
DOC

Red, min alc 10%. White, min alc 10.5%. Max yield 10 tonnes/ha.
Grapes: Red, Terrano 70–100%, other local varieties allowed up to 30%. White, Malvasia Istriana 70–100%, other local varieties allowed up to 30%.
Cabernet Franc: 85–100%; min alc 10.5%.
Cabernet Sauvignon: 85–100%; min alc 10.5%.
Chardonnay: 85–100%; min alc 11%.
Malvasia: Malvasia Istriana 85–100%; min alc 11%.
Merlot: 85–100%; min alc 10.5%.
Pinot Grigio: Pinot Gris 85–100%; min alc 10.5%.
Refosco: Refosco dal Penduncolo Rosso 85–100%; min alc 10.5%.
Sauvignon: Sauvignon Blanc 85–100%; min alc 11.5%.
Terrano: Terrano min 85%, Piccola Nera and/or Pinot Noir 15%; min alc 10%.
Traminer: 85–100%; min alc 11.5%.
Vitovska: 85–100%; min alc 10.5%.

The word "Carso" is more Celtic than Italian and means "land of rock," a reference to a stretch of broken limestone rock, like the corridor between Trieste and the rest of Italy.

Castel Del Monte   *Region: Apulia*
DOC

Red, min alc 12%, max yield 14 tonnes/ha. Rosé, min alc 11%, max yield 14 tonnes/ha. White, min alc 11%, max yield 15 tonnes/ha.
Grapes: Red, Uva di Troia 65–100%, Sangiovese, Montepulciano, Aglianico and Pinot Noir max 35%. Rosé, Bombino Nero and/or Uva di Troia 65–100%, Montepulciano, Aglianico and Pinot Noir max 35%. White, Pampanuto 65–100%, other local white varieties max 35%.
Riserva: min age two years, one of which must be in wood. Min alc 12.5%.
Varietal wines: a minimum of 90% of the named variety; min alc for varietal reds 12.5% (Pinot Noir 11.5%) and for varietal whites 10.5%.

DOC around the "castle of the mountain" near Andria, on the slopes of the Murge Mountains. Vineyards were based around older, indigenous varieties until more recently, when the DOC has included newer grapes like Cabernet, Chardonnay and others. The high allowable yield is not always pushed to the full, but the wines are popular rather than sought after.

Castel San Lorenzo
Region: Campania
DOC
Red and rosé, min alc 11.5%, max yield 12 tonnes/ha. White, min alc 11%, max yield 12 tonnes/ha.
Grapes: Red and rosé, Barbera 60–80%, Sangiovese 20–30%, other local varieties up to 10%. White, Trebbiano 50–60%, Malvasia 30–40%, other local varieties up to 20%.
Barbera: Barbera min 85%.
Barbera Riserva: min age two years before release; min alc 12.5%.
Moscato: Moscato Bianco min 85%; min alc 12%.
Moscato Lambiccato: min alc 13.5%. Sweet, lightly gassy white made from local clones of Moscato.

Sunny DOC in the province of Salerno, where Barbera was introduced a few decades ago and has done very well.

Casteller
Region: Trentino-Alto Adige
DOC
Red only, min alc 11%, max yield 13.5 tonnes/ha.
Grapes: Schiava Grosso and Schiava Gentile min 30%, Merlot up to 20%, Lambrusco a Foglia Frastagliata up to 40%; other permitted varieties up to 10%.

Hilly DOC of around 2,700 acres (1,100 ha) beginning at the border of the province of Verona and extending north along both banks of the Adige River into the province of Trent.

Castelli Romani
Region: Latium
DOC
Red, min alc 11%. Rosé, min alc 10.5%. White, min alc 10.5%. Max yield 12 tonnes/ha.
Grapes: Red, Cesanese, Merlot, Sangiovese, Montepulciano and Nero Buono, with other local varieties up to 15%. White, Malvasia Candia and Puntinata, and Trebbiano, with other local varieties up to 30%.

A recent (1996) DOC which recognizes the popularity of easy-drinking wines. The red styles are dry, sometimes slightly sweet, and *frizzante*. The whites are light, and also dry and slightly sweet, often with a little *pétillance* to underline their freshness.

Cellatica   *Region: Lombardi*
DOC
Red only, min alc 11.5%, max yield 12 tonnes/ha.
Grapes: Marzemino (known locally as Berzemino) 30–50%, Barbera
30–50%, Schiava Gentile 10–30%, Incrocio Terzi No.1 (hybrid) 10–30%,
plus other local grapes including Cabernet Franc up to 10%.
Superiore: min age one year before release; min alc 12%.

Awarded DOC status in 1968, Cellatica is another historic wine region in the
hills – the vines are allowed up to 1,312 feet (400 m). Incrocio Terzi was created by fertilizing Cabernet Franc with pollen from Cabernet Franc. Cellatica
wine is not highly sought after, but the vineyard has a development program
in place which is improving the style and image.

Cerasuolo di Vittoria   *Region: Sicily*
DOC
Red only, min alc 11%, max yield 10 tonnes/ha.
Grapes: Frappato 40–100%, Calabrese up to 60%, Grosso Nero and
Nerello Mascalese permitted to a max of 10%.

A small DOC producing pleasant and enjoyable wine that ages well – 10–20
years is not thought excessive. The DOC is under review for improvement, a
move brought about by local producers.

Cerveteri   *Region: Latium*
DOC
Red, min alc 11%, max yield 15 tonnes/ha. White, min alc 12%, max yield
14 tonnes/ha.
Grapes: Red, Sangiovese and Montepulciano 60%, Cesanese 25%,
Canaiolo Nero, Carignan and Barbera up to 30%. White, Trebbiano
Toscano, Romagnolo and Giallo min 50%; Malvasia di Candia and del Lazio
max 35%, Tocai, Verdicchio, Bellone and Bombino max 15%.

In the province of Rome and part of Viterbo, this DOC serves a fairly commercial range of wines, simple in style, and with a popular following for the
price. The greater yields are considered high for quality wines and some
producers are lowering yields accordingly. Most wines are sold locally.

Cesanese di Affile   *Region: Latium*
DOC
Red only, min alc 12%, max yield 12.5 tonnes/ha.
Grapes: Cesanese di Affile and/or Cesanese Comune.

This is a dry, soft wine, slightly bitter.

Cesanese di Olevano Romano   *Region: Latium*
DOC
Red only, min alc 12%, max yield 12.5 tonnes/ha.

Grapes: Cesanese di Affile and/or Cesanese Comune; Sangiovese, Montepulciano, Barbera, Trebbiano Toscano and Bambino Bianco to a total of 10% is also permitted.

A DOC near Rome producing basic red quaffing wine, the best of which are well regarded and good value. *Frizzante* and sparkling (*spumante*) red wines are also popular with most being a little sweet, and enjoyed young and fresh. Most wines are sold locally.

Cesanese del Piglio   Region: Latium
DOC
Red only, min alc 12%, max yield 12.5 tonnes/ha.
Grapes: Cesanese di Affile and/or Cesanese Comune.

On the outskirts of Rome, the wines are made mostly from red grapes, although some white (max 10%) is included to enable early drinking.

Chianti   Region: Tuscany
DOCG
Red only, min alc 12%, max yield 8 tonnes/ha.
Grapes: Sangiovese 75–100%, Canaiolo up to 10%, Trebbiano and Malvasia up to 10%, other allowed varieties up to 10%.
Riserva: min age two years before release, at least three months in the bottle; min alc 12.5%
Village wine: Besides Chianti Classico, which has its own DOCG (listed below), Chianti has seven other specific subregions, each of which may hyphenate its name to Chianti if the wine comes entirely from within that specific zone. These subregions are Rufina, Montalbano, Colli-Fiorentini, Colline-Pisani, Colli-Aretini, Colli-Senesi and Montespertoli.

Chianti sold in the flasks is generally considered to be for drinking young. It is made by the Governo system, adding back some dried grapes and encouraging a further fermentation. The better Chiantis (some suitable for aging a few years) are almost always in Bordeaux-shape bottles.

Chianti has come through a major evolution over the last 20 years, firstly by withdrawing larger quantities of white wine, including Trebbiano with its slightly bitter character. The addition of Cabernet Sauvignon, Franc and Merlot as an option encouraged producers to change the rules also. Now the wines are more serious, more structured and have a distinctive Chianti tang that works very well with food.

Variations in soil and climate among the eight regions contribute as much to the individuality of each wine as the winemakers' quests for creative styles. Some Chianti is still fairly fresh, easy and quaffable, though a growing portion is more elaborate, more serious and capable of becoming classy with age. Those variables can be confusing; but for drinkers who persist, Chianti offers some of the best quality for value in European wine.

Riserva wine, which has a longer wood maturation before release, tends to be fed with the some of the best of the season's crop. But it does not always require long bottle-age afterwards; the wood content of the maturation does plenty for many wines. Just the same, there should be no hurry to drink it either.

Chianti Classico   Region: Tuscany
DOCG
Red only, min alc 12%, max yield 12 tonnes/ha.
Grapes: Sangiovese 75–100%, Canaiolo up to 10%, Trebbiano and Malvasia up to 6% (until 2005, when the latter two varieties may be phased out), other permitted varieties up to 10%.
Riserva: min age two years before release, at least three months in the bottle; min alc 12.5%.

DOCG representing the original "classical" zone; this doesn't necessarily mean that all the wine in this DOCG is better Chianti than that from other zones, but the zone itself is highly respected. Chianti Classico has a consortium of growers who promote their region using the black rooster on a gold seal on their label and advertising. The wines qualify for DOCG status anyway, so the consortium is a promotional tool, not necessarily an indication of extra quality.

Cilento   Region: Campania
DOC
Red, min alc 11.5%. Rosé and white, min alc 11%. Max yield 12 tonnes/ha.
Grapes: Red, Aglianico 60–75%, Piedirosso and/or Primitivo, 15–20%, Barbera 10–20%, other local red varieties up to 10%. Rosé, Sangiovese 70–80%, Aglianico 10–15%, Primitivo and/or Piedirosso 10–15%, other local red varieties up to 10%. White, Fiano, 60–65%, Trebbiano Toscano 20–30%, Greco and/or Malvasia Bianca 10–15%, other local white varieties up to a max of 10%.
Aglianico: Aglianico 85–100%; Primitivo and/or Piedirosso up to 15%; min age one year before release.

Dry, arid DOC in an area where the vine struggles a little but comes up with good quality fruit.

Cinque Terre   Region: Liguria
DOC
White only, min alc 11%, max yield 9 tonnes/ha.
Grapes: Bosco min 60%, Albarola and/or Vermentino up to 40%.
Sciacchetra: The grapes must be subjected to drying. Requires aging one year. Min alc 17%, max yield 9 tonnes/ha. (A *liquoroso* version is also produced.)

East of Genoa, Cinque Terre is a hilly strip with the vineyards planted on a "rock wall." About 370 acres (150 ha) are under vine. Quite a famous wine in literature, but not widely sought after these days other than in the immediate area. Nevertheless there are also those who visit the region just to buy the wine, which says something.

Cinque Terre Sciacchetra   Region: Liguria
DOC
Refer **Cinque Terre**.

Circeo   Region: Latium
DOC
Red and rose, min alc 11%, max yield 11 tonnes/ha. White, min alc 10.5%, max yield 11 tonnes/ha.
Grapes: Red and rosé, Merlot min 85%, other local red varieties up to 15%. White, Trebbiano min 60%, Malvasia di Candia, up to 30, other local white varieties up to 30%.
Sangiovese: Sangiovese min 85%, other local red varieties up to 15%.
Trebbiano: Trebbiano Toscano min 85%, other local white varieties up to 15%.
Novello: dry and sweet reds, often *frizzante*.

According to legend, the sorceress Circe (from Homer's *Odyssey*) lived on this promontory in the south of Latium, 90 minutes drive from Rome. The wines are not highly regarded, but have a following as easy-drinking styles.

Ciro   Region: Calabria
DOC
Red and rosé, min alc 12.5%, max yield 11.5 tonnes/ha; min age (for red only) nine months. White, min alc 12%, max yield 13.5 tonnes/ha.
Grapes: Red and rosé, Gaglioppo min 90%, Trebbiano Toscano and/or Greco Bianco up to 5%. White, Reco Bianco min 90%, Trebbiano Toscano up to 10%.
Classico: grapes grown in communes of Ciro and Ciro Marina.
Superiore: min alc 13.5%.
Riserva: min age two years; min alc 13.5%.

A region within the province of Catanzaro, where Bacchus (god of wine) is celebrated in a temple. There are some commercial wines, most of which are sold locally and to tourists, which are not regarded as exceptional internationally.

Cisterna d'Asti   Region: Piedmont
DOC
Red only, min alc 11.5%, max yield 12 tonnes/ha.
Grapes: Croatina 80–100%, other local varieties up to 20%.

Superiore: min age 10 months before release.

Cisterna is a small farming town, given DOC status only recently (2002) although wine has a long history here. Croatina, a rather rare grape variety sometimes called Bonarda in error, produces a vibrant red, usually soft and easy to enjoy while young.

Colli Albani
DOC   *Region: Latium*

White only, min alc 11%, max yield 16.5 tonnes/ha.
Grapes: Malvasia Rossa or Bianca max 60%, Trebbiano Toscano, Trebbiano Romagnolo, Trebbiano Giallo and Trebbiano di Soave 25–50%, Malvasia del Lazio 5–45%. Up to 10% of other white grape varieties may be added, with the exclusion of Moscato sub-varieties.
Superiore: min alc 11.5%.
Spumante: sparkling also made, most of which is sold locally.

From the hills south of Rome, Colli Albani produces a range of grapey-flavored white wine in dry (*secco*) and sweeter (*abboccato*, *amabile* and *dolce*) styles. Most wine is sold locally.

Colli Altotiberini
DOC   *Region: Umbria*

Red, min alc 11.5%, max yield 11 tonnes/ha. White, min alc 10.5%, max yield 11 tonnes/ha.
Grapes: Red and rosé, Sangiovese 55–70%, Merlot 10–20%, Trebbiano Toscano and/or Malvasia del Chianti up to 10%, other recommended varieties 15%. White, Trebbiano Toscano 75–90%, Malvasia del Chianti 10%, other recommended white varieties 15%.

Elevated sites overlooking both sides of the Tiber Valley produce a small amount of wine for Colli Altotiberini. "Alto-Tiber," in the DOC name, means upper Tiber, located to the north of Umbria.

Colli Amerini
DOC   *Region: Umbria*

Red, white and rosé, min alc 11.5%, max yield 12 tonnes/ha.
Grapes: Red, Novello and Rosato-Sangiovese, 65–80%, Montepulciano and/or Ciliegiolo and/or Canaiolo and/or Merlot and/or Barbera, up to 30%, other local red varieties up to 15%. White, Trebbiano Toscano, 70–85%, Grechetto and/or Verdello and/or Garganega and/or Malvasia Toscana, up to 30%, other local white varieties up to 15%.
Superiore: min alc 12%.

In a region best known for olive oil and the nearby Orvieto white wine, this is a little known DOC, mostly making simple whites.

Colli Berici   *Region: Veneto*
DOC
Red and white.
Cabernet: Cabernet Franc and/or Cabernet Sauvignon only; min alc 11%,
max yield 12 tonnes/ha. **Cabernet Riserva:** min age three years, min alc
12%.
Chardonnay: Chardonnay min 85%, Pinot Blanc up to 15%; min alc 11%,
max yield 12 tonnes/ha.
Garganega: Garganega min 90%, Trebbiano di Soave (Trebbiano
Nostrano) up to 10%; min alc 10.5%, max yield 14 tonnes/ha.
Merlot: Merlot only; min alc 11%, max yield 13 tonnes/ha.
Pinot Bianco: Pinot Blanc min 85%, Pinot Gris up to 15%; min alc 11%,
max yield 12 tonnes/ha.
Sauvignon: Sauvignon min 90%, Garganega up to 10%; min alc 11%,
max yield 12 tonnes/ha.
Tocai Bianco: Tocai Bianco min 90%, Garganega up to 10%; min alc 11%,
max yield 12 tonnes/ha.
Tocai Rosso: Tocai Rosso min 85%, Garganega up to 15%; min alc 11%,
max yield 12 tonnes/ha. **Tocai Rosso Barbarano:** min alc 11.5%.
Spumante: Garganega min 50%, Pinot Blanc, Pinot Gris, Chardonnay,
Sauvignon up to 50%; min alc 11%, max yield 12 tonnes/ha.

Medium-sized DOC around Vicenza; fairly high-yielding, "safe" wines rather
than great highlights, although there can be some fresh, clean and user-
friendly wines of great value for money.

Colli Bolognesi   *Region: Emilia Romagna*
DOC
Red, min alc 12.5%. White, min alc 10.5%. Max yield for both
13 tonnes/ha.
Grapes: White, Albana, 60–80%, Trebbiano Romagnolo, 20–40%. Varietal
wines, min 85% of named variety; other varieties permitted under the
DOC law, up to a max of 15%.
Riserva: Reds aged for three years, one of which must be in wood.

Small DOC in the hills of Bologna for which there are about 100 variations
on the theme of varieties, subregions and styles, almost out of proportion for
the size of the area. Best wines considered attractive.

Colli di Bolzano   *Region: Trentino-Alto Adige*
DOC
Red only, min alc 11%, max yield 13 tonnes/ha.
Grapes: Schiava min 90%, Lagrein and Pinot Noir max 10%.

Small DOC of about 75 acres (30 ha) around the city of Bolzano in the region of Trentino-Alto Adige.

Colli di Conegliano   **Region: Veneto**
DOC
Red, min alc 12%, max yield 12 tonnes/ha, min age two years before
release. White, min alc 10.5%, max yield 12 tonnes/ha.
Grapes: Red, Cabernet Sauvignon and Franc and/or Marzemino, each at
least 10%, Merlot 10–40%, *incrocio* Manzoni 2.15.0 up to 10%. White,
incrocio Manzoni 6.0.13 min 30%, Pinot Blanc and/or Chardonnay
30–70%, Sauvignon and/or Riesling Renano up to 10%.
Torchiato di Fregona: Prosecco min 30%, Verdiso min 30%, Boschera min
25%, other local non-aromatic white varieties up to 15%; min age
13 months before release.
Refrontolo Passito: (sweet red) Marzemino 95%, other local non-aromatic
red varieties up to 5%.

DOC in the hills of Treviso. Some styles use grapes dried after picking.

Colli dell'Etruria Centrale   **Region: Tuscany**
DOC
Red and rosé, min alc 10.5%. White, min alc 10%. Max yield 14 tonnes/ha.
Grapes: Red and rosé, Sangiovese 50–100%, Cabernet Franc and/or
Cabernet Sauvignon and/or Merlot and/or Pinot Noir and/or Canaiolo
Nero up to 50%, other local varieties up to 25%. White, Trebbiano Toscano
50–100%, Malvasia del Chianti and/or Pinot Blanc or Pinot Gris and/or
Chardonnay and/or Sauvignon and/or Vernaccia di San Gimignano up to
50%, other white varieties up to 25%.
Novello: Sangiovese 50%, Canaiolo Nero and/or Merlot and/or Gamay
and/or Ciliegiolo up to 50%, other local red varieties up to 25%.
Vin Santo Secco or Amabile: Trebbiano Toscano and/or Malvasia del
Chianti 70%, other local varieties up to 30%; min age three years. **Riserva**:
min age four years before release.
Vin Santo Abboccato: min age three years; min alc 15%.
Riserva: min age four years; min alc 15.5%.
Vin Santo Occhio di Pernice: Sangiovese 50%, other local red or white
varieties up to 50%; min age three years before release. Occhio di Pernice
translates as partridge eye, referring to its color.

Geographically covering Chianti DOCG, this DOC from 1990 gives a lower
or "delimited" alternative for wines that might not reach DOCG standards.
Previously such wine would have had to be given VdT status.

Colli Etruschi Viterbesi   **Region: Latium**
DOC
Red, white and rosé, min alc 10%, max yield 14 tonnes/ha.
Grapes: Red, Sangiovese 50–65%, Montepulciano 20–45%, local red varieties
up to 30%. White, Trebbiano 40–80%, Malvasia up to 30%, local white
varieties up to 30%.

Procanico: Trebbiano 85%, local white varieties (not Malvasia) up to 15%.
Grechetto: Greco Bianco (Grechetto) 85%, local white varieties (not Malvasia) up to 15%.
Rosé: Trebbiano Giallo (Rossetto) 85%, local white varieties (not Malvasia) up to 15%.
Merlot: Merlot 85–100%, local approved varieties (not Cioliegiollo) up to 15%; min alc 11%.
Moscatello: Moscato 85%, local white varieties (not Malvasia) up to 15%.
Violone: Montepulciano (locally known as Violone) 85%, local red varieties (not Ciliegiolo) up to 15%; min alc 11%.

A long wine tradition here, which reached fulfilment when it was awarded DOC status in 1996. This is an important region with a multiplicity of styles (some sweet, some *frizzante*) and qualities. Expect it to settle down over the next few years.

Colli Euganei
DOC   *Region: Veneto*
Red, min alc 11% (Superiore min alc 12%), max yield 14 tonnes/ha. White, min alc 10.5%, max yield 12 tonnes/ha.
Grapes: Red, Merlot 60–80%, Cabernet Sauvignon and Franc, Barbera and Raboso Veronese, alone or together, 20–40%. White, Garganega 30–50%, Serprina (Prosecco) 10–30%, Tocai and/or Sauvignon 20–40%, plus Pinella, Pinot Blanc, Riesling and Chardonnay up to 20%.
Spumante (white): Amabile (lightly sweet) min alc 11% or Secco/Asciutto (dry) min alc 12%.
Spumante (red): Amabile (lightly sweet) min alc 11% or Secco/Asciutto (dry) min alc 12%.
Moscato: Moscato Bianco min 95%, allowable white grapes max 5%; min alc 10.5%, max yield 12 tonnes/ha. **Moscato Spumante:** min alc 11.5%.
Pinot Bianco: Pinot Blanc min 90%, other allowable white grapes max 10%; min alc 11%, max yield 12 tonnes/ha. Superiore min alc 12%. **Pinot Bianco Spumante:** Amabile (lightly sweet) min alc 11% or Secco/Asciutto (dry) min alc 12%.
Tocai Italico: Tocai Italico min 90%, other allowable white grapes max 10%; min alc 11%, max yield 12 tonnes/ha. Superiore min alc 12%. **Tocai Italico Spumante:** Amabile (lightly sweet) min alc 11% or Secco/Asciutto (dry) min alc 12%.
Cabernet: Cabernet Sauvignon and Franc min 90%, other allowable red grapes up to 10%. Superiore min age one year, min alc 12.5%.
Merlot: Merlot min 90%, other allowable red grapes max 10%. Superiore min age one year, min alc 12%. **Merlot Spumante:** Amabile (lightly sweet) min alc 11% or Secco/Asciutto (dry) min alc 12%.

A significant DOC of 2,060 acres (835 ha) over a wide range of grapes and styles including lusty sparkling red varietals.

4444

Colli di Faenza
Region: Emilia-Romagna
DOC
Red, min alc 12%, max yield 12.3 tonnes/ha. White, min alc 11%, max yield 14 tonnes/ha.
Grapes: Red, Cabernet Sauvignon 40–60%, Ancellota, Cilegiolo, Merlot and Sangiovese collectively 40–60%. White, Chardonnay 40–60%, Pignoletto, Pinot Blanc, Sauvignon Blanc and Trebbiano collectively 40–60%.
Sangiovese: if varietally named must use 100% Sangiovese.
Riserva: min age 24 months.

Recent (1997) DOC in the hills around the city of Faenza. The reds are well respected, especially the Riserva and Sangiovese Riserva.

Colli di I'mola
Region: Emilia-Romagna
DOC
Red, min alc 11.5%, max yield 12.5 tonnes/ha. White, min alc 11%, max yield 14 tonnes/ha.
Grapes: Red, Cabernet Sauvignon, Barbera, Sangiovese. White, Chardonnay, Pignoletto, Trebbiano.
Riserva: Red and white, min age 17 months before release.
Varietal wines: min 85% of the variety specified. White varietals, min alc 11.5%.
Superiore: White, min alc 11.5%.
Cabernet Sauvignon Riserva: min age 18 months before release. *Dolce, abboccato* and *frizzante* styles are available.

Quite a large DOC in terms of style. At best, pleasant quaffing wines without great character or statement; at worst, thin and lacking definition.

Colli Lanuvini
Region: Latium
DOC
White only, min alc 11.5%, max yield 14 tonnes/ha.
Grapes: Malvasia Bianca and Puntinata max 70%, Trebbiano Toscano, Verde and Giallo min 30%, Bellone and Bonvino max 10%.

From the hills near Lake Nemi to Aprila in the province of Rome, Colli Lanuvini produces dry or semi-sweet white wines with body, however some can be a little flat, and best drunk with food. The best are harmonious and enjoyable.

Colli di Luni
Region: Liguria
DOC
Red, min alc 11.5%, max yield 12 tonnes/ha. White, min alc 11%, max yield 12 tonnes/ha.
Grapes: Red, Sangiovese 60–70%, Canaiolo Pollera Nera and Ciliegiolo Nero collectively min 15%, other local red varieties up to 25%. White,

Vermentino min 35%, Trebbiano 25–40%, other local varieties up to 30%. Wine labeled Vermentino requires a minimum of 90% of that variety. **Riserva**: (red only) min age two years, min alc 12.5%.

The most northern DOC in Tuscany, running into the most southern DOC of Liguria. Some commentators respect this DOC area for its long history and tradition rather than any special qualities in its wine.

Colli Maceratesi   Region: Marche
DOC
Red, min alc 11.5%, max yield 14 tonnes/ha. White, min alc 11%, max yield 15 tonnes/ha.
Grapes: Red, including Novello, Sangiovese min 50%; Cabernet Sauvignon and Franc, Ciliegiolo, Lacrima, Merlot, Montepulciano and Vernaccia Nera up to 50%, other local non-aromatic red varieties up to 15%. White, including Passito and sparkling (*spumante*), Maceratino min 70%, Trebbiano, Verdicchio, Malvasia, Chardonnay, Sauvignon Blanc, *incrocio* Bruni 54, Pecorino and Grechetto up to 30%, other local non-aromatic white varieties up to 15%.
Ribona: Maceratino 85%, other local varieties up to 15%.

The cuisine of the district and town of Macerata, from which this DOC draws its name, is considered an ideal match for the local wines, bold, well-flavored and straightforward.

Colli Martani   Region: Umbria
DOC
Red and white.
Trebbiano: Trebbiano Toscano 85%, Trebbiano Spoletino, Grechetto, Malvasia Bianca di Candia, Malvasia Bianca del Chianti, Garganega and Verdicchio, alone or together, up to 15%; min alc 11%, max yield 12 tonnes/ha.
Grechetto: Grechetto 85%, Trebbiano Spoletino, Malvasia Bianca di Candia, Malvasia Bianca del Chianti, Garganega and Verdicchio, alone or together, up to 15%; min alc 11.5%, max yield 10 tonnes/ha. When the wine is made from grapes exclusively from Todi and has a min alc of 12% it can be labeled with the sub-denomination Grechetto di Todi.
Sangiovese: Sangiovese 85%, Canaiolo, Ciliegiolo, Barbera, Merlot, Montepulciano, Trebbiano Toscano, Trebbiano Spoletino, Grechetto, Malvasia Bianca di Candia, Malvasia Bianca del Chianti, Garganega and Verdicchio, alone or together, up to 15%. White grapes can not exceed 10% of the total; min alc 11.5%, max yield 12 tonnes/ha.
Sangiovese Reserva: min age two years, one of which must be in wood; min alc 12%.

Sunny hills in the Perugia province of Umbria provide the conditions for Colli Martani's single red and three white grapes. The wines are increasingly satisfying (moderate respect and fair prices help), but have not yet gained strong international standing.

Colli Orientali del Friuli
DOC   **Region: Friuli-Venezia Giulia**

Red and white, min alc 12% (except for Picolot), max yield 11 tonnes/ha.
Tocai Friulano: Tocai Friulano min 90%, other allowable white varieties up to 10%.
Verduzzo: (Friulano) Verduzzo min 90%, other allowable white varieties up to 10%.
Ribolla: Ribolla min 90%, other allowable white varieties up to 10%.
Pinot Bianco: Pinot Blanc min 90%, other allowable white varieties up to 10%.
Pinot Grigio: Pinot Gris min 90%, other allowable white varieties up to 10%.
Sauvignon: Sauvignon min 90%, other allowable white varieties up to 10%.
Riesling Renano: Riesling Renano min 90%, other allowable white varieties up to 10%.
Picolot: Picolot min 90%, other allowable white varieties up to 10%; min alc 15%. Riserva requires two years min age before release.
Merlot: Merlot min 90%, other allowable red varieties up to 10%. Riserva requires min two years age before release.
Cabernet: Cabernet Sauvignon and Franc min 90%, other allowable red varieties up to 10%. Riserva requires two years min age before release.
Pinot Nero: Pinot Noir min 90%, other allowable red varieties up to 10%. Riserva requires two years min age before release.
Refosco dal Peduncolo Rosso: Refosco dal Peduncolo Rosso min 90%, other allowable red varieties up to 10%. Riserva requires two years min age before release.

Lots of styles, lots of grapes, and a spread of quality in this major 5,681-acre (2,300-ha) DOC, located in the eastern hills of Friuli in the top-right corner of Italy.

Colli di Parma
DOC   **Region: Emilia-Romagna**

Red and white.
Rosso: Barbera 60–75%, Bonarda Piemontese and Croatina 25–40%, other allowable red varieties max 15%; min alc 11%, max yield 10 tonnes/ha.
Malvasia (Secco or Asciutto): Malvasia di Candia Aromatico min 85%, Moscato Bianco max 15%; min alc 10.5%, max yield 11 tonnes/ha. A *spumante* version is also made.
Malvasia (Amabile): Malvasia di Candia Aromatico min 85%, Moscato Bianco max 15%; min alc 10.5%, max yield 11 tonnes/ha. A *spumante* version is also made.

Sauvignon: Sauvignon only; min alc 11.5%, max yield 7.5 tonnes/ha.

A small red wine DOC in the Parma area, a region noted for its excellent ham, cured by the prevailing breezes. Barbera grows successfully in this area and has given the red a strong reputation.

Colli Perugini   Region: Umbria
DOC

Red and rosé, min alc 11.5%, max yield 12 tonnes/ha. White, min alc 11%, max yield 12 tonnes/ha.

Grapes: Red and rosé, Sangiovese 65–85%, Montepulciano, Ciliegiolo and Barbera, 15–35%, Merlot max 10%. White, Trebbiano Toscano 65–85%; Verdicchio, Grechetto, Garganega and Malvasia del Chianti 15–35% (max yield for Malvasia is 10%).

In the hills of Umbria, on a site compared to the Epernay district of Champagne, a small-volume DOC offers traditional Italian varieties from a cool *terroir*.

Colli Pesaresi   Region: Marche
DOC

Red, rosé and white, min alc 11%, max yield 14 tonnes/ha.

Grapes: Red and rosé, Sangiovese 70%, other local non-aromatic red varieties up to 30%. White, Trebbiano, Verdicchio, Biancame, Pinot Gris, Pinot Noir (vinified off the skins), Riesling Italico, Chardonnay, Sauvignon Blanc and Pinot Blanc min 75%, other local non-aromatic white varieties max 25%.

Sangiovese: Sangiovese 85–100%, Montepulciano and/or Ciliegiolo up to 15%; min alc 11.5%, max yield 11 tonnes/ha.

Focara Rosso: Pinot Noir, Cabernet Sauvignon and Franc, Merlot min 50%, Sangiovese up to 50%, other local non-aromatic red varieties up to 25%.

Focara Pinot Noir: Pinot Noir 90%, other local non-aromatic red varieties, up to 10%.

Roncaglia Bianco: Trebbiano Toscano min 85%, Pinot Noir 15%.

The hills overlooking Pesaro city give their name to this DOC, once the home of that great composer Rossini. Sangiovese is the predominant grape variety here.

Colli Piacentini   Region: Emilia-Romagna
DOC

Red and white.

Gutturnio: Barbera 55–70%, Croatina (Bonarda) 30–45%; min alc 12%, max yield 12 tonnes/ha.

Monterosso Val d'Arda: Malvasia di Candia Aromatica 35–50%, Trebbiano Romagnolo and Ortrugo 20–35%, Moscato Bianco 10–30%, Bervedino

and/or Sauvignon max 20%; min alc 11%, max yield 9 tonnes/ha. A
spumante is also produced.
Trebbiano Val Trebbia: Ortrugo 35–50%, Malvasia di Candia Aromatica
and/or Moscato Bianco 10–30%, Trebbiano Romagnolo and/or Sauvignon
15–30%, other allowable white varieties max 15%; min alc 11%, max yield
9 tonnes/ha. A *spumante* is also produced.
Val Nure: Malvasia di Candia Aromatica 30–50%, Ortrugo 20–35%,
Trebbiano Romagnolo 20–35%, other allowable white varieties max 15%;
min alc 11%, max yield 10 tonnes/ha. A *spumante* is also produced.
Barbera: Barbera 85%, other allowable red varieties max 15%; min alc
11.5%, max yield 13 tonnes/ha.
Bonarda: Bonarda 85%, other allowable red varieties max 15%; min alc
11.5%, max yield 13 tonnes/ha.
Malvasia: Malvasia 85%, other allowable white varieties max 15%; min alc
10.5%, max yield 12 tonnes/ha. A *spumante* is also produced.
Ortrugo: Ortrugo 85%, other allowable white varieties max 15%; min alc
10.5%, max yield 11 tonnes/ha. A *spumante* is also produced.
Pinot Grigio: Pinot Gris 85%, other allowable white varieties max 15%;
min alc 11%, max yield 9 tonnes/ha. A *spumante* is also produced.
Pinot Noir: Pinot Noir 85%, other allowable red varieties max 15%; min
alc 11%, max yield 9 tonnes/ha. A *spumante* is also produced.
Sauvignon: Sauvignon 85%, other allowable white varieties max 15%; min
alc 11%, max yield 10 tonnes/ha.

Hilly DOC of nearly 9,000 acres (3,600 ha) making a wide range of styles,
which are enjoyed as pleasant varietal statements from the area.

Colli di Rimini   *Region: Emilia-Romagna*
DOC
Red, min alc 11.5%, max yield 13 tonnes/ha. White, min alc 11%, max yield
13 tonnes/ha.
Grapes: Red, Sangiovese 60–75%, Cabernet Sauvignon 15–25%, Merlot,
Barbera, Montepulciano, Ciliegiolo, Terrano and Ancellota up to 25%.
White, Trebbiano 50–70%, Biancame and Mostosa 30–50%, other local
white varieties up to 20%.
Cabernet Sauvignon: Cabernet min 85%, other local red varieties up to
15%.
Biancame: Biancame min 85%, Pignoletto, Chardonnay, Riesling Italico,
Sauvignon Blanc, Pinot Blanc, and Müller-Thurgau up to 15%.
Rébola: Pignoletto 85%, Biancame and/or Mostosa and/or Trebbiano
Romagnolo up to 15%.
Riserva: red, including Cabernet; min age two years before release.

Situated in the southeast of the region, towards the border of Marche. A
relatively new (1996) DOC building a name for itself.

Colli della Romagna Centrale
Region: Emilia Romagna
DOC
Red, min alc 12%. White, min alc 11%. Max yield 12 tonnes/ha.
Grapes: Red, Cabernet Sauvignon 50–60%, Sangiovese and/or Barbera
and/or Merlot and/or Montepulciano 40–50%. White, Chardonnay
50–60%, Bombino and/or Sauvignon Blanc and/or Trebbiano and/or Pinot
Blanc 40–50%.
Cabernet Sauvignon: Cabernet Sauvignon min 85%, other local red
varieties up to 15%.
Chardonnay: Chardonnay 100%.
Sangiovese: Sangiovese 100%.
Trebbiano Romagnolo: Trebbiano Romagnolo 85%, other local non-
aromatic white varieties up to 15%.
Riserva: min age two years before release.

A recent (2001) DOC in a hilly area between Forli and Cesena producing
some simple wine as well as some more complex and robust styles.

Colli della Sabina
Region: Latium
DOC
Red and rosé, min alc 11%, max yield 12 tonnes/ha. White, min alc 10.5%,
max yield 12 tonnes/ha.
Grapes: Red and rosé, Sangiovese 40–70%, Montepulciano 15–40%, other
local varieties up to 30%. White, Trebbiano min 40%, Malvasia min 40%, other
local white varieties up to 20%.

This DOC lies in olive oil country. In the 1980s growers planted new varieties
and concentrated on quality, which resulted in qualification for a DOC in
1996. Some sweeter sparkling styles are also produced.

Colli di Scandiano e Canossa
Region: Emilia-Romagna
DOC
White only, min alc 10.5%, max yield 13 tonnes/ha.
Grapes: White, Sauvignon Blanc (known locally as Spergola or
Spergolino) 40–80%, Malvasia, Trebbiano, Pinot Blanc and Pinot Gris
20–60%.
Sauvignon: Sauvignon min 90%, Malvasia di Candia, Pinot Blanc, Pinot
Gris, Trebbiano and Chardonnay, collectively up to 10%.
Pinot: Pinot Blanc and/or Pinot Noir 100%.
Frizzante (Dolce, Amabile or Secco): min alc 10.5%.
Spumante (Semisecco, Secco or Brut): min alc 11%.
Malbo Gentile: Malbo Gentile 85–100%, Croatina or Sgavetta up to 15%.

A 550-acre (220-ha) DOC with a long history as a wine area and a wide mix
of styles.

Colli Tortonesi
Region: Piedmont
DOC
Red and white.
Barbera: Barbera min 85%, Freisa, Bonarda Piemontese and Dolcetto, alone or together, max 15%; min alc 11.5%, max yield 9 tonnes/ha.
Barbera Superiore: min age two years, one of which is in wood; min alc 12.5%.
Dolcetto: Dolcetto min 85%; min alc 11%, max yield 10 tonnes/ha.
Cortese: Cortese only; min alc 10.5%, max yield 10 tonnes/ha. **Frizzante** min alc 10.5% and **Spumante** min alc 11.5%.
White (Bianco): min alc 10%, made from locally grown, non-aromatic white varieties.

DOC of about 30 districts in the Alessandria province, covering about 1,000 acres (400 ha). The Barbera is well respected, but Tortonesi production is mostly sold locally to accompany local cuisine.

Colli del Trasimeno
Region: Umbria
DOC
Red, min alc 11.5%, max yield 12.5 tonnes/ha. White, min alc 11%, max yield 12.5 tonnes/ha.
Grapes: Red, Sangiovese 60–80%, Ciliegiolo and Gamay 40%, Malvasia del Chianti and Trebbiano Toscano 20%. White, Trebbiano Toscano 60–80%, Malvasia del Chianti, Verdicchio Bianco and Verdello and Grechetto, alone or together, up to 40%.
Vendemmia Tardiva: min age 18 months before release.

Well groomed, tidy-looking DOC sloping towards Lake Trasimeno.

Collina Torinese
Region: Piedmont
DOC
Red only, min alc 10.5%, max yield 10 tonnes/ha.
Grapes: Barbera min 60%, Freisa min 25%, other local non-aromatic red varieties max 5%.

Recent (1999) DOC of with an initial planting of just 20 acres (8 ha).

Colline di Levanto
Region: Liguria
DOC
Red and white, min alc 11%, max yield 11 tonnes/ha.
Grapes: Red, Sangiovese min 40%, Ciliegiolo max 20%, other local red varieties up to 40%. White, Vermentino 40–75%, Albarola 20–55%, Bosco 5–40%, other local white varieties up to 35%.

Next to the DOC of Cinque Terre, Colline di Levanto has similar climate and soil. This DOC features quite well-respected wines.

Colline Lucchesi   Region: Tuscany
DOC
Red, min alc 11%, max yield 12 tonnes/ha. White, min alc 10.5%, max yield
11 tonnes/ha.
Grapes: Red, Sangiovese 45–60%, Canaiolo 8–15%, Ciliegiolo and
Colorino 5–15%, Trebbiano Toscano 10–15%, Vermentino and Malvasia
Toscana 5–10%. White, Trebbiano Toscano 50–70%, Greco and/or
Grechetto 5–15%, Vermentino Bianco 5–15%, Malvasia del Chianti up to
5%.
Riserva: (reds only) min age two years before release.

Colorful DOC around Lucca City.

Colline Novaresi   Region: Piedmont
DOC
Red and white, min alc 11%, max yield 10 tonnes/ha.
Grapes: Red, Nebbiolo min 30%, Uva Rara (Bonarda) max 40%, Vespolina
and Croatina max 30%. Varietal wine must carry 85% of the named
variety. White, Erbaluce 100%.

Nebbiolo, known locally as Spanna, and the other varieties of grapes used in
this DOC have been grown in the hills of Novaresi for centuries. This 1994
DOC allowed a small group of growers to enjoy some individual recognition
for their area.

Colline Saluzzesi   Region: Piedmont
DOC
Red only, min alc 10%, max yield 12 tonnes/ha.
Grapes: Red, Pelaverga, Nebbiolo and Barbera min 60%, other local non-
aromatic red varieties up to 40%.
Varietally named Pelaverga and Quagliano must contain 100% of the
named grape.

Northwest Piedmont DOC that uses the fairly rare Quagliano variety, which
ripens as a very sweet grape, and the Pelaverga variety, which produces a
light-colored red with some appeal.

Collio   Region: Friuli-Venezia Giulia
DOC
Refer **Collio Goriziano**.

Collio Goriziano   Region: Friuli-Venezia Giulia
DOC
Red and white, max yield 11 tonnes/ha.
White: Ribollo Gialla 45–55%, Malvasia Istriana 20–30%, Tocai 15–25%;
min alc 11%.
Varietal wines: 100% of the named variety: Riesling Italico, min alc 12%;

Tocai Triulano, min alc 12%; Malvasia, min alc 11.5%; Pinot Blanc, min alc 12%; Pinot Gris, min alc 12.5%; Sauvignon, min alc 12.5%; Traminer, min alc 12%; Cabernet Franc, min alc 12%; Pinot Noir, min alc 12.5%.
Riserva: min age three years for reds, two years for whites.

Also called Collio, a variation on the Italian word for hills or hillsides, this DOC presents a user-friendly range of wines. There are about 3,400 acres (1,375 ha) under production with Pinot Gris and Sauvignon predominating, and Merlot and Cabernet Franc increasing. Along with neighboring Colli Orientali del Friuli, the wines are on the rise in terms of image and quality.

Contea di Sclafani   Region: Sicily
DOC
Red, min alc 11%, max yield 14 tonnes/ha. White, min alc 10.5%, max yield 14 tonnes/ha.
Grapes: Red (including Novello), Nero d'Avola and Perricone 50%, other local red varieties up to 50%. Rosé and sparkling rosé, Nerello Mascalese 50%, other local red varieties up to 50%. White and sparkling white, Catarratto, Inzolia, Grecanico 50%, other local white varieties up to 50%.
Dolce and **Vendemmia Tardiva:** Ansonica, Catarratto, Grecanico, Grillo, Chardonnay, Pinot Blanc and Sauvignon Blanc, 100%.
Varietal wines: must be 85–100% of the named variety. Varietal wines include grapes like Sangiovese, Cabernet Sauvignon and Pinot Noir, and others not shown in the blend list above for the red.

A 1996 DOC divided between the provinces of Caltanissetta and Agrigento, in Sicily. This DOC has old traditional grapes as well as new varieties, and is progressing in its viticulture.

Contessa Entellina   Region: Sicily
DOC
White, min alc 11%, max yield 14 tonnes/ha.
Grapes: Red and rosé, Calabrese and Syrah min 50%, other local varieties up to 50%. White, Ansonica min 50%, Catarratto Bianco Lucido, Grecanico Dorato, Chardonnay, Sauvignon Blanc and Grillo min 30%, other local varieties max 15%.

Named after a small Palermo town high in the hills. A strong grower movement has moved the region forward in terms of improved quality.

Controguerra   Region: Abruzzi
DOC
Red, min alc 12%, max yield 14 tonnes/ha. White, min alc 11%, max yield 14 tonnes/ha.
Grapes: Red and Novello, Montepulciano min 60%, Merlot, Cabernet Sauvignon and Franc 15%, other local red varieties up to 25%. White, Trebbiano Toscano 60%, Passerina min 15%, other local white varieties

up to 25%. Sparkling (Spumante), Trebbiano min 60%, Chardonnay, Verdicchio and Pecorino at least 30%, other local white varieties up to 10%. Varietal wines must carry 85% of the named variety.

Passito Rosso: Montepulciano 60%, other local red varieties up to 25%.

Passito Bianco: Trebbiano Toscano and/or Passerina and/or Malvasia 60%, other local white varieties up to 40%.

Controguerra: (red and Novello) Montepulciano 60%, Merlot and/or Cabernet 15%, other local red varieties up to 25%.

Spumante: Trebbiano Toscano 60%, Chardonnay and/or Verdicchio and/ or Pecorino min 30%, other local white varieties up to 10%.

The hills, valleys and plains of the Abruzzi region reward the dedicated grower. The wines are inexpensive and full of flavor. Lots of fun to discover, too!

Copertino   *Region: Apulia*
DOC
Red and rosé, min alc 12%, max yield 14 tonnes/ha.

Grapes: Negro Amaro, with the possible addition of up to 30% total of Malvasia di Brindisi, Malvasia Nera di Lecce, Montepulciano and Sangiovese. The Sangiovese can not exceed 15%.

Rosso Riserva: min age two years, min alc 12.5%.

Dry, robust and hearty reds that use the qualities of this variety to the fullest. Regarded as very good value most years.

Cori   *Region: Latium*
DOC
Red, min alc 11.5%, max yield 16 tonnes/ha. White, min alc 11%, max yield 16 tonnes/ha.

Grapes: Red, Montepulciano 40–60%, Nero Buono di Cori 20–40%, Cesanese Comune (Bonvino Nero) 10–30%. White, Malvasia di Candia max 70%, Trebbiano Toscano max 40%, Bellone and/or Trebbiano Giallo max 30%.

DOC 1,300 feet (400 m) above sea level in the hills around the town of Cori. Known for sound, straightforward wines, and producing a higher volume of white than red.

Cortese dell'Alto Monferrato   *Region: Piedmont*
DOC
White only, min alc 10%, max yield 10 tonnes/ha.

Grapes: Cortese min 85%, other non-aromatic white grapes max 15%.
Frizzante and *spumante* versions are also produced.

Cortese grapes grown in the provinces of Asti and Alessandria have a long heritage, however red wines and Moscato hold so much of the attention and volume in Piedmont. The wine is tasty and fresh, suitable for drinking with fish and early courses.

Cortona **Region: Tuscany**
DOC
Red, min alc 12%, rosé min alc 11%, max yield 10 tonnes/ha. White, min alc 11%, max yield 11 tonnes/ha.
Grapes: Red, Sangiovese 40–60%, Canaiolo 10–30%, other local non-aromatic red varieties max 30%.
Varietal wines: min 85% of the named variety, including Chardonnay and Sauvignon Blanc.
Vin Santo: Sangiovese min 85%, min age three years. Riserva, min age five years.
Vin Santo Occhio di Pernice: Sangiovese and/or Malvasia min 80%. Min age eight years before release.

Recent (1999) DOC around the town of Cortona on the Tuscan border with Umbria; at least 1,150 feet (350 m) above sea level.

Costa d'Amalfi **Region: Campania**
DOC
Red and rosé, min alc 10.5%. White, min alc 10%. Max yield 12 tonnes/ha.
Grapes: Red and rosé, Piedirosso min 40%, Sciascinoso and Aglianico up to 60%, other red varieties up to 40%. White, Falanghina and/or Biancolella min 60%, other local varieties up to 40%.
Furore, Ravello and Tramonti: This DOC has three subregions, Furore, Ravello and Tramonti, which require a min alc of 11.5% for reds and 11% for whites when these subregional names are used. These subregions have a Riserva with at least two years of aging.

Overlooking the Amalfi coast, the terraced vineyards of Costa d'Amalfi DOC are planted only with the local varieties with a long history in the area. Wines are regarded as distinctive regional statements.

Costa della Sesia **Region: Piedmont**
DOC
Red, min alc 11%. Rosé and white, min alc 10.5%. Max yield 10 tonnes/ha.
Grapes: Red and rosé, Nebbiolo, Bonarda, Vespolina, Croatina and Barbera min 50%, other local non-aromatic varieties up to 50%. White, Erbaluce 100%. Varietal wines must be min 85% of the named variety.

DOC covering 18 communes in the provinces of Verceli and Biella, in the hills overlooking the Sesia River. Not as well known as the adjacent DOC and DOCG, Monti Lessoni and Gattinara.

Delia Nivolelli **Region: Sicily**
DOC
Red, min alc 11.5%, max yield 14 tonnes/ha. White, min alc 11%, max yield 14 tonnes/ha.
Grapes: Red, Nero d'Avola, Pignatello or Perricone, Merlot, Cabernet

Sauvignon, Syrah and Sangiovese min 65%; other local varieties up to 35%. White, Grecanico, Inzolia, Grillo min 65%; other local white varieties up to 35%. Sparkling (*spumante*), Grecanico, Chardonnay, Inzolia, Damaschino and Grillo total 100%. Varietal wines including Cabernet Sauvignon, Merlot, Sangiovese, Chardonnay and others, min 85% of named variety.
Riserva: red only, min age two years before release.

A fairly new DOC of the mid-1990s, part of a restructuring and evolution in the province of Trapani on the island of Sicily, near Marsala on the southwest coast of the island.

Dolceacqua   **Region: Liguria**
DOC
Refer **Rossese di Dolceacqua**

Dolcetto d'Acqui   **Region: Piedmont**
DOC
Red only, min alc 11.5%, max yield 8 tonnes/ha.
Grape: Dolcetto.
Superiore: min age one year before release, min alc 12.5%.

One of seven DOCs based on the Dolcetto grape in Piedmont. A deep-colored and moderately soft wine, generally for drinking in the first three years.

Dolcetto d'Alba   **Region: Piedmont**
DOC
Red only, min alc 11.5%, max yield 9 tonnes/ha.
Grape: Dolcetto.
Superiore: min age one year before release, min alc 12.5%.

The most respected in quality terms of seven DOCs based on the Dolcetto grape in Piedmont. A deep-colored and moderately soft wine, generally for drinking in the first three years.

Dolcetto d'Asti   **Region: Piedmont**
DOC
Red only, min alc 11.5%, max yield 8 tonnes/ha.
Grape: Dolcetto.
Superiore: min age one year before release, min alc 12.5%.

One of seven DOCs based on the Dolcetto grape in Piedmont. A deep-colored and moderately soft wine, generally for drinking in the first three years.

Dolcetto di Diano d'Alba   **Region: Piedmont**
DOC
Red only, min alc 11%, max yield 8 tonnes/ha.
Grape: Dolcetto.
Superiore: min age one year before release, min alc 11%.

One of seven DOCs based on the Dolcetto grape in Piedmont. A deep-colored and moderately soft wine, generally for drinking in the first three years.

Dolcetto di Dogliani   Region: Piedmont
DOC
Red only, min alc 11.5%, max yield 8 tonnes/ha.
Grape: Dolcetto.
Superiore: min age one year before release, min alc 12.5%.

One of seven DOCs based on the Dolcetto grape in Piedmont. A deep-colored and moderately soft wine, generally for drinking in the first three years.

Dolcetto delle Langhe Monregalesi   Region: Piedmont
DOC
Red only, min alc 11%, max yield 7 tonnes/ha.
Grape: Dolcetto.
Superiore: min age one year before release, min alc 12%.

One of seven DOCs based on the Dolcetto grape in Piedmont. A deep-colored and moderately soft wine, generally for drinking in the first three years.

Dolcetto di Ovada   Region: Piedmont
DOC
Red only, min alc 11.5%, max yield 8 tonnes/ha.
Grape: Dolcetto.
Superiore: min age one year before release, min alc 12.5%.

One of seven DOCs based on the Dolcetto grape in Piedmont. A deep-colored and moderately soft wine, generally for drinking in the first three years.

Donnici   Region: Calabria
DOC
Red only, min alc 12%, max yield 12 tonnes/ha.
Grapes: Gaglioppo (Montonico Nero) 50%, Greco Nero 10–20%, Malvasia Bianca and/or Pecorello max 20%.

Small DOC of under 250 acres (100 ha) known for its dark-colored red.

Elba   Region: Tuscany
DOC
Red, min alc 12%, max yield 9 tonnes/ha. White, min alc 11%, max yield 9 tonnes/ha.
Grapes: Red, Sangiovese min 75%, Trebbiano Toscano (locally known as Procanico), Biancone and/or Canaiolo up to 25%. White, Trebbiano Toscano min 90%, other allowable white varieties up to 10%. A little *spumante* is also produced.

DOC with nearly 500 acres (200 hectares) of vineyards on the island of Elba

off the Tuscan coastline, where the windy conditions aren't always condu-
cive for winemaking.

Eloro   Region: Sicily
DOC
Red, min alc 12%, rosé min alc 11.5%. Max yield 12 tonnes/ha.
Grapes: Nero d'Avola, Pignatello and Frappato min 90%, other local red
varieties up to 10%. Other varietal wines must have a minimum of 90%
of the variety named and can include up to 10% of other varieties that are
permitted in this DOC.
Pachino: Nero d'Avola min 80%, Frappato and Pignatello up to 20%.
Pachino Riserva: min age two years before release.
Pignatello: Pignatello min 80%, Frappo and Nero d'Avola up to 20%.

A DOC with indigenous varieties not widely seen elsewhere. This is a historic
area that contains a number of Greek archeological sites.

Erbaluce di Caluso   Region: Piedmont
DOC
White only, min alc 11%, max yield 12 tonnes/ha.
Grape: Erbaluce 100%.
Caluso Spumante: Erbaluce 100%; min alc 11.5%, max yield 12 tonnes/ha.
Caluso Passito: Erbaluce min 95%; 5% Bonarda allowed. Grapes are
subjected to drying. Min alc 13.5%, max yield 12 tonnes/ha. Bottled only
after five years.
Liquoroso: min age five years, min alc 17.5%. During the aging process,
blending of different vintages is permitted.

Unusual DOC of just under 250 acres (100 ha) around Turin, with only one
grape variety. The Caluso Passito is perhaps the nectar of the region, but the
wines are available only in small quantities and are much sought-after.

Esino   Region: Marche
DOC
Red and white, min alc 10.5%, max yield 12 tonnes/ha.
Grapes: Red, Sangiovese and/or Montepulciano min 60%, other local red
varieties min 40%. White, Verdicchio 50–100%, other local authorized
varieties up to 50%.

Recent (1995) DOC. Wines known for freshness and balance, and suited to
a wide range of foods.

Est! Est!! Est!!! di Montefiascone   Region: Latium
DOC
White only, min alc 11%, max yield 13 tonnes/ha.
Grapes: Trebbiano Toscano (Procanico) 65%, Malvasia Bianca Toscana
20%, Rosetto (Trebbiano Giallo) 15%.

The unusual name of this DOC comes from an ancient story (dating back to 1000 A.D.) told in the region, which sets the scene for this 1,000-acre (405-ha) DOC. The wine is considered only average but is fun to drink locally in celebration of the story.

Etna
Region: Sicily
DOC
Red, min alc 12.5%, max yield 9 tonnes/ha. White, min alc 11.5%, max yield 9 tonnes/ha.
Grapes: Red or rosé, Nerello Mascalese min 80%, Nerello Mantellato (Nerello Cappuccio) max 20%, other non-aromatic red varieties up to 10%. White, Carricante min 60%, Catarratto Bianco Comune or Lucido max 40%, Trebbiano Minnella Bianca and other non-aromatic white varieties up to 15%.
Bianco Superiore: Carricante min 80%, Catarratto Bianco Comune or Lucido max 20%, Trebbiano Minnella Bianca and other non-aromatic white varieties up to 15%; min alc 12%.

DOC in the hills around Catania. Its quality is considered just average but improving.

Falerio dei Colli Ascolani
Region: Marche
DOC
White only, min alc 11.5%, max yield 14 tonnes/ha.
Grapes: Trebbiano Toscano max 80%; Verdicchio, Passerina, Malvasia (no more than 7% Malvasia allowed), Pinot Blanc and Pecorino, any or all max 25%.

A fairly well-spread DOC with just 200 acres (80 ha) of actual vineyard in total.

Falerno del Massico
Region: Campania
DOC
Red, min alc 12.5%, max yield 10 tonnes/ha. White, min alc 11%, max yield 10 tonnes/ha.
Grapes: Red, Aglianico 60–80%, Piedirosso 20–40%, Primitivo and/or Barbera max 20%. White, Falanghina 100%. Riserva requires two years of aging, one of which must be in wood.
Primitivo: Primitivo 85%, Piedirosso and Barbera, alone or together, max 15%; min alc 13%. Riserva or Vecchio requires two years of aging, one of which must be in wood.

Based around the famous Falernian or Falernum, a special and well-recorded wine in Roman times, the modern version comes in mixed styles, some made only from Primitivo grapes, some blended red and some whites as well.

Fara
Region: Piedmont
DOC
Red only, min alc 12%, max yield 11 tonnes/ha.
Grapes: Nebbiolo 30–50%, Vespolina 10–30%, Bonarda Novarese up to 40%.

Small DOC of 54 acres (22 ha) in the hills that makes a respected, Nebbiolo-based red, the additional varieties balancing it well.

Faro
Region: Sicily
DOC
Red only, min alc 12%, max yield 10 tonnes/ha.
Grapes: Nerello Mascalese 45–60%, Nerello Cappuccio 15–30%, Nocera 5–10%, optional Calabrese and/or Sangiovese up to 15%.

Looking over the Strait of Messina towards mainland Italy, the region has a long and colorful wine history. Faro is setting out to be quality driven but has just a handful of vineyards at this stage.

Fiano di Avellino
Region: Campania
DOCG
White only, min alc 11.5%, max yield 10 tonnes/ha.
Grapes: Fiano min 85%, Greco, Coda di Volpe Bianca and Trebbiano Toscano up to 15%. The name of the wine can be accompanied by the word "Apianum," a traditional term of classical origin.

A recent (2003) DOCG. Fiano is a strong-flavored variety; it is almost exclusive to this DOCG, where it produces wines of some age, often with nuttiness and honey tones, sometimes gently oxidizing to add character.

Franciacorta
Region: Lombardy
DOCG
Sparkling white and rosé, min alc 11.5%. Max yield 10 tonnes/ha.
Grapes: White, Pinot Blanc, Pinot Noir and/or Chardonnay. Rosé, Pinot Blanc and/or Chardonnay min 85%, Pinot Noir max 15%.
Millesimato: min 85% from year shown.

DOCG working towards quality sparkling wine in the hills south of Lake Iseo. DOCG status has been given to some 2,500 acres (1,000 ha) and expectations are high for future wines of depth and quality.

Frascati
Region: Latium
DOC
White only, min alc 11%, max yield 15 tonnes/ha.
Grapes: Malvasia Bianca di Candia and/or Trebbiano Toscano min 70%, Greco and Malvasia del Lazio up to 30%.
Secco or Ascuitto: dry.
Amabile: lightly sweet.

Dolce or Cannellino: noticeably sweet, grapes botrytis-affected.
Superiore: min alc 11.5%.

Frascati is famous, though not really for its quality. A sensibly-priced quaffing wine produced by this large DOC is widely seen around the world.

Freisa d'Asti   *Region: Piedmont*
DOC
Red only, min alc 11%, max yield 8 tonnes/ha.
Grape: Freisa.
Amabile: lightly sweet.
Superiore: min age one year before release, min alc 12.5%.
A *frizzante* and *spumante* are also produced.

The Freisa grape, indigenous to Piedmont, is used in three DOCs in that region, as well as the large volume of *Vino da Tavola* that comes from a wider Piedmont catchment area. Freisa d'Asti is the largest of the three DOCs and is well regarded.

Freisa di Chieri   *Region: Piedmont*
DOC
Red only, min alc 11%, max yield 8 tonnes/ha.
Grape: Freisa.
Superiore: min age one year before release, min alc 11.5%.
A *frizzante* and a *spumante* are also produced.

The Freisa grape, indigenous to Piedmont, is used in three DOCs in that region, as well as the large volume of *Vino da Tavola* made from a wider Piedmont catchment area. Freisa di Chieri is a tiny DOC.

Friuli Annia   *Region: Friuli-Venezia Giulia*
DOC
Red, rosé and white, min alc 10.5%, max yield 12 tonnes/ha.
Grapes: Red, Cabernet Sauvignon and Franc, Merlot, Refosco. White, Chardonnay, Malvasia, Pinot Blanc, Pinot Gris, Sauvignon Blanc, Tocai Friulano, Verduzzo Friulano. Varietal wine requires the named variety to be 100%. An extensive range of additional varieties is permitted for varietal wine, including Chardonnay, Pinot Blanc, Sauvignon Blanc, Malvasia and Verduzzo.
Riserva: min age two years before release.

An appellation from the mid-1990s, Fruili Annia is a small DOC in Italian terms, best known for its Tocai, but also with extensive other plantings to test conditions and markets.

Friuli Aquileia   *Region: Friuli-Venezia Giulia*
DOC
Red, rosé and white, min alc 10%, max yield 14 tonnes/ha.

Grapes: Red, Cabernet Sauvignon and Franc, Merlot, Refosco. Rosé, Merlot only. White, Chardonnay, Gewürztraminer, Müller-Thurgau, Malvasia, Pinot Blanc, Pinot Gris, Riesling, Sauvignon Blanc, Tocai Friulano, Verduzzo Friulano. Varietal wine requires the named variety to be 100%.
Riserva: Red only, min alc 12%, min age two years, named variety 90–100%.
Superiore: White only, min alc 11%, named variety 90–100%.

A wide range of styles with a long list of varieties is allowed under this DOC, which provides a good choice of clean, fresh and fruity wines.

Friuli Grave   Region: Friuli-Venezia Giulia
DOC
Red, rosé and white, min alc 10.5%, max yield 14 tonnes/ha.
Varietal wines with their own requirements as shown below.
Rosato (rosé): Merlot 70–80%, Cabernet Sauvignon, Refosco dal Peduncolo Rosso and Pinot Noir, alone or together, 20–30%; min alc 11%, max yield 12 tonnes/ha. Superiore, min alc 12%.
Merlot: Merlot 85%, Refosco Nostrano and other allowable red varieties 15%; min alc 11%, max yield 13 tonnes/ha. Superiore, min alc 12%.
Cabernet Franc: Cabernet Franc 85%, Refosco Nostrano and other allowable red varieties 15%; min alc 11%, max yield 12 tonnes/ha. Superiore, min alc 12%.
Cabernet Sauvignon: Cabernet Sauvignon 85%, Refosco Nostrano and other allowable red varieties 15%; min alc 11%, max yield 12 tonnes/ha. Superiore, min alc 12%.
Cabernet: Cabernet Franc and/or Cabernet Sauvignon 85%, Refosco Nostrano and other allowable red varieties 15%; min alc 11%, max yield 12 tonnes/ha. Superiore, min alc 12%.
Pinot Nero: Pinot Noir 85%, Refosco Nostrano and other allowable red varieties 15%; min alc 11%, max yield 12 tonnes/ha. Superiore, min alc 12%.
Refosco dal Peduncolo Rosso: Refosco dal Peduncolo Rosso 85%, Refosco Nostrano and other allowable red varieties 15%; min alc 11%, max yield 13 tonnes/ha. Superiore, min alc 12%.
Tocai Friulano: Tocai Friulano 85%, other allowable white varieties 15%; min alc 11%, max yield 13 tonnes/ha. Superiore, min alc 12%.
Pinot Bianco: Pinot Blanc 85%, other allowable white varieties 15%; min alc 11%, max yield 12 tonnes/ha. Superiore, min alc 12%.
Pinot Grigio: Pinot Gris 85%, other allowable white varieties 15%; min alc 11%, max yield 13 tonnes/ha. Superiore, min alc 12%.
Chardonnay: Chardonnay 85%, other allowable white varieties 15%; min alc 10.5%, max yield 13 tonnes/ha. Superiore, min alc 11.5%.
Verduzzo Friulano: Verduzzo Friulano 85%, other allowable white varieties 15%; min alc 11%, max yield 13 tonnes/ha. Superiore, min alc 12%.
Riesling Renano: Riesling Renano 85%, other allowable white varieties

15%; min alc 11%, max yield 12 tonnes/ha. Superiore, min alc 12%.
Sauvignon: Sauvignon 85%, other allowable white varieties 15%; min alc 11%, max yield 12 tonnes/ha. Superiore, min alc 12%.
Traminer Aromatico: Traminer Aromatico 85%, other allowable white varieties 15%; min alc 11%, max yield 12 tonnes/ha. Superiore, min alc 12%.

A major DOC on a plain beside the DOC Friuli Isonzo. Its name comes from the sandy, gravelly soil from the mountains above. Merlot is the most planted variety.

Friuli Isonzo   *Region: Friuli–Venezia Giulia*
DOC
Red and white, min alc 10.5%, max yield 13 tonnes/ha. A red and a white *frizzante* are also produced.
Grapes: Red, Merlot 60–70%, Cabernet Franc and/or Cabernet Sauvignon 20–30%, Refosco dal Peduncolo Rosso and Pinot Noir up to 20%. White, Tocai Friulano 40–50%, Malvasia Istriana and/or Pinot Blanc 25–30%, Chardonnay 25–30%.
Tocai Friulano: Tocai Friulano 100%; min alc 10.5%, max yield 13 tonnes/ha.
Malvasia Istriana: Malvasia Istriana 100%; min alc 10.5%, max yield 13 tonnes/ha.
Verduzzo Friulano: Verduzzo Friulano 100%; min alc 10.5%, max yield 13 tonnes/ha.
Chardonnay: Chardonnay 100%; min alc 11%, max yield 12 tonnes/ha.
Pinot Bianco: Pinot Blanc 100%; min alc 11%, max yield 12 tonnes/ha.
Pinot Grigio: Pinot Gris 100%; min alc 11%, max yield 12 tonnes/ha.
Riesling Italico: Riesling Italico 100%; min alc 11%, max yield 12 tonnes/ha.
Riesling Renano: Riesling Renano 100%; min alc 11%, max yield 12 tonnes/ha.
Sauvignon: Sauvignon 100%; min alc 11%, max yield 12 tonnes/ha.
Traminer Aromatic: Traminer Aromatic 100%; min alc 11%, max yield 12 tonnes/ha.
Merlot: Merlot 100%; min alc 10.5%, max yield 13 tonnes/ha.
Cabernet, Cabernet Franc and Cabernet Sauvignon: Cabernet, Cabernet Franc and/or Cabernet Sauvignon; min alc 11%, max yield 12 tonnes/ha.
Franconia: Franconia 100%; min alc 11%, max yield 12 tonnes/ha.
Pinot Noir: Pinot Noir 100%; min alc 11%, max yield 12 tonnes/ha.
Refosco dal Peduncolo Rosso: Refosco dal Peduncolo Rosso 100%; min alc 11%, max yield 12 tonnes/ha.

Similar to Friuli Grave, the neighboring DOC. Glacial erosion has provided sandy, gravelly soil in the basin drained by the Isonzo River. Wide styles, lots of grapes, relatively high yields.

Friuli Latisana   Region: Friuli-Venezia Giulia
DOC
Red and white.
Rosato: Merlot 70–80%, Cabernet Franc and Sauvignon, Refosco Nostrano or Refosco dal Peduncolo Rosso, alone or together 20–30%; min alc 10.5%, max yield 13 tonnes/ha.
Merlot: Merlot min 85%, other varieties max 15%; min alc 10.5%, max yield 13 tonnes/ha.
Cabernet: Cabernet Franc and/or Cabernet Sauvignon min 90%, other varieties max 15%; min alc 10.5%, max yield 12 tonnes/ha.
Cabernet Franc: Cabernet Franc min 90%, min alc 10.5%. **Riserva:** min alc 11.5%; min age two years before release.
Cabernet Sauvignon: Cabernet Sauvignon min 90%, min alc 10.5%. **Riserva:** min alc 11.5%; min age two years before release.
Refosco: Refosco Nostrano and/or Refosco dal Peduncolo Rosso min 85%, other red varieties max 15%; min alc 10.5%, max yield 13 tonnes/ha.
Tocai Friulano: Tocai Friulano min 85%, other varieties max 15%; min alc 10.5%, max yield 13 tonnes/ha.
Pinot Bianco: Pinot Blanc min 85%, other white varieties max 15%; min alc 11%, max yield 13 tonnes/ha.
Pinot Grigio: Pinot Gris min 85%, other white varieties max 15%; min alc 10.5%, max yield 12 tonnes/ha.
Verduzzo Friulano: Verduzzo Friulano min 85%, other allowed varieties max 15%; min alc 10.5%, max yield 13 tonnes/ha.
Traminer Aromatico: Traminer Aromatico min 85%, other allowed varieties max 15%; min alc 11%, max yield 12 tonnes/ha.
Chardonnay: Chardonnay min 85%, other allowed varieties max 15%; min alc 11%, max yield 12 tonnes/ha.

This DOC is on the left bank of the Tagliamento River, known for sound, sometimes simple wines, at best clean, fresh and fruity. Some barrel maturation is a new development.

Gabiano   Region: Piedmont
DOC
Red only, min alc 12%, max yield 8 tonnes/ha.
Grapes: Barbera 90–95%, Freisa and Grignolino 5–10%.
Riserva: min age two years, min alc 12.5%.

A tiny, 17 acre (7 ha) DOC, given status in the late 1990s, situated in the hilly districts of the communes of Gabiano and Moncestino in the province of Alessandria. A broadly appealing red style.

Galatina   Region: Apulia
DOC
Red and rosé, min alc 11.5%. White, min alc 11%. Max yield 12 tonnes/ha.

Grapes: Red, Negro Amaro min 65%, with other local varieties up to 35%. White, Chardonnay min 55%, with other local non-aromatic varieties up to 45%. Varietal wines must contain a minimum of 85% of the labeled variety.
Riserva: red only; min age two years before release.

Salento, the heel of Italy's boot, is the location of this 1997 DOC. This is the home of a grape called Negro Amaro (meaning black and bitter), which produces a lively red style.

Galluccio
DOC
Region: Campania

Red and rosé, min alc 11.5%, max yield 7 tonnes/ha. White, min alc 11%, max yield 8 tonnes/ha.
Grapes: Red, Aglianico min 70%, other local red varieties max 30%. White, Falanghina min 70%, other local white varieties max 30%.
Riserva: red only; min age two years before release.

DOC around the extinct volcano of Roccamonfina in volcanic soil southeast of Naples. Low yields and quality orientation set high standards but the wines are not yet widely known.

Gambellara
DOC
Region: Veneto

White only, min alc 10.5%, max yield 14 tonnes/ha.
Grapes: Garganega min 80%, Trebbiano max 20%.
Superiore: min alc 11.5%.

DOC near Soave (which has a similar dry wine style) of around 2,220 acres (900 ha) growing Garganega, known locally as Gambellara.

Garda
DOC
Region: Lombardy

Red, min alc 11%. Rosé and white, min alc 10.5%. Max yield 14 tonnes/ha.
Grapes: There are 18 varieties allowed, and each may be labeled varietally provided they are made from a minimum of 85% of the stated variety. Other grapes from the DOC are permitted up to 15%.
Frizzante: can only be made from Garganega or Chardonnay.
Bianco Classico: Riesling and/or Riesling Italico min 85%, other local non-aromatic white varieties up to 15%.
Rosso Classico (Chiaretto Classico and Rosé): Groppello 30–85%, Marzemino 5%–60%, Sangiovese 5%–60%, Barbera 5%–60%, other local non-aromatic varieties up to 10%.
Chardonnay Spumante Amabile: min alc 11%, lightly sweet sparkling.
Superiore (Rosso Classico): min age two years before release, min alc 12%.
Riserva (Groppelo Classico): min age two years before release, min alc 12%.

To the east of Lake Garda lies Veneto, to the west lies Lombardy; this catchment area allows a lot of ordinary wine to attain the respectability of a DOC. This is a relatively young DOC (1996) allowing 18 varieties, each to be chosen where it does best.

Garda Colli Mantovani DOC
Region: Lombardy and Veneto

Red, rosé and white, min alc 10.5%, max yield 14 tonnes/ha.
Grapes: Red, Cabernet 20–50%, Merlot 20–40%, Rondinella 20–30%, Sangiovese, Molinara, Negrara and Trentina up to 15%. Rosé, Merlot max 45%, Rondinella max 40%, Cabernet max 20%, Sangiovese, Molinara, Negrara and Trentina max 15%. White, Garganega max 35%, Trebbiano max 35%, Chardonnay max 15%, Sauvignon, Riesling Renano and Riesling Italico up to 15%.
Riserva: Cabernet and Merlot varietals min 85% of named variety; min age two years before release, min alc 12%.

The hills of the "Mantuan Morainic Amphitheatre" near the southern banks of Lake Garda provides this sloping DOC with a lake-affected *terroir*. High yields allow bounty, and the quality is pleasant and easy.

Gattinara DOCG
Region: Piedmont

Red only, min alc 12.5%, max yield 7.5 tonnes/ha. Min age three years.
Grapes: Nebbiolo min 90%, Bonarda di Gattinara max 10% with or without Vespolina max 4%.
Riserva: min age four years, min alc 13%.

Famous 250-acre (100-ha) DOCG from 1990 just one-twelfth the size of adjacent DOCG Barolo. Wines regarded highly, and most vintages age very well.

Gavi or Cortese di Gavi DOCG
Region: Piedmont

White only, min alc 10.5%, max yield 9.5 tonnes/ha.
Grape: Cortese 100%.
Frizzante and *spumante* are also produced.

Covers about 1,850 acres (750 ha) of hills on both sides of the Lemme River near the town of Gavi. This DOCG was given status in 1998. The Cortese grape (an indigenous Italian variety) is thought to be the best white variety in the Piedmont region.

Genazzano DOC
Region: Latium

Red, min alc 11%. White, min alc 10.5%. Max yield 14 tonnes/ha.
Grapes: Red, Sangiovese 70–90%, Cesanese 10–30%, other local red

varieties up to 20%. White, Malvasia di Candia 50–70%, Bellone and Bombino 10–30%, other local white varieties up to 40%.

DOC on the southern slopes of Monti Prenestini overlooking the Valle del Sacco, 31 miles (50 km) south of Rome.

Ghemme
Region: Piedmont
DOCG
Red only, min alc 12%, max yield 8 tonnes/ha. Min age four years, of which at least three must be in wood.
Grapes: Nebbiolo (locally known as Spanna) min 75%, Vespolina and/or Bonarda Novarese up to 25%.
Riserva: min alc 12.5%, 25 months in casks, four years aging.

The sub-alpine Navarra hills in the north of Piedmont offer 210 acres (85 ha) of vineyards for this DOCG, which was promoted to this status in 1997.

Gioia del Colle
Region: Apulia
DOC
Red, min alc 11.5%, max yield 12 tonnes/ha. Rosé, min alc 11%, max yield 12 tonnes/ha. White, min alc 10.5%, max yield 13 tonnes/ha.
Grapes: Red, Primitivo 50–60%, Montepulciano and/or Sangiovese and/or Negro Amaro and/or Malvasia Nera 40–50% (Malvasia Nera max 10%). Rosé, Primitivo 50–60%, Montepulciano and/or Sangiovese and/or Negro Amaro and/or Malvasia Nera 40–50% (Malvasia Nera max 10%). White, Trebbiano Toscano 50–70%, other local allowable white varieties 30–50%.
Primitivo: Primitivo 100%; min alc 13%, max yield 8 tonnes/ha.
Riserva: min age two years, min alc 14%.
Aleatico Dolce: Aleatico 85%, Negro Amaro and/or Malvasia Nera and/or Primitivo max 15%; min alc 15%, max yield 8 tonnes/ha. **Riserva:** min age two years, one of which must be in wood; min alc 16%. A *liquoroso* is also made, with a min alc of 18.5%.

There are some rather morbid legends about Gioia's geography, but it produces a fairly famous and sought-after wine. Some strong, robustly flavored reds that have charm and distinction are emerging from this DOC.

Giro di Cagliari
Region: Sardinia
DOC
Red only, min alc 14.5% (*secco* 14%), max yield 12 tonnes/ha. Min age nine months before release.
Grape: Giro 100%.
Liquoroso Dolce Naturale and **Liquoroso Secco:** min age nine months, min alc 17.5%. **Riserva:** min age two years, one of which must be in wood.

DOC in the Oristano area of the Cagliari province. Giro de Cagliari produces mainly smooth wine to accompany desserts, but there is also a dry (*secco*) style for main courses. As a wine style, this is something different.

Golfo del Tigullio
DOC
Region: Liguria

Red, rosé and white, min alc 10.5%, max yield 13 tonnes/ha.
Grapes: Red and rosé, Ciliegiolo 20%–70%, Dolcetto 20%–70%, other non-aromatic local varieties up to 40%. White, Vermentino 20%–70%, Bianchetta Genovese 20%–70%, other non-aromatic local varieties up to 40%.
Passito: from non-aromatic local varieties; min alc 16.5%.
Muscato: Moscato Bianco, min alc 10%. **Muscato Passito**: min alc 15.5%.
Spumante: same variety requirement as white; min alc 11%.

Established in 1997, this DOC uses only traditional local varieties. It covers a wide area between Genoa and the province of La Spezia to the south, and includes a number of valleys, like Val Graveglia and Val Petronio, where wine growing has very ancient roots. Wines are regarded as pleasant local styles.

Grave del Friuli
DOC
Region: Friuli-Venezia Giulia

Now known as **Friuli Grave**.

Gravina
DOC
Region: Apulia

White only, min alc 11%, max yield 15 tonnes/ha.
Grapes: Malvasia del Chianti 40–65%, Greco di Tufo and/or Bianco d'Alessano 35–60%, Bombino Bianco and/or Trebbiano Toscano and/or Verdeca up to 10%.
Spumante: made in *secco* (dry) and *amabile* (lightly sweet) styles; same grape requirements and min alc level as white.

DOC Gravina (which means ravine) is based around the town of the same name, an area with a long wine heritage.

Greco di Bianco
DOC
Region: Calabria

White only, min alc 17%, max yield 10 tonnes/ha. Min age one year before release.
Grapes: Greco Bianco min 95%, other allowable white varieties up to 5%.

Greco di Bianco is considered one of the most significant wines from Calabria, sometimes rated amongst the best of Italian dessert wines. A DOC of a few well-defined vineyards in the province of Reggio Calabria. Grapes are partially dried after picking to raise sugar levels.

Greco di Tufo
DOCG
Region: Campania

White only, min alc 11.5%, max yield 10 tonnes/ha.

Grapes: Greco di Tufo 85–100%, Coda di Volpe Bianca up to 15%. A *spumante* is also produced.

A recent (2003) DOCG given some respect for its full-bodied wine.

Grignolino d'Asti   Region: Piedmont
DOC
Red only, min alc 11%, max yield 8 tonnes/ha.
Grapes: Grignolino min 90%, Freisa up to 10%.

Light colored red to be enjoyed young and fresh, with some noticeable tannin from the many pips in the Grignolino grape.

Grignolino del Monferrato Casalese   Region: Piedmont
DOC
Red only, min alc 11%, max yield 7.5 tonnes/ha.
Grapes: Grignolino min 90%, Freisa up to 10%.

A well-respected DOC offering quality red wine, light and tannic from the many pips in the Grignolino grape.

Guardia Sanframondi (Guardiolo)   Region: Campania
DOC
Red, min alc 11.5%, max yield 12 tonnes/ha. White, min alc 11%, max yield 12 tonnes/ha.
Grapes: Red and rosé, Sangiovese min 80%, other local red varieties max 20%. White, Malvasia Bianco 50–70%, Falanghina 20–30%, other local varieties up to 10%. *Spumante* (sparkling), Falanghina min 70%, other local white varieties max 30%.
Aglianico: Aglianico min 90%, min alc 11.5%.
Riserva: min age two years, min alc 12.5%.

DOC named after the old town of the same name, east of Naples. Highly regarded wines, especially the red.

Ischia   Region: Campania
DOC
Red and white.
Grapes: Red, Guarnaccia 50%, Piedirosso (known locally as Per'e Palummo) 40%, Barbera 10%; min alc 11.5%, max yield 10 tonnes/ha. White, Forastera 65%, Biancolella 20%, other grapes 15%; min alc 11%, max yield 10 tonnes/ha.
Bianco Superiore: Forastera 50%, Biancolella 40%, San Lunardo 10%; min alc 12%, max yield 8 tonnes/ha from selected subareas.

The island of Ischia is the base of this 420-acre (170-ha) DOC, where white wine is about 80% of production. Site selection for DOC qualifying wines is precise, requiring favorable exposures and soils of crumbly rock of volcanic origin with a great deal of fossil material and a high pumice content. Phosphorus and potassium tend to be high.

Isonzo   Region: Friuli-Venezia Giulia
DOC
Refer Friuli Isonzo.

Lacrima di Morro d'Alba   Region: Marche
DOC
Red only, min alc 11%, max yield 14 tonnes/ha.
Grapes: Lacrima min 85%, Montepulciano, Verdicchio up to 15%.

Lacrima (which means "tears") is almost exclusively grown here; do not be confused by the d'Alba part of the name, which might suggest that it is grown in Alba in Piedmont. The wine is idiosyncratic, not particularly sought-after.

Laga di Corbara   Region: Umbria
DOC
Red only, min alc 12.5%, max yield 12 tonnes/ha.
Grapes: Red, Cabernet Sauvignon, Merlot, Pinot Noir and Sangiovese min 70%, Aleatico, Barbera, Cabernet Franc, Canaiolo, Cesanese, Ciliegiolo, Colorino, Dolcetto and Montepulciano up to 30%.
Varietal wine: min 85% of named variety; up to 15% is allowed from other varieties of this DOC.

Lake (Lago) Corbara was formed from the building of a dam on the Tiber River, which caused a mild change to the *terroir* of the surrounding hills and vineyards.

Lambrusco Grasparossa di Castelvetro   Region: Emilia-Romagna
DOC
Red only, min alc 10.5%, max yield 14 tonnes/ha.
Grapes: Lambrusco Grasparossa 85%, other Lambrusco and Uva d'Oro up to 15%.

Light, frothing, fun wine, usually fruity with a little sweetness for enjoying young. The Grasparossa clone is said to be fuller in style than other clones.

Lambrusco Mantovano   Region: Lombardy
DOC
Red only, min alc 10.5%, max yield 15 tonnes/ha.
Grapes: Lambrusco Viadanese or Groppello Ruberti, Lambrusco Maestri, Lambrusco Marani and Lambrusco Salamino 85%, Ancellota and Fortana or Uva d'Oro 15%.

Light, frothing, fun wine, usually fruity with a little sweetness for enjoying young.

Lambrusco Reggiano   *Region: Emilia-Romagna*
DOC
Refer **Reggiano.**

Lambrusco Salamino di Santa Croce   *Region: Emilia-Romagna*
DOC
Red only, min alc 11%, max yield 15 tonnes/ha.
Grapes: Lambrusco Salamino 90%, other Lambrusco and Uva d'Oro up to
10%.

Light, frothing, fun wine, usually fruity with a little sweetness for enjoying
young.

Lambrusco di Sorbara   *Region: Emilia-Romagna*
DOC
Red only, min alc 11%, max yield 14 tonnes/ha.
Grapes: Lambrusco di Sorbara 60%, Lambrusco Salamino 40%.

Light, frothing, fun wine, usually fruity with a little sweetness.

Lamezia   *Region: Calabria*
DOC
Red only, min alc 12%, max yield 12 tonnes/ha.
Grapes: Nerello Mascalese and/or Nerello Cappuccio 30–50%, Gaglioppo
(known locally as Magliocco) 25–35%, Greco Nero (known locally as
Marsigliana) 25–35%, other allowable varieties up to 5%.

DOC of 370 acres (150 ha) making a cherry-red wine that has delicate flavors yet retains a mouth-filling texture.

Langhe   *Region: Piedmont*
DOC
Red, min alc 11%. White, min alc 10.5%. Max yield 10 tonnes/ha.
Grapes: "Local varieties" are specified. This includes Nebbiolo and Dolcetto
for red, while white offers Chardonnay, Favorita and Arneis. Grapes can be
grown within the Cuneo province.
Langhe Arneis: Arneis 100%; min alc 10.5%.
Langhe Chardonnay: Chardonnay 100%; min alc 10.5%. If a vineyard is
named, 100% of the grapes must come from there, and max yield is
8 tonnes/ha.
Langhe Dolcetto: Dolcetto 100%; min alc 11%.
Langhe Favorita: Favorita 100%; min alc 10.5%. If a vineyard is named,
100% of the grapes must come from there, and max yield is 8 tonnes/ha.
Langhe Fresia: Fresia 100%; min alc 11%. **Amabile:** sweeter.
Langhe Nebbiolo: Nebbiolo 100%; min alc 11.5%. If a vineyard is named,
100% of the grapes must come from there, and max yield 8 tonnes/ha.
Amabile: sweeter.

In the restructuring of Piedmont appellations in 1994, the Langhe name, associated with classic Barolo and other respected Piedmont DOCs, provided an opportunity for other surrounding vineyards to have a home, and even for internal DOCs and DOCGs (like Barolo) to "declassify" or "commercialize" their wines into a DOC with lower alcohol and higher yield requirements. So DOC Langhe provides a home for whites and reds that were previously homeless, and gives options to growers inside the territory to have a wider, broader (and presumably cheaper) outlet, but still remain under DOC discipline. About 1,800 acres (750 ha) of vineyard are covered by this DOC in addition to those of the internal DOCs and DOCGs, which may also declassify.

Latisana   *Region: Friuli-Venezia Giulia*
DOC
Refer **Friuli Latisana.**

Lessini   *Region: Veneto*
DOC
Refer **Monti Lessini.**

Lessini Durello   *Region: Veneto*
DOC
Refer **Monti Lessini.**

Lessona   *Region: Piedmont*
DOC
Red only, min alc 12%, max yield 8 tonnes/ha, min two years aging.
Grapes: Nebbiolo min 75%, Vespolina and Bonardo max 25%.

A small 16-acre (6.5-ha) DOC in the Vercelli hills to the north of Piedmont. Not well known, Lessona became a DOC in 2000.

Leverano   *Region: Apulia*
DOC
Red, min alc 12%. Rosé, min alc 11.5%. White, min alc 11%. Red, rosé and white, max yield 15 tonnes/ha. Riserva, min alc 12.5%, min age two years.
Grapes: Red, Negro Amaro min 65%, Malvasia Nera di Lecce, Sangiovese and/or Montepulciano and/or Malvasia Bianca allowed up to 35%, (Malvasia Bianca cannot exceed 10%). Rosé, Negro Amaro min 65%, Malvasia Nera di Lecce, Sangiovese and/or Montepulciano and/or Malvasia Bianca allowed up to 35%. White, Malvasia Bianca min 65%, Bombino Bianco and Trebbiano Toscano allowed up to 35%.

Located in the Apulia region this is mostly a red wine DOC. Leverano produces a hearty, robust style made in warm conditions, although it is not widely known.

Lison-Pramaggiore   **Region: Veneto, Friuli-Venezia Giulia**
DOC
Red and white, min alc 11%.
Tocai Italico: Tocai Italico min 90%, other varieties up to 10%; max yield
12 tonnes/ha.
Classico: Tocai Italico 100%; grapes come from vineyards situated in the
most ancient production areas; min alc 11.5%.
Pinot Bianco: Pinot Blanc min 90%, other varieties up to 10%; max yield
13 tonnes/ha. A *spumante* is also produced.
Chardonnay: Chardonnay min 90%, other varieties up to 10%; max yield
13 tonnes/ha. A *spumante* is also produced.
Pinot Grigio: Pinot Gris 90%, other varieties up to 10%; max yield
10 tonnes/ha. A *spumante* is also produced.
Riesling Italico: Riesling Italico min 90%, other varieties up to 10%; max
yield 12 tonnes/ha. A *spumante* is also produced.
Sauvignon: Sauvignon min 90%, other varieties up to 10%; max yield
12 tonnes/ha. A *spumante* is also produced.
Verduzzo: Verduzzo min 90%, other varieties up to 10%; max yield
13 tonnes/ha. A *spumante* is also produced.
Merlot: Merlot min 90%, other allowed red varieties 10%; max yield
11 tonnes/ha. **Riserva:** min alc 11.5%.
Cabernet: Cabernet Franc and/or Cabernet Sauvignon min 90%, other
allowed red varieties 10%; max yield 12 tonnes/ha. **Riserva:** min age three
years, min alc 11.5%.
Cabernet Franc: Cabernet Franc 90%, other allowed red varieties 10%;
max yield 12 tonnes/ha. **Riserva:** min age three years, min alc 11.5%. A
spumante is also produced.
Cabernet Sauvignon: Cabernet Sauvignon 90%, other allowed red
varieties 10%; max yield 12 tonnes/ha. **Riserva:** min age three years, min
alc 11.5%.
Refosco dal Peduncolo Rosso: Refosco dal Peduncolo Rosso min 90%,
other varieties up to 10%; max yield 12 tonnes/ha.

A DOC that crosses the provincial borders of Veneto and Fruili, and a new
blend of two previous DOCs, the Cabernet of Pramaggiore and Tocai di
Lison. The new DOC has a clumsy appearance with a wide spectrum of
grapes and styles; but it has been accepted by those that know it, and the
wines are regarded as fresh, and usually good value.

Lizzano   **Region: Apulia**
DOC
Red, min alc 11.5%, max yield 14 tonnes/ha. Rosé, min alc 11.5%, max yield
14 tonnes/ha. White, min alc 10.5%, max yield 12 tonnes/ha.
Grapes: Red, Negro Amaro 60–80%, Montepulciano, Sangiovese,
Bombino Nero and Pinot Noir, alone or together, up to 40%, Malvasia
Nera di Brindisi and/or di Lecce up to 10%. *Frizzante* is also produced.

Rosé, Negro Amaro 60–80%, Montepulciano, Sangiovese, Bombino Nero and Pinot Noir, alone or together, up to 40%, Malvasia Nera di Brindisi and/or di Lecce allowed up to 10%. *Frizzante* also produced. White, Trebbiano Toscano 40–60%, Chardonnay and/or Pinot Blanc at least 30%, Malvasia Lunga Bianca up to 10%, Sauvignon and/or Bianco di Alessano up to 25%. *Frizzante* or *spumante* also produced.

Negro Amaro Rosso: Negro Amaro min 85%, Malvasia Nera di Brindisi and/or Lecce, Montepulciano, Sangiovese and Pinot Noir allowed, alone or together, up to 15%; min alc 12%, max yield 14 tonnes/ha. **Superiore:** min age one year, min alc 13%.

Negro Amaro Rosso (red) and **Negro Amaro Rossato (rosé):** Negro Amaro min 85%, Malvasia Nera di Brindisi and/or Lecce, Montepulciano, Sangiovese and Pinot Noir allowed, alone or together, up to 15%; min alc 12%, max yield 14 tonnes/ha.

Malvasia Nera: Malvasia Nera di Brindisi and/or Lecce min 85%, Negro Amaro, Montepulciano, Sangiovese and Pinot Noir allowed, alone or together, up to 15%; min alc 12%, max yield 14 tonnes/ha. **Superiore:** min age one year, min alc 13%.

High-yielding DOC in the heel of Italy's boot, not regarded as anything but simple regional wines from a warm Mediterranean climate.

Loazzolo   *Region: Piedmont*
DOC
White only, min alc 13%, max yield 2.5 tonnes/ha.
Grape: Moscato Bianco.

Late-harvested Moscato, essentially a *passito* from this DOC in the hills overlooking Liguria. Grown in high elevation, the grapes must be processed within the DOC area, dried out a little after picking and made into a raisiny, late-meal wine. Released after two years, Loazzolo is considered best with at least one extra year of bottle age. With 5 acres (2 ha) of allocated vineyard, it is supposedly the smallest DOC in Italy, and the lowest-yielding.

Locorotondo   *Region: Apulia*
DOC
White only, min alc 11%, max yield 13 tonnes/ha.
Grapes: Verdeca 50–65%, Bianco d'Alessano 35–50%, Fiano, Bombino and Malvasia Toscana allowed up to 5%. *Spumante* is also produced.

A highly-regarded DOC in Apulia of about 4,000 acres (1,650 ha) producing a delicately fruity style.

Lugana   *Region: Lombardy-Veneto*
DOC
White only, min alc 11.5%, max yield 12.5 tonnes/ha.
Grapes: Trebbiano Veronese min 90%, non-aromatic white varieties are

permitted up to 10%. *Spumante* is also produced, with min alc 12%.

DOC of average Trebbiano dry white, said to be most enjoyable with the fish from Lake Garda nearby.

Malvasia di Bosa
Region: Sardinia
DOC
White only, min alc 15%, max yield 8 tonnes/ha. Min age two years.
Grapes: Malvasia di Sardegna 100%.
Dolce Natural (Passito): min alc 15%.
Liquoroso Dolce Naturale and **Liquoroso Secco (Dry):** min age two years (often given three), min alc 17.5%.

White made near the town of Bosa from grapes grown in the northwest of the island of Sardinia. The sweeter styles especially can become a lovely golden yellow.

Malvasia di Cagliari
Region: Sardinia
DOC
White only, min alc 14%, max yield 11 tonnes/ha. Min age nine months.
Liquoroso Dolce Naturale and **Liquoroso Secco (dry):** min alc 17.5%.
Riserva: min age two years, one of which must be in oak.

Similar in style to Malvasia di Bosa but a little more intense in its aromas and flavors, this DOC is in the southeast corner of Sardinia.

Malvasia di Casorzo d'Asti
Region: Piedmont
DOC
Red only, min alc 10.5%, max yield 11 tonnes/ha.
Grapes: Malvasia Nera di Casorzo, with additions of Barbera, Freisa and Grignolino up to 10%. *Spumante* is also produced, min alc 11%.

Hilly DOC using the red version of the Malvasia grape family. One-third of the sugar is fermented first; the juice is then cleaned and filtered before a slow secondary fermentation, which may go on for several months including further filtering. The wine is sweetish, pink or dark red, and quite fragrant.

Malvasia di Castelnuovo Don Bosco
Region: Piedmont
DOC
Red only, min alc 10.5%, max yield 11 tonnes/ha.
Grapes: Malvasia di Schierano min 85%, Freisa allowed up to 15%.
Spumante is also produced, min alc 11%.

DOC within Asti province producing a pink, sweet style of wine, something different and rather unusual, considered best when it accompanies pastries, ice cream or dessert. A DOC of 200 acres (80 ha) covering the area commonly named the "white lands"; the soil here is full of sediment, with clay, limestone and sand, very similar to the soil in the Langhe DOC nearby.

Malvasia delle Lipari   Region: Sicily
DOC
White only, min alc 11.5%, max yield 9 tonnes/ha.
Grapes: Malvasia di Lipari max 95%, Corinto Nero 5–8%.
Secco: dry.
Dolce Natural (Passito): grapes are dried after picking, losing about half their initial volume; min alc 18%.
Liquoroso: sweeter than Dolce Natural, min alc 20%.

DOC on the Lipari islands off the north coast of Sicily. A small quantity of much-treasured wine is made using old methods to produce dinner wine, a dessert wine and a liqueur.

Mandrolisai   Region: Sardinia
DOC
Red and rosé, min alc 11.5%, max yield 12 tonnes/ha.
Grapes: Bovale Sardo min 35%, Cannonau 20–35%, other varieties up to 10%.
Superiore: min age two years before release, at least one in wood; min alc 12.5%.

DOC of about 500 acres (200 ha) in the central part of Sardinia, where the Spanish Bovale Sardo is known locally as Muristellu.

Marino   Region: Latium
DOC
White only, min alc 11%, max yield 16.5 tonnes/ha.
Grapes: Malvasia Bianca di Candia (Malvasia Rosso) max 60%, Trebbiano Toscano, Trebbiano Romagnolo, Trebbiano Giallo and Trebbiano di Soave, alone or together, 25–55%, Malvasia del Lazio (Malvasia Puntinata) 5–45%, other allowed white varieties max 10%.
Superiore: min alc 11.5%. A *spumante* is also produced.

One of six DOCs in the volcanic hills east of Rome. This is big-volume, high-yielding, low-priced territory, with sales helped by having Rome nearby.

Marsala   Region: Sicily
DOC
Red and white.
Oro and **Ambra:** Grillo and/or Catarratto (all sub-varieties and clones) and/or Ansonica (or Inzolia) and/or Damaschino; max yield 10 tonnes/ha.
Rubino: mainly Perricone (or Pignatello) and/or Calabrese (or Nero d'Avola) and/or Nerello Mascalese; other allowed white varieties max 30%; max yield 9 tonnes/ha.
Fine: min age one year, min alc 17%.
Superiore: min age two years in wood, min alc 18%. **Superiore Riserva:** min age four years.

Vergine and/or **Soleras:** min age five years, min alc 18%. As with sherry, this is made using the *solera* system, aging wine in a progressive succession of barrels to gain an aged complexity by mixing younger with older wines.
Stravecchio or **Riserva:** wine aged for a period of not less than 10 years.

Marsala is a fortified dessert wine, its volume now dwindling. Some yield figures for the base wine are set but are not relevant for comparisons. The technique of making Marsala varies by manufacturer, and the DOC laws allow this flexibility within limits. Essentially a fortified wine (with grape spirit added), Marsala has progressed from a heavy, oxidized wine to a stylish wine in the best examples, with a positive burnt-almond after-flavor. There are dry, sweet and long-aged styles, much of it until recently confined to the kitchens of knowledgeable restaurants. Marsala can be a great aperitif or after dinner wine; it is also used to add character to Zabaglione, a sweet Italian dessert made from egg whites.

Martina   *Region: Apulia*
DOC
Refer **Martina Franca.**

Martina Franca   *Region: Apulia*
DOC
White only, min alc 11%, max yield 13 tonnes/ha.
Grapes: Verdecca 50–65%, Bianco d'Alessano 35–50%, Fiano, Bombino, Malvasia Toscana up to 5%. A *spumante* is also produced.

The community of Martina Franca, from which the DOC takes its name, is the gateway to the fertile valley of the Itria. This wine starts fresh and lively but develops an amber color after three or four years, producing a different, more solid style.

Matino   *Region: Apulia*
DOC
Red and rosé, min alc 11.5%, max yield 12 tonnes/ha.
Grapes: Negro Amaro min 70%, Malvasia Nera and Sangiovese allowed up to 30%.

Hearty, robust red wine from a DOC in southeast Italy.

Melissa   *Region: Calabria*
DOC
Red, min alc 12.5%, max yield 11 tonnes/ha. White, min alc 11.5%, max yield 12 tonnes/ha. Superiore, min age two years, min alc 13%.
Grapes: Red, Gaglioppo 75–95%, Greco Nero, Greco Bianco, Trebbiano Toscano and Malvasia Bianca, alone or together, 5–25%. White, Greco Bianco 80–95%, Trebbiano Toscano and/or Malvasia Bianca 5–20%.

Melissa is Greek for "sweetness" (in a ripe sort of way, not sugar-sweet). This is a small DOC with a long history.

Menfi
Region: Sicily
DOC
Red and white, min alc 11.5%, max yield 12 tonnes/ha.
Grapes: Red, Nero d'Avola, Sangiovese, Merlot, Cabernet Sauvignon, Syrah 70%, other local red varieties up to 30%. White, Inzolia, Chardonnay, Catarratto Bianco Lucido, Grecanico min 75%, other local non-aromatic white varieties up to 25%.
Vendemmia Tardiva: from the group or a blend of Chardonnay, Catarratto Bianco Lucido, Inzolia, Ansonica and Sauvignon, all subjected to light drying, 100%.
Feudo dei Fiori: Chardonnay, Inzolia, Ansonica 80%, other local white varieties up to 20%.
Bonera: Cabernet Sauvignon and/or Nero d'Avola and/or Merlot and/or Sangiovese and/or Syrah 85%, other local varieties up to 15%. **Bonera Riserva:** min alc 12.5%.
Varietal wine: min 85% of variety on the label.

A strong, innovative 1995 DOC, Menfi developed as part of an initiative to revitalize areas of Sicily, where procrastination had led to mediocre wine being produced in areas where much better quality could be expected. Traditional varieties have been linked with new grapes that have potential in the region.

Merlara
Region: Veneto
DOC
Red and white, min alc 11%, max yield 12 tonnes/ha.
Grapes: Red and Novello, Merlot min 50–70%, other local non-aromatic red varieties up to 50%. White, Tocai Friulano min 50–70%, other local non-aromatic white varieties up to 50%. Other varietal wines must carry 85% of the named variety.
Marzemino Frizzante: a dryish red with a light sparkle, Marzemino min 85%.

Surrounding the town of Merlara, this area near Veneto received DOC status in 2000. Some Cabernet Sauvignon has made a strong name for itself; this is a DOC with a growing image, set to establish its wine style in the next few years.

Meranese di Collina or Meranese
Region: Trentino-Alto Adige
DOC
Red only, min alc 10.5%, max yield 12.5 tonnes/ha.
Grapes: Several clones of Schiava, including Grossa, Media, Piccola or Gentile, Grigia and Tschaggele.

Bulgraviato or **Burggräfler:** The wine produced in the former Contea (Castello) di Tirolo.

This DOC covers the high altitude area around the town of Merano. The wine is an idiosyncratic light, fresh, red style based on the Schiava grape family.

Molise   *Region: Molise*
DOC
Red, min alc 11%. White, min alc 10.5%, max yield 12 tonnes/ha.
Grapes: Red, Montepulciano min 85%, plus other local red varieties up to 15%.
Riserva: min age two years before release. White, Chardonnay, Pinot Blanc and Moscato min 50%, other local white varieties up to 50%.
Red varietal wines: min 85% of named variety; grapes include Aglianico (**Riserva:** min age two years before release), Cabernet Sauvignon, Sangiovese.
Tintilia: Bovale Grande min 85%, other approved local varieties up to 15%. **Riserva:** min age two years before release.
White varietal wines: min 85% of named variety; grapes include Chardonnay, Falanghina, Greco Bianco, Moscato, Pinot Blanc, Sauvignon Blanc, Trebbiano.
Passito: a sweet white made from Moscato grapes.

Molise is a mountainous region in the southeast of Italy below Abruzzi. There are two DOCs within its boundaries, but the Molise DOC has a much wider catchment. This DOC, which attained its status in 1998, was considered a bold move as part of an initiative to improve wine quality instigated by some producers in recent years.

Monferrato   *Region: Piedmont*
DOC
Red, min alc 11%; rosé (known locally as *chiaretto* or *ciaret*), min alc 10.5%; max yield for both 11 tonnes/ha. White, min alc 10%, max yield 12 tonnes/ha.
Grapes: Red and rosé, one or more local non-aromatic red varieties 100%; if varietally labeled, 85–100% of the named variety, including Barbera, Bonarda, Cabernet Sauvignon and Franc, Dolcetto, Freisa, Grignolino, Pinot Noir and Nebbiolo, with max 15% of other local varieties. White, one or more local non-aromatic white varieties 100%; if varietally labeled, 85–100% of the named variety, including Chardonnay and Sauvignon Blanc, plus max 15% of other local varieties.
Casalese Cortese: Production is limited to some defined villages in the province of Alessandria; min alc 10.5%.

A large catchall DOC that extends from the Po River to the southern boundary of Piedmont. This DOC, which has several other DOCs and DOCGs within, around and overlapping it, offers a wide spectrum of grapes that can be blended, but varietal wines are also made. The area takes in the whole Asti province, including a large part of Alessandria, a total of about 98,800 acres (40,000 ha); vineyards are planted on hills at an altitude of between 650–1,650 feet (200–500 m).

Monferrato Freisa   Region: Piedmont
DOC
Red only, min alc 11%, max yield 8 tonnes/ha.
Grape: Freisa.

A new DOC for this grape, which is indigenous to Piedmont. Sometimes sold as *frizzante* (gassy) or *spumante* (sparkling).

Monica di Cagliari   Region: Sardinia
DOC
Red only, min alc 14.5%, max yield 11 tonnes/ha. Min age nine months.
Grape: Monica 100%.
Liquoroso Dolce Naturale and **Liquoroso Secco (dry):** min alc 17.5%.
Riserva: Min age two years, one of these in wood.

DOC of 250 acres (100 ha), regarded as pleasant and best enjoyed young.

Monica di Sardegna   Region: Sardinia
DOC
Red only, min alc 11%, max yield 15 tonnes/ha. Min age six months.
Frizzante is also produced.
Grapes: Monica min 85%, plus grapes grown on the island, usually Pascale de Cagliari and Carignan.
Superiore: min age one year, min alc 12.5%.

Twelve times the size of Monica di Cagliari, a little blending is allowed in this DOC. But otherwise, like its smaller partner DOC, its wines are best enjoyed young and fruity.

Monreale   Region: Sicily
DOC
Red, min alc 12%, max yield 11 tonnes/ha. White, min alc 11%, max yield 13 tonnes/ha.
Grapes: Red, Calabrese, Nero d'Avola, Perricone min 50%, other local red varieties up to 50%. White, Catarratto, Ansonica, Inzolia min 50%, other local white varieties up to 50%.
Varietal wines: min 85% of variety shown; other varieties of this DOC allowed up to 15%.

Large DOC which was carved out of an an even larger number of vineyards in time for 2000 approval; its first vintage was 2001. A long-time producing area, Monreale generally produces simple wines, but is now hoping to increase its quality under DOC status. New varieties for the region, including Cabernet Sauvignon, Merlot, Syrah, Pinot Noir, Sangiovese, Pinot Blanc, Chardonnay and others are all making an impact. Much is still to be settled.

Montecarlo   Region: Tuscany
DOC
Red and white, min alc 11.5%, max yield 10 tonnes/ha.
Grapes: Red, Sangiovese 50–75%, Canaiolo Nero 5–15%, Ciliegiolo, Colorino, Malvasia Nera and Syrah, alone or together, 10–20%, other allowed varieties up to 15%. White, Trebbiano Toscano 60–70%.

Northwest Tuscan DOC producing smooth, dry wine. Some effort has gone into raising the quality of wine in this part of Tuscany. Wood age is not required, but wines are commonly given two years.

Montecompatri Colonna   Region: Latium
DOC
White only, min alc 11%, max yield 15 tonnes/ha.
Grapes: Malvasia Bianca di Candia and Puntinata up to 70%, Trebbiano Toscano, Verde and Giallo at least 30%, Bellone and Bonvino up to 10%.
Superiore: min alc 11.5%. *Frizzante* is also produced.

A sound, fairly typical mid-Italian DOC of about 750 acres (300 ha) with well-priced, straightforward wine.

Montecucco   Region: Tuscany
DOC
Red, min alc 11.5%, max yield 12 tonnes/ha. White, min alc 11.5%, max yield 11 tonnes/ha.
Grapes: Red, Sangiovese min 60%, other non-aromatic local red varieties up to 40%. White, Trebbiano min 60%, other local white varieties up to 40%. Varietal wines, Vermentino min 85%; Sangiovese min 85%; each with other local varieties up to 15%.
Riserva: min age two years before release.

This DOC between the south of Brunello di Montalcino and the southern border of Tuscany uses traditional Tuscan grapes and techniques, and is pushing upwards in quality.

Montefalco Sagrantino   Region: Umbria
DOCG
Red only, min alc 13%, max yield 8 tonnes/ha.
Grapes: Sagrantino min 95%, Trebbiano Toscano up to 5%.
Passito: Sagrantino min 95%, Trebbiano Toscano up to 5% made from grapes partially dried; min alc 14.5%, max yield 8 tonnes/ha. Min age 29 months before release.

DOCG in the hills around Montefalco, to the south of Perugia, best known for its intense red wine and a dessert style (*passito*) produced from dried grapes.

Montello and Colli Asolani DOC
Region: Veneto

Red and white.

Prosecco: Prosecco min 85%, Pinot Blanc and/or Pinot Gris and/or Riesling Italico and/or Verduzzo Trevigiano and/or Bianchetta Trevigiano 15%; min alc 10.5%, max yield 12 tonnes/ha.

Prosecco Spumante: Prosecco min 85%, Pinot Blanc and/or Pinot Gris and/or Riesling Italico and/or Verduzzo Trevigiano and/or Bianchetta Trevigiano 15%; min alc 11%, max yield 12 tonnes/ha.

Merlot: Merlot min 85%, Malbec and/or Cabernet Franc and/or Cabernet Sauvignon max 15%; min alc 11%, max yield 12 tonnes/ha.

Cabernet: Cabernet min 85%, Cabernet Franc and/or Cabernet Sauvignon and/or Malbec up to 15%; min alc 11.5%, max yield 10 tonnes/ha.

Provincial DOC above the city of Treviso where the Piave River divides the hills. On the left bank is DOC Prosecco di Conegliano-Valdobbiadene and on the right bank DOC Montello and Colli Asolani.

Montepulciano d'Abruzzo DOC
Region: Abruzzi

Red only, min alc 12%, max yield 14 tonnes/ha.

Grapes: Montepulciano min 85%, Sangiovese up to 15%. Min age five months before release.

Vecchio: min age two years in wood.

Cerasuolo: rosé.

An 18,000-acre (7,500-ha) DOC providing a large amount of light to medium red, usually tasty and vibrant, and enjoyable in the first two or three years following vintage. Seldom expensive.

Monteregio di Massa Marittima DOC
Region: Tuscany

Red, min alc 11.5%. Rosé, min alc 11%; max yield 12 tonnes/ha. White, min alc 11%, max yield 12 tonnes/ha.

Grapes: Red and rosé, Sangiovese min 80%, other local varieties up to 20%. White, Trebbiano min 50%, Vermentino, Malvasia, Ansonica max 30%, other local varieties max 30%.

Riserva: min age two years before release, min alc 12%.

Vermentino: Vermentino min 90%, other varieties max 10%.

Vin Santo, Secco or **Amabile:** Trebbiano and/or Malvasia min 70%, other local white varieties max 30%. Min age three years before release. **Riserva:** min age four years before release.

Vin Santo Occhio di Pernice: Sangiovese 50–70%, Malvasia Nera 10–50%, other local red varieties max 30%. Min age three years before release.

Hilly DOC to the north of Tuscany with nine wine styles. Best known for Vermentino and Vin Santo.

Montescudaio
DOC   **Region: Tuscany**

Red, min alc 11.5%, max yield 11 tonnes/ha. White, min alc 11.5%, max yield 12 tonnes/ha.

Grapes: Red, Sangiovese 65–85%, Trebbiano Toscano and Malvasia del Chianti, alone or together, 15–25%, other allowed red varieties up to 10%. White (*bianco*), Trebbiano Toscano 70–85%, Malvasia del Chianti and Vermentino, alone or together, 15–30%, other allowed white varieties up to 10%.

Vin Santo: The same grapes as *bianco*, but subjected to natural drying; min alc 17%.

DOC of 618 acres (250 ha) near the city of Volterra. Not widely known but produces sound, pleasant wines.

Monti Lessini
DOC   **Region: Veneto**

Red, min alc 12%, max yield 14 tonnes/ha. White, min alc 11.5%, max yield 16 tonnes/ha.

Grapes: Red, Merlot min 50%, Pinot Noir, Corvina, Cabernet Sauvignon and Franc, Carmenère up to 50%. White, Chardonnay min 50%, Pinot Blanc, Pinot Noir, Pinot Gris and Sauvignon up to 50%.

Superiore: white only, min alc 12.5%

Riserva: red only, min alc 12.5%.

Spumante: Chardonnay min 50%, Pinot Blanc and/or Pinot Noir up to 50%. A rosé (*rosato*) sparkling is also included which contains the same varieties; in theory this would not require any red grapes, but some Pinot Noir is implicated in order to get the rosé color.

Durello: White only, Durella min 85%, Garganega, Trebbiano di Soave, Pinot Blanc, Pinot Noir, Chardonnay up to 15%; min alc 10.5%. Superiore 11.5%, Spumante 11%.

This DOC is mainly about Durella, a late-ripening, high-acid grape, grown only here. Much of it was previously shipped to Germany for use in *Sekt*. Now, under this DOC, the growers are getting more return and developing an image. The sparkling (*spumante*) version of Durella is gaining popularity. The other reds and whites of this DOC are relatively minor in volume.

Montuni del Reno
DOC   **Region: Emilia-Romagna**

White only, min alc 10.5%, max yield 18 tonnes/ha. *Frizzante* is also made.

Grapes: Montu 85%, other allowed non-aromatic white varieties up to 15%.

The Montu or Montuni grape produces plenty of yield and a pleasant straw-yellow colored white wine.

Morellino di Scansano   Region: Tuscany
DOC
Red only, min alc 11.5%, max yield 12 tonnes/ha.
Grape: Sangiovese 85–100%, other local varieties up to 15%.
Riserva: min age two years, one of which must be in wood; min alc 12%.

DOC covering about 1,250 acres (500 ha) of vineyard in a strip of hills between the Ombrone and Albegna rivers in the province of Grosseto, towards the coast of Tuscany. Near DOC Bolgheri. A reasonably recent wine region in Italian terms. It has shown some strength through the 1990s and could easily become a premium region.

Moscadello di Montalcino   Region: Tuscany
DOC
White only, min alc 10.5%, max yield 10 tonnes/ha.
Grapes: Moscato Bianco 85–100%, other local varieties up to 15%.
Moscadello di Montalcino Vendemmia Tardiva: late picked grapes, high in sugar. Min age two years before release; min alc 15%.
May be produced in *frizzante* and *liquoroso* versions. The *liquoroso* must have a min alc of 12% and be bottled for at least six months.

This DOC uses the same Moscato grape as the surrounding DOCs, but is small and not well known. A light, easy-drinking, semi-sweet white style.

Moscato d'Asti   Region: Piedmont
DOCG
White only, min alc 4.5–6.5%, max yield 11 tonnes/ha. A *frizzante* version is also made.
Grape: Moscato Bianco.

In 1993 this became a DOCG covering fresh, lightly sweet white, the plain version usually with a hint of *pétillance* (gas) only, the *frizzante* with a little more. At the same time as this DOCG was given its status, DOCG Asti (with more sparkle than DOCG Moscato d'Asti) took over from Asti Spumante and was given separate status.

Moscato di Cagliari   Region: Sardinia
DOC
White only, min alc 15%, max yield 11 tonnes/ha. Min age five months.
Grape: Moscato Bianco.
Liquoroso Dolce Naturale: min age five months, min alc 17.5%.
Riserva: min age one year.

Famous wine on the island of Sardinia. The grapes are picked very ripe but before raisining.

Moscato di Noto Naturale or *Moscato di Noto* DOC
Region: Sicily

White only, min alc 11.5%, max yield 12.5 tonnes/ha.
Grape: Moscato Bianco.
Spumante: min alc 13%.
Liquoroso: min age five months after the addition of alcohol; min alc 22%.

A DOC producing a small quantity; highly sought-after as a prestige wine.

Moscato di Pantelleria and *Passito di Pantelleria* DOC
Region: Sicily

White only, min alc 8%, max yield 7 tonnes/ha, min sugar 40 g/L.
Grape: Moscato (known locally as Zibibbo) 100%.
Passito Moscato: Moscato min 95%, other local grapes up to 5%.
Passito: min alc 14%, min sugar 110 g/L.
Vino Naturalmente Dolce: min alc 14%.
Liquoroso: min age one year; min alc 21.5%.

DOC on Pantelleria, a volcanic island at the southern limit of Italy, in fact closer to Africa than Italy's south coast! Plantings cover 3,460 acres (1,400 ha). "Extra" is sometimes produced with grapes picked at 23.5° Baumé; this is pretty sweet and luscious, and requires a minimum age of one year before release.

Moscato di Sardegna Spumante DOC
Region: Sardinia

White only, min alc 11.5%, max yield 13 tonnes/ha.
Grapes: Moscato Bianco min 90%, other allowed white varieties up to 10%.

Popular DOC with a long wine history on the island. Sweetish whites from Moscato grapes.

Moscato di Scanzo DOC
Region: Lombardy

Red only, min alc 17%.
Grape: Moscato de Scanzo.

DOC around the town of Scanzorosciate in the province of Bergamo. It provides a red *passito* wine, made by careful choosing of suitable grapes, which are then dried for several weeks on special racks in ventilated rooms before crushing and fermenting. Aging of at least two years is then required. This gives a warm, generous style of red wine, naturally sweet from the residual sweetness left from the dried grapes.

Moscato di Siracusa
Region: Sicily
DOC
White only, min alc 14%, max yield 7.5 tonnes/ha.
Grape: Moscato Bianco.

Officially just half a hectare of vineyard. A legendary name but almost no production.

Moscato di Sorso-Sennori
Region: Sardinia
DOC
White only, min alc 15%, max yield 9 tonnes/ha. Min age five months.
Grape: Moscato Bianco. A sweet *liquoroso* version is also produced.

Tiny DOC covering the two villages in the DOC name. Very little wine produced at present.

Moscato di Trani
Region: Apulia
DOC
White only, min alc 12.5%, max yield 12 tonnes/ha. Min age five months before release.
Grapes: Moscato Bianco min 85%, other allowed white varieties max 15%.
Liquoroso: min age one year, min alc 18%.

Another tiny Moscato DOC, less than 100 acres (40 ha).

Nardo
Region: Apulia
DOC
Red and rosé, min alc 12.5%, max yield 18 tonnes/ha.
Grapes: Negro Amaro 80–100%, Malvasia Nera di Lecce, Montepulciano max 20%.

High-yielding DOC from a grape whose name translates as "black and bitter." Usually a robust, hearty red.

Nasco di Cagliari
Region: Sardinia
DOC
White only, min alc 13.5% for *dolce* (sweet), 14.5% for *secco* (dry); max yield 10 tonnes/ha.
Grape: Nasco 100%.
Liquoroso Dolce Naturale and **Liquoroso Secco or Dry:** min alc 17.5%.
Riserva: min age two years, one of which must be in wood.

Nasco has a long history on the island but has been cut right back by phylloxera. Today the DOC is small, barely 100 acres (40 ha).

Nebbiolo d'Alba
Region: Piedmont
DOC
Red only, min alc 12%, max yield 9 tonnes/ha. *Spumante* is also produced.

Grape: Nebbiolo 100%.

A single variety DOC produced on both sides of the Tanaro River in Cuneo province next to the city of Alba, close to Barolo and Barbaresco. This vine is cultivated predominantly on sand and clay soils from a DOC of about 1,250 acres (500 ha). A dry, good-aging style of red that is well-respected.

Nuragus di Cagliari   *Region: Sardinia*
DOC
White only, min alc 10.5%, max yield 20 tonnes/ha. *Frizzante* is also produced.
Grapes: Nuragus min 85%, other allowed white varieties up to 15%.

With a fairly simple indigenous grape (Nuragus) and one of the highest allowed yields in Italy, this DOC is regarded as unspectacular, but part of the colorful fabric of Italian viticulture and winemaking.

Offida   *Region: Marche*
DOC
Red only, min alc 12%, max yield 10 tonnes/ha.
Grapes: Montepulciano min 50%, Cabernet Sauvignon min 30%, other local non-aromatic red varieties max 20%.
Pecorino: Pecorino 85%, other local non-aromatic white varieties, up to 15%.
Passerina: Passerina 85%, other local non-aromatic white varieties, up to 15%.
Passerina Vin Santo: min age three-and-a-half years before release.

A recent (2001) DOC, which allows some speciality wines (Pecorino and Passerina) from specified communes within the DOC region; the Vin Santo is allowed only from two communes, the red from 17 others. A bit divisional by style and thus a rather unusual DOC.

Oltrepò Pavese   *Region: Lombardy*
DOC
Red, min alc 11.5%, max yield 11 tonnes/ha. Rosé, min alc 10.5%, max yield 11 tonnes/ha. White, refer to individual listings below for alcohol and yield requirements.
Grapes: Red and rosé, Barbera max 65%, Uva Rara and/or Ughetta and/or Pinot Noir max 45%, Croatina min 25%.
Riserva: min age two years, min alc 12%. The year in which the grapes were grown must be shown on the label.
Buttafuoco: Barbera max 65%, Uva Rara and/or Ughetta and/or Pinot Noir max 45%, Croatina min 25%; min alc 12%, max yield 10.5 tonnes/ha.
Sangue di Giuda: Barbera max 65%, Uva Rara and/or Ughetta and/or Pinot Noir max 45%, Croatina min 25%; min alc 12%, max yield 10.5 tonnes/ha.

Barbera: Barbera min 85%, other allowed red varieties permitted up to 15%; min alc 11.5%, max yield 12 tonnes/ha.
Bonarda: Croatina (Bonarda) min 85%, other allowed red varieties permitted up to 15%; min alc 11%, max yield 10.5 tonnes/ha.
Riesling Italico: Riesling Italico min 85%, Riesling Renano up to 15%; min alc 10.5%, max yield 11 tonnes/ha.
Riesling Renano: Riesling Renano min 85%, Riesling Italico up to 15%. *Spumante* is also produced.
Cortese: Cortese min 85%, other allowed white varieties up to 15%; min alc 10.5%, max yield 11 tonnes/ha. *Spumante* is also produced.
Moscato: Moscato Bianco min 85%, Malvasia di Candia up to 15%; min alc 10%, max yield 11 tonnes/ha. Moscato types are *abboccato* or *amabile*, *dolce*, *spumante*, and *liquoroso dolce natural*, min alc 17.5–22%, *liquoroso secco*, min alc 18–22%.
Pinot Noir: Pinot Noir min 85%, other allowed red varieties up to 15%; min alc 10.5%, max yield 10 tonnes/ha. *Spumante* (white or rosé) is also produced, min alc 11.5%.
Pinot Grigio: Pinot Gris min 85%, Pinot Noir, Pinot Blanc, Riesling Italico and Riesling Renano up to 15%.

Looked on as a simple wine-producing DOC, yet all commentators say it has potential to rise from the ranks of supplying a wide range of quaffing styles.

Orcia   *Region: Tuscany*
DOC
Red and white, min alc 12%, max yield 10 tonnes/ha.
Grapes: Red, Sangiovese min 60%, other local varieties up to 40%, of which no more than 10% may be white. White and Vin Santo, Trebbiano min 50%, other local grape varieties up to 50%.

DOC that lies between two DOCGs, a strip between Brunello di Montancino and Vino Nobile de Montepulciano with the Orcia River flowing through it. Orcia is said to have remained traditional, producing a red based on Sangiovese and a white based on Trebbiano, as their forefathers made, along with a little Vin Santo.

Orta Nova   *Region: Apulia*
DOC
Red, min alc 12%, max yield 15 tonnes/ha. Rosé, min alc 11.5%, max yield 15 tonnes/ha.
Grapes: Sangiovese min 60%, Uva di Troia, Montepulciano, Lambrusco Maestri, Trebbiano Toscano, any or all, up to 40%. However, the Trebbiano Toscano and Lambrusco Maestri are limited to max 10% of each.

Orta Nova DOC is a rather small DOC, which takes its name from a commune located to the south of Foggia.

Orvieto
DOC   *Region: Umbria*

White only, min alc 11.5%, max yield 11 tonnes/ha.
Grapes: Trebbiano Toscano 50–65%, Verdello 15–25%, Grechetto,
Drupeggio and/or Malvasia Toscana 20–30% (Malvasia limited to max
20%).
Classico: Specified area of production. Produces about a third of Orvieto
wines.

A big-volume DOC producing an accessible, easy-drinking style at best. Not
highly regarded, but the volume says it all, satisfying millions of people.
Regardless, it is definitely a region on the move – while the Orvieto white is
struggling to keep up the pace as a blend with Trebbiano, new blends along
with some red wines are being developed that are moving away from the
Orvieto style.

Ostuni
DOC   *Region: Apulia*

Red and white, min alc 11%; max yield for both 11 tonnes/ha.
Grapes: White, Impigno 50–85%, Francavilla 15–50%, Bianco de Alessano
and/or Verdeca 10%. Red, refer Ottavianello below.
Ottavianello: Cinsault (locally known as Ottavianello) min 85%, Negro
Amaro, Malvasia Nera, Notar Domenico, Sussumariello up to 15%.

DOC based on three small mountains in an area extending from the end
of the Murge Mountains to the Adriatic Sea, around the town of Ostuni. A
small international interest grows larger as the quality improves.

Pagadebit di Romagna
DOC   *Region: Emilia-Romagna*

White only, min alc 10.5%, max yield 14 tonnes/ha.
Grapes: Bombino Bianco (locally known as Pagadebit or Pagadebito) min
85%, other allowed white varieties up to 15%.

Once a blending variety, the main grape of this DOC has captured the im-
agination of merchants and growers. DOC status in 1989 was earned by the
hard work put in to develop image and quality.

Parrina
DOC   *Region: Tuscany*

Red, min alc 11.5%. Rosé, min alc 11%. Max yield for both 11 tonnes/ha.
White, min alc 11.5%, max yield 12 tonnes/ha.
Grapes: Red and rosé, Sangiovese min 80%, Canaiolo Nero,
Montepulciano and Colorino up to 20%. White, Trebbiano Toscano min
80%, Ansonica and/or Malvasia del Chianti up to 20%. **Riserva:** min age
three years, min alc 12%.

Small DOC of about 300 acres (120 ha) in the Tuscan Maremma, with an ancient wine heritage. The area is bounded in part by the Albegna River. Traditional Tuscan varieties Sangiovese and Trebbiano are used, and this DOC's following is diminished only by the small volume produced.

Passito di Pantelleria
DOC
Region: Sicily

Refer **Moscato di Pantelleria.**

Penisola Sorrentina
DOC
Region: Campania

Red, min alc 10.5%, max yield 14 tonnes/ha. White, min alc 10%, max yield 14 tonnes/ha.
Grapes: Red, Piedirosso, Sciascinso, Aglianico, min 60%, other local red varieties max 40%. White, Falanghina 40–100%, Biancolella, Greco Bianco up to 60%, other local varieties max 40%.

The "Peninsula of Sorrento" provides the name for this coastal DOC, with three subzones, Lettere, Gragnano and Sorrento. Light, fresh, slightly gassy red wine is popular here.

Pentro di Isernia or Pentro
DOC
Region: Molise

Red and rosé, min alc 11%, max yield 11 tonnes/ha. White, min alc 10.5%, max yield 11 tonnes/ha.
Grapes: Red and rosé, Montepulciano 45–55%, Sangiovese 45–55%, other allowed varieties up to 10%. White, Trebbiano Toscano 60–70%, Bombino Bianco 30–40%, other allowed varieties up to 10%.

Pentro di Isernia is a tiny DOC, produced on the hills of the province of Isernia near the city of the same name.

Piave or Vini del Piave
DOC
Region: Veneto

Red and white.
Vecchio: min age two years, min alc 12.5%.
Cabernet: Cabernet Franc and/or Cabernet Sauvignon 95%; min alc 11.5%, max yield 11 tonnes/ha. **Riserva:** min age two years before release, min alc 12.5%.
Merlot: Merlot min 95%, other allowed red varieties up to 5%. Min alc 11%, max yield 13 tonnes/ha. **Riserva:** min age two years, min alc 12.5%.
Pinot Blanc: Pinot Blanc min 95%; min alc 11%, max yield 12 tonnes/ha.
Pinot Grigio: Pinot Gris min 95%; min alc 11.5%, max yield 12 tonnes/ha.
Pinot Nero: Pinot Noir min 95%; min alc 11.5%, max yield 12 tonnes/ha.
Raboso: Raboso Piave and/or Raboso Veronese min 95%; min alc 11.5%, max yield 14 tonnes/ha.

Tocai: Tocai min 95%; min alc 11%, max yield 11 tonnes/ha.
Verduzzo: Verduzzo Trevigiano and Verduzzo Friulano min 95%.

A DOC situated just north of Venice selling mostly red wine, though the full selection is available. Wines are fruity and enjoyable, with Merlot a strength.

Piemonte
DOC
Region: Piedmont

Red, white and sparkling.
Grapes: Sparkling (*spumante*), Muscato 100%. Varietal wine must carry a minimum of 85% of the variety named with up to 15% of other DOC varieties.
Pinot Blanc Spumante: Pinot Blanc min 85%, Chardonnay, Pinot Gris, Pinot Noir up to 15%.
Pinot Grigio Spumante: Pinot Gris min 85%, Chardonnay, Pinot Blanc, Pinot Noir up to 15%.
Pinot Nero Spumante: Pinot Noir min 85%, Chardonnay, Pinot Gris, Pinot Blanc up to 15%.

DOC covering the provinces of Asti, Cuneo and Alessandria, created to help the sparkling wines falling outside the well-known areas and the wine from Barbera, which was good enough for a DOC but which didn't have a home.

Pinerolese
DOC
Region: Piedmont

Red only, min alc 10.5%, max yield 10 tonnes/ha.
Grapes: Barbera, Bonarda, Nebbiolo, Neretto min 50%, other local varieties up to 50%.
Ramie: Avana min 30%, Avarengo min 15%, Neretto min 20%, other local red varieties up to 35%.
Varietal wines: min 85% of variety named, other DOC varieties max 15%.
Dolcetto: Dolcetto min 85%.
Doux d'Henry: wine from a tiny yet famous vineyard.

DOC in the provinces of Turin and Cuneo below the Alps, famous for Doux d'Henry, a tiny vineyard of about 2.5 acres (1 ha), and Ramie from specific parts of the DOC. In total there are about 200 acres (80 ha) of fascinating wines, which are particularly sought-after for their heritage.

Pollino
DOC
Region: Calabria

Red only, min alc 12%, max yield 11 tonnes/ha.
Grapes: Gaglioppo (Arvino, Aglianico, Aglianico di Cassano and Lacrima types) 60–100%, Greco Nero, Malvasia Bianca (Verdeca and Luvarella types), Montonico Bianco and Guarnaccia Bianca up to 40%, with white varieties limited to 20%.

Superiore: min age two years, min alc 12.5%.

Pollino DOC is in the southernmost production area of Calabria, and is named after the mountain that dominates the whole region and affects the climate.

Pomino   *Region: Tuscany*
DOC
Red, min alc 12% (Riserva, min alc 12.5%). White, min alc 11%. Max yield 10.5 tonnes/ha.
Grapes: Red, Sangiovese 60–75%, Canaiolo, Cabernet Sauvignon and Cabernet Franc 15–25%, Merlot 10–20%, other red varieties permitted up to 15%. One year of aging required. White, Pinot Blanc and/or Chardonnay 60–80%, Trebbiano Toscano up to 30%, other white varieties are allowed up to 15%.
Riserva (red): min age three years, of which 18 months must be in wood.
Vin Santo Bianco: grape varieties same as white, but subjected to drying; min alc 15.5%. Three years aging in wood. Types are *secco* (dry), *amabile* (sweetish) and *dolce* (sweet).
Vin Santo Rosso: grape varieties same as red, but subjected to drying; min alc 15.5%. Three years aging in wood. Types are *secco* (dry) *amabile* (sweetish) and *dolce* (sweet).

Pomino DOC was born in the early 1970s, allowing newer grape varieties to meld into the scene in the famous Rufina sub-district of Tuscany. Not a large number of producers, but this is a DOC with a band of enthusiastic supporters around the world.

Pramaggiore   *Region: Veneto, Friuli-Venezia Giulia*
DOC
Refer **Lison-Pramaggiore.**

Primitivo di Manduria   *Region: Apulia*
DOC
Red only, min alc 14%, max yield 9 tonnes/ha.
Grape: Primitivo 100%.
Dolce Naturale: min age nine months, min alc 16%.
Liquoroso Dolce Naturale: min age two years, min alc 17.5%.
Liquoroso Secco: min age two years, min alc 18%.

Primitivo is the grape known as Zinfandel in California. The high minimum alcohol and low yield of this DOC tells all, a big, bold red should be the norm!

Prosecco di Conegliano-Valdobbiadene   *Region: Veneto*
DOC
White only, min alc 10.5%, max yield 12 tonnes/ha.

Grapes: Prosecco min 85%, Verdiso, Pinot Blanc, Pinot Gris and Chardonnay may be added.
Superiore di Cartizze: grapes must come from the territory known as Cartizze; min alc 11%.
Frizzante: min alc 10.5% for Prosecco di Conegliano-Valdobbiadene; 11% min alc for the type labeled Superiore di Cartizze.
Spumante: min alc 11% for Prosecco di Conegliano-Valdobbiadene; 11.5% min alc for the type labeled Superiore di Cartizze.

Provincial DOC above the city of Treviso where the Piave River divides the hills. On the left bank is DOC Prosecco di Conegliano-Valdobbiadene and on the right bank DOC Montello and Colli Asolani.

Ramandolo   *Region: Friuli-Venezia Giulia*
DOCG
White only, min alc 14%, max yield 10 tonnes/ha.
Grape: Verduzzo Friulano 100%.

DOCG to the north of the Udine, in the hills above Nimis, a region famous for a rather unique sweet wine from the Verduzzo grape. At its best, this is a very special white dessert wine, elegant, fragrant, full-bodied, not too sweet, and slightly tannic, all characteristics that are enhanced when the vintage is delayed and the grapes are allowed to dry a little.

Recioto di Soave   *Region: Veneto*
DOCG
White only, min alc 12%, max yield 9 tonnes/ha.
Grapes: Garganega min 70%, Pinot Blanc, Chardonnay, Trebbiano di Soave up to 30%, other local white varieties up to 5%. Light drying after picking allowed.
Classico: grapes from a defined area, min age 12 months before release.
Spumante: sweet white, min age one year age before release, min alc 11.5%.

A recent (2001) white wine DOCG in Verona, making the Amarone style of dried-grape wines. Both styles require a min of 14% potential alcohol at picking.

Reggiano   *Region: Emilia-Romagna*
DOC
Mostly red, min alc 10.5%, max yield 16 tonnes/ha.
Lambrusco: Lambrusco Marani, Lambrusco Salamino, Lambrusco Montericco, Lambrusco Maestri, Lambrusco di Sorbara 85–100%, Ancellotta, Malbo Gentile, up to 15%.
Lambrusco Salamino: Lambrusco Salamino 85–100%, Ancellotta and/or Lambrusco Marani, Lambrusco di Sorbara, Malbo Gentile, up to 15%.
Bianco Spumante: Lambrusco Marani, Lambrusco Maestri, Lambrusco

Salamino, Lambrusco Montericco, Lambrusco di Sorbara, Malbo Gentile, 100%; min alc 11%.

Popular Lambrusco DOC, light red, and usually slightly fizzy (*frizzante* or *spritzig*). A great party drink, which enjoyed fashion status in the Western world in the 1970s and 1980s. Fun wine.

Reno   **Region: Emilia-Romagna**
DOC
Refer **Montuni del Reno**

Riesi   **Region: Sicily**
DOC
Red, min alc 11.5%, max yield 14 tonnes/ha. White, min alc 11%, max yield 15 tonnes/ha.
Grapes: Red, Calabrese and/or Cabernet Sauvignon, 80–100%, other local red varieties up to 20%. Rosé, Calabrese 50–75%, Nerello Mascalese, Cabernet Sauvignon 25–50%, other local non-aromatic varieties up to 25%. White, Ansonica and/or Chardonnay 75–100%, other local non-aromatic white varieties up to 25%.
Superiore: Calabrese min 85%, other local non-aromatic red varieties up to 15%; min age two years, min alc 12%.

Riesi was first included in the Cerasuolo di Vittoria DOC. In 2001 it was given separate DOC status because of its rising quality and growing interest in the wine. Some vineyards have been purchased by a new wave of producers keen to exploit quality before quantity. A combination of old and new grape varieties is used in both the red and the white wines.

Riviera del Garda Bresciano   **Region: Lombardy**
DOC
Red and rosé, min alc 11%, max yield 12.5 tonnes/ha.
Grapes: Groppello Gentile, Groppellone and Mocasina 30–60%, Sangiovese 10–25%, Barbera 10–20%, Berzamino (Marzemino) 5–30%.
Superiore: min age one year, min alc 12%.
Chiaretto: min alc 11.5%.

DOC on the western side of Lake Garda. The lake tempers the climate of the region, which encourages the producers in this DOC to stay with the old, long-established traditional varieties.

Riviera Ligure di Ponente   **Region: Liguria**
DOC
Red and white.
Ormeasco: Ormeasco (a clone of Dolcetto) min 95%, non-aromatic red grapes up to 5%; min alc 11%, max yield 9 tonnes/ha. **Superiore:** min alc 12.5%; min age one year. Made only in the Riviera dei Fiori subzone.

Pigato: Pigato min 95%, non-aromatic white grapes up to 5%; min alc 11%, max yield 11 tonnes/ha.
Rossese: Rossese min 95%, with the possible addition of other non-aromatic red grapes allowed; max yield 9 tonnes/ha.
Vermentino: Vermentino min 95%, with the possible addition of other non-aromatic white grapes allowed; max yield 11 tonnes/ha.

The province of La Spezia accounts for the greater part of Liguria's wine production but many famous wines, such as the Pigato, Vermentino and Ormeasco are made on the Riviera di Ponente, the western stretch of the Ligurian coast. Those wines, along with Rossese di Albenga, were recently united under the single DOC of Riviera Ligure di Ponente, which includes the three geographical subzones Albenga, Finale and Riviera dei Fiori.

Roero   *Region: Piedmont*
DOC
Red and white, min alc 11.5%, max yield 8 tonnes/ha. Min age eight months.
Grapes: Nebbiolo with the possible addition of Arneis 2–5%, grapes allowed for the province may be added up to max of 3%; min alc 11.5%, max yield 8 tonnes/ha. Min age eight months.
Roero Arneis: Arneis 100%; min alc 10.5%, max yield 10 tonnes/ha. A *spumante* is also produced.

A special DOC to the locals, Roero is based around the Arneis grape – "white Nebbiolo" to the devoted, the local name means "a friendly rebel." A DOC of about 1,100 acres (450 ha) and wines that are able to attract a high price, even for the sparkling.

Romagna Albana Spumante   *Region: Emilia-Romagna*
DOC
Sparkling white, min alc 15%, max yield 14 tonnes/ha.
Grape: Albana.

An unusual situation in Italy, this DOC comes from the same region and varieties as DOCG Albana di Romagna; but it is seen as a "fun" drink, while the DOCG is considered "serious."

Rossese di Dolceacqua or Dolceacqua   *Region: Liguria*
DOC
Red only, min alc 12%, max yield 9 tonnes/ha.
Grapes: Rossese (known locally as Rossese di Ventimiglia) min 95%. Other non-aromatic red varieties may be used up to 5% max.
Superiore: min age one year, min alc 13%.

Small but fairly famous DOC around the town of Dolceacqua, steeped in history and traditional winemaking methods. Its wine has a strong following but is not always consistent.

Rosso Barletta
DOC   *Region: Apulia*

Red only, min alc 12%, max yield 15 tonnes/ha.
Grapes: Uva di Troia min 70%, Montepulciano and/or Sangiovese and/or Malbec allowed up to 30%. (The Malbec can not exceed 10%.)
Invecchiato: min age two years, one of which must be in wood.

DOC of 150 acres (60 ha) on a very historic site representing "the challenge of Barletta," when 13 Italian knights fought 13 French knights over the quality of the local red wine! Now considered a safe, tasty red.

Rosso Canosa (or Canasium)
DOC   *Region: Apulia*

Red only, min alc 12%, max yield 14 tonnes/ha.
Grapes: Uva di Troia 65%, Montepulciano and/or Sangiovese 35% (Sangiovese can not exceed 15%), other red grape varieties allowed up to 5%.
Riserva: min age two years, one of which must be in wood; min alc 13%.

Rosso di Canosa is produced in the community of the same name situated in Bari province. Its label often bears the ancient Latin name of the city, Canusium. A small DOC of 250 acres (100 ha) offering a robust red style, hearty and alcoholic.

Rosso di Cerignola
DOC   *Region: Apulia*

Red only, min alc 12%, max yield 14 tonnes/ha.
Grapes: Uva di Troia min 55%, Negro Amaro, 15–30%, Sangiovese, Barbera, Montepulciano, Malbec, Trebbiano Toscano up to 15%.
Riserva: min age two years in wood, min alc 13%.

Adriatic coast DOC with the relatively low-yielding Uva di Troia, highly regarded as a major influence on the character and style of wine from this DOC.

Rosso Conero
DOC   *Region: Marche*

Red only, min alc 11.5%, max yield 14 tonnes/ha.
Grapes: Montepulciano 85–100%, Sangiovese max 15%.
Riserva: min age two years before release, min alc 12.5%.

Big volume DOC offering safe, tasty wines at a very good price, sometimes far ahead of expectations based on the price.

Rosso di Montalcino
DOC   *Region: Tuscany*

Red only, min alc 12%, max yield 10 tonnes/ha. Min age one year.
Grape: Brunello di Montalcino (Sangiovese Grosso).

From the same region as DOCG Brunello di Montalcino, this DOC is essentially a cheaper, younger and higher-yielding version of one of Italy's most prestigious wines.

Rosso di Montepulciano DOC
Region: Tuscany

Red only, min alc 11.5%, max yield 10 tonnes/ha. Min age five months.
Grapes: Sangiovese (known locally as Prugnolo Gentile) 70–100%, Canaiolo Nero up to 20%, other authorized varieties up to 20%.

From the same region as DOCG Vino Noble di Montepulciano, this DOC is essentially a cheaper, younger and higher-yielding version of one of Italy's most prestigious wines.

Rosso Orvietano DOC
Region: Umbria

Red only, min alc 10.5%, max yield 12 tonnes/ha.
Grapes: Aleatico, Cabernet Franc, Cabernet Sauvignon, Canaiolo, Ciliegiolo, Merlot, Montepulciano, Pinot Noir, Sangiovese min 70%, Barbera, Cesanese Comune, Colorino, Dolcetto up to 30%.
Varietal wines: min 85% of the named variety, other varieties up to 15%.

Essentially this is the red wine DOC for the white wine area of Orvieto. Developed late, this red wine using old traditional varieties and newer grapes like Cabernet and Pinot Noir has done pretty well. Some is sold by variety, some as blends.

Rosso Piceno DOC
Region: Marche

Red only, min alc 11.5%, max yield 14 tonnes/ha.
Grapes: Sangiovese 60–100%, Montepulciano max 40%, Trebbiano and Passerino up to 15%.
Superiore: grapes come from a specific area in the province of Ascoli Piceno; min age one year, min alc 12%.
Riserva: min age two years before release.
Sangiovese: Sangiovese 85–100%, other local varieties up to 15%.

Hilly DOC up to 2,300 feet (700 m) high, typically offering a cheerful, no-fuss, easy-drinking red.

Rubino di Cantavena DOC
Region: Piedmont

Red only, min alc 11.5%, max yield 10 tonnes/ha.
Grapes: Barbera 75–90%, Grignolino and Freisa alone or together up to 25%.

Historic and romantic DOC of just 30 acres (12 ha) which are planted in a circular formation round the amphitheater-shaped hill of Cantavenna.

Ruché di Castagnole Monferrato   Region: Piedmont
DOC
Red only, min alc 12%, max yield 9 tonnes/ha.
Grapes: Ruché 90–100%, Barbera and/or Brachetto up to 10%.

DOC in the Asti province of Piedmont, a wide production zone for just 70 acres (28 ha) of vineyard! Ruché or Rouchet is a local grape with some similarities to Nebbiolo.

Salice Salentino   Region: Apulia
DOC
Red and rosé, min alc 12%, max yield 12 tonnes/ha.
Grapes: Negro Amaro 80–100%, Malvasia Nera di Brindisi, Malvasia Nera di Lecce up to 20%.
Riserva: min age two years in wood.
Aleatico Dolce: Aleatico di Puglia 85–100%, Malvasia Nera, Negro Amaro, Primitivo up to 15%; min alc 15%.
Salentino Bianco: Chardonnay min 70%, other local varieties up to 30%. Min alc 11%.
Salentino Pinot Bianco: Pinot Blanc min 85%, Chardonnay, Sauvignon up to 15%. Min alc 10.5%.
Rosé: min alc 12%.
Prodotto Invecchiato: min age one year.

The DOC of a small community to the north of Lecce, about 2,000 acres (800 ha).

San Colombano al Lambro or San Colombano   Region: Lombardy
DOC
Red only, min alc 11%, max yield 11 tonnes/ha.
Grapes: Croatina 30–45%, Barbera 25–40%, Uva Rara 5–15%, other allowed red varieties up to 15%.

DOC named after a local castle. This is a small region, barely 250 acres (100 ha). Wines are considered interesting but are not widely exported.

San Gimignano   Region: Tuscany
DOC
Red, white and rosé, min alc 11.5%, max yield 13 tonnes/ha.
Red: Sangiovese 50%, other local red varieties up to 50%.
Sangiovese: Sangiovese 85%, other local red varieties up to 15%.
Rosé: Sangiovese 60%, Canaiolo Nero up to 20%, Trebbiano Toscano, Malvasia del Chianti, Vernaccia di San Gimignano up to 15%, other local red varieties up to 15%.
Vin Santo Secco or **Amabile:** Malvasia del Chianti 50%, Trebbiano Toscano 30%, Vernaccia di San Gimignano up to 20%, other local varieties up to 10%.

Vin Santo Occhio di Pernice: Sangiovese 70–100%, other local red varieties up to 30%.

In the same territory as DOCG Vernaccia di San Gimignano, this is a high and hilly DOC with no special claim to vinous fame.

San Martino della Battaglia   Region: Lombardy
DOC
White only, min alc 11.5%, max yield 12.5 tonnes/ha.
Grapes: Tocai Friulano 80–100%, other local varieties up to 20%.
Liquoroso: min alc 15%.

Situated to the south of Lake Garda, this is a DOC that ages well. Area is about 175 acres (70 ha).

San Severo   Region: Apulia
DOC
Red and rosé, min alc 11.5%. White, min alc 11%. Max yield 14 tonnes/ha.
Grapes: Red and rosé, Montepulciano d'Abruzzo 70–100%, Sangiovese up to 30%. White, Bombino Bianco 40–60%, Trebbiano Toscano 40–60%, Malvasia Bianca Lunga (Malvasia del Chianti) and/or Verdeca up to 20%. A *spumante* is also produced.

Situated to the north of Foggia, the town of San Severo is surrounded by fields that are almost entirely planted with vines, part of a vast zone known as the Capitanata di Puglia. San Severo DOC is regarded as pleasant wine, sometimes rather neutral. A decent size DOC, covering about 5,000 acres (2,000 ha).

Sangiovese dei Colli Pesaresi   Region: Marche
DOC
Refer **Colli Pesaresi**

Sangiovese di Romagna   Region: Emilia-Romagna
DOC
Red only, min alc 11.5%, max yield 11 tonnes/ha.
Grapes: Sangiovese 85–100%.
Superiore: wine from a specified area; min alc 11.5%.
Riserva: min age two years.

DOC of 2,500 acres (1,000 ha). Some very good wine is seen under this DOC, although strangely some is also sold as *Vino da Tavola*.

Sannio   Region: Campania
DOC
Red and rosé, min alc 11%, max yield 12 tonnes/ha. White, min alc 10.5%, max yield 14 tonnes/ha.
Grapes: Red and rosé, Sangiovese 50%, other local red varieties, including

Piedirosso and Sciascinoso, up to 50%. White, Trebbiano Toscano 50%, other local white varieties, including Samnium-Aglianico, Coda di Volpe, Falanghina, Fiano, Greco and Moscato up to 50%.

Spumante Metodo Classico: Greco and Falanghina grape blend, with a second ferment in the bottle. Min age one year in the bottle before release.

This is a hilly DOC in the heart of Campania where the best land has a long grape history. The regulations for Sannio provide for historic varieties. The local speciality is the *spumante*.

Sant'Ágata dei Goti   Region: Campania
DOC

Red and rosé, min alc 11.5%, max yield 12 tonnes/ha. White, min alc 11%, max yield 12 tonnes/ha.

Grapes: Red and rosé, Aglianico 40–60%, Piedirosso 40–60%, other local red varieties up to 20%. White, Falanghina 40–60%, Greco 40–60%, other local white varieties up to 20%.

Varietal wines: min 90% of variety named and max 10% allowed varieties.

Aglianico Riserva: min age three years before release.

Piedirosso Riserva: min age two years before release.

Tiny DOC well down Italy's boot boasting beautiful countryside and some quite distinctive delicate wine styles with a loyal following.

Sant'Anna di Isola Capo Rizzuto   Region: Calabria
DOC

Red and rosé, min alc 12%, max yield 12 tonnes/ha.

Grapes: Gaglioppo 40–60%, Nocera, Nerello Mascalese, Nerello Cappuccio, Malvasia Nera, Malvasia Bianca, Greco Bianco, alone or together, 40–60% (with the white-grape varieties limited to 35%).

A *capo* (cape) on the heel of the Italian boot sets up the territory for this small (less than 100 acres/40 ha) DOC which is working on a development plan to accentuate the quality and style of the regional wine.

Sant'Ántimo   Region: Tuscany
DOC

Red, min alc 12%, max yield 12 tonnes/ha. White, min alc 11.5%, max yield 12 tonnes/ha.

Grapes: Red, blends of Cabernet Sauvignon, Merlot and Pinot Noir in any proportions, and including traditional Tuscan varieties. White, blends of Chardonnay, Sauvignon and Pinot Gris in any proportions, and including traditional Tuscan varieties.

Varietal wine: must be 85–100% of variety labeled, other varieties admitted under DOC law up to 15%.

Vin Santo Secco or Amabile: Trebbiano Toscano and/or Malvasia Bianca 70%, other local white varieties up to 30%. **Riserva:** min age four years

before release.
Vin Santo Occhio di Pernice: Sangiovese 50–70%, Malvasia Nera
30–50%, other local red varieties up to 20%. **Riserva:** min age four years
before release.

A DOC which gets its name from the Romanesque Abbey of Sant'Ántimo
of Montalcino, which is surrounded by vineyards and olive trees. With the
exception of a small area to the northeast, the Sant'Ántimo DOC covers
exactly the same territory as Montalcino's Brunello, Rosso and Moscadello
wines. The Sant'Ántimo appellation has helped establish those local wines
that didn't fit the bill for Montalcino's better-known reds, and it has allowed
the winemakers to experiment.

Santa Maddalena DOC   *Region: Trentino-Alto Adige*

Red only, min alc 11.5%, max yield 12.5 tonnes/ha.
Grapes: Schiava min 90%, Lagrein, Pinot Noir up to 10%.
Classico: wines produced in the oldest zone.

Well-known DOC in Alto Adige, named after the hill of the same name to
the east of the city of Bolzano. This DOC is known as "Saint Magdalener" by
local Germans. The best wines are highly regarded.

Sardegna Semidano DOC   *Region: Sardinia*

White only, min alc 11%, max yield 10 tonnes/ha.
Grapes: Semidano 85%, other local grapes up to 15%.
Mogoro: grapes must come from a specific subzone; other requirements
are the same.
Superiore: min alc 13%.
Passito: min alc 15%.
Spumante (sparkling): an *amabile* (lightly sweet) and a *dolce* (sweeter)
version are made; min alc 11.5%.

Found only on the island of Sardinia, Semidano is grown mostly in the
southern territories of the province of Oristano as well as in some areas of
Campidano di Cagliari. The DOC regulation, however, sets no geographical
limits to its cultivation and the Semidano is expected to spread through the
island.

Sassicaia DOC   *Region: Tuscany*
Refer **Bolgheri-Sassicaia.**

Savuto DOC   *Region: Calabria*
Red and rosé only, min alc 12%, max yield 11 tonnes/ha.

Grapes: Gaglioppo (known locally as Magliocco and Arvino) 35–45%, Greco Nero, Nerello Cappuccio, Magliocco Canino, Sangiovese 30–40% (Sangiovese is limited to max 10%), Malvasia Bianca and/or Pecorino up to 25%.
Superiore: min age two years before release, min alc 12.5%.

DOC on the slopes that descend from the mountains to the banks of the Savuto River. Wine regarded as pleasant.

Scavigna   *Region: Calabria*
DOC
Red, min alc 11.5%. Rosé, min alc 11%. White, min alc 10.5%. Max yield for all is 12 tonnes/ha.
Grapes: Red and rosé, Gaglioppo max 60%, Nerello Cappuccio max 40%, Aglianico max 20%, other local red varieties up to 35%. White, Trebbiano Toscano max 50%, Chardonnay max 30%, Greco Bianco max 20%, Malvasia max 10%, other local white varieties up to 35%.

Scavigna DOC lies between Nocera Terinese and Falerna in the province of Catanzaro. This is one of the most highly regarded DOCs in Calabria.

Sciacca   *Region: Sicily*
DOC
Red, min alc 11.5%, max yield 12 tonnes/ha. White and rosé, min alc 10.5%, max yield 13 tonnes/ha.
Grapes: Red, Merlot, Cabernet Sauvignon, Nero d'Avola and Sangiovese min 70%, other local non-aromatic red varieties max 30%. Rosé, same varieties as for red but some white varieties can be blended. White, Inzolia, Grecanico, Chardonnay and Catarratto Lucido min 70%, other local non-aromatic white varieties max 30%.
Riserva Rayana: Catarratto Lucido and/or Inzolia min 80%, other local non-aromatic white varieties max 20%; min alc 13%. Min age two years before release, including one year in the bottle.
Varietal wine: min 85% of named variety. Cabernet Sauvignon (min alc 12%), Chardonnay (min alc 11.5%), Grecanico (min alc 10%), Inzolia (min alc 10.5%), Merlot (min alc 12%), Nero d'Avola (min alc 11.5%), Sangiovese (min alc 11.5%).

Sciacca is a small harbor in the province of Agrigento, Sicily. The Sciacca DOC was established in 1998. It covers the entire territory of Sciacca and the neighboring town of Caltabellotta. This area enjoys a climate and soil that are highly favorable to growing vines of any kind and the DOC allows the production of the usual white, red and rosé wines, as well as seven other varieties, some obtained from traditional local grapes and others from recently imported varieties.

Sforzato (or Sfursat) di Valtellina   *Region: Lombardy*
DOCG
Refer **Valtellina Superiore.**

Sizzano   *Region: Piedmont*
DOC
Red only, min alc 12%, max yield 10 tonnes/ha.
Grapes: Nebbiolo (known locally as Spanna) 40–60%, Vespolina 15–40%,
Bonarda Novarese up to 25%. Min age three years, of which two must be
in wood.

A tiny (for Italy) DOC of barely 50 acres (20 ha) but a rather sought-after
and historic wine.

Soave   *Region: Veneto*
DOC
White only, min alc 10.5%, max yield 14 tonnes/ha.
Grapes: Garganega min 70%, Trebbiano di Soave (Nostrano) up to 30%
and/or Trebbiano Toscano up to 15%.
Classico: grapes grown within a defined area.
Recioto: grape proportions as for Soave, but left to dry by water
evaporation. Sweetish in style; min alc 14%. Some *spumante* is produced
also.
Liquoroso: grapes left longer to dry, which results in greater sweetness and
a min alc of 16%.

A DOC famous for its white wine, historic and almost as well known as
Chardonnay in some markets; but the heavier Soave style lost favor in the
1980s and 1990s as other fresher and fruitier styles invaded the traditional
Soave market. However, changes in local style are happening. Soave can still
offer complex, developed whites at a good price which are excellent value.
Some of the more clumsy cooperatives, however, have adjustments to make
in style and maturation.

Soave Superiore   *Region: Veneto*
DOCG
Dry white only, min alc 11.5%, max yield 10 tonnes/ha.
Grapes: Garganega min 70%, Pinot Blanc, Chardonnay and Trebbiano up
to 30%, local varieties up to 5%.
Classico: grapes grown within a defined central area.
Riserva: min age 24 months before release, including three months in the
bottle; min alc 12.5%.

Separate from the 1968 Soave DOC, Soave Superiore was awarded DOCG
status in 2001 (effective 2002 vintage) after the producers made a strong,
positive endeavor to produce something superior to other local wine.
However, in late 2003 few wineries were using the DOCG.

Solopaca   **Region: Campania**
DOC
Red, min alc 11.5%, max yield 13 tonnes/ha. White, min alc 12%, max yield
15 tonnes/ha.
Grapes: Red, Sangiovese 45–60%, Aglianico 10–20%, Piedirosso 20–25%,
Sciascinoso and other red varieties max 10%. White, Trebbiano Toscano
50–70%, Malvasia di Candia 20–40%, Malvasia Toscana, Coda di Volpe
Bianco and other white varieties up to 10%.

Like so many Italian DOCs, Solopaca is based on vineyards in the hills; this
one is on both sides of the Calore River.

Sorni   **Region: Trentino-Alto Adige**
DOC
Red and white, max yield 14 tonnes/ha.
Rosso: Schiava min 70%, Teroldego 20–30%, Lagrein max 10%; min alc
10.5%.
Scelto: varieties as above; min alc 11%. Scelto is not quite the same as a
riserva but close.
Bianco: Nosiola 70%, Müller-Thurgau, Sylvaner Verde and Pinot Blanc up
to 30%.

A tiny Trentino DOC. Sorni Rosso is a fresh young-drinking red, Scelto a little
more serious and able to develop.

Sovana   **Region: Tuscany**
DOC
Red and rosé, min alc 11%, max yield 10 tonnes/ha.
Grapes: Sangiovese min 50%, other grapes up to 50% to allow Aglianico,
Cabernet and Merlot, which may also be labeled varietally as Superiore; min
age two years; min alc 12%.

A recent DOC that is helping the strong-willed locals to get themselves or-
ganized for producing red wine in a specific subregion.

Squinzano   **Region: Apulia**
DOC
Red and rosé, min alc 12.5%, max yield 14 tonnes/ha.
Grapes: Negro Amaro 70–100%, Malvasia Nera di Brindisi, Malvasi Nera di
Lecce and Sangiovese, alone or together, up to 30% (Sangiovese max 15%).
Riserva: the Squinzano Rosso may be labeled as Riserva if it has a min alc
of 13% and aging of two years, six months of which must be in wood.

A well-liked DOC providing robust, hearty reds with the pleasantly bitter
finish of Negro Amaro. The vineyards to the south of Apulia have been
planted almost exclusively with Negro Amaro since the sixth century BC.

Taburno
DOC
Region: Campania

Red and rosé, min alc 11.5%, max yield 13 tonnes/ha.
Grapes: Red, Sangiovese 40–50%, Aglianico 30–40%, other local varieties up to 30%. White, Trebbiano Toscano 40–50%, Falanghina 30–40%, other local white varieties up to 30%.
Riserva: min age three years before release, min alc 12%.
Spumante: Coda di Volpe and/or Falanghina 60%, other local white varieties up to 40%.

Aglianico del Taburno has its own related but almost separate DOC, which is in the same area but respects a heritage and a style. Taburno has embarked on a new beginning, with centuries of winemaking settling into a style that is becoming widely appreciated as new techniques and equipment play their part.

Tarquinia
DOC
Region: Latium

Red, min alc 10.5%, max yield 12 tonnes/ha. White, min alc 10.5%, max yield 12 tonnes/ha.
Grapes: Red, Sangiovese and/or Montepulciano min 60%, Cesanese up to 25%, other local red varieties up to 30%. White, Trebbiano Toscano (known locally as Procanico) and/or Trebbiano Giallo min 50%, Malvasia di Candia and/or Malvasia del Lazio up to 35%, up to 30% other local white varieties are allowed, but grapes of the Pinot Grigio variety are specifically excluded.
Novello: new red wine sold fresh and young; min alc 11%.
Frizzante: dry with a little sparkle.

A very wide DOC area, not just limited to the land around Tarquinia, which lies between the provinces of Rome and Viterbo. Along the Tyrrhenian coast it goes from Montalto di Castro to Fiumicino, and inland it reaches the Monti Cimini to the northeast and the Monti della Tolfa to the northwest.

Taurasi
DOCG
Region: Campania

Red only, min alc 12%, max yield 10 tonnes/ha. Min age three years before release, at least one of which must be in wood.
Grapes: Aglianico min 85%, Piedirosso, Sangiovese and Barbera, alone or together, up to 15%.
Riserva: min age four years before release, at least two of these in wood; min alc 12.5%.

Well regarded wine in southern Italy where DOCGs are rare. DOC Tourasi is situated in Campania and covers less than 1,000 acres (400 ha); however, it is one winemaker, Mastroberadino, who produces most of the wine under this label.

Terlano   **Region: Trentino-Alto Adige**
DOC
White only, max yield 13 tonnes/ha.
Terlano: Pinot Blanc and/or Chardonnay 50%, Riesling Italico, Riesling
Renano, Sauvignon, Sylvaner and Müller-Thurgau up to 45%, other whites
up to 5%; min alc 11.5%. A *spumante* is also produced.
Pinot Blanc: Pinot Blanc min 90%, other allowed white varieties up to 10%;
min alc 11.5%.
Chardonnay: Chardonnay min 90%, other allowed white varieties up to
10%; min alc 11%.
Riesling Italico: Riesling Italico min 90%, other allowed white varieties up
to 10%; min alc 10.5%.
Riesling Renano: Riesling Renano min 90%, other allowed white varieties
up to 10%; min alc 11.5%.

Terlano, or Terlaner in German, offers whites from around the town of this
name in the German-speaking part of Alto Adige. There is a Terlano grape
variety, almost extinct but still cultivated, which was once thought to produce therapeutic wine.

Teroldego Rotaliano   **Region: Trentino-Alto Adige**
DOC
Red and rosé, min alc 11.5%, max yield 17 tonnes/ha.
Grape: Teroldego 100%.
Superiore: min alc 12%.
Riserva: min age two years before release, at least one of these in oak.

Historic Teroldego wine was known for centuries as "princely wine," and the
grape variety is barely known outside the DOC. Lively, with low tannins and
plenty of color.

Terralba   **Region: Sardinia**
DOC
Refer **Campidano di Terralba.**

Terre di Franciacorta   **Region: Lombardy**
DOC
Red and white, min alc 11%, max yield 12.5 tonnes/ha.
Grapes: Red, Cabernet Sauvignon or Franc 40–50%, Barbera 20–30%,
Nebbiolo 15–25%, Merlot 10–15%, other red varieties up to 15%
permitted. White, Pinot Blanc and/or Chardonnay.

A region noted for its sparkling wine, which has DOCG status (*refer*
Franciacorta); but these still wines under the Terre di Franciacorta DOC are
growing in importance.

Tocai di San Martino della Battaglia   **Region: Lombardy**
DOC
Refer **San Martino della Battaglia.**

Torgiano   **Region: Umbria**
DOC
Red, min alc 12%, max yield 12 tonnes/ha. White, min alc 10.5%, max yield
12 tonnes/ha.
Grapes: Red, Sangiovese 50–70%, Canaiolo 15–30%, Trebbiano Toscano
10%, Ciliegiolo and Montepulciano 10%. White, Trebbiano Toscano
50–70%, Grechetto 15–35%, Malvasia Toscana, Malvasia di Candia,
Verdello up to 15%.
Cabernet Sauvignon: Cabernet Sauvignon min 85%, other local red
grapes up to 15%; min alc 12%.
Chardonnay: Chardonnay min 85%, other local white grapes up to 15%;
min alc 10.5%.

A hilly DOC of growing popularity; the best red in this area has been given
DOCG status (*refer* following entry).

Torgiano Rosso Riserva   **Region: Umbria**
DOCG
Red only, min alc 12.5%, max yield 10 tonnes/ha. Min age three years.
Grapes: Sangiovese 50–70%, Canaiolo 15–30%, Trebbiano, Ciliegiolo and
Montepulciano up to 10%.

A fairly tiny (400 acres/160 ha) DOCG up in the hills, but very highly regarded. Wines are often not released until after the three-year minimum.
Other wines in the area use the "plain" DOC above.

Trebbiano d'Abruzzo   **Region: Abruzzi**
DOC
White only, min alc 11.5%, max yield 17.5 tonnes/ha.
Grapes: Trebbiano d'Abruzzo (Bombino Bianco) and/or Trebbiano Toscano.
Malvasia Toscana, Cococciola and Passerina are allowed up to 15%. Min
age five months before release.

Simple quaffing white wine DOC from the same area that produces voluminous quantities of Montepulciano d'Abruzzo. Note the high yield permitted
for this Trebbiano.

Trebbiano di Romagna   **Region: Emilia-Romagna**
DOC
White only, min alc 11.5%, max yield 14 tonnes/ha.
Grape: Trebbiano.

No-fuss white wine from a DOC to the east of Emilia-Romagna.

Trentino   ***Region: Trentino-Alto Adige***
DOC
Red and white.
Grapes: Red, Cabernet 50–85%, Merlot 15–50%; min alc 11.5%, max yield
14 tonnes/ha. White, Chardonnay 50–85%, Pinot Blanc 15–50%; min alc
11%, max yield 15 tonnes/ha.
Chardonnay: Chardonnay only; min alc 11%, max yield 15 tonnes/ha.
Moscato Giallo: Moscato Giallo only; min alc 11.5%, max yield
12 tonnes/ha.
Moscato Rosa: Moscato Rosé only; min alc 12.5%, max yield
10 tonnes/ha.
Müller-Thurgau: Müller-Thurgau only; min alc 11%, max yield
14 tonnes/ha.
Nosiola: Nosiola only; min alc 10.5%, max yield 14 tonnes/ha.
Pinot Blanc: Pinot Blanc only; min alc 11%, max yield 15 tonnes/ha.
Pinot Grigio: Pinot Gris only; min alc 11%, max yield 14 tonnes/ha.
Riesling Italico: Riesling Italico only; min alc 10.5%, max yield
15 tonnes/ha.
Riesling Renano: Riesling Renano only; min alc 11%, max yield
14 tonnes/ha.
Traminer Aromatico: Traminer Aromatico only; min alc 11.5%, max yield
14 tonnes/ha.
Cabernet: Cabernet Sauvignon and Franc; min alc 11%, max yield
13 tonnes/ha. **Riserva:** min alc 11.5%, two years of aging.
Cabernet Franc: Cabernet Franc only; min alc 11%, max yield
13 tonnes/ha. **Riserva:** min alc 11.5%, two years of aging.
Cabernet Sauvignon: Cabernet Sauvignon only; min alc 11%, max yield
13 tonnes/ha. **Riserva:** min alc 11.5%, two years of aging.
Lagrein: Lagrein only; min alc 11%, max yield 14 tonnes/ha. **Riserva:** min
alc 11.5%, two years of aging.
Marzemino: Marzemino only; min alc 11%, max yield 13 tonnes/ha.
Riserva: min alc 11.5%, two years of aging.
Merlot: Merlot only; min alc 11%, max yield 15 tonnes/ha. **Riserva:** min
alc 11.5%, two years of aging.
Pinot Nero: Pinot Noir only; min alc 11%, max yield 12 tonnes/ha.
Riserva: min alc 11.5%, two years of aging.
Vin Santo: Nosiola only; the grapes must be subjected to light drying
according to the traditional method; min alc 16%, max yield 14 tonnes/ha,
three years of aging.

A large province-wide DOC covering Trentino, the southern half of Trentino-
Alto Adige, with a wide range of varietal wines. There are a small number
of internal DOCs with their own status but essentially Trentino is a catchall
for the province, with fairly large yields producing generally clean, pleasant
wines without a lot of intensity. It is an important DOC for its volume, and
will be more important if the DOC grows in style and recognition.

Trento   **Region: Trentino-Alto Adige**
DOC
Dry white and sparkling rosé, min alc 11.5%, max yield 12 tonnes/ha.
Grapes: Pinot Noir, Chardonnay, Pinot Meunier and Pinot Blanc in
proportions to suit the producer. Minimum time on lees is 15 months.
Riserva: minimum time on lees 36 months; min alc 12%.

A new DOC making traditional method sparkling wine.

Val d'Arbia   **Region: Tuscany**
DOC
White only, min alc 11%, max yield 13 tonnes/ha. Min age five months.
Grapes: Trebbiano Toscano 75–85%, Malvasia del Chianti 15–25%, other
allowed white varieties up to 15%.
Vin Santo: grapes as above, but subjected to drying; min alc 17%. Min
age three years in wood.

A DOC in Siena province, including a little land in Chianti territory.

Val di Cornia   **Region: Tuscany**
DOC
Red, min alc 11.5%, max yield 12 tonnes/ha. White, min alc 11%, max yield
12 tonnes/ha.
Grapes: Red, Sangiovese, Cabernet Sauvignon, Merlot. White, Trebbiano,
Vermentino.

Situated in coastal Tuscany, with Bolgheri DOC nearby. This is quite a large
DOC, newly promoted, and known for light, pleasant wines to be enjoyed
young.

Val Polcevera   **Region: Liguria**
DOC
Red, min alc 10.5%, max yield 14 tonnes/ha. White, min alc 10%, max yield
12 tonnes/ha.
Grapes: Red, Dolcetto, Sangiovese and Ciliegiolo min 60%, Barbera up
to 40%. White (*spumante, passito* and *coronata*), Vermentino, Bianchetta
Genovese and Albarola min 60%, Pigato and/or Rollo and/or Bosco up to
40%.
Coronata: made from grapes grown in the old village of the same name.

New DOC (1999) in an area with a long wine tradition but whose vineyards
have been replaced by commercial enterprises. Coronata, a major source of
wine in the past, is now particularly small.

Valcalepio   **Region: Lombardy**
DOC
Red, min alc 11.5%, max yield 10 tonnes/ha. White, min alc 11.5%, max
yield 9 tonnes/ha.

Grapes: Red, Merlot 55–75%, Cabernet Sauvignon 25–45%. Min age two years, one of which in wood. White, Pinot Blanc 55–75%, Pinot Gris 25–45%.

New varietal plantings after phylloxera have worked well for this DOC, which is in the mountains to the north of Bergamo. A well-regarded wine.

Valdadige
DOC
Region: Veneto and Trentino-Alto Adige

Red, rosé and white, max yield 14 tonnes/ha.
Grapes: Red, Schiave and Lambrusco, alone or together, up to 30% (Schiave must be at least 20%), Merlot, Pinot Noir, Lagrein, Teroldego and Negrara to make up the difference; min alc 11%. Rosé, Schiave and Lambrusco, alone or together, up to 30% (Schiave must be at least 20%), Merlot, Pinot Noir, Lagrein, Teroldego and Negrara, alone or together, to make up the difference; min alc 10.5%. White, Pinot Blanc, Pinot Gris, Riesling Italico, Müller-Thurgau and Chardonnay, alone or together, in an amount of not less than 20%, Bianchetta Trevigiana, Trebbiano Toscano, Nosiola, Vernaccia, Sylvaner and Veltliner Bianco, alone or together, to make up the difference; min alc 10.5%.
Pinot Grigio: Pinot Gris min 85%, plus other non-aromatic white varieties from the area; min alc 10.5%.
Schiava: Schiava Grossa, Schiava Gentile and Schiava Grigio, alone or together, up to 85%, other red varieties from the area.

Valdadige (the name comes from "Valley of Adige," *Etschtaler* in German) has a production area shared by three provinces in two regions: Bolzano and Trento in Trentino-Alto Adige and Verona in Veneto, with the small subzone Terra dei Forti across the border of both Trento and Verona. The vineyards on the Trentino side may also use the DOC Alto Adige. Wines have a wide range of styles as well as many varieties.

Valdichiana
DOC
Region: Tuscany

Red, min alc 11.5%, max yield 12 tonnes/ha. White, min alc 11%; max yield 12 tonnes/ha.
Grapes: Red, Sangiovese min 50%, Cabernet and/or Merlot and/or Syrah up to 50%, other local non-aromatic red varieties up to 15%.
Bianco Vergine: Trebbiano min 20%, Chardonnay, Pinot Blanc, Grechetto and Pinot Gris max 80%, other local non-aromatic white varieties max 15%.
Vin Santo: Trebbiano and Malvasia Bianca 50%, other local non-aromatic white varieties up to 50%; min age three years before release. **Riserva Vin Santo:** min age four years before release.
Varietal wines: must carry at least 85% of the named variety.

The name breaks down into "Valley of Chiana," which lends its name to

Chianti. This DOC in the provinces of Arezzo and Siena is best known for Bianco Vergine, regarded as highly medicinal, a white wine prescribed for liver and stomach complaints.

Valle d'Aosta   Region: Aosta Valley
DOC
Red and white.
Grapes: Red and rosé, red grapes authorized for the region; min alc 9.5%, max yield 12 tonnes/ha. Six months aging. White, white grapes authorized for the region; min alc 9%, max yield 12 tonnes/ha. Six months aging.
Müller-Thurgau: Müller-Thurgau min 90%, other allowed white varieties may be added up to 10%; min alc 10%, max yield 11 tonnes/ha. Three months aging.
Gamay: Gamay min 90%, other allowed red varieties may be added up to 10%; min alc 11%, max yield 12 tonnes/ha. Six months aging.
Pinot Nero: Pinot Noir min 90%, other allowed red varieties may be added up to 10%; min alc 11.5%, max yield 8.5 tonnes/ha. Six months aging.
Arnad-Montjovet: Nebbiolo min 70%, Dolcetto, Vien de Nus, Pinot Noir, Neyret and Freisa, alone or together, max 30%; min alc 11%, max yield 8 tonnes/ha. Eight months aging. **Superiore:** two years aging, min alc 12%.
Blanc de Morgex et de la Salle: Blanc de Morgex only; min alc 9%, max yield 9 tonnes/ha. Three months aging.
Chambave Moscato: Moscato di Chambave only; min alc 11%, max yield 10 tonnes/ha. Three months aging in wood.
Chambave Moscato Passito: Moscato di Chambave only; grapes must be subjected to light drying; min alc 16.5%, max yield 10 tonnes/ha. Two years aging in wood.
Chambave Rosso: Petit Rouge min 60%, Dolcetto, Gamay, Pinot Noir, alone or together, up to 25%; min alc 11%, max yield 10 tonnes/ha. Six months aging in wood.
Donnas: Nebbiolo min 85%, Freisa, Vien de Nus and Neyret, alone or together, max 15%; min alc 11%, max yield 7.5 tonnes/ha. Two years aging.
Enfer d'Arvier: Petit Rouge 85%, Vien de Nus, Neyret, Dolcetto, Pinot Noir, Gamay, alone or together, up to 15%.
Nus Pinot Gris or **Nus Malvoisie:** Pinot Gris only; min alc 12%, max yield 8 tonnes/ha. Three months aging.
Nus Pinot Gris or **Nus Malvoisie Fletri:** Pinot Gris only; must be subjected to light drying; min alc 16.5%, max yield 8 tonnes/ha. Two years aging in wood.
Nus Rosso: Vien de Nus min 50%, Petit Rouge and Pinot Noir, alone or together, up to 40%; min alc 11%, max yield 8 tonnes/ha. Six months aging in wood.
Torrette: Petit Rouge min 70%, Pinot Noir, Gamay, Fumin, Neyret, Vien de

Nus and Dolcetto, alone or together, min 30%; min alc 11%, max yield 10 tonnes/ha. Six months aging in wood. **Superiore:** eight months aging in wood, min alc 12%.

The Aosta Valley is one of the smallest of Italy's wine regions, and this DOC covers all but a tiny proportion of DOC wine, within which a couple of specialized DOCs exist. Tucked high in the north of Italy the valley has a strong passing trade that, along with tourists and locals, manages to consume most of its production, even though it can be pricey.

Valle Isarco   Region: Trentino-Alto Adige
DOC
White only.
Traminer Aromatico: Gewürztraminer only; min alc 11%, max yield 10 tonnes/ha.
Pinot Gris: Pinot Gris only; min alc 11%, max yield 10 tonnes/ha.
Veltliner: Veltliner only; min alc 10.5%, max yield 12 tonnes/ha.
Sylvaner: Sylvaner only; min alc 10.5%, max yield 13 tonnes/ha.
Müller-Thurgau: Müller-Thurgau only; min alc 10.5%, max yield 13 tonnes/ha.

A DOC with strong German heritage, as reflected in the grapes used.

Valpolicella   Region: Veneto
DOC
Red only, min alc 11%, max yield 12 tonnes/ha.
Grapes: Corvina Veronese 40–70%, Rondinella 20–40%, Molinara 5–25%, Rossignola, Negrara Trentina, Barbera and Sangiovese allowed up to 15%.
Classico: grapes grown in defined subregion.
Superiore: min age one year in wood, min alc 12%.

Near Lake Garda, Valpolicella is one of the best known Italian DOCs but struggles to keep up with its own success. Light, fresh, tangy reds form the basic style, but it is a style that Chianti and other DOCs have run away with while Valpolicella remains unchanged. The region will catch up.

Since 2002, Amarone styles made within the same region and with the same grape varieties have been given their own DOC; *refer* **Amarone della Valpolicella.**

Valsusa   Region: Piedmont
DOC
Red only, min alc 11%, max yield 9 tonnes/ha.
Grapes: Avanà, Barbera, Dolcetto and Neretta min 60%, other local varieties 40%.

A remarkably small DOC in a country with so many vineyards! Valsusa wine is grown in 19 rural districts, from the town of Almese up to Exilles, over a vine-bearing surface that in 2000 officially registered just 22 acres (9 ha).

Valtellina
Region: Lombardy
DOC
Red only, min alc 11%, max yield 12 tonnes/ha.
Grapes: Nebbiolo (known locally as Chiavennasca) min 80%, other local
varieties up to 20%. Min age two years before release. **Riserva** (under
subzone names): min age three years.

Part of Valtellina has DOCG status (*refer* following entry), and this part of
the area is pushing hard for recognition. Larger than the Superiore vineyards
and requiring 1% less alcohol, the plain style is considered simpler and ready
for drinking earlier.

Valtellina Superiore
Region: Lombardy
DOCG
Red only, min alc 12%, max yield 8 tonnes/ha.
Grapes: Nebbiolo (known locally as Chiavennasca) min 90%, other local
varieties up to 10%. Min age two years before release. **Riserva** (under
subzone names): min age three years.

A very northern DOCG within Italy, Valtellina is in a narrow valley around the
Adda River, which flows into Lake Como. Subzones are Grumello, Inferno,
Sassella, Stagafassi and Valgella (part of the Riserva status). Distinctive
Nebbiolo grapes are used, but these are a little sharper, with less body and
power than in Piedmont's best wines. Valtellina has divided into two: this
DOCG Superiore, with extra alcohol (and it is hoped, more ripeness), and
the plain Valtellina DOC (*refer* previous entry) which can be a little lighter
and is suitable for drinking early.

Velletri
Region: Lazio
DOC
Red, min alc 11.5%, max yield 16 tonnes/ha. White, min alc 11%, max yield
16 tonnes/ha.
Grapes: Red, Montepulciano 30–50%, Sangiovese 30–45%, Cesanese
Comune and Cesanese di Affile min 15%, Bombino Nero and/or Merlot
and/or Ciliegiolo max 10%. White, Malvasia Bianca di Candia and/or
Malvasia Puntinata max 70%, Trebbiano Tosacano, Verde and Giallo up to
30%, Bellone and Bonvino up to 10%.
Superiore: min alc 11.5%.

DOC Velletri in the Lazio region produces sound, honest wine. Whites are
generally preferred, but in the right year the DOC can offer reds that satisfy
and age well.

Verbicaro
Region: Calabria
DOC
Red, min alc 12%, max yield 11 tonnes/ha. Rosé and white, min alc
10.5%, max yield 12 tonnes/ha.

Grapes: Red and rosé, Gaglioppo (Guarnaccia Nera) and Greco Nero
60–80%, Malvasia Bianca, Guarnaccia Bianca and Greco Bianco 20–40%,
other local non-aromatic red varieties up to 20%. White, Greco Bianco
and/or Malvasia Bianca and/or Guarnaccia Bianca min 70%, other local
white varieties up to 30%.
Riserva: min age three years before release.

Wine district with a long heritage. The DOC is regarded as producing sound
honest wine. Note the low yields.

Verdicchio dei Castelli di Jesi
DOC
Region: Marche

White only, min alc 11.5%, max yield 15 tonnes/ha.
Grapes: Verdicchio min 85%, Malvasia Toscana and Trebbiano Toscano
may be added up to 15%.
Classico: wine from grapes grown within a traditional area; alcohol and
yield the same.
Riserva: min alc 12.5%.
Spumante: dry sparkling; min alc 11.5%
Passito: sweeter style; min alc 15%.

Almost 6,500 acres (2,600 ha) of DOC given to good, cheerful but simple
white wine. Well priced for sound, local quaffing.

Verdicchio di Matelica
DOC
Region: Marche

White only, min alc 11.5%, max yield 13 tonnes/ha. A *spumante* version is
also made.
Grapes: Verdicchio 85–100%, Malvasia Toscana and Trebbiano Toscano up
to 15%.
Riserva: min age two years before release; min alc 12.5%.
Passito: a sweeter wine, aged at least one year. Light drying of grapes allowed;
min alc 15%.

DOC in the hills around Macerata and the town of Matelica which normally
produces light dry whites.

Verduno Pelaverga
DOC
Region: Piedmont

Red only, min alc 12%, max yield 11 tonnes/ha.
Grape: Pelaverga.

A 22-acre (9-ha) DOC in Verduno ("hill of flowers") with a rare grape variety
that is peppery to smell and thought to have aphrodisiac qualities. The wine,
more pink than red, is suited to light lunches and nighttime snacks.

Vermentino di Gallura   Region: Sardinia
DOCG
White only, min alc 12%, max yield 10 tonnes/ha.
Grapes: Vermentino 95–100%, other allowed white varieties up to 5%.
Superiore: min alc 13%, max yield 9 tonnes/ha.

This DOCG region in the north of Sardinia is affected by the fierce Mistral wind, and the barren soils won't successfully grow much else other than the Vermentino grape. The granite soil is said to provide the distinctive bouquet of the wine.

Vermentino di Sardegna   Region: Sardinia
DOC
White only, min alc 10.5%, max yield 20 tonnes/ha.
Grapes: Vermentino min 85%, other allowed white varieties up to 15%.
Spumante: min alc 11%.

A much broader catchment area than the Vermentino di Gallura DOCG but uses the same grape, though with a lighter style.

Vernaccia di Oristano   Region: Sardinia
DOC
White only, min alc 15%, max yield 8 tonnes/ha. Min age two years in wood.
Grape: Vernaccia di Oristano.
Liquoroso: dry and sweeter *liquoroso* styles available, both min alc 18%.

The Sardinians, it is said, have resisted both malaria and misgovernment by drinking Vernaccia! With two years minimum age, much of it in the barrel, the dry (*secco*) style is robust and mouth-filling, and it has been compared to sherry. Sweeter (*dolce*) wines can be golden and yet robust.

Vernaccia di San Gimignano   Region: Tuscany
DOCG
White only, min alc 11%, max yield 9 tonnes/ha.
Grapes: Vernaccia di San Gimignano min 90%. Other grapes allowed in Siena, up to 10%; min alc 11.5%.
Riserva: min age one year. A *liquoroso* is also produced.

Despite its DOCG status, this region does not produce anything particularly exciting. While it has a low yield and the promise of a province like Tuscany, this is a fairly simple wine.

Vernaccia di Serrapetrona   Region: Marche
DOCG
Red only, min alc 11.5%, max yield 12 tonnes/ha.
Grapes: Vernaccia di Serrapetrona 85%, Sangiovese, Montepulciano and Ciliegiolo 15%.

A recent (2003) DOCG making dry, sweet and light, sometimes fizzy, reds from a variety that seems to defy definition! Confusingly, "Vernaccia" is a name used for other Italian grape varieties as well. Wine writer Jancis Robinson tells us the root of the name is the same as "vernacular," meaning "indigenous."

Vesuvio   Region: Campania
DOC
Red, min alc 10.5%. White, min alc 11%. Max yield for both 10 tonnes/ha.
Grapes: Red and rosé, Piedirosso and Sciascinose min 80% (Piedirosso must be min 50%), Aglianico 20%. White, Coda di Volpe, Verdeca min 80% (Coda di Volpe must be min 35%), Falanghina Greco up to 20%.
Lacryma Christi del Vesuvio: same grapes as red and white; min alc 12%.

Large DOC of volcanic soil with exposed vineyards obtaining plenty of warm sun. Despite a relatively low allowable yield for Italy, this is a DOC of straight-forward, lower-priced wines, at best very quaffable and pleasant, at worst a little thin and bitter.

Vicenza   Region: Veneto
DOC
Red and rosé, min alc 11%. White, min alc 10.5%. Max yield for both 14 tonnes/ha.
Grapes: Red and rosé, Merlot 50–100%, other local non-aromatic red varieties up to 50%. White and Passito, Garganega 50%, other local non-aromatic white varieties up to 50%.
Varietal wines: (12 varieties) min 85% of the named variety, up to 15% other similar varieties are permitted under the DOC law; min alc 11%.
Cabernet: Cabernet Sauvignon and/or Franc and/or Carmenère min 85%, other local varieties up to 15%.
Riserva: available in Rosso, Cabernet, Cabernet Sauvignon, Merlot, Pinot Noir and Raboso. Min age two years, min alc 12%.

New (2000) DOC with five other DOCs surrounding it; Vicenza was developed to raise the regional percentage of DOC wine. Still becoming established by making a recognizable foray in a wide range of styles from riesling to sparkling, and cabernet to pinot noir.

Vin Santo del Chianti   Region: Tuscany
DOC
Vin Santo: Trebbiano and Malvasia min 70%, other authorized varieties up to 30%; min alc 16%, max yield 10 tonnes/ha; min age three years before release. **Riserva:** min age four years before release.
Vin Santo Occhio di Pernice: Sangiovese 50–100%, other local authorized grapes, white or red, up to 50%; min alc 17%. **Riserva:** min age three years before release.

Village wines: As with Chianti DOCG, each of the seven subregions, Rufina, Montalbano, Colli-Fiorentini, Colline-Pisani, Colli-Aretini, Colli-Senesi and Montespertoli, may hyphenate its name to the DOC if the wine comes entirely from within that specific region.

A range of dry and sweet *Vin Santo* wines from the same territories as the Chianti DOCG. The list of variations (*dolce, abboccato, riserva,* etc.) is a long one.

Vin Santo di Gambellara   **Region: Veneto**
DOC
Refer **Gambellara.**

Vino Nobile di Montepulciano   **Region: Tuscany**
DOCG
Red only, min alc 12.5%, max yield 8 tonnes/ha. Min age two years in wood before release.
Grapes: Sangiovese (known locally as Prugnolo Gentile) 70–90%, Canaiolo Nero, up to 20%, other local non-aromatic varieties (with the exception of Malvasia del Chianti) up to 20% (white varieties up to 10%).
Riserva: min age three years in wood; min alc 13%.
Riserva Speciale: min age four years in wood.

A well respected DOCG from a hilly area south of Chianti, near DOCG Brunello di Montalcino. One of the first DOCGs but quality development continues to retain old respect.

Zagarolo   **Region: Latium**
DOC
White only, min alc 11.5%, max yield 15 tonnes/ha.
Grapes: Malvasia max 70%, Trebbiano min 30%, Bellone and Bonvino max 10%.
Superiore: min alc 12.5%.

DOC offering a light, easy wine, Frascati-like, to be enjoyed young and fresh.

Indicazione Geographica Tipica (IGT)

The following is a list of regions in Italy referred to as *Indicazione Geographica Tipica* (IGT). Some of these, like the VDQS in France, may be given quality wine status as DOCs and DOCGs in the future. Others in the list will not; they are less-specific area names giving identity to wines that are supposedly "typical" of where they come from, and may be similar to the French *Vin de Pays* wines. In yet other instances, some of the IGTs are regional names like Tuscany and Umbria, and give a broad catchall recognition to wines "typical of the region" that may not fit varietally or geographically into an internal DOC(G).

As the DOC(G) systems emerged, it became clear that some *Vino da Tavola* wines had substantial qualities and were claiming demand and high prices well beyond the local DOC wines. A simple example can be found in Tuscany, where some producers blended Cabernet Sauvignon with Sangiovese in varying proportions, then using small oak maturation produced a substantial, complex wine, referred to as "Supertuscan." But because both the grapes and the techniques did not conform to that of the local DOC(G) such wines had to use the "Vino da Tavola" designation on the label, a classification originally planned for simple, country styles without much identity.

Thus the need became apparent for a category that stood alone, gave recognition to the quality and perhaps awaited changes or additions to DOCs and DOCGs that would allow these wines to qualify. (Chianti DOC, for example, did make changes, by allowing other varieties.) This is gradually taking place – in Tuscany, for example, the new specific DOCs of Bolgheri and Bolgheri-Sassicaia were formed.

Now that the IGT system is in place, it has become a mechanism to foster creativity and experimentation that will perhaps lead to better things. (France, of course, has no such system and may be the worse for it.) Though officially just "table wine" under EU law, IGTs can offer some fine, interesting and sometimes bargain-value wines and, speaking romantically, some of the most interesting future additions to Italian wine evolution and lore.

As of 2003, Italy has the following IGTs:

Allerona	Umbria	Basilicata	Basilicata
Alta Valle della Greve	Tuscany	Benaco Bresciano	Lombardy
Alto Livenza	Friuli-Venezia Giulia	Beneventano	Campania
		Bergamasca	Lombardy
Alto Mincio	Lombardy	Bettona	Umbria
Alto Tirino	Abruzzi	Bianco di Castel Franco Emilia	Emilia-Romagna
Arghilla	Calabria		
Atesino delle Venezie	Trentino-Alto Adige	Calabria	Calabria
Barbagia	Sardinia	Camarro	Sicily

Cannara	Umbria
Civitella d'Agliano	Latium
Colli Aprutini	Abruzzi
Colli Cimini	Latium
Colli Ericini	Sicily
Colli del Limbara	Sardinia
Colli di Salerno	Campania
Colli del Sangro	Abruzzi
Colli della Toscana Centrale	Tuscany
Colli Trevigiani	Veneto
Collina del Milanese	Lombardy
Colline Frentane	Abruzzi
Colline Pescaresi	Abruzzi
Colline Savonesi	Liguria
Colline Teatine	Abruzzi
Condoleo	Calabria
Conselvano	Veneto
Costa Viola	Calabria
Daunia	Apulia
Del Vastese or Histonium	Abruzzi
Delia Nivolelli	Sicily
Delle Venezie	Friuli-Venezia Giulia
Dugenta	Campania
Emilia or dell'Emilia	Emilia-Romagna
Epomeo	Campania
Esaro	Calabria
Fontanarossa di Cerda	Sicily
Forlì	Emilia-Romagna
Fortana del Taro	Emilia-Romagna
Frusinante or del Frusinante	Latium
Grottino di Roccanova	Basilicata
Irpinia	Campania
Isola dei Nuraghi	Sardinia
Lazio	Latium
Lipuda	Calabria
Locride	Calabria
Marca Trevigiana	Veneto
Marche	Marche
Maremma Toscana	Tuscany
Marmilla	Sardinia
Mitterberg	Trentino-Alto Adige
Modena or Provincia di Modena	Emilia-Romagna
Montenetto di Brescia	Lombardy
Murgia	Apulia
Narni	Umbria
Nettuno	Latium
Nurra or Nurra Algherese	Sardinia
Ogliastra	Sardinia
Osco or Terre degli Osci	Molise
Paestum	Campania
Palizzi	Calabria
Parteolla	Sardinia
Pellaro	Calabria
Planargia	Sardinia
Pompeiano	Campania
Provincia di Mantova or Mantova	Lombardy
Provincia di Nuoro or Nuoro	Sardinia
Provincia di Pavia or Pavia	Lombardy
Provincia di Verona or Veronese	Veneto
Puglia	Apulia
Quistello	Lombardy
Ravenna	Emilia-Romagna
Roccamonfina	Campania
Romangia	Sardinia
Ronchi di Brescia	Lombardy
Rotae	Molise
Rubicone	Emilia-Romagna
Sabbioneta	Lombardy
Salemi	Sicily
Salento	Apulia
Salina	Sicily
Scilla	Calabria
Sebino	Lombardy
Sibiola	Sardinia
Sicilia	Sicily
Sillaro or Bianco del Sillaro	Emilia-Romagna
Spello	Umbria
Tarantino	Apulia
Terrazze Retiche	Lombardy
Terre di Chieti	Abruzzi
Terre di Veleja	Emilia-Romagna
Terre del Volturno	Campania

Tharros	Sardinia		Valle del Crati	Calabria
Toscano or Toscana	Tuscany		Valle d'Itria	Apulia
Trexenta	Sardinia		Valle Peligna	Abruzzo
Umbria	Umbria		Valle del Tirso	Sardinia
Val di Magra	Tuscany		Valli di Porto Pino	Sardinia
Val di Neto	Calabria		Veneto	Verona
Val Tidone	Emilia-Romagna		Veneto Orientale	Verona
Valdamato	Calabria		Venezia Giulia	Fruili-Venezia Giulia
Vallagarina	Veneto and Trentino-Alto Adige		Vigneti delle Dolomiti	Veneto and Trentino-Alto Adige
Valle Belice	Sicily			

CHAPTER 3

Spain

Denominación de Origen (DO)
Denominación de Origen Calificada (DOCa)
Denominación de Origen de Pagos Vitícolos Determinados (DO de PVD)
Vino de la Tierra (VdlT)
Vino de Mesa (VdM)

The country with the biggest vineyard in the world, Spain has 2.9 million acres (1.2 million ha) under vine. This figure was once even higher, but has decreased as European consumption dropped and new wine-producing countries encroached on part of their markets.

The people of Spain are passionate about their wine. Like the French and the Italians, they also recognize the region, the "land," by certifying them as *Denominación de Origen* (DO). It's not always easy for the newcomer to Spanish wine to make sense of the wine region names, as some don't coincide with political and geographical boundaries of the same names. Spain even has a hint of a top tier grade similar to the DOCG in Italy: this is called *Denominación de Origen Calificada* (DOCa), though so far only two DOs (Rioja and Priorato) have risen to that level.

Yet Spain is evolving and is now investing in wine. There is a decade of major change ahead for the wine industry in a country that has absorbed wine as part of its culture for thousands of years. Many vineyards have gone already and new ones have been planted; there are changes in grape varieties; blends have been added; and modern equipment is now available that gives the winemaker more control.

Spain has its own indigenous varieties, like Tempranillo and Parellada, which very much form part of the local wine culture. As in Italy, there is also major growth in "new" varieties in regions that have not had grapes like Chardonnay and Cabernet until recently. Many of these newcomers are blended with the indigenous varieties, sometimes working well.

Spain is in the midst of a sequence of changes. Large quantities of vineyards have been pulled out over the past 30 years and subsidies are still a part of life for some growers whose basic production is generally "wasted" in distillation. Yet this change has brought about a new wave in Spain: vineyards are producing low yields, often very low, and the benefits in terms of wine quality are beginning to show. Yield is not limited under the DO system; but yield has come down, and this lowering has brought a resurgence of flavors and styles, and a new awareness of quality.

Whatever the reason, international interest in Spanish wines has reached a new level. Even the sherry producers, whose market was literally dying, have revamped everything from alcohol levels and packaging to the sales message and the advertising to alert younger people to the pleasures of a cool, crisp sherry.

Who would have thought that an area in the uplands of Spain could find a waiting list for its US$100-a-bottle red upon its release at 10, or even 20 years old? That red, Vega Sicilia, has also lifted the profile of DO Ribera del Duero and has highlighted the interest and excitement in Spanish wines generally. What has happened in the past 10 years is just the beginning.

Spain can now justly be celebrated not only for its heritage, but also for its promising wine future.

Wine Classifications

Denominación de Origen (DO)
Denominación de Origen Calificada (DOCa)
Before joining the EU (which has its own wine requirements) in 1986, Spain introduced (in 1970) the DO system to qualify what are now about 60 areas of vineyard as *Vinos de Calidad Producido en Regiones Determinades* (VCPRD). This is the Spanish translation of the French VQPRD or "Quality Wine" under the EU (refer "The European Way" on page 19). The laws came into effect in 1979 and have been adjusted since, some of them several times, to bring them into working order and keep up with trends.

The DO system – which also covers olive oil, cheese and other agricultural products – is administered and policed by the *Instituto Nacionel de Denominaciónes de Origen* (INDO), who ensure compliance with EU requirements under the direction of the Spanish Ministry of Agriculture and Fisheries in Madrid.

In each region, there is a regulatory council, the *Consejo Regulador de la Denominación*, responsible for the day-to-day work of checking wines at various stages and providing analysis for the higher bodies. Most councils have sophisticated laboratories and experimental vineyards for testing clones, new varieties, rootstocks and methods.

A "DO" is a defined area of land within which grapes must be grown in order to qualify to use the name of the DO on the label. This is similar in principle to the systems of France and Italy except that, unlike those two countries, Spain does not have a "maximum yield" restriction (no maximum tonnes or hectoliters per hectare), at least at this stage. Spain is, generally speaking, a low-yielding wine nation when it comes to its finer wines.

The top tier, for which only Rioja and Priorato have so far qualified, adds *Calificada* to the DO, which is then shortened to DOCa. The similarity to DOCG in Italy is obvious. Spain is also a region working well and producing consistent quality; wineries have agreed on their rules and are doing the job responsibly with checks and audits.

Denominación de Origen de Pagos Vitícolos Determinados (DO de PVD)

DO de PVD is like the DO and DOCa classifications, but it was created for single estates "in a gesture that guarantees their complexity and special characters." So far, just two estates have been recognized in this way. Their wines are externally audited just like regional DOs.

Vino de la Tierra (VdlT)

Country wine, the equivalent of French *Vin de Pays*, VdlT is the step between *Vino de Mesa* (table wine) and DO wine. This classification requires wines using regional names to conform to local practices and grape varieties, but it does not impose the stringent requirements of a DO.

Vino de Mesa (VdM)

Table wine for which no vintage date or place of origin is required to be shown on the label. The VdM classification is for wine made from unclassified vineyards and a small number of other wines that have not been able to comply with local rules for the DO in which they were produced. These latter wines may be quite expensive, perhaps using "new" grape varieties or methods outside the norm.

Wine Terms

Airén	Grape variety used almost entirely in Spain; Airén is the most planted grape in the world.
Anejo	Aged.
Bodega	Cellar where wine is made and from which it is sold.
Casa	House.
Cavista	Underground cellar, especially for maturing sparkling wine.
Cencibel	Name used in southern Spain for the Tempranillo grape.
Cepa	Vine name, grape variety.
Collita	Harvest or vintage in Catalan.
Cosecha	The year of harvest, the vintage.
Crianza	Wine with a minimum of six months in *barriques* and matured further before release, usually for two years, but winemakers may exceed this. Reds often spend a minimum of one year in *barriques* and one year in the bottle, and are not released before their third year. Some DOs specify longer than six months and sometimes larger vessels than *barriques*. In essence, the term *crianza* lies between no status (sometimes termed *joven*, young) and *reserva* status. *Crianza* wines are not generally expensive but have had some development before release to ensure drinkability.
De licor	Liquor – strong, usually distilled wine.
Dolce	Sweet.
Garancha	Grenache (grape).
Godello	Verdelho (grape).
Gran Reserva	Red wine from a highly-rated vintage, which has had at least two years in oak and three more years in tank or bottle, and is not released before the sixth year after harvest. White *gran reserva*, from a highly-rated vintage, must have at least six months in the cask, a minimum of four years in cask and bottle, and is not released before the fifth year after harvest.
Joven	Young, as in *vino joven*. Wine for drinking young and fresh.

Macabeo	Alternative name for Viura (grape).
Mazuela	Spanish name for Carignan (grape).
Monastrell	Spanish name for Mourvèdre (grape).
Negre	Red (wine) in Catalan.
Rancio	Rancid (as in rancid butter), where the various methods of heating and/or storing wine give a particular oxidized character with a distinctive smell.
Reserva	Reserve; red *reserva* must have at least one year in the cask, sometimes two, and is not released until at least the fourth year after harvest; white *reserva* requires six months in the cask, and is not released before the third year after harvest.
Ribeiro	Riverbank or riverside.
Roble, poure	Oak.
Rosado	Rosé (wine).
Seco, seca	Dry.
Tinto	Red (wine).
Valle	Valley.
Vendimia	Harvest or vintage.
Vidccpa	Vine.
Vinedo	Vineyard.
Vino joven	Young wine, usually with no oak treatment, for drinking young and fresh.
Viura	Spanish name for Macabeo (grape).

Appellations of Spain

Abona
Region: Canary Islands
DO
Min alc, red 11.5%, rosé 11%, white 10.5%, *dulce clasico* 15%, *de licor* (min 55 g/L sugar) 15%.
Grapes: Red, Listán Negro, Negramoll, Moscatel Negro, Bastardo Negro, Malvasia, Tintilla, Vijariego. White, Bermejuela, Malvasia, Mou.

DO on Tenerife Island, Europe's highest delimited vineyard at 5,250 feet (1,600 m) above sea level. Generally plain.

Alella
Region: Catalonia
DO
Min alc, red, rosé and white 11.5%.
Grapes: Red, Tempranillo, Grenache, Pansa Rosada. White, Pansa Blanca, Grenache Blanc.

DO of about 1,480 acres (600 ha) near Barcelona, the city suburbs claiming some of the vineyards. The biggest volume wine is the white; Chardonnay is being experimented with.

Alicante
Region: Valencia
DO
Min alc, red and rosé 12%, white 11%.
Grapes: Red, Bobal, Cabernet Sauvignon, Grenache, Mourvèdre, Merlot, Tempranillo, Pinot Noir. White, Airén, Chardonnay, Merseguera, Muscat of Alexandria, Macabeo, Planta Fina.
Fondillón: Min alc 15%, Mourvèdre grape, min age 8 years in the cask.

Alicante is a DO with a decent-sized vineyard, 32,120 acres (13,000 ha), and lots of good honest wine. Its speciality is Fondillón, a long-aged, high-alcohol Mourvèdre. The country is dry, and yields are low (about 25 hl/ha).

Almansa
Region: Castilla-La Mancha
DO
Min alc, red 12%, rosé 12.5%, white 11.5%.
Grapes: Red, Grenache, Mourvèdre. White, Merseguera.

An elevated DO in the heartland of Spain, with an altitude range of 1,640–3,940 feet (500–1,200 m) and covering 18,780 acres (7,600 ha). Red predominates and this is sold mainly for drinking young, but there's evolution happening here.

Ampurdan-Costa Brava
Region: Catalonia
DO
Min alc, red, rosé and white 11.5%.

Grapes: Red, Grenache, Carignan. White, Macabeo, Pansa Blanca.

Situated on the far top-right edge of Spain around the city of Perelada, with the Pyrénées to the north and the Mediterranean on the east. Lots of rosé, but red is growing in importance.

Bierzo   **Region: Castilla y Léon**
DO
Min alc, red and rosé 11%, white 10%.
Grapes: Red, Grenache, Mencia. White, Dona Blanca, Godello, Malvasia, Palomino.

Neighbor of Valdeorras to the west, an 8,400-acre (3,400-ha) DO nicely elevated at 1,640–2,300 feet (500–700 m) with great views across the Sil River. Cool nights and warm days produce a robust, hearty red, still evolving as part of the "new Spanish wines."

Binissalem-Mallorca   **Region: Balearic Islands**
DO
Min alc, red 11.5%, rosé 11%, white 10.5%.
Grapes: Red, Manto Negro min 50%, Mourvèdre, Tempranillo, Callet, Cabernet Sauvignon. White, Moll min 70%, Muscat, Parellada, Macabeo, Chardonnay.

Once with tens of thousands of hectares of vineyards, Majorca (Mallorca locally), the famous island to the east of Spain in the Mediterranean, now has less than a tenth of its original plantings, and even then less than 740 acres (300 ha) qualify for the DO Binissalem. The lovely climate suits grapes as well as holiday-makers.

Bullas   **Region: Murcia**
DO
Min alc, red 12%, rosé 11%, white 10%.
Grapes: Red, Mourvèdre, Tempranillo. White, Macabeo, Airén.

An elevation of 2,000–2,600 feet (600–800 m) doesn't seem unusual for a DO in Spain. The Mourvèdre (known locally as Monastrell) has the biggest impact in this DO of some 6,425 acres (2,600 ha), and it provides a fruity, young and vibrant style.

Calatayud   **Region: Aragón**
DO
Min alc, red 11%, rosé 12%, white 10.5%.
Grapes: Red, Grenache, Carignan, Tempranillo, Mourvèdre. White, Macabeo, Malvasia, Muscat, Grenache Blanc.

Elevated vineyards up to 2,950 feet (900 m) in a DO of some capacity, covering 18,000 acres (7,300 ha). Still experimenting with styles, including

Cabernet Sauvignon and Chardonnay. Growers are required to supply one of nine cooperatives locally. Some Syrah is grown, and is looking good but not allowed DO status.

Campo de Borja   Region: Aragón
DO
Min alc, red 12%, rosé 11%, white 10.5%.
Grapes: Red, Grenache, Cabernet Sauvignon, Carignan, Tempranillo.
White, Muscat, Macabeo.

On the south side of the Ebro River in central Spain, this DO of 17,300 acres (7,000 ha) is another decent-sized vineyard region. It has hot, dry summers and the sandy soil over limestone found in many Spanish vineyard areas. Best known for red.

Cariñena   Region: Aragón
DO
Min alc, red 12%, rosé and white 11%, *rancios* 15%, *de licor* 15%.
Grapes: Red, Grenache, Carignan (Mazuela), Tempranillo, Juan Ibanez, Mourvèdre, Cabernet Sauvignon. White, Macabeo, Grenache Blanc, Parellada, Muscat.

Large DO of more than 49,400 acres (20,000 ha), built around Carignan grapes but now diversifying and reestablishing its style. Lots sold as young-drinking red.

Cava   Several separate regions
DO
Min alc, red, rosé and white 9.5%. Min age on lees nine months; Reserva, "when the wine is ready" (usually longer than nine months); Gran Reserva, 30 months.
Grapes: Red, Grenache, Mourvèdre. Rosé, Pinot Noir, Trepat. White, Macabeo, Xarel-lo, Parellada, Chardonnay, Subirat, Malvasia Riojana.
Brut Nature: No sweetness in the dosage; more of the same wine from another bottle is used to top-up after disgorgement.

In EU terms, Cava is a quality sparkling wine produced in a specified region. That region encompasses 159 villages, most of them in the Penedès and other parts of Catalonia. Cava is also made in some wineries in La Rioja, Aragón, the Basque Country, Valencia and Extremadura; in total about 79,000 acres (32,000 ha), though this is an approximation because of the spread and variables of the DO. Cava is a style, a traditional-method wine, sold in the bottle in which the second ferment occurred.

Chacolí de Bizkaia (Bizkaiko-Txakolina)   Region: País Vasco
DO
Min alc, red, rosé and white 9.5%.

Grapes: Red, Ondarrabi Beltza. White, Folle Blanche, Ondarrabi Zuri.

Tiny DO, less than 250 acres (100 ha), in northern Spain. Faces more towards the south and the sun than Chacolí de Guetaria (*refer* next entry), but is still a little vintage-variable. Tourists like to try the small quantities available.

Chacolí de Guetaria (Getariako-Txakolina) DO
Region: País Vasco

Min alc, red, rosé and white 9.5%.

Grapes: Red, Ondarrabi Beltza. White, Ondarrabi Zuri.

DO in northern Spain of 435 acres (175 ha) known for its white wine, Chacolí (Txakolina in Basque, the regional language). A vintage-variable region facing north, the wrong way for best sun use. Works well in the right years.

Cigales DO
Region: Castilla y Léon

Min alc, red 12%; for white see individual wines below.

Grapes: Red, Grenache and Tempranillo min 85%. White, Albillo, Verdelho, Macabeo (known locally as Viura).

Cigales Nuevo: Tempranillo min 60%, white varieties min 20%; min alc 10.5%.

Cigales: Tempranillo min 60%; white varieties min 20%; min alc 11%.

Best known for rosé but red is on the rise. Cigales DO has 7,410 acres (3,000 ha) of vineyard at 2,625 feet (800 m) above sea-level.

Conca de Barberà DO
Region: Catalonia

Min alc, red 10.5%, rosé 10%, white 10%, varietal Parellada 10%, sparkling 10.8%.

Grapes: Red, Grenache, Trepat, Tempranillo, Cabernet Sauvignon, Pinot Noir. White, Macabeo, Parellada, Chardonnay.

With almost 22,240 acres (9,000 ha) of vineyard, this DO is far from tiny. A DO under change, with new varieties bringing more wine styles able to stand on their own. Much has been used for *cava*.

Condado de Huelva DO
Region: Andalucía

White only, min alc 11%, Condado Palido 15–17%, Condado Viejo 15–23%.

Grapes: Garrido Fino, Muscat, Palomino, Zalema.

A DO that historically supplied the sherry region around the coast, but this is no longer allowed. With 14,800 acres (6,000 ha) under vine, the region provides some white table wine (*joven*), and a range of fortified and *rancio* styles.

Costers del Segre
Region: Catalonia
DO
Min alc, red, rosé and white 9.5%, *espumoso* 10.8%, Vino de Aguja 9%.
Grapes: Red, Cabernet Sauvignon, Grenache, Carignan, Merlot,
Mourvèdre, Tempranillo, Trepat. White, Chardonnay, Grenache Blanc,
Macabeo, Parellada.

Well regarded DO of almost 9,880 acres (4,000 ha) in four zones around
Lerida on the Segre River.

Dominio de Valdepusa
Region: Toledo
DO de PVD
Min alc, red only, 13.5%.
Grapes and max yield: Syrah 13 tonnes/ha, Cabernet Sauvignon
10 tonnes/ha, Petit Verdot 12 tonnes/ha, Merlot.

One of just two single-estate DO de PVDs (*Denominación de Origen de Pagos
Vitícolos Determinados*) to date, the other is Finca Elez. An estate of 105 acres
(42 ha), Dominio de Valdepusa sells varietal wines, including their flagship
Emeritus, a blend of varieties.

El Hierro
Region: Canary Islands
DO
Min alc, red 12%, rosé 10.5%, white 11%, *dulce clasico* 14%.
Grapes: Red, Bastardo Negro, Listán Negro, Malvasia Rosada, Negramoll,
Tintilla, Vijariego Negro. White, Albillo, Bastardo Blanco, Bermejuela.

Down off the coast of Africa, this DO covers the whole of the El Hierro island,
with about 1,235 acres (500 ha) under vine. Quite a hilly region and difficult
to cultivate because mechanization is almost impossible.

Finca Elez
Region: Albacete
DO de PVD
Min alc, red 12.5%, white 12%.
Grapes: Red, Cabernet Sauvignon, Merlot, Tempranillo, Syrah. White,
Chardonnay.

One of just two single-estate DO de PVDs (*Denominación de Origen de Pagos
Vitícolos Determinados*) to date, the other is Dominio de Valdepusa. Finca Elez
is an 85-acre (35-ha) estate at about 3,100 feet (950 m) towards the south
of Spain. Wines are labeled in large print as Manuel Manzaneque, the name
of the owner, and sold both as varietal wines and blends.

Jerez-Xérès-Sherry y Manzanilla-Sanlúcar
Region: Southeast Spain
de Barrameda
DO
Min alc, *fino* 15–18%, *amontillado* 16–22%, *oloroso* 17–22%, *palo cortado*
and *raya* 17–22%, *manzanilla* 15–19%.

Grapes: Palomino de Jerez, Palomino Fino, Pedro Ximénez, Muscat of Alexandria.

VOS or VORS: Rare and small quantity sherry, depicted by a special seal on the bottle. Strictly controlled and no more than one-third of stock allowed to be sold to ensure continuity. Min age three years before release, but usually much older.

Fino: Straw or golden-colored, a sharp but delicate almond-like aroma, dry and light to the palate, with aging under the *velo de flor*.

Manzanilla: Straw-colored with sharp aroma, dry and light to the palate, with aging under the *velo de flor* exclusively in wine cellars located in Sanlúcar de Barrameda.

Amontillado: Amber-colored, with a sharp but subtle hazelnut-like aroma. Smooth and light to the palate. Alcohol content around 17.5%.

Oloroso: Initially dry, amber-to-mahogany colored, with a pronounced aroma as its name, *oloroso* (fragrant), would indicate. Nutty, with a full body.

Palo Cortado: Wine of a bright-mahogany color with an almond-like aroma and dry palate; balanced, elegant and very persistent. It combines the smooth, delicate and sharp characteristics of Amontillado and the thick and true wine qualities of *oloroso*.

Pale Cream: A smooth wine, with a pale color, and a sharp but delicate sweet aroma.

Cream: A sweet, dark-colored wine, made from *oloroso*. It has a sharp but subtle aroma and a full body.

Pedro Ximénez: A dark-mahogany colored wine, with deep raisiny aromas. Smooth and sweet in the mouth. Full, vigorous and perfectly balanced. Made from Pedro Ximénez grapes that have been set out in the sun for drying.

Sherry territory covers 27,180 acres (11,000 ha) on Spain's south coast overlooking the Mediterranean. Qualifying wines (in terms of area, grape varieties and production) may carry the Jerez-Xérès-Sherry name, which is written the same way in Spanish, French and English. Wines may carry the term "Manzanilla-Sanlúcar de Barrameda" only if they were actually *aged* in the Sanlúcar de Barrameda area, although grapes can be grown anywhere in sherry territory. But some Manzanilla producers stick to the standard "Jerez-Xérès-Sherry" term, mostly for simplicity.

Jumilla   ***Region: Murcia and Albacete provinces***
DO
Min alc, red 12%, rosé 11.5%, white 11%.
Grapes: Red, Mourvèdre, Cabernet Sauvignon, Tempranillo, Grenache, Merlot. White, Airén, Macabeo, Pedro Ximénez

Jumilla Monastrell or Jumilla Seleccion: Mourvèdre (known locally as Monastrell) min 85%, with up to 15% of the red grapes listed; min alc, red 12.5%, rosé 12%.

An arid DO of some size, about 106,250 acres (43,000 ha). Its wine style is still evolving, as part of the changes taking place in the Spanish wine industry, and is yet to be taken seriously, although the indications are there for tasty, well-priced wine. Some carbonic maceration and double-skinning; but the push towards quality and a stronger image drives the evolution.

La Mancha   *Region: Castilla-La Mancha*
DO
Min alc, red 11%, rosé and white 10%, sparkling 10.5%.
Grapes: Red, Tempranillo (known locally as Cencibel), Cabernet Sauvignon, Grenache, Merlot, Moravia. White, Airén, Macabeo, Pardilla.

Large DO of 444,800 acres (180,000 ha). More than double that is planted in the area but the rest does not qualify for the DO. In fact not all the qualifying 444,800 acres are utilized for DO wine either.

This is a vast area with some elevation, featuring Airén, the world's most-planted grape variety. Some red from Tempranillo grapes is developing a decent reputation.

La Palma   *Region: Canary Islands*
DO
Min alc, red 12%, rosé and white 11%.
Grapes: Red, Negramoll, Almuneco, Bastardo Negro, Malvasia Rosada, Moscatel Negro, Tintilla. White, Malvasia, Gual, Verdelho Bastardo Blanco, Bermejuela, Albillo, Burra Blanca, Forestera Blanca, Listán Blanco, Moscatel, Pedro Ximénez, Sabro, Torrontés.

This DO covers the whole of "La Isla Bonita" and has magnificent views, with the Atlantic as a backdrop. About 1,480 acres (600 ha) under qualifying vineyards, producing a mixed bag of young-drinking wines grown on volcanic soil.

Lanzarote   *Region: Canary Islands*
DO
Min alc, rosé 11%, white 10.5%, sparkling red 11%.
Grapes: Red, Listán Negro, Negramoll. White, Malvasia, Burrablanca, Breval, Diego, Listán Bianca, Moscatel, Pedro Ximénez.

A DO covering the whole of Lanzarote Island where 4,940 acres (2,000 ha) are under vine. As a result of a volcanic eruption in 1820, the soil is black lava and ash, with some richer, fertile soil underneath. No phylloxera here, and vines are not grafted. About 80 percent of plantings are in Malvasia grapes.

Málaga
Region: Andalucía
DO
Min alc, 15%–23%.
Grapes: Pedro Ximénez, Moscatel.

A DO in the southeast of Spain, 2,225 acres (900 ha) of gravelly, chalky vineyards in the hills behind the city of Málaga where the wines must be made. Most grapes are dried further in the sun after picking, before making a fairly sweet fortified wine, although a little drier style is also made.

Manchuela
Region: Castilla-La Mancha
DO
Min alc, red 12%, white 11%.
Grapes: Red, Bobal, Tempranillo, Cabernet Sauvignon, Grenache, Merlot, Syrah, Mourvèdre, Moravia. White, Albillo, Macabeo, Chardonnay, Sauvignon Blanc.

A new (2000) DO of almost 4,940 acres (2,000 ha) adjacent to both La Mancha DO and Utiel-Requena DO. A brave new start for a long-established wine area on the south-central plateau, now seeking its own recognition.

Mentrida
Region: Castilla-La Mancha
DO
Min alc, red 12%, rosé 11.5%.
Grapes: Grenache, Tinto Bastio, Tempranillo.

On almost barren land with low-yielding vines subject to severe drought at times, this DO in central Spain of more than 32,125 acres (13,000 ha) grows only red grapes. Some investment is being made in better equipment and improving on the slightly oxidized style the region is known for.

Mondejar
Region: Castilla-La Mancha
DO
Min alc, red and rosé 11%, white 10%.
Grapes: Red, Tempranillo, Cabernet Sauvignon. White, Malvar, Macabeo, Torrontés.

A DO of 11,120 acres (4,500 ha) in Central Spain regarded as producing good average wines, mainly red.

Monterrei
Region: Galicia
DO
Min alc, red 10%, white 10%.
Grapes: Red, Gran Negro, Grenache, Mencia, Merenzao (also known locally as Bastardo and Maria Ardona). White, Dona Blanca, Godello, Treixadura, Palomino.
Superior: Red from Mencia and Merenzao only, min alc 10.5%. White contains no Palomino, min alc 11%.

DO on the northern Portuguese border. There are 6,550 acres (2,650 ha) under vine but not a lot of bottled wine at this stage. Some Portuguese grapes play their part.

Montilla-Moriles
Region: Andalucía
DO
Min alc, white 10–12%, *fino* 15–17.5%, *amontillado* 16–22%, *oloroso* 16–20%, *palo cortado* 16–18%, *raya* 16–20%, *pedro ximénez* and Moscatel min 15%.
Grapes: Airén, Baladi, Moscatel, Pedro Ximénez, Torrontés.

In the south of Spain, near Málaga, this is a large DO of more than 24,700 acres (10,000 ha). The Pedro Ximénez grape predominates, as does *solera* maturation. But some light white (*joven*) is also made. The fully fortified wines need to be sold as "liqueur wines" in the U.K. to avoid being mistaken for sherry. Elsewhere, they are sold as *fino, oloroso*, and so on. A range of aperitif and dessert styles, sold as dry, medium, pale cream and cream wines below 15% alcohol, are also popular.

Montsant
Region: Catalonia
DO
Min alc, red 12%, white 11.5%.
Grapes: Red, Grenache, Carignan, Cabernet Sauvignon, Syrah, Merlot. White, Grenache Blanc.

A new (2001) DO taking part of Priorato territory (including Falset) with different, sandy soil giving it its own status. Covers about 4,200 acres (1,700 ha) including the mountain that gives this DO its name. Best known for robust, big-bouquet reds that are fragrant, concentrated, alcoholic and mouth-filling.

Navarra
Region: Navarra
DO
Min alc, red, rosé and white 10%, Moscatel *licor* 15%.
Grapes: Red, Cabernet Sauvignon, Grenache, Graciano, Merlot, Carignan, Tempranillo. White, Grenache Blanc, Chardonnay, Malvasia, Moscatel, Macabeo (Viura).

Important northern Spain DO near the Pyrénées with five subregions: Ribera Alta, Ribera Baja, Valdizarbe, Baja Montana, Tierra de Estella, all of which, some say, deserve their own DO. Navarra has 33,360 acres (13,500 ha) under vine. This is a major wine region with about 90 percent red grapes, although a lot of rosé is made here.

Penedès
Region: Catalonia
DO
Min alc, red and rosé 10%, white 9%, sparkling 10.8%.
Grapes: Red, Cabernet Sauvignon, Grenache, Carignan (known locally as

Mazuela), Mourvèdre, Samso, Ull de Liebre. White, Macabeo, Parellada, Xarel-lo.

A large and famous DO of 61,780 acres (25,000 ha), with a wide spectrum of wines and styles through red, rosé and white. Some strong players have led the way with wine of prestige, and been followed by winemakers determined to make the Penedès name famous.

Pla de Bages
Region: Catalonia
DO
Min alc, red 11.5%, rosé 10.5%, white 10%.
Grapes: Red, Cabernet Sauvignon, Grenache, Merlot, Sumoll, Ull de Liebre. White, Chardonnay, Macabeo, Parellada, Picapoll.

Fairly small DO for Spain, about 1,360 acres (550 ha), still developing its own image and reputation.

Pla i Llevant
Region: Marjorca
DO
Min alc, red 12%, white 11.5%.
Grapes: Red, Callet, Fogoneu, Tempranillo, Manto Negro, Mourvèdre, Merlot, Cabernet Sauvignon. White, Macabeo, Parellada, Chardonnay, Moscatel, Prensal Blanc.

A small, fairly recent DO of about 520 acres (210 ha), this is the second DO on the island of Marjorca in the Balearic Islands and is seeking to establish its own identity.

Priorato
Region: Catalonia
DOCa
Min alc, red, rosé and white 13.75%, generoso (fortified) 14–18%, rancio 14–20%.
Grapes: Red, Grenache, Carignan, Cabernet Sauvignon, Merlot, Syrah. White, Grenache Blanc, Macabeo, Pedro Ximénez, Chardonnay.

A mountainous area of low rainfall, the dry conditions keep the crops of this 4,450-acre (1,800-ha) DOCa at a low-yielding level, although the Siurana River, a tributary of the Ebro River, aids irrigation. Mostly red wine is produced here, and there is some ongoing development with Cabernet Sauvignon. Priorato is a hot star on the rise.

Rías Baixas
Region: Galicia
DO
Red, min alc 10%, min age three years in oak. White, Albariño 11.3%, other white 11%.
Grapes: Red, Caino Tinto, Souson, Espedeiro, Loureira Tinta, Brancellao, Mencia. White, Albariño, Loureira Blanca, Treixadura, Caino Blanco, Torrontés, Godello.

Rías Baixas is in top-left corner of Spain on the coast, a damp corner getting more rain than most of Spain, but helped by easy-draining soil. A 4,450-acre (1,800-ha) DO of mainly white, which has evolved to pair with the local fish. A sought-after wine, it is made predominantly from the Albariño grape. A wine labeled "Albariño" must be made 100 percent from the grape. *Rías* translates to "estuaries," and the area has some beautiful fjords from the Atlantic with mountainous country above.

Ribera del Duero   *Region: Castilla y Léon*
DO
Min alc, red 11.5%, rosé 11%.
Grapes: Tinta del Pais, Garancha Tinta, Cabernet Sauvignon, Malbec, Merlot.

Quite a large DO of more than 27,180 acres (11,000 ha) of elevated terrain 1,640–2,620 feet (500–800 m) above sea-level. Has gained a strong reputation over the past decade and prices have risen in line with the image. The Duero River runs into Portugal and on to the sea, creating the valley where so much port is made. On the Spanish side, helped by Vega Sicilia's strong image over 20 years, the whole Ribera del Duero DO has now been able to ride the wave; though a few wines have missed the boat, at their peril. The best are tasty, alive, long-lived, and getting expensive. Much still to evolve and settle.

Ribera del Guadiana   *Region: Extremadura*
DO
Min alc, red 11%, white and rosé 10%.
Grapes: Red, Bobal, Cabernet Sauvignon, Garancha Tinta, Graciano, Carignan, Merlot, Mourvèdre, Syrah, Tempranillo, Tinto Fino. White, Alarijen, Borba, Cayetana Blanca, Chardonnay, Chelva (Montua), Eva (Beba de Los Santos), Malvar, Parellada, Pedro Ximénez, Verdelho, Macabeo (known locally as Viura).

There are six important zones here, each with its own strengths and preferred grapes from the above lengthy list. The zones are Ribera Alta, Tierra de Barros, Matanegra, Ribera Baja, Montánchez and Cañamero.

Ribera del Jucar   *Region: Castilla-La Mancha*
DO
Min alc, red only, 12.5%.
Grapes: Tempranillo, Cabernet Sauvignon, Merlot, Syrah and Bobal. Max yield is 63–70 hl/ha, depending on variety.

Almost 22,240 acres (9,000 ha) of rocky, clay soil on the eastern side of La Mancha, beside the Jucar River. A new (2003) DO containing six cooperatives and just a handful of individual wineries, Ribera del Jucar is said to provide easy drinking but has full-flavored reds to rival Australia.

Ribeira Sacra   **Region: Galicia**
DO
Min alc, red and white from one variety 11%, other red and white 10%.
Grapes: Red, Brancellao, Grenache, Mencia, Merenzao, Mouraton
(Negreda). White, Albariño, Dona Blanca, Godello, Loureira, Palomino,
Torrontés, Treixadura.

This DO has an emphasis on red wine, rare in Galicia. Situated in the top-left
corner of Spain, this is a DO of 2,965 acres (1,200 ha) that doesn't reach
the Atlantic coast, so far inland it shares a border with Portugal. Crisp whites
complement fruity, delicate reds.

Ribeiro   **Region: Galicia**
DO
Min alc, red and white 9%.
Grapes: Red, Brancellao, Caino, Ferron, Garancha Tinta, Mencia, Souson,
Tempranillo. White, Albariño, Albilla, Godello, Palomino, Loureira,
Macabeo, Torrontés, Treixadura.

This DO on the Mino River and its tributaries is going through some change.
New styles are emerging from replanted vineyards.

Rioja   **Region: La Rioja**
DOCa
Min alc, red 11%, white and rosé 10.5%; Rioja Alta red 11.5%, rosé 11%,
white 10.5%; Rioja Baja red 12%, rosé 11.5%, white 11%. Reserva and
Gran Reserva red 12%, rosé and white 11%.
Grapes: Red, Granacha, Graciano, Carignan, Tempranillo, Cabernet
Sauvignon. White, Granacha Blanca, Malvasia Riojana, Macabeo (known
locally as Viura).
Joven: Unaged wines, often without oak, sold in their second year.
Crianza: Min age one year in *barriques*, plus some bottle age, release not
before the third year.
Reserva: Min age one year in *barriques*, plus bottle age, release not before
the fourth year.
Gran Reserva: Min age two years in *barriques* and three years in the bottle,
release not for at least five years.

With 118,600 acres (48,000 ha) under vine (about 60% Tempranillo,) this
DO plays a vitally important part in Spanish wine development. The higher
vineyards are subzoned Rioja Alta, giving way to Rioja Alavesa and down to
Rioja Baja, the three zones all with their own qualities and contributions. The
whole territory has developed magnificently over the past two decades and
is a credit to Spain. Its recognition raised it to the status of DOCa, the first
DO in Spain to attain this level. Quality control, consistency, self-policing
and high standards have much to do with this, along with settled management systems and higher grape prices.

Rueda   Region: Castilla y Léon
DO
Min alc, white only 11%, Superior (min 85% Verdelho) 11.5%, sparkling
11.5%, Palido Rueda 15%, Dorado Rueda 15%.
Grapes: Verdelho, Sauvignon Blanc, Palomino, Macabeo (known locally as
Viura).

A DO of different, iron-rich soils, extremes in climate from searingly hot summers to bitterly cold winters, and a low rainfall. Almost 14,820 acres (6,000
ha) under vine. Considered best as a light, fruity white wine, but other styles
are made.

Sherry   Region: Southeast Spain
Refer **Jerez-Xérès-Sherry y Manzanilla-Sanlúcar de Barrameda**

Somontano   Region: Aragón
DO
Min alc, red 11.5%, rosé 11%, white 10%.
Grapes: Red, Cabernet Sauvignon, Grenache, Moristel, Parellada,
Tempranillo. White, Alcanon, Chardonnay, Grenache Blanc, Macabeo.

Literally "under the mountains," Somontano DO is in the foothills of the
Pyrénées and is building an image that surpasses its older reputation of rustic, loose wines.

Tacoronte-Acentejo   Region: Canary Islands
DO
Min alc, red 12%, rosé 10.5%, white *joven* 10%, white *macerado tradicional*
12%.
Grapes: Red, Listán Negro, Negramoll. White, Listán Blanca, Gual,
Verdelho, Malvasia, Moscatel, Vijariego.

DO on the north coast of Tenerife, with vineyards of mixed elevation up the
sides of the volcano, as high as 2,620 feet (800 m). The altitude is perhaps
balanced by the latitude of the DO, which is one of the closest to the equa-
tor. About 2,470 acres (1,000 ha) are under vine.

Tarragona   Region: Catalonia
DO
Two subzones, Tarragona Campo and Falset, each with different blends
and requirements.
Tarragona Campo: Red and rosé, Grenache, Tempranillo; min alc 11%.
White, Grenache Blanc, Macabeo, Parellada, Xarel-lo; min alc 11%.
Falset: (Situated near the town of this name) Reds only, Grenache,
Carignan; min alc 13%, *clasico* 13.5%, *rancio* 14%.

Another big Spanish DO of more than 24,700 acres (10,000 ha) producing a
mixed range of wine from "poor man's port" and communion wine through

to pleasant white wine. A lot of wine in the area is sold to *cava* houses, which reduces the volume in the Tarragona DO. Falset, an important subzone, was included in the new Montsant DO from 2001.

Terra Alta   *Region: Catalonia*
DO
Min alc, red and rosé 12%, white 12.5%.
Grapes: Red, Carignan, Grenache. White, Grenache Blanc, Muscat.

"Terra Alta" means high lands, and these vineyards are 1,310 feet (400 m) up. Quite a large and mixed DO of 27,170 acres (11,000 ha) on the south of the Ebro River. This is a region struggling for identity, but with adaptation to the regional *terroir*, it could have some strong potential.

Toro   *Region: Castilla y León*
DO
Min alc, red 12.5%, rosé and white 11%, *rancio* up to 15%.
Grapes: Red, Tempranillo (known locally as Tinto de Toro), Grenache. White, Malvasia, Verdelho.

Very hot summer temperatures and little rainfall, and an altitude of 1,970–2,460 feet (600–750 m), create quite severe conditions for this 7,410-acre (3,000-ha) DO around the town of the same name. At their best, the reds are strong, robust and oak-matured with longevity, sometimes with very high alcohol. Considered a rising star.

Utiel-Requena   *Region: Valencia*
DO
Min alc, red, rosé and white 10%, sparkling 11%, sparkling aromatics 7%, de Aguja 10%. Superior from 100%, Muscat or Bobal 10.5%, Tinto from Grenache and Tempranillo 11.5%.
Grapes: Red, Bobal, Cabernet Sauvignon, Grenache, Merlot, Tempranillo, White, Chardonnay, Macabeo, Merseguera, Planta Nova.

Large DO of 98,800 acres (40,000 ha) on the plateau above and to the west of the city of Valencia. Three-quarters of the vineyards are planted with Bobal, and Grenache produces lots of dry, full and fruity rosé as well as some hearty reds. White wine production is just 5 percent.

Valdeorras   *Region: Galicia*
DO
Min alc, red, rosé and white 9%, *embotellado* 10%.
Grapes: Red, Grenache (known locally as Alicante), Mencia, Gran Negro, Maria Ardona, Merenzao. White, Verdelho, Palomino, Dona Blanca.

A DO tucked up north of Portugal, 93 miles (150 km) inland from the Atlantic, this has about 3,700 acres (1,500 ha) of vineyard. Hot summers can produce fairly intense, dark reds from Grenache.

Valdepenas   **Region: Southeast Spain**
DO
Min alc, red 11%, rosé 10.5%, white 10%.
Grapes: Red, Tempranillo, Cabernet Sauvignon, Grenache. White, Airén, Macabeo.

"Valley of the stones" is in the foothills of the Sierra Morena. Soft, red soil and lots of stones help both heat and irrigation. This is a big DO, covering 74,130 acres (30,000 ha), which has some light, easy wines and some more serious Reserva and Gran Reserva. "The sleeping beauty is waking up," Jose Ramón Martinez wrote in 1998 in *Spain Gourmet Tour* magazine. Martinez was referring to the change from contentment with simple wines sold in bulk or demi-johns towards "what may be the region's last chance to embrace modernity."

Valencia   **Region: Valencia**
DO
Min alc, red and rosé 10.5%, white 10%, *rancio* and *licor* 15%, sparklings 11%, Muscat 10%, *licor* Muscat 15%.
Grapes: Red, Grenache, Mourvèdre, Tempranillo, Tintorera, Bodal, Cabernet Sauvignon, Forcallat. White, Macabeo, Malvasia, Merseguera, Muscat of Alexandria, Pedro Ximénez, Planta Fina de Pedralba, Planta Nova, Tortosi, Verdil.

An area of about 39,500 acres (16,000 ha) with fruity red and easy drinking white, both considered DYA (drink youngest available). However, in a region this large, there will be many variations on the theme, especially with the recent emphasis on development in wine quality.

Valle de Guimar   **Region: Canary Islands**
DO
Min alc, red 11.5%, rosé 10.5%, white 10%, *dulce clasico* and *malvasía de licor* 15%.
Grapes: Red, Listán Negro, Malvasia, Moscatel Negro, Negramoll, Bastardo Negro, Vijariego Negro. White, Gual, Malvasia, Verdelho, Listán Blanco, Muscat, Vijariego.

Area to the south of Tenerife, mostly small winemakers making predominantly white wine.

Valle de la Orotava   **Region: Canary Islands**
DO
Min alc, red 11.5%, white and rosé 11%, *dulce clasico* and *de licor* 15%.
Grapes: Red, Listán Negro, Malvasia Rosada, Negramoll, Tintilla, Vijariego Negra. White, Gual, Malvasia, Verdelho, Vijariego, Pedro Ximénez, Torrontés, Bastardo Blanco, Forestera Blanca, Listán Blanco, Marmajuelo, Moscatel, Pedro Ximénez, Torrontés.

In northwest Tenerife this is a well-respected DO of about 2,470 acres (1,000 ha), in a lovely valley. Red seems to do well, especially while young.

Vinos de Madrid   **Region: Central Spain**
DO
There are three subzones in this DO, Arganda, Navalcarnero and San Martin de Valdeglesias, each with different requirements:
Arganda: min alc, red 11.5%, white 10%, rosé 11%, sparkling 11.5%.
Navalcarnero: min alc, red 12%, white 11%, rosé 11.5%, sparkling 11.5%.
San Martin de Valdeglesias: min alc, red 12%, white 11%, rosé 11.5%, sparkling 11.5%.
Grapes: Red, Grenache, Tinto Fino, Cabernet Sauvignon, Merlot, Tempranillo. White, Albillo, Malvar, Airén, Parellada, Torrontés, Viura.

Vineyards on the south side of Madrid form the basis of this DO, but no great quantity is produced. Most of the wine it produces is enjoyed in the city, but with 32,000 acres (13,000 ha), this is not a small region and evolution and development of quality is pushing out the sphere of interest. The three subregions are important to the local winemakers and drinkers. Freezing winters and scorching summers, the typical climate of central Spain, are tough on the vines, which are planted at an elevation of about 1,970–2,600 feet (600–800 m).

Ycoden-Daute-Isora   **Region: Canary Islands**
DO
Min alc, red 12%, rosé 11.5%, white 11%.
Grapes: Red, Listán Negro, Negramoll, Trousseau, Malvasia, Tintilla, Vijariego Negro. White, Gual, Malvasia, Verdelho, Bastardo Bianco, Bermejuela, Forestera, Listán Bianca, Muscat, Pedro Ximénez, Sabro, Torrontés, Vijariego.

South of the islands of Madeira, at about 28 degrees north latitude, the Canary Islands lie just off the coast of Morocco. This DO of a little over 2,470 acres (1,000 ha) on Tenerife (an island with many fascinations apart from wine) may have a white wine strength, but opinions vary.

Yecla   **Region: Levante**
DO
Min alc, red 12%, white and rosé 11.5%.
Grapes: Red, Mourvèdre, Grenache. White, Merseguera, Verdil.

DO in southeast Spain near Jumilla and Alicante. Mourvèdre (locally known as Monastrell) substantially predominates and offers a robust red style.

CHAPTER 4

Portugal

Denominação de Origem Controlada (DOC)
Indicação de Proveniencia Regulamentada (IPR)
Vinho Regional (VR)
Vinho de Mesa (VdM)

Portugal is the fourth largest European country in vineyard area after Italy, France and Spain. Almost 4 percent of Portuguese land is under vine, about 600,000 acres (240,000 ha) – vineyards in Italy cover 3 percent of the country's land. Yet throughout the 1990s a lot of vineyards were pulled up, reducing Portugal's vineyard area by about one-quarter.

However, in terms of wine production by volume, Portugal drops to about number eight in the world because its yield – the number of tonnes per hectare that it produces – is among the lowest. Statistics show that Portugal averages just 21 hectoliters (555 gallons) of wine per hectare (2.5 acres) of vineyard. Compared with Bordeaux, where the best appellations have a theoretical maximum yield of more than twice that, Portugal's yields are indeed very low.

Portugal's Atlantic coast enjoys a maritime climate; but inland, through the hills towards the Spanish border, it gets hotter for longer periods. Southeastern areas have hot summers also, and little rainfall. The vine often struggles, yet can sometimes perform at its best. With better knowledge and investment in people and equipment, Portugal is making a new statement; currently this development is happening only in a few committed regions and by some committed people, but this seems poised to run on throughout the country, helped by the competitive needs of all wine-producing countries to survive in demanding international markets.

Portugal has a wide range of wines and styles: its port, for example, is as far away stylistically as we could imagine from the *vinho verde* produced in the neighboring region. Approximately 125,000 acres (50,600 hectares) of the Vinho Verde region produce almost 90 million gallons (340 million L) each year of crisp, bracing low-alcohol white wine, four times more wine than the whole of New Zealand produces. This quantity of white is surprising given that Portugal's wine production is 70 percent red!

But what is Portugal? The country that sent its explorers into the world has been described politically in the last decade as an unimportant nation at the edge of Europe. Yet in wine terms, Portugal has had a great decade, pushing up its styles, and taking its small yields and sometimes strong wines into the limelight. It may not have the prestige sought by some of the world's new wine markets, but it does have a heritage, marked by old vines and a certain individuality. Now a new spirit is taking hold in its people and winemakers. What has been pulled out is gone; what is left may be ready to be rediscovered.

In the wider wine evolution that has occurred in Europe recently, Portugal has had to keep up, make changes, make new investments in its wineries and consider marketing as a means of survival. Joining the European Union brought its own challenges and opportunities. Portugal already had a wine appellation system in place; but in 1988 the country established its quality regions, called *Denominação de Origem Controlada* (DOC), a system in line with the other EU wine countries. It has also installed a second level, *Indicação de Proveniencia Regulamentada* (IPR), not as simple table wine but as quality wine.

Portugal uses its own indigenous grape varieties and has imported relatively small proportions of "new" varieties like Chardonnay and Cabernet Sauvignon. It has not sent many of its own varieties out into the wider world either. The largest national producer, Sogrape, has put special effort into the indigenous Portuguese varieties, trying hard to build on their uniqueness rather than competing in a world full of Cabernet, Merlot and Chardonnay. Alongside the efforts of Sogrape there has been a small but gathering momentum from individual winemakers seeking to add their own dimension, partly by investment, which is certainly evident in wine quality. All this is having the required effect – Portugal is on the rise.

Thus Portuguese wine remains unique in the world. There is much to be enjoyed, and still much to be discovered; a new chapter is evolving after thousands of years of viticulture. As with Spain, Portugal will once again be famous for its wine.

Wine Classifications

Denominação de Origem Controlada (DOC)
The standard appellation of Portugal, a DOC is a defined area containing vineyards with only specified grape varieties planted in order to qualify for use of the DOC name on the label. This is a VQPRD or "quality wine"

classification under the European Union rules. The *Instituto da Vinha e do Vinho* (IVV) administers DOCs. A list of DOCs with notes follows.

Indicação de Proveniencia Regulamentada (IPR)

The next level appellation, often something of an apprenticeship level for defined regions which hope to later go to DOC stage. This is a VQPRD or "quality wine" classification under the European Union rules. The *Instituto da Vinha e do Vinho* (IVV) administers IPRs.

Vinho Regional (VR)

This is for "table wine" under EU rules, recognizing defined areas which can be quite large (nine cover Portugal) with less consistency in the wine as a result. These are administered by the IVV like the DOC and IPR categories. These regions are currently, from north to south, Minho (or Rios do Minho), Trás-os-Montes, Beiras, Estremadura, Ribatejano, Terras do Sado, Alentejano and Algarve.

Vinho de Mesa (VdM)

Simple table wine, with few controls and no geographic requirements; grapes may come from any part of Portugal. Often these are blends of regions.

Wine Terms

Adega	A cellar or winery.
Branco	White wine.
Castelão	Grape variety also known as Periquita.
Caves	Winery.
Cepa	Vine.
Claro	New wine.
Doce	Sweet wine.
Espumante	Sparkling wine.
Garrafa	Bottle.
Garrafeira	This word refers in Portugal to either a wine or a blend of wines from more than one region with no restriction on the varieties of grape unless indicated as a "Garrafeira RD." The wine must be of good quality. Red wine is aged in wood for two years, white wine is aged for six months.
Licoroso	Wine with high alcohol content.
Maduro	Mature table wine.

Periquita	Grape variety also known as Castelão.
Quinta	Estate, usually single-vineyard.
Reserva	Older wine of a good year.
Rosado	A rosé wine.
Seco	Dry wine.
Selo de Origem	The seal of origin guaranteeing the authenticity of a demarcated wine.
Talia	Grape variety also known as Trebbiano.
Tinto	Red wine.
Trebbiano	Grape variety also known as Talia.
Uva	Grape.
Velho	Old wine.
VEQPRD	Quality sparkling wine produced in a denominated region.
VLQPRD	Quality liqueur wine produced in a denominated region.
Vinha	Vineyard.
Vinho	Wine.
Vinho de Mesa (VdM)	Table wine.
Vinho Regional (VR)	Regional wines; wines that are not DOC or IPR and are produced in a specific region from at least 85 percent of locally grown grapes.
Vinho verde	"Green wine," a young white wine. There is also a Vinho Verde DOC, named for this style.

Appellations of Portugal

Alenquer   *Region: Estremadura*
DOC
Red, min alc 11.5%, max yield 80 hl/ha. White, min alc 11%, max yield
90 hl/ha.
Grapes: Red, Castelão, Camarate, Truncadeira Preta, Preto Martingo, Tinta
Miuda. White, Rinto, Fernão Pires, Jampal, Vital.

Separated by the Serra de Montejunto, which shelters the DOC from the
winds off the Atlantic, Alenquer (named after the town) carries a good–
average reputation. Some winemakers are experimenting with varieties other
than those allowed in the DOC (including Chardonnay, Cabernet, Syrah and
others) which precludes them from using the DOC, for now at least.

Alentejo   *Region: Alentejano*
DOC
Red, min alc 11.5%, max yield 55 hl/ha. Rosé, min alc 11.5%, max yield
60 hl/ha. White, min alc 11%, max yield 55 hl/ha.
Grapes: Red, Aragonez, Periquita, Trincadeira min 75%, Alfrocheiro,
Alicante Bouschet, Cabernet Sauvignon, Carignan, Grand Noir, Moreto,
Tinta Caiada up to 25%. White, Antao Vaz, Arinto, Perrum, Siria collectively
min 75%, Diagalves, Fernão Pires, Malvasia Rei, Robo de Ovelha,
Trincadeira das Pratas collectively up to 25%.

Alentejo, as well as being a DOC, is also the provincial name of a wine
region, a *Vinho Regional*. To avoid confusion the latter is generally known
as Alentejano. It covers a third of mainland Portugal (with one-sixth of the
population) south of the Tagus. Within this region are what were previously
eight separate DOCs, but since 2000 these have now been linked as subregions under DOC Alentejo. While these subregions may hyphenate their
name to Alentejo, some wines on sale still carry the old nomenclature.

A group of mountains and foothills, elevated sites and lower lands with a
wide spread of styles give the 35,000 acres (14,000 ha) of vineyards in the
Alentejo DOC some very good wines. The best of these wines are not often
exported, but they are sold in Lisbon restaurants. The lesser wines are more
simple but developing, helped recently by stainless steel and refrigeration.
Many makers prefer to use the regional name, Alentejano rather than claim
their right to a subregional DOC.

The following eight subregions are now linked under the Alentejo DOC:

Borba: About 7,500 acres (3,000 ha) of vineyards on both limestone and
schist make Borba a very significant subregion within the Alentejo DOC, and
some Borba estates make distinguished and highly regarded wine. White
wine grapes are Antao Vaz, Arinto, Perrum, Rabo de Ovelha, Siria, Trincadeira
das Pratas collectively a min of 95%, and Alicante Branco up to 5%.

Evora: On the plain adjacent to Redondo and Reguengos, Evora covers about 2,500 acres (1,000 ha). The most-planted variety is Castelão (Periquita). Average vineyard size in this subregion is well above the regional average.

Granja-Amareleja: Arid country east of Guadiana River with low rainfall and infertile soils and thus low-yielding vineyards. This is said to help the quality of the Moreto plantings (more than in other parts of Portugal) and the subregion enjoys a good reputation for its reds. Red wine grapes are Alfrocheiro, Aragonez, Moreto min of 80%, Carignan, Tinta Canada, Trincadeira up to 20%. For whites, Rabo de Ovelha is added to the majority blend (min 65%). Manteudo is allowable in the minority blend (up to 35%).

Moura: Named after a local town, this subregion has two vineyard groupings, one around Moura, the other around Serpa (an area famous for its sheep cheese). Fertile soil generally can give high yields, and this subregion is not regarded as especially significant. Red wine grapes are Alfrocheiro, Perequita, Aragonez, Moreto, Trincadeira min of 75%, Alicante Bouschet, Cabernet Sauvignon, Tinta Cavalla up to 20%. For white wine, Rabo de Ovelha may be included in the majority blend (up to 70%), grapes for minority blend (max 30%) are Alicante Branco, Bical, Chardonnay, Moscatel Grado, Perrum, Trincadeira das Pratas.

Portalegre: Cool, elevated vineyards on the approaches to the Serra de Sao Mamede. This subregion covers both slopes and plains. Red wines allow Grand Noir in the major part of the blend; the minority part allows Alicante Bouschet, Cinsault, Moreto up to 25%. White wines differ from the regional allowances in that they do not allow Antao Vaz. Minority blend (max 25%) includes Manteudo.

Redondo: About 3,700 acres (1,500 ha) east of the town of the same name, Redondo produces mostly red wine, which is not highly regarded. As well as those red grapes listed for this DOC, Redondo is allowed to include Tinta Caiada and Alfrocheiro in the majority blend up to 70%, the minority blend also includes up to 30% Grand Noir. For white, only Diagalves and Manteudo are allowed.

Reguengos: About 8,000 acres (3,200 ha) of schist and granite soils makes Reguengos the largest subregion in the Alentejo DOC. Its mixed collection of fine and ordinary wine seems ready to evolve through good leadership, perhaps from single estates or the large cooperative. For red, Tinta Caiada may be included in the majority part of the blend up to 70%, the minority (up to 30%) allows Alfrocheiro, Alicante Bouchet, Cabernet Sauvignon, Carignan, Corropia, Grand Noir and Moreto.

Vidigueira: With some of the hottest climate and most arid land in Portugal, this subregion struggles to make fine wine but does quite well in some well-managed estates. Despite the heat here, a surprising quantity of white grapes are planted. Red also allows Alfrocheiro, Tinta Grossa and Moreto in the majority blend (up to 75%) and in the minority blend (up to 25%) Grand Noir and Carignan are excluded. For white, Lariao, Manteudo and Mourisco Branco may be added to the minority blend (up to 25%).

Almeirim   Region: Ribatejano
DOC
Since 2000 this has become part of DOC **Ribatejo**.

Arruda   Region: Estremadura
DOC
Red, min alc 11.5%, max yield 80 hl/ha. White, min alc 11%, max yield 90 hl/ha.
Grapes: Red, Castelão, Camarate, Preto Martinho, Tinta Miuda. White, Arinto, Fernão Pires, Jampal, Vital.

Sitting in the middle of DOCs Alenquer, Torres Vedras and Bucelas, Arruda is named after the town of Arruda dos Vinhos. A hilly area, much of the vineyards supplying the local cooperative. Light, peppery reds of good quaffing standard predominate here.

Bairrada   Region: Beiras
DOC
Red, white and rosé, min alc 11%; max yield, red 55 hl/ha, rosé and white 70 hl/ha.
Grapes: Red, Baga min 50%, Bastardo, Camarate, Jaen. White, Arinto, Bical.
Sparkling: Cannot be released until nine months after secondary fermentation.

Situated close to the Atlantic coast, this is a popular DOC, especially for sparkling wine, but new efforts are building the whole image.

Beira Interior   Region: Douro
DOC
Red, min alc 12%, rosé and white, min alc 11%, max yield 55 hl/ha.
Grapes: Red, Bastardo, Marufo, Rufete, Touriga Nacional. White, Bical, Cerceal, Fonte Cal, Malvasia, Siria, Tamarez, Rabo de Ovelha.

Previous IPRs Castelo Rodrigo, Pinhel (on the upper reaches of the Coa River, a tributary of the Douro) and Cova de Beira (further south) come together in this new DOC, with the three names retained as subregions where appropriate.

Borba   Region: Alentejano
DOC
Previously with DOC status, but now a subregion of DOC **Alentejo**.

Bucelas   **Region: Estremadura**
DOC
White only, including sparkling, min alc 10.5%, max yield 70 hl/ha.
Grapes: Arinto, Esgana Cão, Rabo de Ovelha.

A small DOC of only 435 acres (175 ha) just north of Lisbon. Dry, crisp white, often with a hint of *pétillance*. The Arinto grape has a slightly bitter style.

Carcavelos   **Region: Estremadura**
DOC
Red and white, min alc 15–22%, max yield 55 hl/ha.
Grapes: Red, Periquita, Trincadeira Preta. White, Arinto, Galego Dourado, Boal, Rabo de Ovelha.
Carcavelos Vinho Generoso: White grapes fortified and sweetened by partly fermented juice. Sweet and aged at least 10 years before release; not unlike a madeira or aged tawny port; min alc 18%.

Situated on the Costa do Sol, at the mouth of the Targus (Tejo) River, this DOC is right at the edge of Lisbon. *Generoso*, the fortified style, is the flagship of this DOC, but its dry, unfortified wines are gaining a greater acceptance. Currently only small quantities are made and the wine is not highly regarded.

Cartaxo   **Region: Ribatejano**
DOC
Since 2000 this has become part of DOC **Ribatejo**.

Chamusca   **Region: Ribatejano**
DOC
Since 2000 this has become part of DOC **Ribatejo**.

Colares   **Region: Estremadura**
DOC
Red and white, min alc 10%, max yield red 55 hl/ha, white 70 hl/ha.
Grapes: Red, Ramisco. White, Arinto, Jampal, Galego, Dourado, Malvasia.

Tiny coastal Atlantic DOC with two subzones: Chão-de-Areia ("sandy ground"), a region of dunes with sandy soil as deep as 33 feet (10 m), and Chão Rijo ("hard ground"), which has brown, calcareous soil. Much of the sandy soil missed the phylloxera epidemic 120 years ago but has its own modern viticultural problems today. Red and white Colares wines are slow to mature, but can be fine with time. This DOC is much smaller than it used to be.

Coruche   **Region: Ribatejano**
DOC
Since 2000 this has become part of DOC **Ribatejo**.

Dão   *Region: Beiras*
DOC
Red, min alc 11.5% (Reserva, min alc 12.5%), max yield 60 hl/ha. Rosé,
min alc 11%, max yield 70 hl/ha. White, min alc 11%, max yield 80 hl/ha.
Grapes: Red, Touriga Nacional min 20%, Alfrocheiro Preto, Bastardo, Jaen,
Tinta Pinheira, Tempranillo (Tinta Roriz). White, Encruzado, Assario Branco,
Barcelo, Borrado das Moscas (Bical), Cerceal (Sercial) Verdelho.
Garrafeira: "Fine wine" requiring an extra 0.5% alcohol and min age of
two years in the cask for red, six months for white.

A DOC around the city of Viseu in north-central Portugal enclosed by
mountains, which shelter it from the Atlantic winds and rain; the rugged
hilly vineyards enjoy a degree of "sun-trap." Low bush-vines on infertile soils
of mixed schist and granite make the most of the conditions in this *terroir*.
Named from the Dão River, south of the Douro, Dão DOC has evolved and
continues to do so; its hearty, robust reds are edging forward through better
techniques and less dependence on cooperatives, which may have reduced
the overall quality in the recent past.

Douro   *Region: Trás-os-Montes*
DOC
Red, min alc 11%, white and rosé, min alc 10.5%. Max yield, red and rosé
55 hl/ha, white 65 hl/ha.
Grapes: Red, Touriga Nacional min 20%, Touriga Francesa, Tinta Roriz
(Tempranillo), Tinta Barroca, Tinta Cão, Tinta Amarela, Tinta Pinheira,
Alfrocheiro Preto, Jaen (Mencia), Mourisco Tinto, Bastardo. White,
Encruzado, Verdelho (Gouveio), Viosinho, Rabigato, Malvasia Fina,
Donzelinho, Douro Superior.

DOC of the table wines in the Douro Valley, inland from Oporto (port has a
separate DOC). A wide range of grape varieties and styles emerge from the
diverse range of soils and *terroir* throughout the valley.

Demarcated for unfortified wine in 1982, the Douro Valley, especially
the eastern end towards Spain, has been given much credit for lively and
interesting variations.

Evora   *Region: Alentejano*
DOC
Evora previously held DOC status, but is now a subregion of DOC
Alentejo.

Granja-Amareleja   *Region: Alentejano*
DOC
Granja-Amareleja previously held DOC status, but is now a subregion of
DOC **Alentejo.**

Lafoes
Region: North Atlantic Coast
DOC
Red and white, min alc 10%, max yield 50 hl/ha.
Grapes: Red, Jaen, Touriga, Amaral. White, Arinto, Cerceal, Dona Branca, Esgana Cão, Rabo de Ovelha.

DOC near Vinho Verde in the Vouga Valley. Quite a wet area, it is known for light reds that tend to be a little *spritzig* and have a definite acidic bite. Whites are a little like *vinho verde*, with low alcohol and a little gassiness. Simple wines.

Lagoa
Region: Algarve
DOC
Red, min alc 12%, white, min alc 11.5%. Max yield for both 60 hl/ha.
Grapes: Red, Negra Mole, Periquita (known locally as Castelão), Bastardo, Moreto. White, Crato Branco (known locally as Siria), Perrum, Diagalves, Tamarez.

In Algarve on the very south of Portugal, where the Atlantic narrows before becoming the Mediterranean, there are four DOCs: Tavira, Portimao, Lagos and Lagoa. Some commentators have criticized the region as being too warm for the allowed grapes.

The four DOCs are based around cooperatives, but the cooperative wineries at Tavira and Portimao have closed recently because of a shortage of grapes. If the vineyards of the deep south have been neglected somewhat, a bright inspirational beacon has been the planting of Vida Nova in the Algarve by Sir Cliff Richard, although his vineyard uses grapes that do not qualify for DOC status.

Lagos
Region: Algarve
DOC
Red, min alc 12%, white, min alc 11.5%. Max yield for both 60 hl/ha.
Grapes: Red, Negra Mole, Periquita (known locally as Castelão), Bastardo, Moreto. White, Crato Branco (known locally as Siria), Perrum, Diagalves, Tamarez.

In Algarve on the very south of Portugal, where the Atlantic narrows before becoming the Mediterranean, there are four DOCs: Tavira, Portimao, Lagos and Lagoa. Some commentators have criticized the region as being too warm for the allowed grapes.

The four DOCs are based around cooperatives, but the cooperative wineries at Tavira and Portimao have closed recently because of a shortage of grapes. If the vineyards of the deep south have been neglected somewhat, a bright inspirational beacon has been the planting of Vida Nova in the Algarve by Sir Cliff Richard, although his vineyard uses grapes that do not qualify for DOC status.

Lourinha
Region: Estremadura
DOC
Although a DOC, Lourinha only produces brandy.

Madeira
Region: Madeira
DOC
Red and white, min alc 17%, max yield 80 hl/ha
Grapes: Red, Tinta Negra Mole, Bastardo, Malvasia Roso, Verdelho Tinto.
White, Sercial, Verdelho, Boal, Malvasia, Terrantez.
Standard Madeira: Based around the Tinta Negra Mole grape, this comes in dry, medium dry, medium sweet and rich (or sweet).
Boal: Min 85% Boal grape, medium-rich and raisiny.
Malmsey: Min 85% of the two Malvasia varieties, usually quite sweet.
Sercial: Min 85% of Sercial grape, usually dryish.
Verdelho: Min 85% Verdelho grape; smoky, medium style.
Colheita: Madeira styles with min 20 years in cask.
Reserva Extra: Madeira varietal styles with min 15 years in cask.
Reserva Velha: min age 10 years in cask and bottle before release.
Reserva: min age five years before release.

Famous wine from the island of Madeira, off the African coast. Madeira is usually sweet, fortified with brandy and carrying reasonable acidity, which helps it through long maturation in casks. The gentle oxidation or "maderisation" with time produces mellow wines. The development of the Madeira style is in itself a fascinating study over hundreds of years.

Moura
Region: Alentejano
DOC
Previously with its own DOC status, but now a subregion of DOC **Alentejo**.

Musca
Region: Terras do Sado
DOC
Refer **Setubal**.

Obidos
Region: Estremadura
DOC
Red, min alc 11%, max yield 70 hl/ha. White, min alc 11%, max yield 90 hl/ha.
Grapes: Red, Baja, Alicante Bouschet, Boal, Camarate (Castelão Nacional), Castelão Frances (Periquita), Trincadeira (Tinta Amarela). White, Arinto, Boal, Alicante Branco, Cabinda, Fernão Pires (Maria Gomes), Malvasia, Rabo de Ovelha, Chardonnay.

Not a large DOC yet with some differing soils, from sandy to calcareous and alluvial. Like other parts of Portugal, viticultural efforts have increased since the mid-1980s and are now showing in wine improvement.

Palmela   ***Region: Terras do Sado***
DOC
Red, min alc 12.5%, rosé, min alc 11%, white, min alc 10%, max yield
100 hl/ha.
Grapes: Red, Periquito, Afrocheiro, Bastardo, Cabernet Sauvignon,
Trincadeira. White, Arinto, Fernão Pires, Rabo de Ovelha, Moscatel de
Setubal, Tamares, Vital.

Small DOC with some exciting wines.

Port (Porto e Douro)   ***Region: Trás-os-Montes***
DOC
Fortified red and white, min alc 19–22%, max yield 55 hl/ha. Red may
have some white grapes included.
Grapes: Red, Touriga Francesa, Touriga Nacional, Bastardo, Mourisco,
Tinto Cão, Tinta Roriz, Tinta Amarela, Tinta Barroca. White, Verdelho,
Malvasia Fina, Rabo de Ovelha, Viosinho, Donzelinho, Roupeiro (Codega).

Vintage: The top wine of the top years, with vintage shown on the bottle,
this is developed to be bottled early (20 months) and do its maturing in
the bottle rather than the cask. Thus bottles are sold early but need 10 to
20 years aging or they are likely to be chewy, hot and a little rough. This
doesn't put off many enthusiasts, however! The cork is a normal table wine
stopper to enable the vintage port to be lain on its side. It will throw a sediment and is best stood up for three days before use to allow the sediment
to settle; the wine is then decanted in one pouring motion leaving the sediment behind. Only about 4 percent of a top vintage goes into vintage port,
making it a small volume, expensive wine.

Late-bottled vintage (LBV): Sound port from a good year is allowed four
to six years in the cask before bottling. Generally LBVs are ready for drinking after bottling; they are filtered of sediment and require no further age;
they don't usually have the right type of cork for laying down anyway. The
vintage and year of bottling will appear on the label.

Single quinta: Made from a single vineyard in a year that was not declared
as "vintage" by the producing winery or house. Treated like vintage port
and released when almost mature, usually about eight years. Vintage will be
shown on the label.

Colheita: Tawny port from long barrel age but one vintage, with the year
shown on the label; usually the bottling date is also shown.

Vintage character: Barrel-matured port, usually ruby in color, supposedly
similar to port but aged in the cask. Can be premium port, but in practical
terms not really "vintage" character at all.

Crusting port: A little like vintage port, but not from a single year. Bottle age
does result in a sediment, so decanting is practical.

Aged tawny: Usually labeled as 10, 20, 30 or 40 years old, these are barrel-aged ports with their average age shown on the label. So, in simple terms, a "20-year old" may have some 30-year-old wine, freshened by some 10-year-old. The older styles are pale with age, delicate, often lovely and a remarkable comparison with a vintage port of around the same age. Aged tawny is bottled after filtering and thus ready for drinking immediately; it is not for further cellaring.

Tawny: The cheaper port style, traditionally the same as ruby but aged longer in the cask, which produces the tawny color. More recently, a simple blend has been produced, using some white port to lighten the color. Ideally, tawny port should be a little more mellow than ruby and suited to creamier, softer cheeses. Ready for drinking when bottled.

Ruby: Another cheaper style, and yet the greatest volume of port is sold under ruby or similar labels. Usually averaging about three years of age, the color is ruby red and the acid fresh, offering a style that is better matched to more tasty cheeses. Ready for drinking when bottled.

Port may contain 40 grape varieties, 28 of them red, 12 white. Normal red port is red. The fermentation of the grape sugar is stopped before it is all converted to alcohol by adding back some brandy, grape spirit, to kick the alcohol level up to 17–20 percent, and thus beyond the ability of the yeast to convert further sugar into alcohol. The result is a sweet red with fortification. What happens then determines the style, which can vary from a robust, alive, frisky young red (ruby) style through to aged, light-colored port with delicacy and mellowness from long cask age with its slow oxidation.

Port carries a traditional heritage of the after-dinner drink that accompanies good stories and cigars, but the younger generation does not want higher alcohol drinks, nor do they need yet another wine category to understand. So in the new millennium the region and its houses face a challenge that has evolved throughout the 1990s. It's worth noting that many of the major port houses are English based, a reflection of the very English history of this wine style. Hence we see English names like Dow, Cockburn, Smith-Woodhouse, Graham, Taylor, Sandeman and others among the major brands.

Portalegre   *Region: Alentejano*
DOC
Previously with DOC status, but now a subregion of DOC **Alentejo**.

Portimao   *Region: Algarve*
DOC
Red, min alc 12%, white, min alc 11.5%. Max yield for both 60 hl/ha.
Grapes: Red, Negra Mole, Periquita (known locally as Castelao), Bastardo, Moreto. White, Crato Branco (known locally as Siria), Perrum, Diagalves, Tamarez.

In Algarve on the very south of Portugal, where the Atlantic narrows before becoming the Mediterranean, there are four DOCs: Tavira, Portimao, Lagos and Lagoa. Some commentators have criticized the region as being too warm for the allowed grapes.

The four DOCs are based around cooperatives, but the cooperative wineries at Tavira and Portimao have closed recently because of a shortage of grapes. If the vineyards of the deep south have been neglected somewhat, a bright inspirational beacon has been the planting of Vida Nova in the Algarve by Sir Cliff Richard, although his vineyard uses grapes that do not qualify for DOC status.

Redondo   Region: Alentejano
DOC
Previously with DOC status, but now a subregion of DOC **Alentejo**.

Reguengos   Region: Alentejano
DOC
Previously with DOC status, but now a subregion of DOC **Alentejo**.

Ribatejo   Region: Ribatejano
DOC
Red and rosé, min alc 11.5%, max yield 80 hl/ha. White, min alc 11%, max yield 90 hl/ha.
Grapes: Red and rosé, Baga, Camarate, Trincadeira, Perequita min 80%, Cabernet Sauvignon, Tinta Miuda max 20%. White, Arinto, Fernão Pires, Trebbiano, Trincadeira das Pratas collectively to min 80%, Tamarez, Vital, Cerceal Branco, Malvasia up to 20%.

DOC around the city of Santarém, from Abrantes in the north down to Vila Franca de Xira. This area is handy to Lisbon, near the Atlantic coast of central Portugal, the DOC name coming from the valley of the River Tejo (Tagus). Almost 90,000 acres (36,000 ha) were given DOC Ribatejo status in 2000 with the addition of six subregions that had previously had their own DOCs and which sometimes use differing grape varieties. There are still earlier wines available from these subregions that carry their original DOC names on the labels.

The difficult issue is that the size and mix of Ribatejo DOC carries a spread of *terroirs* not properly recognized under one catchall DOC. The flood plain of the Tagus, for example, offers much fertility and high yield; the drier, sandy heartland (*charneca*) is much less fertile, while the rolling plains (*bairro*) north of the Tagus – including Tomar and Cartaxo – seem less important yet have some excellent sites suited to wine. In terms of style identification, the six subregions, with a little modification, may have been better left to their own DOCs. Perhaps because of this, about 80 percent of Ribatejo is not sold under the DOC label but as Vinho de Mesa, simple table wine.

The six subregions in this DOC are as follows:

Almeirim: Large subregion of Ribatejo making predominantly white wine, some considered good, especially from vineyards on the terraces away from the river. Wines are usually low-priced and appeal for that reason. Whites include Rabo de Ovelha in the 80% min group, with only Tamarez in the minority part of the blend.

Cartaxo: A subregion offering big volumes of wine, favored by Lisbon restaurants. Style is generally light to medium body for enjoying young. Red grapes include Preto Martinho in the 80% min group while Baga goes to the minority of the blend with Cabernet and Tinta Miuda.

Chamusca: A subregion regarded as of little importance in quality wine but there are promising signs, especially from Tramagal, up the river near Abrantes. Red wine puts Baga in the minority 20% of the blend with Cabernet and Tinta Miuda. No Malvasia or Vital is used in the white wine.

Coruche: Subregion named after the town. Regarded as having much potential for wine quality but, so far, little wine is labeled with the Coruche name. For the white wine, Rabo de Ovelha becomes a minority variety (up to 20%) along with Tamarez, and there is no Cerceal Branco or Vital.

Santarém: Subregion around the city of the same name. Its wine is not highly regarded. Reds include Preto Martinho in the 80% majority group; Baga is not included at all. Bastardo included in the minority of the blend, with Cabernet and Tinta Miuda. Whites use no Vital or Malvasia.

Tomar: The most northern (and coolest) subregion of Ribatejo, Tomar is working towards an improved reputation for red wines. Whites are considered undistinguished, they use only Rabo de Ovelha in the minority (up to 20%) part of the blend.

Santarém   *Region: Ribatejano*
DOC
Since 2000 this has become part of DOC **Ribatejo**.

Setubal (also known as Moscatel de Setubal)   Region: Terras do Sado
DOC
White only, min alc 16.5% to 22%, max yield 70 hl/ha.
Grapes: As of 2002 only Moscatel de Setubal (also known as Muscat of Alexandria) and Moscatel Roxo may be used in this DOC. Prior to that, other varieties were allowed up to 30%.

Setubal and Moscatel de Setubal are both used to name the wine of this DOC, situated just south of Lisbon. There are about 850 acres (330 ha) of the grape called Moscatel de Setubal in the DOC and barely 30 acres (12 ha) of Moscatel Roxo. Like making port, the method for Setubal adds some grape spirit before all the fermentation is over, thus stopping the fermenting process and retaining sugar. What is different is that the skins are left to soak in the Setubal for several months and these add character. The wine is then transferred to horizontal vats made from oak or mahogany. Most is bottled a couple of years later but some is left in wood to age further. A famous old DOC that has been somewhat left behind in the growth of unfortified wine but still has an eager market of enthusiasts.

Tavira
Region: Algarve
DOC
Red, min alc 12%, white, min alc 11.5%. Max yield for both 60 hl/ha.
Grapes: Red, Negra Mole, Periquita (known locally as Castelao), Bastardo, Moreto. White, Crato Branco (known locally as Siria), Perrum, Diagalves, Tamarez.

In Algarve on the very south of Portugal, where the Atlantic narrows before becoming the Mediterranean, there are four DOCs: Tavira, Portimao, Lagos and Lagoa. Some commentators have criticized the region as being too warm for the allowed grapes. The four DOCs are based around cooperatives, but the cooperative wineries at Tavira and Portimao have closed recently because of a shortage of grapes. If the vineyards of the deep south have been neglected somewhat, a bright inspirational beacon has been the planting of Vida Nova in the Algarve by Sir Cliff Richard, although his vineyard uses grapes that do not qualify for DOC status.

Tavora-Varosa
Region: Douro
DOC
Red and white, min alc 10.5%, max yield 50 hl/ha.
Grapes: Red, Alvarelhao, Tinta Barroca, Tinta Roriz, Touriga Francesa, Touriga Nacional. White, Malvasia Fina, Arinto, Borrado das Moscas, Cerceal, Gouveio, Fernão Pires, Folgosao.

Hilly DOC around the city of Lamego at an elevation of 1,650–2,625 feet (500–800 m). Some light reds, which can be astringent, are not highly regarded. White wines are thought more promising, though are not yet increasing in volume. Much is made into sparkling wine, which also uses Pinot Noir and Chardonnay. Three cooperatives produce most of the volume.

Tomar
Region: Ribatejano
DOC
Since 2000 this has become part of DOC **Ribatejo**.

Torres Vedras
Region: Estremadura
DOC
Red, min alc 11.5%, max yield 80 hl/ha. White, min alc 11%, max yield 90 hl/ha.
Grapes: Red, Camarate, Mortagua, Periquita, Tinta Miuda. White, Seara Nova, Vital, Jampal, Rabo de Ovelha, Arinto, Fernão Pires

Almost a coastal DOC, making mostly white wine. Named after the town of Vedras, this DOC is known more for volume than quality. The high yield says it all; this DOC and DOC Obidos have the highest yield in Portugal.

Vidigueira
Region: Alentejano
DOC
Previously with DOC status, but now a subregion of DOC **Alentejo**.

Vinho Verde
Region: Minho
DOC
Red, rosé and white, min alc 8%, max yield 80 hl/ha. Alvarinho, min alc 11%, max yield 60 hl/ha. Espumante, min alc 10%.
Grapes: Red, Vinhao (Sousao), Espedeiro, Azal Tinto, Borracal (Caino Tinto), Brancelho, Pedral. White, Loureiro, Trajadura, Paderna, Azal, Avesso, Alvarinho.

The typical *vinho verde* is a light, fresh and slightly gassy white wine sold in an easily recognized squat bottle. Although a small amount of similar red wine is also made, little of it is exported. Vinho Verde is a large DOC in northwest Portugal of some 143,300 acres (58,000 ha) up to the Spanish border. Another 29,650 acres (12,000 ha) in the Minho wine region are estimated to be making wine that doesn't qualify as DOC. In such a fertile, green land with that huge volume under one delimited area, diversity in grape growing is natural. Vines are growing on trees, many of them old thick vines; some are trellised, some grow on fences, in some areas, anything goes! Quality and style varies also, from light, dry and with a little acid, to harder, greener wines, some clearly thin from over-cropping, which has prevented full ripeness. As André Dominé says in his book *Wine*: "Even the best, well-made Verdes with alcohol close to 11.5% have an after-taste that is more or less restrained in acidity. For lovers of seafood who want to quench their thirst, this is a positive, not a negative quality. Verde is not a wine to taste, sip and contemplate. It is a wine which definitely encourages the appetite."

Indicação de Proveniencia Regulamentada (IPR)

IPRs are also quality wines under EU rules, although secondary (at least in theory) to the DOC status. As Portugal reestablishes its wine industry, many of the following names will become DOCs.

Alcobaça	Graciosa
Biscoitos (Terceira)	Pico
Chaves	Planalto Mirandes
Encostas d'Aire	Valpaços

CHAPTER 5

Germany

Deutscher Landwein
Deutscher Tafelwein
Qualitätswein bestimmter Anbaugebiete (QbA) (quality wine)
Qualitätswein garantierten Ursprungs (QgU) (quality wine with "guarantees")
Qualitätswein mit Prädikat (QmP) (quality wine with special attributes)

Perhaps wrongly thought of as the land of sweet white, Germany today offers a fairly full spectrum of wine styles, especially for its northerly latitude of between 48 and 52 degrees. There is robust Pinot Noir (*spätburgunder*) and also some lighter, elegant white styles: deliciously rich, intense and expensive sweet wines; charming rieslings with 10 percent alcohol that are wonderful afternoon sippers at three to five years of age; and some dry wines as well. Despite their low alcohol, often down at 7 or 8 percent, German wines of good pedigree can age marvelously. Sometimes (but not always) they can look quite dark in color, almost startlingly so, yet they still hold their balance and fruit-interest.

Germany has many variables. One vineyard may have several grape varieties and thus be difficult to classify in quality terms as is done in France. Vineyard sites also vary, from those on flat or rolling topography to others that are etched into a steep river bank, which requires the earth to be taken back up the slope after each rainfall. The soil varies from rocky and schisty to more alluvial soils, some are more fertile than others, some are reddish, some are largely clay and others are limestone. As a result, the spectrum of German wine styles is a wide one.

The Germans have a regulatory system that is very precise, but a little different than that of France, Italy and Spain. Regions and vineyards are still considered to be important and there are restrictions on the use of vineyard and regional names. But a lot of emphasis is put on the sugar-weight, the "must" weight at the time of picking. This can, of course, vary from site to site, vintage to vintage and even grape to grape.

So rather than have a *grand cru* vineyard as in Burgundy that can use the title regardless of vintage, the German system recognizes what the vineyard has produced in any given year; an *Auslese* level this year may follow a *Kabinett* level last year.

The long history of German wine continues to evolve. In both wine styles and wine law, development is ongoing. Based on a full review and new wine laws in 1971, the current labeling system is still under scrutiny and further changes are likely, although getting agreement among wide opinion has slowed the progress. Most agree that the present system has drawbacks, yet after more than 30 years, there is at least some understanding of it. The 1971 laws replaced some well-known names and expanded some famous vineyard names to include the surrounding area, though it was questionable whether some wines thus included were in fact at the same quality level.

Reading a German wine label used to be more difficult because of the tendency to use old-fashioned script typefaces in which some letters could be difficult to tell apart; this is now less of a problem because modern typefaces are being used more frequently, which is an advance in itself. In order to understand the information given on a German wine label it is important to be aware of several factors: the region (*anbaugebiet*), of which there are 13 defined; the grape variety (which must make up at least 85 percent if its name appears on the label); the status in the quality system; the vintage (wine content must be 85 percent minimum of that vintage) and the vineyard or group of vineyards.

First look for the quality level, say QmP Auslese; then the region (the *anbaugebiet*), say Rheingau; and finally the grape variety, say Riesling. This example gives us three very good signals of quality wine: a classy region, a variety that does very well there and a quality level that suggests nicely ripe fruit. The price for this wine may be US$18 or it may be US$40. Both these wines will have passed analysis and a taste test in order to qualify for the designated quality level; the price variation will reflect the pedigree of the vineyard and the vintage.

German Grape Varieties

There are about 100 German grape varieties of commercial significance. Riesling became the most-planted in 1996 when it overtook Müller-Thurgau. However, the higher yields of the latter can still provide greater volume. These two varieties account for more than 40 percent of Germany's 260,000 acres (105,000 hectares). Grapes and the regions suited to them are important to Germany's wine heritage. Crossing one grape with another to get qualities from both is quite common, and a number of crossed varieties appear on the list below. The early-ripening Silvaner, for example, can be crossed with a later-ripening variety like Riesling to give some of Riesling's richness in a grape that ripens before the frosts that can damage it. Many thousands of such crosses are needed to find one that works well commercially and provides benefits to the industry. Some of the more commonly used varieties follow.

Bacchus: White wine cross of Silvaner, Riesling and Müller-Thurgau, named after the Latin name for the god of wine. A big-yielding commercial variety, aromatic when ripe with light Muscat tones.

Chardonnay: A relatively new variety for Germany, officially permitted only in 1991, but plantings now exceed 1,500 acres (600 ha), well under 1 percent of the country's vineyards. Very much in the make-or-break stage. It's worth remembering that in the right location and with effort, Pinot Noir, the other Burgundian grape, can do very well in Germany.

Domina: A red grape cross of Portugieser and Spätburgunder (Pinot Noir). About 600 acres (240 ha) are planted, mostly in Franken.

Dornfelder: A red grape cross of Helfensteiner and Heroldrebe, this is Germany's third most-planted red grape. Its wine is considered easy-drinking and thus very popular.

Dunkelfelder: A dark-skinned red variety useful in adding color to lighter reds.

Elbling: High-acid white grape, mostly planted in Mosel-Saar-Ruwer (about 2,500 acres/1,000 ha) and considered by some commentators as outdated. However, it does qualify in Mosel-Saar-Ruwer as an approved "Classic" variety.

Faberrebe: A white grape cross of Weissburgunder (Pinot Blanc) and Müller-Thurgau. More of a volume grape yet can produce good, flavorsome and refreshing white wine. Mostly grown in Pfalz, Rheinhessen and Nahe.

Frühburgunder: Early-ripening clone of Pinot Noir, as opposed to Spätburgunder, the traditional variety as grown in Burgundy.

Gewürztraminer: White grape, although pink in skin color. *Gewürz* is German for spicy, and Tramin is a village in Tyrol, Italy, where what is thought of as a mutation of a less spicy (and less pink) variety called Roter-Traminer became known. The variety can do well in Germany, as it can in Alsace with a quite different style, but it is variable in yield and intensity.

Grauburgunder: Known around the world as Pinot Gris, Pinot Grigio or Rulander.

Gutedel: Called Chasselas in most of the world, Fendant in Switzerland. Planted in Baden.

Huxelrebe: A white-wine cross of Gutedel and Courtillier Musque from 1927. A simple wine with big yields; if yields are controlled, Huxelrebe can reach a high level of sugar and flavor, to *Auslese* standard.

Kerner: A white cross of Trollinger and Riesling. This is a bigger yielding grape than Riesling and though not as classy or deep in its flavors, will grow satisfactorily in more difficult vineyard conditions. At best, its wines are fruity and fresh, and do not usually gain extra tones from bottle age.

Lemberger: Red variety also called Blauer Limberger and Blaufrankisch. Considered of Austrian origin. There are about 3,000 acres (1,250 ha) under vine in Germany, mostly in Württemberg.

Morio-Muskat: A white grape cross of Silvaner and Weissburgunder, made by Peter Morio whose surname forms part of the grape name. The strong bouquet is reminiscent of Muscat. Not big on the planting list these days but still used in Rheinhessen and the Pfalz.

Müller-Thurgau: Also known as Rivaner. A cross by Hermann Müller from the Swiss canton (village) of Thurgau, which gives it its name. Thought of initially as a cross and several re-crosses of Silvaner and Riesling to bring the early-ripening attributes of Silvaner to some of the fruit depth of Riesling, Müller-Thurgau is now considered by German authorities to be a cross of Riesling and Gutedel. Can offer a fruity, uncomplicated style. This is the second most-planted variety in Germany, and in some years the higher yields make it the most prolific in terms of volume.

Ortega: A white variety cross of Müller-Thurgau and Siegerrebe, early ripening with plenty of sweetness. Mostly planted in Rheinhessen and the Pfalz, but also in Mosel-Saar-Ruwer.

Portugieser: Thought to be an Austrian variety, a black grape producing much rosé. The second most-planted red variety in Germany after Pinot Noir.

Rieslaner: A cross of Silvaner and Riesling, with the late-ripening characteristics of the latter. When fully ripe makes a pleasant, balanced wine. Planted mostly in Franken.

Riesling: The most noble and respected of Germany's white grapes, late in ripening and potentially rich and fresh yet also with a great deal of longevity. Germany's most-planted variety, differing in styles from dry to richly sweet and with some variation between regions.

Rivaner: Alternative name for Müller-Thurgau.

Rulander: Pinot Gris, but also called Grauburgunder in some parts of Germany.

Saint Laurent: Red variety with depth in its color, thought to be related to Pinot Noir and mostly grown in Austria, but also used in Germany's Pfalz region, where it is an approved "Classic" variety.

Scheurebe: A white cross, taking its name partly from Georg Scheu, who crossed Silvaner with Riesling in 1916, creating a late-ripening variety (a Riesling trait) with some commercial value.

Schwarzriesling: Literally, "black Riesling," but in fact it is Meunier or Pinot Meunier (as used in Champagne). Also known as Müllerrebe.

Silvaner: White grape with a long German history, early ripening compared with Riesling but a little too neutral in flavor to be exciting. Quite widely planted, accounting for some 7 percent of German vineyards.

Spätburgunder: Pinot Noir, "*spät*" in the front of the word indicates a later-ripening clone. Almost 8 percent of German vineyards are planted in this variety. Ahr and Baden use it extensively.

Trollinger: Red grape, named after Triol; known as Schiava in Italy and Vernatsch in Austria.

Weissburgunder: Known outside of Germany as Pinot Blanc. Grown in what was the East Germany region and also in Baden and the Pfalz.

Quality Levels

Tafelwein: Table wine. Not necessarily German; can be a blend of wines from EU countries. No A.P. number on the label.

Deutscher Tafelwein: German table wine. Contains only German produce. Grapes picked at a minimum of 44.5° *oechsle* (except in Baden, where the minimum is 50°). Can be chaptilized (sugar added) to raise alcohol; minimum alcohol 8.5 percent. No A.P. number on the label.

Deutscher Landwein: German country wine. Contains only German produce. Grapes picked at a minimum of 47.5° *oechsle*. Only dry (*trocken*) or semi-dry (*halbtrocken*) styles are produced. Country wine can be chaptilized to raise alcohol within EU limits.

Qualitätswein bestimmter Anbaugebiete (QbA): Quality wine from one of the 13 *anbaugebiete* (specified wine regions), the relevant name to be shown on the label. Grapes picked at a minimum of 51° *oechsle*; in some regions and with some grape varieties this can be up to 72° *oechsle*. Can be chaptilized to raise alcohol. Each label carries an A.P. number to certify that it has passed taste and other tests.

Qualitätswein garantierten Ursprüngs (QgU): Quality wine, as in QbA, that comes from a specific *bereich*, *grosslage* or *einzellage* (district, village or vineyard) with a consistent taste profile (typicity) for its area. This classification was added in 1994, long after the 1971 law, to recognize regional grape and style, sugar, acidity and alcohol levels. The classification is yet to be fully demonstrated, but its use is potentially on the rise; a small bridge, perhaps, between the existing system and *terroir*-based recognition.

Qualitätswein mit Prädikat (QmP): Quality wine with *prädikats*, attributes, special qualities. Wine can not be chaptilized, no sugar may be added, but a little *süssreserve* (sweet juice) is allowable; so QmP wines are highly regarded. The region (one of the 13 *anbaugebiete*) must also be shown on the label. All QmP wines must also show one of the following six "subdivision" classifications, indicating the wine type:

- QmP Kabinett: From the idea "good enough to lock in a cabinet" (that is, away from staff and young family members), *kabinett* wines may be low in alcohol, light and easy, the first step in the no-sugar-added QmP ladder. Minimum is 70° *oechsle* at picking for Riesling, 74° in warmer regions, 76° in Baden.

- QmP Spätlese: Technically this means "late picked," but if Germany is placed on a world scale, "later picked" might be closer to the mark, as these usually are not the late-picked, superripe grapes with botrytis knocking on their skins one would find in warmer countries. Higher sugar (at least 76° *oechsle*) can be fermented out into dryer whites (*spätlese-trocken*) with higher alcohol and less residual sweetness, or made into a light, lower alcohol, easy-drinking white with appeal at any time of the day. Minimum 76° *oechsle* at picking for Riesling, 85° in warmer regions, 100° in Baden.

- QmP Auslese: Made from grapes with 83° *oechsle* (even higher in some grapes and regions) and often but not necessarily with some botrytis affecting them. These very ripe grapes should give quite concentrated flavors and may be a little sweet, or very sweet, from a delicious afternoon sipper to a rich dessert style. Minimum 83° *oechsle* at picking for Riesling, 92° to 95° in warmer regions, 76° in Baden.

- QmP Beerenauslese (sometimes abbreviated in the wine trade as BA): Picked with a must weight of at least 110°, as high as 125° in some regions. Some botrytis, perhaps bunch-picked (the inside berries in the bunch not fully botrytized) or with a selection of the berries that are carrying botrytis, to give a rich, sweet, dessert wine. Alcohol-content is variable, but it is usually a magnificent wine, especially that made from Riesling, and is able to mature very well. The right conditions – weather, humidity, botrytis and ripeness – do not occur every year.

- QmP Eiswein (Icewine): Made from grapes at *beerenauslese* ripeness but which are harvested after a frost, which freezes the water in the grape's juice, and picked early in the morning before the ice in the juice defrosts. Only the water freezes during a frost, not the nectar of fruit and sugar, so a gentle press – in modern times an airbag is used – lightly crushes the grapes to make a wine with sweetness, lusciousness and usually with only a trace of botrytis. In the right year this can be a rare and special wine.

- QmP Trockenbeerenauslese (sometimes abbreviated in the wine trade as TBA): a rare wine made from botrytis-affected grapes, individually selected from raisined grapes giving long-lived, luscious, honeyed wines. Riesling at picking must be 150° *oechsle*, which comes from berry selection several times through the vineyard to choose the most botrytis-affected grapes.

Recognizing Quality

German wine law may seem strict in its requirements, and in some requirements it goes further than any other country's labeling system. However, among the thousands of vineyards in Germany, some deserve more attention than others. When the grape grower is also quality oriented, some fine wines can result. Recognizing this, a system to identify two levels of quality came into force in 2001. "Classic" status and

"Selection" status are now available to some vineyards; these two appellations have correspondingly higher requirements in grape sugar levels at picking and in overall quality.

There is also a separate private scheme involving 200 vineyard owners who have strong sites for quality grapes. The requirements on sugar levels and winemaking for this private scheme are similar to those for Classic and Selection status levels, and the operators of the scheme carry out their own quality audit before a VBG seal may be applied. This seal will only be seen on appropriate wines dating from the 2002 vintage.

"Classic" and "Selection" Appellations

As of the 2000 vintage, the terms **"Classic"** and **"Selection"** have been introduced and shown on labels. These terms are intended to simplify matters for consumers. Winemakers in all 13 German wine growing regions can use these terms on labels, provided the wines they produce are above average in quality, harmoniously dry in taste, and made from a traditional grape variety for each region. The allowed varieties are shown in the regional (*anbaugebiete*) list that follows.

The intention behind labeling certain wines as Classic wines is to enable consumers to easily find uncomplicated, dry varietal wines with reliable taste and quality at an affordable price. Selection wines are premium quality, dry varietals available in limited quantities and priced accordingly. For both of these appellations, production standards are above those set for non-qualifying wines, that is, they have lower yields, higher sugar levels at picking date, and so on. They also must taste typical of their region when being approved.

Classic wines must be picked with a sugar level of 8° *oechsle* higher than for other grapes in the same region, and as finished wines they must have at least 12 percent alcohol (11.5 percent in Mosel-Saar-Ruwer). The requirement to be "harmoniously dry in taste" recognizes that a light sugar content can be offset by higher acidity, and the rule for Classic wines is that the residual sugar content (in grams of sugar per liter of wine) can be twice as high as the acidity. So a higher-acid wine can be balanced by higher sugar. However, there is a maximum imposed: 15 grams of sugar per liter of wine is the ceiling. Because all Classic and Selection wines are harmoniously dry in style, the terms *trocken* (dry) and *halbtrocken* (off-dry) are superfluous.

Classic wines are identified on the label by the Classic logo next to the name of the grape variety. The name of the producer and the wine growing regions are also mentioned, but vineyard names have been deliberately omitted.

Selection wines must meet additional quality criteria: grapes must originate from an individual and carefully selected vineyard site (named on the label) and be harvested by hand; yields are lower than prescribed by law; and first release is September 1 of the year following the harvest.

Wine growers who intend to produce grapes for a Selection wine must fulfill many quality-oriented criteria. The wine's individual vineyard site (or parcels thereof) must be registered with authorities and be clearly demarcated as a Selection site by May 1 prior to the harvest.

The sugar level of grapes for Selection wines are set at *Auslese* level although the final wines will be dry, or "harmoniously dry in taste," as in Classic wines. Yields are restricted to a maximum of 60 hectoliters per hectare. Grapes must be hand-picked and selectively harvested to weed out unripe or rotten berries. In terms of style, Selection wines are dry, with up to 9 grams per liter of residual sugar. There is one exception to this rule: for riesling, the residual sugar content can be 1.5 times as high as the acidity, up to a maximum of 12 grams per liter. The goal is to achieve a balance of sweetness and acidity.

Verband Deutscher Prädikatsweingüter (VDP)

The Verband Deutscher Prädikatsweingüter (VDP) is an association that empowers its members to use an emblem showing a stylized eagle with a cluster of grapes and the letters VDP on bottles of qualifying wine (a little like the Chianti Classico Consortium in Italy, whose emblem with a black cockerel on a gold background indicates membership). VDP identifies top quality vineyards and imposes strict quality conditions on yield and winemaking before the emblem or seal can be used. A VDP seal on the label indicates the epitome of German wine quality.

The prestige and image of such membership has been building strongly since 2002. The association has a much longer heritage; but in 2002 the visual recognition and meaning of the status were enhanced (including a phase-in period to 2004 where necessary) and wines now need to qualify through an extensive screening process to carry the status. Such status, however, is private – it has no recognition in law, and the normal German labeling rules must apply as well. These conditions are shown on a back label, while the VDP information is on the front.

Membership requires that grape varieties in the vineyard are traditional for the region, and quality levels and standards set by law must be well exceeded by the VDP wines. Must weights (sugar levels at harvest time), for example, must reach a far higher level than those required under law. Yields are required to be very low. All these facets of quality are monitored by the association to protect their image.

VDP is an exclusive club of 200 top vineyard owners; but even for these owners, some blocks within their vineyards may not qualify. VDP says: "Our label makes it possible for drinkers and wine buyers to distinguish between quality and top quality." This indicates the dual aim of the VDP membership, a top site and stringent winemaking conditions.

There is a hierarchy in the recognition of VDP wines: The lowest level is **Gutsweine** or **Ortsweine** (house wine). The second level is **Klassifizierte Lagenweine** (wine from a classified site). At the top is

Grosses Gewächs (meaning "great growth"). This term is used in the Rheingau only, elsewhere it is called **Erstes Gewächs**.

Mosel-Saar-Ruwer members have a small dispensation because of their cooler conditions: dry wines from this region may be chaptilized; that is, sugar can be added (as under QbA rules), while for members in other regions chaptilizing is not permitted.

Wine Terms

Abfüller	Commercially bottled (not bottled on the estate).
Affenthaler Spätburgunder Rotwein	A Spätburgunder (Pinot Noir) from specific parts of the Baden region, near Baden-Baden and Buhl.
Anbaugebiete	Wine regions. There are 13 of them, and the name of the relevant *anbaugebiete* must appear on all wine labels that are of a quality level above *Tafelwein*. Notes on the *anbaugebiete* are given at the end of this chapter. Two new regions from the old East Germany have been added recently.
A.P. Nr (Number)	Abbreviation for *Amtliche Prüfungsnummer,* the idenification number for the wine allocated as it comes through the "quality wine" approval system. This number is shown on the label of all QbA, QgU and QmP level wines. (*Refer* "Quality Levels" on page 263.) The number is in five parts, but these parts are often lumped together. First is the number of the application committee that reviewed the wine; the next three digits identify the village where the wine was bottled; the next three digits identify the producer's identification number for his or her wine; then two or three digits represent the application number, followed by the last two digits which show the year the application was made. The year of application may be the year of vintage, or after bottle maturation, or some years later when the wine is released.
Bereich	A district, that is, smaller than an *anbaugebiete* (region) but larger than, and often containing, *grosslagen* (villages). A defined geopolitical district.
Classic	*Refer* "Recognizing Quality" on page 264.
Einzellage	An individual site, or vineyard (collectively referred to as *einzellagen*). A single vineyard, however, does not necessarily mean a single owner; there may be

several owners, just as there are with vineyards in Burgundy.

Erzeugerabfüllung   Estate bottled, bottled on the property where the wine was grown and made.

German Wine Seal   An optional extension of the A.P. number during judging is to award applying wines with higher standards (above the level required for approval for their A.P. status) with the *Deutscher Weinsiegel* (German Wine Seal). The German Wine Seal on a label provides a useful clue about sweetness levels. A bright yellow seal indicates a dry (*trocken*) wine, a lime-green seal identifies off-dry or half-dry (*halbtrocken*) wines and a red seal indicates sweeter wines.

Grosslage   A large site, or more specifically a group of vineyards, is entitled to use the name of the *grosslage* (village). This is part of the 1971 law that attracts criticism, because it allows "lesser" sites within the defined *grosslage* to use the prestigious name. There are about 150 defined and named *grosslagen* in Germany.

Gutsabfüllung   Bottled by the winery where the wine was made, a group of estates perhaps, using one winemaker and bottling on site.

Halbtrocken   Semi-dry.

Hochgewachs   A term used only rarely with riesling to show a higher sugar-level, supposedly indicating that the wine is of better quality than the QbA shown on the label.

Lage   Site or vineyard (plural *lagen*) with a name. Also *Einzellage* (single site, single vineyard).

Liebfraumilch   QbA that can be from one or more of the regions of Rheingau, Nahe, Rheinhessen or Pfalz. At least 70 percent of the content must be from Riesling, Müller-Thurgau, Sylvaner or Kerner grapes. No varietal description is allowed on the label.

Loreley   Mittelrhein wine made from 100 percent Riesling with residual sweetness between nine and 18 grams of sugar per liter of wine. Must pass a taste test to qualify.

Moseltaler   A blend of Riesling, Müller-Thurgau, Ebling and/or Kerner produced in the Mosel-Saar-Ruwer region. No varietal description is allowed on the label. The wine is slightly sweet, between 15 and 30 grams of sugar per liter of wine. Must pass a taste test to qualify.

Must weight   Sugar level in the juice of the freshly picked grapes. *Refer* **Oechsle**.

Oechsle   The must weight, reflective of the sugar content in the juice at picking. Denser grape juice (with a higher specific gravity) has more sugar. Outside of Germany, grape juice sugar is usually measured in degrees Baumé or Brix. In Germany, *oechsle* is very important to the status of the finished wine. *Tafelwein*, for example, requires an *oechsle* of 44.5° while a *Trockenbeerenauslese* requires at least 150°. An *oechsle* of 44° would ferment into just 5 percent alcohol, so sugar will need to be added when grapes are picked at that level.

Perlwein   *Tafelwein* or QbA with a little gas (*pétillance*).

Selection   *Refer* "Recognizing Quality" on page 264.

Sekt   A simple level of sparkling wine, *schaumweine*.

Süssreserve   "Sweet reserve," natural grape juice held back from fermentation (so it is high in natural grape sugar), which can be added back to fermented wines for sweetness and/or balance. Because this is "juice" rather than "sugar," it is allowable in QmP wines.

Trocken   *Trocken* wine is dry wine, with no or very low sugar. However there is an inconsistency in the language when this word is used in the construction *trockenbeerenauslese*: "*trockenbeeren*" means "dry berries," berries in which the water level has been reduced by botrytis, leaving the fruit very sweet. So despite the fact that *trocken* means "dry," *trockenbeerenauslese* is very sweet wine!

VDP   *Refer* "Recognizing Quality" on page 264.

Weissherbst   Rosé from one grape, which is at least QbA quality.

Winzersekt   "Wine growers' sparkling wine." Sparkling wine made by the traditional method as used in Champagne. Winzersekt is either made from Riesling (especially to the north of Germany) or from Pinot Noir and Chardonnay. Usually estate grown and bottled, but the final disgorgement may be contracted out.

Germany's Wine Regions (*Anbaugebiete*)

Ahr
Vineyard area: approximately 1,300 acres (525 ha).
Approved grapes for Classic and Selection wines: Riesling, Frühburgunder, Pinot Noir.

Named after the river that flows east from the Eifel ranges into the Rhine River near Remagen. Pinot Noir is the highlight of the region's growing reputation. Sound, firm Pinot Noir like this is well regarded and the increasing influence of outsiders coming in as winemakers is adding to its character. Ahr seems to be all about red wine, basically Pinot Noir, though some Portugieser does well when helped by a good year and good winemaking, but a spectrum of white wines also deserves attention. A small region, with little exported.

Baden
Vineyard area: approximately 40,000 acres (16,200 ha).
Approved grapes for Classic and Selection wines: Riesling, Silvaner, Müller-Thurgau (Rivaner), Gutedel, Pinot Gris (Grauburgunder), Pinot Noir (Spätburgunder), Pinot Blanc (Weissburgunder).
Selection wines only: Auxerrois, Chardonnay, Meunier (Schwarzriesling), Saint Laurent.

Germany's most southern region, Baden reaches south from Franken to Lake Constance with some parts of Baden lower in latitude than Alsace in France. Cities of Baden-Baden, Heidelberg and Freiberg are included in this region. The most-planted grape here is Müller-Thurgau. Pinot Noir and Pinot Gris are the image-setters, although Riesling (called Klingelberger in some parts of Baden) can excel here also.

Franken
Vineyard area: approximately 15,000 acres (6,075 ha).
Approved grapes for Classic and Selection wines: Müller-Thurgau, Silvaner, Pinot Blanc (Weissburgunder), Pinot Noir (Spätburgunder).
Classic wines only: Domina.
Selection wines only: Pinot Gris (Grauburgunder), Riesling, Rieslaner.

Franken (known in English as Franconia) is in central Germany, east of Frankfurt on the south-facing slopes lining the Main River and its tributaries, around the city of Würzburg.

An unusual region in Germany because Riesling is not a major contributor here. Rieslings that are given full attention can play a big part in the Franken premium image; but in quantity terms, other varieties serve well, such as Müller-Thurgau, Sauvignon Blanc, Bacchus and other crosses like Rieslaner and Kerner.

Hessische Bergstrasse
Vineyard area: approximately 1,200 acres (460 ha).
Approved grapes for Classic and Selection wines: Riesling, Pinot Gris (Grauburgunder), Pinot Noir (Spätburgunder), Pinot Blanc (Weissburgunder).
Selection wines only: Müller-Thurgau, Rivaner, Silvaner.

A northern region in Germany, on the slopes of the Odenwald River, this region produces only a small volume of wine. More than half is in Riesling which (with a little Pinot Noir) is based around a cooperative. Not widely seen internationally because of its small size, Hessische Bergstrasse lacks a notable identity but has producers striving for quality and recognition. The best wines here are considered as good as those of Rheingau region.

Mittelrhein
Vineyard area: approximately 1,500 acres (610 ha).
Approved grapes for Classic and Selection wines: Riesling, Pinot Gris (Grauburgunder), Pinot Noir (Spätburgunder), Pinot Blanc (Weissburgunder).

Literally "middle-Rhine," the Mittelrhein begins just south of Bonn, following the Rhine River on slopes often steep and difficult to work. Despite its length, it's a small region in terms of plantings. Much of the grape growing is a part-time occupation and a big part of the winemaking is done through cooperatives. Riesling predominates, a crisp style with high acidity from cool temperatures.

Mosel-Saar-Ruwer
Vineyard area: approximately 30,000 acres (12,150 ha).
Approved grape for Classic and Selection wines: Riesling.
Classic wines only: Pinot Gris (Grauburgunder), Pinot Blanc (Weissburgunder), Elbling, Rivaner.

A region of three rivers: the Saar and the Ruwer flow into the Mosel (which begins in France as the Moselle) and the Mosel flows into the Rhine at Koblenz. Some steep almost cliff-like vineyards overlook the rivers and conditions make it difficult in many vineyards to work and retain the soil after rainfall. Some commentators say only one vintage in nine is "great" in Mosel-Saar-Ruwer but that one vintage is worth the wait! The frequency of "very good" vintages is a saving grace but when things go wrong here, it's difficult to make fine wine. The Mosel-Saar-Ruwer offers a lighter, paler, crisper style than the Rhine regions but each year has its own story. The fragrant aromatics can be very compelling. Longevity is very good in all but the worst vintages, and sometimes amazingly young-tasting styles can emerge at 12 to 15 years, tasting as though they are only three or four years. Higher acidity clearly helps. But Mosel-Saar-Ruwer is a famous region with some amazing wines in the right vintages. The slaty soil of some parts (Saar particularly) and the similar but earthy soil of Ruwer can complement the style of the collective region: Saar and Ruwer make up about 12 percent (depending on vintage) of the total region, with the balance along the longer Mosel River.

Nahe
Vineyard area: approximately 11,500 acres (4,650 ha).
Approved grapes for Classic and Selection wines: Riesling, Pinot Gris (Grauburgunder), Pinot Blanc (Weissburgunder), Pinot Noir (Spätburgunder).
Classic wines only: Rivaner, Scheurebe, Müller-Thurgau, Silvaner, Dornfelder, Portugieser.

Vineyard region on both sides of the Nahe River, which flows into the Rhine at Bingen. Some flat but mostly hilly vineyards, some quite steep in the German tradition. Predominantly white grapes, led by Riesling and Sylvaner, with about 10 percent in red varieties. Overall, Nahe is considered pleasant commercial wine, but the best can achieve much higher prices and respect.

Pfalz (once called Rheinpfalz and/or Palatinate)
Vineyard area: approximately 60,000 acres (24,300 ha).
Approved grapes for Classic and Selection wines: Riesling, Pinot Gris (Grauburgunder), Pinot Blanc (Weissburgunder), Pinot Noir (Spätburgunder).
Classic wines only: Rivaner, Dornfelder.
Selection wines only: Chardonnay, Gewürztraminer, Saint Laurent, Meunier (Schwarzriesling).

Bordered by Rheinhessen on the north and France on the south and west, Pfalz has been home for a lot of ordinary wine, but this region has been pulling itself up since the 1980s. Planted with a lot of German crossings like Kerner and Scheurebe, the Pfalz has started to come to terms with the mix of bulk and simple wines and stronger, more powerful styles resulting from lower yields and higher prices. Riesling plantings have increased significantly. Some Pinot Noir and Dornfelder form most of the red vineyards; about 20 percent of the region. Pfalz is on the rise, even though a lot of the low-priced ordinary wine that is the norm here will take longer to evolve.

Rheingau
Vineyard area: approximately 8,000 acres (3,240 ha).
Approved grape for Classic and Selection wines: Riesling.
Selection wines only: Pinot Noir (Spätburgunder).

Twenty miles (32 km) across from east to west, from Wicker to Hochheim, Rheingau is one of the smaller regions of Germany's highly regarded Rhine River valley and the most highly regarded overall of the 13 regions in quality terms. This is fine wine territory. The wines are Riesling-based (about

80 percent) although Pinot Noir (10 percent) is also significant. The Riesling style is richer, more concentrated overall than other regions, sometimes with a delicious spicy fruitiness which shows in the fragrance. Here the vineyards are run by full-time workers, the wines sold in bottles rather than in bulk. The consumer generally pays more for Rheingau wines but they provide the extra in the fruit and aromatics, although such a statement must be taken as general and vintages, of course, do vary.

Rheinhessen
Vineyard area: approximately 66,000 acres (26,700 ha).
Approved grapes for Classic and Selection wines: Riesling, Silvaner, Pinot Blanc (Weissburgunder), Pinot Gris (Grauburgunder), Pinot Noir (Spätburgunder), Portugieser.
Classic wines only: Dornfelder.
Selection wines only: Chardonnay, Gewürztraminer, Frühburgunder.

The biggest German wine region. Mostly on rolling hills, although with some steep slopes and some flatter lands. Soil overall is quite fertile and well planted with other crops as well as grapes. Best vineyards tend to be closer to the Rhine. Rheinhessen makes a lot of high-volume labels including Liebfraumilch, and has a big proportion of plantings (about 85 percent) in white varieties with higher yields like Müller-Thurgau, while Riesling has only a small proportion. In a region this size, however, there are vineyards producing top-class wines and although commentators see Rheinhessen as commercial, with simple wines, there are also many that are excellent, being both refreshing and very good value.

Saale-Unstrut
Vineyard area: approximately 1,285 acres (520 ha).
Approved grapes for Classic wines only: Müller-Thurgau, Gewürztraminer, Kerner, Portugieser.
Approved grapes for Selection wines only: Riesling, Silvaner, Pinot Blanc (Weissburgunder), Pinot Noir (Spätburgunder).

Situated at 51 degrees north latitude in the valleys of the Saale and Unstrut rivers, about equidistant between Weimar and Leipzig in what was East Germany. A well-spread area under vine with an emphasis on simple white varieties like Müller-Thurgau, Sylvaner, Pinot Blanc, Chasselas and others, generally dry and light in alcohol. Work goes on to raise the quality in the region and make more styles that have individuality, but the recent heritage under Communist economics has been the production of bulk, cheap wine, and quality and individuality will take longer to evolve.

Sachsen
Vineyard area: approximately 900 acres (365 ha).
Approved grapes for Classic and Selection wines: Riesling, Pinot Gris

(Grauburgunder), Pinot Blanc (Weissburgunder), Gewürztraminer, Pinot Noir (Spätburgunder).

Sachsen (Saxony) is the smallest and most eastern of the 13 regions. Well north (51 degrees latitude) in the upper Elbe Valley the region extends some 34 miles (55 km) north and south of Dresden in the old East Germany. Sachsen is cooperative-based and still finding an identity. More than 90 percent of vineyards are planted in white varieties (mostly dry) from Müller-Thurgau, Riesling, Traminer and Pinot Blanc to a little historic grape variety called Goldriesling (Riesling crossed with Courtiller Musque). Sachsen wines are not widely sought after, but following the political changes in East Germany, winemakers and growers here are seeking to build a new industry and reputation.

Württemberg
Vineyard area: approximately 28,000 acres (11,300 ha).
Approved grapes for Classic and Selection wines: Riesling, Kerner, Silvaner, Trollinger, Lemberger, Dornfelder, Pinot Noir (Spätburgunder), Meunier (Schwarzriesling), Pinot Gris (Grauburgunder).

Region towards the south of Germany and the Neckar River. Like the Mosel-Saar-Ruwer, many of the region's vineyards are steep, river-flanking slopes. The main vineyard part of the region is between Stuttgart and Heilbronn up to Baden and lots of small growers work through a cooperative. The most planted variety is Riesling, just ahead of Trollinger, a simple red grape. Pinot Meunier or simply Meunier (known here as Müllerrebe) is on the rise, but Müller-Thurgau and Kerner are also significant. The Württemberg white style is lesser known but when made cleanly it is entirely satisfying; the reds are thought of as indistinctive, with Pinot Noir on the rise when given full attention.

Part Two

The New World Way:

Wine of the Grape

The New World Way:

Wine of the Grape

Unlike Europe, when countries like the United States or Australia enthusiastically embarked on their wine industries, the history of the land was not there to guide them. Which grape was suitable for which area, which variety, rootstock and trellising would be required for each *terroir*, all this had to be learned first-hand.

Although New World countries have made a lot of fast progress, the matching of wines and styles to areas and conditions is very much an ongoing process. To come up with a formula that the Europeans may have had 200 years ago, vineyards must be allowed to grow older and methods need to be proven over decades of searching for the right clones and rootstocks, and testing vintages with different types of oak.

This is a sizeable difference between the Old World and the New World in wine terms. European history names wine from the vineyard, whether Margaux, Chianti, Champagne, Rheingau or estates or Châteaux within these. The new kids on the vineyard use many varieties and blend regions, so they are not limited by single-site emphasis.

A wine from the Sonoma Valley in the U.S. or from Hawke's Bay in New Zealand may be named after varieties like Cabernet, Syrah, Zinfandel, Merlot or Pinot Noir, and thus the "varietal minimum" becomes an issue. If wine is going to be named by the grape, then how much of the wine is made from the grape or grapes named on the label needs to be defined. Sometimes local rules and the rules of overseas markets are not the same, however. New Zealand and Chile, for example, have a varietal minimum of 75 percent of the named variety, with the proviso that exported wine must conform to the requirements of the destination market. Most markets, however, require 85 percent and it may only be a matter of time before countries like New Zealand and Chile will come into line for domestic requirements also.

Another issue are the wine areas themselves. Regions, subregions, districts, "viticultural areas" and even "geographic indicators" are all in the process of evolution, and deciphering the designation of wine areas varies from one country to the next. This highlights the differences between the New World and Europe. In Australia, for example, a winemaker like Penfolds will happily blend wine from regions thousands of miles apart, even in an expensive wine like Grange; if it makes the wine better, they say, why not? To the European, this recognition of the grape is a far cry from the traditional philosophy of *terroir*, the "wine of my land."

Such are the differences, styles and variety of international wines. It is these differences that enhance our choices when we buy wine from around the world.

CHAPTER 6

United States

American Viticultural Area (AVA)

The rediscovery of wine in California during the 1970s has led to a burgeoning industry with growing enthusiasm on the part of winemakers and wine drinkers. While nationwide consumption is not at European levels, the big dollar purchase is not just restricted to first-growth Bordeaux and Grand Cru Burgundy. There are drinkers happy to pay hundreds of dollars for special bottles of local wine, and a growing range of such is available from United States' wineries. There are also thriving industries, especially in the northeast, and in California, Washington and Oregon states, where more affordably-priced wine is available in varieties as vastly different as concord, niagara, chardonnay, cabernet sauvignon and merlot.

American Appellations

In the 1980s, the United States developed a system of recognizing "delimited grape growing areas" and registering them as "American Viticultural Areas" or AVAs. The official definition of an AVA is "...a delimited grape-growing region distinguishable by geographic features. Viticultural features such as soil, climate, elevation, and topography distinguish it from surrounding areas."

Currently the list of AVAs exceeds 150. These appellations vary in size considerably, and sometimes include a lot of land unsuited to viticulture (in contrast to the French system, for example, which only recognizes specific vineyard sites for AOCs). The largest AVA is Ohio River Valley, which covers 16.64 million acres (6.7 million ha) and crosses the borders of four states. Twelve other AVAs also cross state borders. At the other end of the scale, the smallest AVA is Cole Ranch covering about

150 acres (60 ha). It is important to note that some AVAs overlap and others sit inside one another.

AVAs have not found total acceptance with critics and wine commentators, and rational arguments abound as to why many AVAs should not exist, or should not bear the name they do. Condemnations vary from irrelevance and "lacking meaning" to the way some overlap while others cover too wide a region to have any consequence; in the eyes of other commentators the entire AVA system lacks direction, and is fragmented and unhelpful. Bureaucratic needs are part of the difficulty: when some growers petition for an AVA, neighboring areas that may have little in common tend to apply to be included, sometimes for historic reasons. Also, some AVAs are groups of smaller AVAs, wide enough for the conglomerate name to be meaningless, but giving the larger companies an identity for wine blended from the AVAs within.

Regardless of these criticisms, for now the AVA system does exist – partly because of pressure from the important EU markets – and will improve and evolve with time. And while AVAs may be "shaped" over future generations, this chapter attempts to tie together what a wine drinker might want to know about current labeling.

The larger AVAs, covering wide variations in soil and climate (in fact a multiplicity of the whole *terroir* concept), do not help consumers much in identifying a style of wine they might expect from a given AVA. But the majority of AVAs are more sensible in size and can make a contribution to consumer understanding. Comparing the chardonnays of AVA Russian River Valley with the more inland AVA Alexander Valley, for example, can highlight quite striking differences in *terroir*.

However, it needs to be made very clear that the registering of an AVA by the Alcohol and Tobacco Tax and Trade Bureau (known as the TTB, which in 2003 replaced the jurisdiction of the Bureau of Alcohol, Tobacco and Firearms) under the Federal Alcohol Administration Act is not a designation of quality. The TTB has no mandate to grade or regulate quality. The AVA is a statement about where the wine came from. There are no restrictions on grape varieties that can be grown within an AVA nor on viticultural or winemaking practices, yield per acre or minimum alcohol. There may sometimes be local regulations on spraying and other things but these have nothing to do with AVA rules or requirements.

Just the same, the clear implication is that winemakers within an AVA will want to achieve a standard of quality that will enhance the reputation of their AVA, making it a recognized wine-producing region known for quality wines. This image is in the hands of the growers within an AVA and their own quality control and standards, administered by local committees. It is not a requirement of law that an AVA represents quality, so each of the 150-plus regions must achieve their own recognition and standing in the eyes of the consumers.

Indeed, while all this might suggest that an AVA is but a formality, an application to register an area as an AVA may take years and great expense. Applicants must work with committees of local growers, winemakers and others who might be affected by an AVA; historic studies will need to be done on the proposed name for the AVA; weather people and in some instances soil experts will have to be employed; and all information must be pulled into shape by an attorney of law. Registering an AVA is far from a formality.

One of the interesting aspects of AVAs is that there is no legal need to use the name of the AVA on the label, even when the requirement is met that at least 85 percent of the grapes came from within the specified AVA. Some winemakers consider their own name, their brand, identifies the wine (and image) perfectly well without putting the AVA name on the label. And even when the AVA name is used on the label, the classification "AVA" does not need to appear underneath as it does on an AOC wine from France or a DOC wine from Italy. But when the AVA *is* on the label, the rules of that AVA apply.

No wine can be labeled with a city name; where vineyards come from within a city, the county name should be used unless there is a qualifying AVA. There are almost 60 counties in California alone and about three-quarters of them have vineyards.

There is no hierarchy of AVAs; all are equal. But there can be times when two AVAs overlap and the grapes are grown from within the overlap. Also, within Napa County in California, the several AVAs must also show "Napa Valley" as well as the specific AVA. For example, wine from the AVA Stags Leap will also show Napa Valley. This is a requirement under state law.

Where two AVAs are represented in a wine, there is very often a catch-all AVA for the wider net. Long Island is an AVA, for example, where two separate AVAs represent specific parts of Long Island. A blend of those two can therefore use the Long Island AVA.

It's appropriate here to mention "Meritage" in relation to labels on U.S. wines. This term is not related to the AVA system and is not an official rule in any way. There is a group of winemakers of some number that uses the term "Meritage" on wines from "Bordeaux" blends, Cabernet Sauvignon, Cabernet Franc, Merlot, Malbec and/or Petit Verdot for reds, and Sémillon and Sauvignon Blanc for whites. They have registered the name, and its appearance tells us that this is sold as a quality wine, blended by two or more of those grapes, by a member of the Meritage Association. One requirement is that member-wineries should use "Meritage" only on their most-expensive or second-most-expensive wines. Another requirement is that production must not exceed 25,000 cases of each Meritage wine per year.

Terms Used In Association With AVA Wine

Estate Bottled: Grapes grown and wine made within an AVA, where the vineyards are owned or controlled by the wine company making the wine. "Estate Bottled" on the label doesn't exclude bought-in grapes; as long as the winery's viticultural team controls the viticulture, then the wine may be labeled "Estate Bottled" if the other requirements are met. The requirements are that the wine must not leave the premises, but must be fermented, matured, cleaned and bottled in the winery. *Refer* **Proprietor Grown.**

Proprietor Grown: When a winery is outside an AVA but the winery owns or controls a vineyard entitled to the AVA, "Proprietor Owned" or "Vintner Owned" are allowable designations instead of "Estate Bottled." Other requirements of "Estate Bottled" must be met.

Reserve (Proprietor's Reserve, etc.): No legal meaning, but when used appropriately this is applied to a wine of higher standing than a plain label or non-Reserve wine.

Vineyard Designation: Vineyard names may appear on the label only if the vineyard is within an AVA and at least 95 percent of the grapes have come from the named vineyard.

Vintner Grown: *Refer* **Proprietor Grown.**

Grape Variety Families

Most California, Washington and Oregon wineries use European (*vinifera*) grape varieties: Merlot, Cabernet, Pinot Noir, Chardonnay, Riesling, and so on. Further east, however, other families of grapes are grown as well. There is no requirement under the AVA structure on the use of specific grape varieties, but where appropriate, reference to grape varieties has been made in the AVA notes below.

Despite their long history, hybrid and *labrusca* varieties have made little impact on the U.S. in terms of quality wine, and there is more experimentation being done in the eastern states with *vinifera*. However, there are exceptions in some states, such as the Hudson Valley in New York, Pennsylvania and Missouri where hybrids and American native vines do excel.

The following grape variety families are found in the U.S.:

Hybrid: French (*Vitis vinifera*)-American crosses are hybrids, the American varieties giving the hybrid resistance to phylloxera and mildews. The EU term is "inter-specific cross," a cross of two species or families. Hybrid varieties include Aurora, Cayuga, Seyval Blanc, Vignoles, Baco Noir, Chambourcin, Chancellor, Rosette, Villiard Noir, Chardonell, Traminette and others.

Labrusca: *Vitis labrusca* varieties include Catawba, Concord, Delaware, Diamond, Duchess, Elvira, Isabella, Ives, Niagara, Steuben and others.

American Native Varieties: Difficult to precisely define separately as many of the above *labrusca* and native hybrids are referred to as "Native American Vines" when some (or their derivatives) have come from Europe. But Norton, which is bred in Virginia and originally called Cynthiana, and still known as such in some places, can be an outstanding red worth seeking out in the eastern states.

American Viticultural Areas (AVAs)

Alexander Valley   *California*
AVA: 32,600 acres (13,200 ha)
Within Sonoma County, Alexander Valley AVA is wide, has fertile soils and
runs alongside the Russian River valley. Warm enough to ripen Cabernet
Sauvignon properly, and some fine Zinfandel have attracted attention as
well.

Altus   *Arkansas*
AVA: 12,800 acres (5,180 ha)
Altus AVA sits inside the Ozark Mountain AVA. Half a dozen wineries, most
on a mountain plateau above the Arkansas River around the town of Altus
(population barely 500), provide a selection of wines, mostly from American
native varieties but with some *vinifera* developing.

Anderson Valley   *California*
AVA: 600 acres (245 ha)
Cool, coastal AVA within Mendocino on California's North Coast. A small AVA,
yet almost as diverse as other local regions in altitude (it is not literally a "valley") and heat summation. This AVA is known for fine dark Zinfandels, along
with intense white wines and sparklings.

Applegate Valley   *Oregon*
AVA: Area not available
Warm and dry higher-altitude AVA with Cabernet and Merlot added to the
Oregon mix of Pinot Noir, Chardonnay, Pinot Gris and Riesling. A well-re-
garded area, especially for wineries concentrating on low yields and fruit
intensity.

Arkansas Mountain   *Arkansas*
AVA: 2.88 million acres (1.17 million ha)
Arkansas Mountain is huge but sits within the even larger Ozark Mountain
AVA. Tiny vineyard plantings (south of the Ouchita Mountains) mixing
vinifera with hybrids and American native varieties. Altus AVA is within its
borders.

Arroyo Grande Valley   *California*
AVA: 42,880 acres (17,370 ha)
AVA within the Central Coast catchment, an area just a little warmer than its
neighbors in San Luis Obispo County, south of San Francisco. Cool-climate
varieties like Pinot Blanc and Pinot Noir have done well here, but some wineries have also made successful wines from Zinfandel and other varieties.
Sparkling wine has also been successful.

Arroyo Seco   *California*
AVA: 18,240 acres (7,380 ha)
AVA in the Central Coast catchment, within Monterey's Salinas Valley around
– but mainly west of – the town of Greenfield. Cabernet Sauvignon is developing quickly in plantings but not on its own; Chardonnay is doing very
well also.

Atlas Peak   *California*
AVA: 11,400 acres (4,620 ha)
An AVA in Napa Valley's eastern mountains, named for the highest point of
Foss Valley, known as Atlas Peak. A pioneer AVA in introducing Sangiovese
to California.

Augusta   *Missouri*
AVA: Area not available
Augusta AVA sits inside Ozark Mountain AVA. Barely 600 acres (243 ha) of
vineyard grow in Missouri, just to the west of St Louis. Not much of the
plantings are *vinifera* but there are varieties like Norton, Seyal and Vidal,
varieties of superb quality and lots of interest. The *vinifera* family shows well
when cared for properly and clearly also has a future here.

Bell Mountain   *Texas*
AVA: 3,200 acres (1,300 ha)
One of six AVAs in Texas, Bell Mountain is in Gillespie County, just north of
AVA Fredericksburg. Cabernet Sauvignon is the star here, but this is a small
AVA.

Ben Lomond Mountain   *California*
AVA: 38,400 acres (15,540 ha)
Within the AVA of Santa Cruz Mountains, Ben Lomond Mountain sits to the
northwest, with only about 75 acres (30 ha) under vines. Fruit coming from
here is highly respected; but because of the small volume, Ben Lomond is
somewhat unknown.

Benmore Valley   *California*
AVA: 1,440 acres (580 ha)
Small AVA between Mendocino and Clear Lake within the North Coast of
California. One vineyard sets the scene with a small volume. This is an AVA
criticized for its "irrelevance."

Bennett Valley   *California*
AVA: 8,140 acres (3,300 ha)
New (late 2003) AVA with 650 acres (265 ha) already planted, just south of
Santa Rosa city and within Sonoma County. Temperatures are a little cooler
than the surrounding area and fog-affected. Although extensively planted in

the late 1880s, the area was decimated by both phyloxera and prohibition, and replanting only began in 1975.

California Shenandoah Valley   *California*
AVA: 10,000 acres (4,050 ha)
The California prefix is important, as there is also a Shenandoah Valley in West Virginia. The California site, tucked under the Sierra Foothills inland from Sacramento, is really more of a flattish table than a valley. This is Zinfandel territory in particular, but also grows Italian varieties and Chardonnay. Containing less than 1,500 acres (600 ha) of vineyard, the AVA overlaps El Dorado and Amador counties. The Sierra Nevada Range affects the climate, which is warm during ripening, balanced with cool nights.

Capay Valley   *California*
AVA: 102,400 acres (41,500 ha)
A new (2003) AVA in northwestern Yolo County, bordering Napa, Lake and Colusa Counties. "Capay" comes from the local Indian word for "stream." Cache Creek runs the entire length of the valley. Only 25 acres (10 ha) are currently planted and only one winery makes Capay-only wine.

Carmel Valley   *California*
AVA: 19,200 acres (7,770 ha)
AVA within AVA Monterey in the Central Coast catchment, basically facing the coast. Some small wineries by California standards do well, plus some grapes sold under contract to wineries outside the AVA.

Carneros
Refer Los Carneros

Catoctin   *Maryland*
AVA: 170,000 acres (68,800 ha)
On the lower, northern end of the Blue Ridge Mountains. Chardonnay and Cabernet do quite well here but there are plantings of French-American hybrid varieties as well. Small but energetic wine industry.

Cayuga Lake   *New York*
AVA: 460 acres (186 ha)
Within the Finger Lakes AVA, Cayuga Lake is the most easterly lake. Cayuga has scores of fairly small wineries, mostly on the western side, growing *labrusca* and hybrid grapes. There has also been steady experimentation with *vinifera* in the last decade.

Central Coast   *California*
AVA: 1 million acres (404,700 ha)
From San Francisco to Santa Barbara, Central Coast makes a decent-sized

strip down the Pacific coast and includes a healthy number of AVAs with their own identity: Livermore Valley, Santa Cruz Mountains, Santa Clara Valley, San Ysidro District, Pacheco Pass, Monterey, Santa Lucia Highlands, Arroyo Seco, San Lucas, San Benito, Paicines, Cienega Valley, Lime Kiln Valley, Mount Harlan, Carmel Valley, Chalone, Hames Valley, Paso Robles, York Mountain, Edna Valley, Arroyo Grande Valley, Santa Maria Valley, Santa Ynes Valley. Central Coast AVA is used for a few vineyards falling outside the above list, and mainly for blends of wines from two or more of the above mentioned vineyards.

Central Delaware Valley   *New Jersey and Pennsylvania*
AVA: 96,000 acres (39,000 ha)
There are vineyards both sides of the Delaware River between New Jersey and southeast Pennsylvania, but the area is not widely planted with vineyards.

Chalk Hill   *California*
AVA: 22,400 acres (9,070 ha)
An AVA within Sonoma, north of Santa Rosa, southeast of Healdsburg, in the foothills behind the Russian River valley. A little more than 800 acres (320 ha) with a high proportion of Chardonnay and Sauvignon Blanc.

Chalone   *California*
AVA: 8,540 acres (3,460 ha)
AVA in the Central Coast catchment, within Monterey and high in the Gavilan Mountains on the east of the Salinas River valley. Cooler varieties do well here, Pinot Noir, Chardonnay, Pinot Blanc. There is only one vineyard and winery.

Chiles Valley   *California*
AVA: 6,000 acres (2,430 ha)
Within the Central Coast AVA, Chiles Valley is a medium-sized vineyard district in the Napa, a little to the east of Rutherford AVA. There are 800 acres (300 ha) under vine and five local wineries, best known for Zinfandel. A little higher above sea-level than Napa.

Cienega Valley   *California*
AVA: Area not available
In the Central Coast catchment and within San Benito County, Cienega Valley AVA is something of a parallel AVA with Mount Harlan AVA, at differing elevations. Cienega Valley is not a widely used AVA.

Clarksburg   *California*
AVA: 64,640 acres (26,200 ha)
Southwest of Sacramento (including some islands in the delta), Clarksburg is

an AVA producing a wide range of grapes and styles, Chenin Blanc being the most highly regarded. This part of the California Delta has lots of channels and a high water table, providing peat-like organic soils that can be very fertile for grapes. These soils and the excess water in the area require a different type of vineyard management. Merritt Island AVA is within its borders.

Clear Lake   California
AVA: 168,960 acres (68,400 ha)
North Coast California AVA, named after a large freshwater lake. Most vineyards are in Big Valley southwest of the lake. Zinfandel country but Sémillon and Sauvignon Blanc also, adding up to a spread of grapes doing well.

Cole Ranch   California
AVA: 150 acres (60 ha)
Situated within Mendocino, Cole Ranch is the smallest AVA in the U.S., one vineyard and one winery.

Columbia Valley   Oregon and Washington
AVA: 1.15 million acres (465,000 ha)
Includes AVAs of Yakima Valley and Walla Walla Valley in Washington state. Protected by the Cascade Range, the area is very low in rainfall, but the Yakima and Snake rivers, flowing into the Columbia River, collectively provide irrigation water, which is essential to the area. A big AVA with a wide range of angles and elevations, heat summations and soils, Columbia Valley is complex, its best wines very highly regarded.

Cucamonga Valley   California
AVA: 109,400 acres (44,300 ha)
In the Los Angeles basin, Cucamonga AVA used to have far more vineyards than it has today. Demand for quality wine and the pressure of rising land prices has caused volumes to diminish. Wines from this AVA are not widely seen.

Cumberland Valley   Pennsylvania and Maryland
AVA: 765,000 acres (310,000 ha)
In the south of Pennsylvania, Cumberland Valley AVA lies near the Maryland border and stretches from the west bank of the Susquehanna River at Harrisburg to the Potomac River in Washington County in Maryland. Only about 100 acres (40 ha) are planted in grapes, *vinifera* and hybrid, and the area supports a handful of wineries.

Diablo Grande   California
AVA: 30,000 acres (12,150 ha)
Within San Joaquin Valley (inside the Central Valley AVA), Diablo Grande is a

defined area around Modesto. Not widely planted as a region but is home to the huge Gallo winery (which doesn't use the AVA because grapes are drawn from elsewhere as well) and other vineyards. The region is quantity-wine oriented and is successful at it. Few labels use the AVA.

Diamond Mountain   California
AVA: 5,000 acres (2,025 ha)
Subregional AVA of the Napa Valley on steep slopes of the Macayamas Mountains to the southwest of Calistoga. The slopes help the sunny ripening period and Cabernet Sauvignon does well.

Dry Creek Valley   California
AVA: 80,000 acres (32,400 ha)
Northeast of Healdsburg, Dry Creek Valley is a strip about 15 miles (25 km) long and barely 2 miles (3.2 km) wide. The valley floor is given over to white grapes, especially Sauvignon Blanc, while the edges up on the hillsides are more versatile and include some highly-rated Zinfandel.

Dunnigan Hills   California
AVA: 89,000 acres (36,000 ha)
Around the town of Dunnigan, west of Sacramento on the edge of the Sacramento Valley in the Central Valley.

Edna Valley   California
AVA: 22,400 acres (9,070 ha)
A cooler climate during ripening, Edna Valley is an AVA in the Central Coast catchment within San Luis Obispo County, best known for Chardonnay and Pinot Noir.

El Dorado   California
AVA: 416 acres (168 ha)
One of the first California AVAs, El Dorado has less than 20 wineries. Tucked in towards the Sierra Foothills, Italian varieties have done well in a well-spread mix of styles and grapes.

Escondido Valley   Texas
AVA: 32,000 acres (13,000 ha)
Cooler part of Texas in Pecos County near Fort Stockton.

Fair Play   California
AVA: 21,120 acres (8,550 ha)
Fairly new (2001) AVA to the south of El Dorado County, known locally as "South County." Zinfandel, Syrah and some Italian varieties share the limelight. About 15 smallish wineries, quite highly regarded.

Fennville   Michigan
AVA: 75,000 acres (30,350 ha)
Many of the world's finest regions are near water and Lake Michigan helps
Fennville on the south side. The AVA produces a lot of fruit juice from grapes,
and also a worthwhile range of *vinifera* from Pinot Gris to Cabernet Franc.

Fiddletown   California
AVA: 11,500 acres (4,660 ha)
AVA in the Sierra Foothills tucked in beside AVA California Shenandoah
Valley. Known best for Zinfandel but also producing a wide range of varieties
and styles. Rain and frost can make life difficult for quality wine growers.

Finger Lakes   New York
AVA: 8,400 acres (3,400 ha)
Covering two Finger Lakes, Keuka and Canandaigua (but not Cayuga and
Seneca, which have their own AVA), this AVA has more than 50 wineries,
mostly small in scale (with the odd exception) and is growing hybrids and
labrusca varieties, with increasing experimentation in *vinifera*.

Fredericksburg Texas Hill Country   Texas
AVA: 70,400 acres (28,500 ha)
One of six AVAs in Texas, this AVA sits within Texas Hill Country, the largest
AVA in the United States. It offers a good reputation for Chardonnay and
Cabernet Sauvignon but is tiny in volume.

Grand River Valley   Ohio
AVA: 125,000 acres (50,600 ha)
Within the large multi-state Lake Erie AVA, Grand River Valley is south of the
lake, near Ashtabula. A big area but contains less than 200 acres (80 ha) of
vineyards. An AVA considered to be climatically significant in its potential.

Grand Valley   Colorado
AVA: 32,000 acres (13,000 ha)
Grand Valley lies on the western side of the Rocky Mountains. An elevated
yet dry AVA with small vineyard plantings, less than 200 acres (80 ha), in
both *vinifera* and hybrids.

Guenoc Valley   California
AVA: 4,400 acres (1,780 ha)
Near Clear Lake AVA in Lake County, east of Mendocino County. A little
warmer than districts around it, with some hot daytime temperatures in
summer fluctuating to quite cold overnight. The entire AVA, which has
about 340 acres (140 ha) of vineyard, is within the larger property of the
Magoon family, and is all one winery.

Hames Valley   California
AVA: 10,240 acres (4,150 ha)
AVA within the Central Coast catchment, in Monterey County near San Luis
Obispo. Fairly hot ripening weather, and tiny production. The wine can be
fine but is not considered significant in terms of volume.

Hampton   New York
AVA: 136,450 acres (55,220 ha)
Known locally as The Hamptons, this is the smaller of two AVAs within
the Long Island AVA (the other one is North Fork). The Hamptons has less
than 150 acres (60 ha) under vine. Some interesting wines from Bordeaux
grapes.

Hermann   Missouri
AVA: 51,200 acres (20,700 ha)
A small vineyard zone between St Louis and Jefferson City, Hermann AVA
sits inside Ozark Mountain AVA. Perhaps 200 acres (80 ha) under vine but
overtly successful in Norton, Chambourcin and other non-*vinifera* varieties.

Howell Mountain   California
AVA: 14,080 acres (5,700 ha)
To the east of the Napa Valley, this mountainous AVA reaches as high as
1,500 feet (430 m). There is some accent on red wine; Zinfandels and
Cabernet also show strength and richness.

Hudson River   New York
AVA: 224,000 acres (90,650 ha)
The Hudson River running north of New York has a big AVA catchment in its
valley. A couple of dozen mainly small wineries offer both *vinifera* and hybrid
varieties.

Isle St George   Ohio
AVA: 640 acres (260 ha)
The Isle St George AVA is a very small part of the Lake Erie AVA on North
Bass Island, just south of the Canadian border. It has a long viticultural his-
tory because of the help given by the Great Lakes, and grows mostly *vinifera*
varieties.

Kanawha River Valley   Ohio and West Virginia
AVA: 64,000 acres (26,000 ha)
Tiny plantings, mostly on ridges across the river, provide barely 100 acres
(40 ha) of vineyard within the Ohio River Valley AVA. Planted mostly with
hybrids.

Knights Valley   *California*
AVA: 36,240 acres (14,700 ha)
AVA in the north of Sonoma, down near the northern edge of the Napa, Knights Valley is best known for Cabernet Sauvignon but other varieties are also on the increase.

Lake Erie   *New York, Pennsylvania and Ohio*
AVA: 2.24 million acres (907,000 ha)
The most extensive of New York's vineyards are on the banks of Lake Erie, well inland. There are more than 20 wineries. However, wine production is relatively small as most plantings are used for grape juice. Within Lake Erie is the Isle St George AVA on North Bass Island.

Lake Michigan Shore   *Michigan*
AVA: 1.28 million acres (518,000 ha)
In the southern part of Michigan along with much smaller AVA Fennville, Lake Michigan Shore has a spread of varieties including a fair amount of Cabernet Franc. Pinot Gris, Chardonnay and Riesling also do well as dinner wines. In some years, Icewine is made.

Lake Wisconsin   *Wisconsin*
AVA: 28,000 acres (11,340 ha)
AVA in Dane and Columbia counties, where hot summers allow grapes to ripen. A handful of wineries growing hybrids and some *vinifera*. Less than 50 acres (20 ha) under vine.

Lancaster Valley   *Pennsylvania*
AVA: 225,000 acres (91,050 ha)
The Lancaster Valley AVA, located in the Lancaster-Frederick lowland in the south of Pennsylvania near the Maryland border. About 220 acres (85 ha) of commercially-planted grapes, and three wineries.

Leelanau Peninsula   *Michigan*
AVA: 211,200 acres (85,500 ha)
On the eastern shores of Lake Michigan around the city of Traverse, Leelanau Peninsula AVA carries a handful of wineries with *vinifera* and hybrids. The coolness of the region gives higher acidity, which is well suited to sparkling wine – and some cellaring. Nearby is Old Mission Peninsula AVA.

Lime Kiln Valley   *California*
AVA: 2,300 acres (930 ha)
AVA within the Central Coast catchment within San Benito County and Cienega Valley. A cool AVA with just one vineyard, and thus rated as an "inconsequential" AVA by some commentators.

Linganore   Maryland
AVA: 57,600 acres (23,330 ha)
AVA in central Maryland, with three wineries on elevated vineyards, north and west of Mount Airy.

Livermore Valley   California
AVA: 96,000 acres (38,880 ha)
AVA within the Central Coast catchment, east of San Francisco Bay in Alameda County, with about 5,000 acres (2,000 ha) under vine. A warm region that is being squeezed by urban growth. Whites do well here but reds are not far behind.

Lodi   California
AVA: 551,500 acres (223,185 ha)
A warm but not hot AVA spanning Sacramento and San Joaquin counties in northern California, with rich, fairly fertile soil. A little underrated at present because of various issues and problems, but high quality wine is made here by winemakers careful of yield and winemaking practices. Zinfandel has done especially well. Lodi is a big volume AVA providing a wide range of grapes and styles. A further 93,500 acres (37,870 ha) south and west were added in 2002 (included in the above figures). However, a movement has begun proposing Lodi be divided into as many as nine separate AVAs, and certainly the volume of the vineyards seems to encourage this. The application and appeals will probably take until 2005 to be completed.

Long Island   New York
AVA: 749,150 acres (303,170 ha)
Almost entirely surrounded by water, this AVA has a relatively mild climate compared with some inland AVAs. Bordeaux grapes work quite well here. There are two AVAs within the broad one, Hampton and North Fork. The AVAs share 3,000 acres (1,200 ha) of vineyards and almost 30 wineries.

Loramie Creek   Ohio
AVA: 3,600 acres (1,460 ha)
A tiny vineyard area in Shelby County. Since the AVA was approved in 1982, most vineyards have closed.

Los Carneros   California
AVA: Area not available
Straddling part of the Napa Valley and Sonoma Valley, Carneros has made a name for itself particularly with its Chardonnay and Pinot Noir, leading also to widespread use of these grapes for sparkling wines. It is a "cool" region, thus not warm enough for Cabernet to ripen regularly.

Madera   *California*
AVA: 230,000 acres (93,100 ha)
In the San Joaquin Valley (within Central Valley AVA) just north of Fresno, Madera contributes a wide range of styles including some bigger-volume labels and some fortifieds. There were no wineries within the AVA at the time of writing, but there are active vineyards.

Malibu-Newton Canyon   *California*
AVA: 850 acres (345 ha)
Above the very fashionable Malibu beach, this is a tiny AVA with just one vineyard and winery.

Martha's Vineyard   *Massachusetts*
AVA: 64,000 acres (25,900 ha)
Island AVA producing some Viognier, Chardonnay and Cabernet, with just one winery.

McDowell Valley   *California*
AVA: 540 acres (220 ha)
Within Mendocino, south of the city of Ukiah, McDowell Valley is best known for its Syrah.

Mendocino   *California*
AVA: 275,200 acres (111,500 ha)
The most northern of California's wine regions, holding within it the AVAs of Potter Valley, Anderson Valley, McDowell Valley, Cole Ranch and Clear Lake.

Mendocino Ridge   *California*
AVA: 87,470 acres (35,400 ha)
Area to the east of the Mendocino AVA, stretching from the eastern border of Anderson Valley out towards the coast. Although covering a large area, the AVA is restricted to elevated vineyards above about 1,200 feet (370 m).

Merritt Island   *California*
AVA: 5,000 acres (2,000 ha)
Part of the California Delta's zone of water channels, Merritt Island is entirely within the Clarksburg AVA. Not much volume.

Mesilla Valley   *Texas and New Mexico*
AVA: 284,800 acres (115,250 ha)
A handful of wineries, more in New Mexico than Texas, has created interest in this AVA. About 220 acres (80 ha) under vine, mostly *vinifera*, irrigated from the Rio Grande.

Middle Rio Grande Valley **New Mexico**
AVA: 278,400 acres (112,700 ha)
Spreading from Santa Fe in the north to Belen in the south, most vineyards in this AVA lie above the Rio Grande at an elevation of 4,000–5,000 feet (1,200–1,500 m). A cool, dry AVA suited to hybrids.

Mimbres Valley **New Mexico**
AVA: 636,800 acres (258,000 ha)
Not many local wineries draw on these vineyards, which amount to about 450 acres (180 ha) around the town of Deming in southwest New Mexico. A high percentage of grapes go to wineries further south. Mostly *vinifera* grown, but with some hybrids.

Mississippi Delta **Mississippi, Louisiana and Tennessee**
AVA: 3.84 million acres (1.56 million ha)
A long AVA running down the Mississippi River through three states, even though the official "Delta" is where the river empties into the Gulf of Mexico. Muscadine varieties do well here.

Monterey **California**
AVA: 35,760 acres (14,500 ha)
A county AVA within the Central Coast catchment, south of San Francisco. Low rainfall means irrigation is important, and this is helped by the Salinas River. Within the Monterey County AVA are some individual AVAs with their individual statements: Arroyo Seco, Carmel Valley, San Lucas, San Lucas Highlands, Hames Valley and Chalone. A growing region in volume and importance with a wide range of grapes doing well.

Monticello **Virginia**
AVA: 800,000 acres (324,000 ha)
Around the city of Charlottesville on the eastern slope of the Blue Ridge Mountains, Monticello AVA is named after Jefferson's mansion. More than half Virginia's vineyards lie within this AVA, mainly *vinifera* varieties, and the AVA attracts growing interest as its quality increases.

Mount Harlan **California**
AVA: 7,440 acres (3,010 ha)
AVA in the Central Coast catchment and within San Benito County. Mount Harlan is an elevated AVA cooler than its neighboring (and overlapping) Cienega Valley AVA. Pinot Noir does well. One winery only.

Mount Veeder **California**
AVA: 15,000 acres (6,075 ha)
Subarea AVA of the Napa Valley on the slopes of Mount Veeder, with vineyards as high as 2,500 feet (800 m) above sea-level. With its volcanic soils it

is not a big yielding area but is highly respected for well-fruited Chardonnay and Cabernet.

Napa Valley   *California*
AVA: 225,280 acres (91,200 ha)
Famous district north of San Francisco, helped by its accessibility to such a large center of population and the fact that the region is very tourist-oriented. The 40 mile (65 km) curved strip with about 36,000 acres (14,600 ha) under vine is home to many fine vineyards, which reflect in high prices and sought-after status. Within the strip are more varied *terroirs* (many different soil types, heat summation variations, etc.) and some parts of the Napa have their own AVA: Howell Mountain, Mount Veeder, Oakville, Rutherford, Stags Leap, Wild Horse, Spring Mountain, Diamond Mountain and Carneros. Despite this, however, some wineries choose to use the more famous Napa Valley AVA.

The climate follows a cool-to-warm gradient from the southern end to the northern end, and recent plantings of varieties have been based more on the particular conditions of a site than they were 10 to 20 years ago. A wide range of grape varieties are grown; the most planted is Cabernet Sauvignon, but Merlot is catching up. Sauvignon Blanc, Pinot Noir and Zinfandel are also well-planted and the range of prices varies from US$8 to US$800 a bottle. There are legal battles over the use of Napa names on wines whose heritage goes back before 1987; this leads to a little confusion, but the biggest volume of wine using "Napa" and its sub-appellations come from within the specified AVA. Only a few do not, for reasons that are currently under legal scrutiny.

North Coast   *California*
AVA: 3.01 million acres (1.22 million ha)
North Coast is the umbrella AVA north of San Francisco's Golden Gate Bridge. It covers the Sonoma and Napa valleys, Clear Lake, and up to Mendocino. While it seems unlikely that a winery using grapes from Sonoma or Rutherford would choose to use the North Coast AVA, it is their right to do so if they wish. This AVA name is also used for blends of wines from AVAs within North Coast.

North Fork of Long Island   *New York*
AVA: 101,440 acres (41,100 ha)
With the much smaller Hampton AVA, North Fork AVA lies within the broader Long Island AVA. About 1,500 acres (600 ha) are under vine, mostly *vinifera* varieties.

North Fork of Roanoke   *Virginia*
AVA: Area not available
One of six AVAs in Virginia, covering the northern fork of the Roanoke River

down to the city of Roanoke. There are a small number of vineyards, but no wineries within this AVA.

North Yuba   *California*
AVA: 22,400 acres (9,075 ha)
In the Sierra Foothills, AVA North Yuba has relatively high rainfall but easily-draining soils. Some respected wines are made, from Cabernet Sauvignon to Sauvignon Blanc.

Northern Neck George Washington Birthplace   *Virginia*
AVA: 590,080 acres (240,000 ha)
One of six AVAs within Virginia. To the north of Virginia state (and thus accessible to residents of Washington, DC). A peninsula formed by the Potomac and Rappahannock rivers. Just one winery so far.

Northern Sonoma   *California*
AVA: 348,000 acres (141,000 ha)
A collective of six AVAs, motivated by Gallo, history has it, to cover all their Sonoma plantings. As a catchall, it includes almost all the AVAs of Sonoma County Green Valley, Russian River Valley, Chalk Hill, Knights Valley, Alexander Valley and Dry Creek Valley. The AVA has drawn criticism because it has hotter and cooler areas within it, reducing typicity.

Oakville   *California*
AVA: 5,760 acres (2,330 ha)
Overlaps part of Rutherford AVA, but essentially Oakville is a little cooler, and has a different soil type. Well regarded for Cabernet.

Ohio River Valley   *Indiana, Kentucky, Ohio and West Virginia*
AVA: 16.64 million acres (6.7 million ha)
Running alongside the Ohio River, in terms of area this is the largest AVA in North America but it has just 500 acres (200 ha) planted with grapes, mostly in hybrid varieties.

Old Mission Peninsula   *Michigan*
AVA: 19,200 acres (7,780 ha)
On the east side of Lake Michigan in Grand Traverse County, the cool climate of this AVA increases acidity to produce wines that are crisp and fresh (or suitable for aging), as well as sparklings. There are 200 acres (80 ha) under vine, mostly *vinifera*, with some hybrids.

Ozark Highlands   *Missouri*
AVA: 1.28 million acres (520,000 ha)
AVA inside Ozark Mountain AVA, about 100 miles (160 km) southeast of St Louis. Has about 200 acres (80 ha) planted, though very little in *vinifera*.

Ozark Mountain   *Missouri, Oklahoma and Arkansas*
AVA: 3.52 million acres (1.5 million ha)
Another mega-AVA covering the southern half of Missouri, the northwest corner of Arkansas and northeast Oklahoma, collectively almost 90 counties! Grows *vinifera* and hybrids, with plenty of Chardonnay and red Bordeaux varieties, with about 5,000 acres (2,000 ha) under vine. Within Ozark Mountain AVA are the AVAs of Altus, Arkansas Mountain, Augusta, Hermann and Ozark Highlands.

Pacheco Pass   *California*
AVA: 3,200 acres (1,300 ha)
Small, minor AVA, technically in San Benito County but close to Santa Clara Valley, near the town of Hollister. Its steep hills and thin topsoil have attracted little attention.

Paicines   *California*
AVA: 4,500 acres (1,820 ha)
An AVA in the Central Coast catchment, Paicines is one of five AVAs within San Benito County, located inland from Monterey County. Small plantings only.

Paso Robles   *California*
AVA: 666,600 acres (270,000 ha)
Within the Central Coast catchment, Paso Robles attracts increased attention as plantings increase. Italian grape varieties and some Syrah, Grenache and others are being experimented with and developed. Zinfandel, a variety that also has an Italian connection, does well in mature vineyards. About 20,000 acres (8,100 ha) under vine.

Potter Valley   *California*
AVA: 27,500 acres (11,140 ha)
Within Mendocino, north of the city of Ukiah, Potter Valley AVA is directly east of Redwood Valley AVA. It is best known for its Pinot Noir and white varieties, including botrytis-affected styles. About 1,000 acres (400 ha) under vine, but no wineries.

Puget Sound   *Washington*
AVA: 5.54 million acres (2.24 million ha)
North of the city of Seattle, with a well-respected 50 acres (20 ha) of vineyard that give Puget Sound some fame. This AVA is on the Pacific coast near Vancouver Island and the Canadian border, west of the Cascade Range.

Red Mountain   *Washington*
AVA: 4,040 acres (1,640 ha)
Red Mountain is part of the Yakima Valley and sits on a southwest-facing

slope east of the Yakima River. Being on the eastern side of the Cascade Range, it comes into Benton County. Warm enough to ripen Cabernet but also known for a wide *vinifera* range. Less than 1,000 acres (400 ha) are planted, but the potential is to almost double the planted area. "Power, strength and richness" is the style motto of the local growers.

Redwood Valley   *California*
AVA: 22,400 acres (9,065 ha)
North of Ukiah in Mendocino County, Redwood Valley is elevated and is cooler than surrounding areas, with an afternoon wind that blows through the mountains. However, Cabernet Sauvignon ripens quite well and forms the basis of the AVA, along with Barbera.

River Junction   *California*
AVA: 1,300 acres (525 ha)
A recent (2001) AVA in the southern Joaquin Valley, with about 700 acres (283 ha) planted mostly in Chardonnay. The "junction" is the meeting of the Stanislaus and San Joaquin rivers. Although small and fairly dry, it has a mix of soils, different to surrounding vineyards.

Rockpile   *California*
AVA: 15,400 acres (6,240 ha)
The latest (2002) of 12 AVAs in Sonoma County. Named after a "Rock Pile Ranch" from the 1800s, about 160 acres (65 ha) are planted with an emphasis on Zinfandel. Above the fog line in elevation, Rockpile AVA is a little warmer in summer than areas around it.

Rocky Knob   *Virginia*
AVA: 9,000 acres (3,650 ha)
In Southwest Virginia on the eastern side of the Blue Ridge Mountains, this small AVA has attracted growing interest recently as *vinifera* varieties (including Pinot Noir) have increased. Rocky Knob AVA is one of six AVAs in Virginia.

Rogue Valley   *Oregon*
AVA: Area not available
In the south of Oregon state, close to the California border, Rogue Valley AVA is warmer than the northern AVAs, higher in altitude, and fairly dry. Roughly a 70 x 60 mile (120 x 100 km) rectangle encompassing a handful of wineries with varied rainfall and mesoclimates within.

Russian River Valley   *California*
AVA: 96,000 acres (39,000 ha)
A highly respected AVA on the western side of Sonoma County, producing almost a third of the grapes grown within the county. This AVA has the

Russian River running through the center. A coolish California AVA, affected by the coming and going of fog, and also the variation of lowland and hilly vineyards. Its Pinot Noir and Chardonnay are both well sought-after. Inside the AVA is the Sonoma County Green Valley AVA.

Rutherford   *California*
AVA: 6,650 acres (2,700 ha)
A river terrace between Oakville and St Helena on the western side of Napa, with about 5,000 acres (2,000 ha) of vineyard very well respected for Cabernet Sauvignon in particular. Part of the AVA is the Rutherford Bench, some well-drained, infertile soil that has achieved a reputation especially for the quality of its Cabernet.

Saint Helena   *California*
AVA: 9,060 acres (3,670 ha)
Highly respected AVA in the northern half of Napa Valley although the range of wines runs from quaffing level to expensive and sought-after. The town of Saint Helena is popular with restaurant-goers and houses the Napa Wine Library.

San Benito   *California*
AVA: 45,000 acres (18,225 ha)
An AVA in the Central Coast catchment within San Benito County, something of a continuation of the Santa Clara Valley. San Benito County has one winery and about 2,000 acres (800 ha) of vineyard, spread over five AVAs: San Benito AVA, which encompasses Cienega Valley AVA and Paicines AVA, Mount Harlan AVA, and Lime Kiln AVA. Vineyards have come and gone in this region, and the majority of the crop is these days taken elsewhere for winemaking.

San Francisco Bay   *California*
AVA: 1.57 million acres (635,350 ha)
Since 1999, this AVA has included Contra Costa County, but it also overlaps four other counties around the San Francisco Bay region: San Francisco, San Mateo, Santa Clara and Almada, as well as parts of Santa Cruz and San Benito. Almost 6,000 acres (2,500 ha) are under vine, supplying about 40 local wineries. A wide range of styles with the white varieties showing best overall, but some fine reds are also produced here.

San Lucas   *California*
AVA: 33,920 acres (13,750 ha)
Within Monterey, this AVA has seldom, if ever, been used on labels to date. There are 5,000 acres (2,000 ha) of vineyards here, but most of the output is blended and sold under other names or AVAs.

San Pasqual Valley   *California*
AVA: 9,000 acres (3,650 ha)
AVA south of Temecula, down towards San Diego in the South Coast AVA. A small, relatively insignificant AVA at this stage but has potential.

Santa Clara Valley   *California*
AVA: 332,800 acres (134,700 ha)
South of San Francisco Bay, an AVA in the Central Coast catchment, with the San Ysidro AVA and Pacheco Pass AVA inside it. Santa Clara Valley is a warm region with some highly regarded vineyards and wines. "Silicon Valley," a major center for the computer industry, lies within it, so much of the viticulture has given way to expensive housing.

Santa Cruz Mountains   *California*
AVA: Area not available
A cool-climate AVA within the Central Coast catchment, running around the Santa Cruz Mountain range from Half Moon Bay in the north to Mount Madonna near Watsonville in the south. The minimum qualifying altitude is 400 feet (120 m) and a lot of the delimited area is too steep for vines. It's a large area but only 300 acres (120 ha) are under vines. This AVA in the San Francisco Bay area and around the coast to the south has produced some exceptional wines. Ben Lomond Mountain AVA is within its borders.

Santa Lucia Highlands   *California*
AVA: 22,000 acres (8,900 ha)
AVA in the Central Coast catchment, within Monterey. A warm, elevated area in the lee of the Tularcitos Mountains, able to ripen Cabernet Sauvignon most years.

Santa Maria Valley   *California*
AVA: 80,000 acres (32,400 ha)
AVA within the Central Coast catchment to the north of Santa Barbara County, containing about 5,000 acres (2,000 ha) of vineyards. A dry region, well respected and often attracting high prices for grapes.

Santa Rita Hills   *California*
AVA: 30,720 acres (12,440 ha)
Santa Rita Hills AVA is in the northern part of Santa Barbara County, between Buellton and Lompoc. About 700 acres (285 ha) are planted. This is a relatively new (2001) AVA, which had some dispute but now reflects the enthusiastic efforts of its winemakers to produce quality wine.

Santa Ynez Valley   *California*
AVA: 76,800 acres (31,100 ha)
AVA within the Central Coast AVA catchment, well to the south near Lompoc,

in Santa Barbara County. The Santa Ynez River (draining the Santa Ynez Mountains) drops elevation through the AVA area, giving a mix of temperatures and soils to suit a range of grapes from Merlot to Cabernet Sauvignon, Sauvignon Blanc and Syrah. These do well in different years, though some producers are criticized for over-cropping.

San Ysidro District   California
AVA: 2,340 acres (950 ha)
AVA in the Central Coast catchment, and within Santa Clara Valley AVA. Contains just one vineyard and no wineries. The vineyard is highly regarded.

Seiad Valley   California
AVA: 2,160 acres (875 ha)
In the north of California, with some elevation, this AVA has only tiny plantings, less than 3 acres (1 ha), which are regarded as insignificant.

Seneca Lake   New York
AVA: 204,600 acres (82,800 ha)
This is a new (2003) AVA recognizing the different wine character from the vineyards surrounding Seneca Lake. Seneca Lake is one of the 11 "Finger Lakes" and only the second to have its own AVA (along with neighboring Cayuga Lake). The others use the Finger Lakes AVA. Seneca is the deepest of the lakes and has a moderating impact on the harsh winters, although the AVA must be considered "cool" during ripening. About 3,700 acres (1,500 ha) of vineyards with almost 40 wineries. Riesling predominates.

Shenandoah Valley   Virginia and West Virginia
AVA: 2.4 million acres (971,250 ha)
There is also a Shenandoah Valley AVA in California, but that has the state name prefixed to it to distinguish it. In Virginia, the vines, growing *vinifera*, are tucked into the Blue Ridge Mountains. Volumes are increasing along with quality, and the AVA has quickly attracted growing interest.

Sierra Foothills   California
AVA: 2.6 million acres (1.05 million ha)
This AVA is east of Sacramento at the foot of the Sierra Nevada Range, although it is also just above the Central Valley AVA. The area is called "gold country" for its gold, "the retirement home" for obvious reasons, and is equally known for its hydro-electric power.

Solano County Green Valley   California
AVA: 2,560 acres (1,040 ha)
Not to be confused with the quite separate Sonoma County Green Valley AVA. Solano County is in the Bay area of San Francisco, a small vineyard area with little to say so far as an AVA.

Sonoita   *Arizona*
AVA: 208,000 acres (84,175 ha)
Arizona's only AVA, southeast of Tucson near the Mexican border. Four wineries around the town of Elgin, which have had mixed results so far.

Sonoma Coast (County)   *California*
AVA: 480,000 acres (194,250 ha)
A big umbrella Sonoma AVA, within which lie the AVAs of Sonoma Valley (including Sonoma Mountain), Russian River Valley, Sonoma County Green Valley, Chalk Hill, Knights Valley, Dry Creek Valley, Alexander Valley and Bennett Valley.

Sonoma County Green Valley   *California*
AVA: 32,000 acres (13,000 ha)
A small, almost elite AVA building on a strong and growing image. Just 1,000 acres (405 ha) under vine in a keen, dedicated industry. Some grapes are used in other wider appellations.

Sonoma Mountain   *California*
AVA: 5,000 acres (2,025 ha)
Another fairly elite AVA with just 700 acres (285 ha) under vine, much of which is blended and sold without the name Sonoma Mountain. But with its elevation, 400–1,600 feet (120–500 m) just above the fog line, the day/night temperature variations are lower than on the Sonoma Valley floor. This makes for stylistic differences, and there is potential for wineries to exploit this in the future.

Sonoma Valley   *California*
AVA: 4,000 acres (1,620 ha)
A very famous and highly respected AVA, Sonoma Valley in northern California runs 15 miles (25 km) from San Pablo Bay north to Mendocino. Sonoma Mountain AVA is within its borders. Sonoma Valley celebrates a wide range of grape varieties and styles, from Zinfandel, Cabernet, Merlot and Syrah, with Chardonnay heading the list.

South Coast   *California*
AVA: 115,200 acres (46,700 ha)
Running down from Los Angeles south to the Mexican border, this AVA is not widely planted but includes San Pasqual Valley AVA in San Diego County and Temecula AVA.

Southeastern New England   *Connecticut, Rhode Island and*
AVA: 1.88 million acres (760,800 ha)   *Massachusetts*
Along the Atlantic coast north of New York from New Haven in Connecticut, past Cape Cod to Plymouth in Massachusetts, this AVA spreads inland only

about 15 miles (25 km), so it is influenced by the maritime conditions. The coolness suits some varieties well and, with its mixed soil types, Southeastern New England AVA has shown some highlights with both *vinifera* and non-*vinifera* varieties.

Spring Mountain District   California
AVA: 8,600 acres (3,500 ha)
Subregion of Napa on the Macayamas Mountains, west of St Helena. Does well with a range of red and white varieties, especially powerful Zinfandel.

Stags Leap District   California
AVA: 2,700 acres (1,095 ha)
Subarea AVA to the north of the Napa Valley. Red soil adds a dimension to Cabernet Sauvignon and Merlot. A highly respected AVA commanding premium prices.

Suisun Valley   California
AVA: 15,360 acres (6,220 ha)
One of two AVAs within Solano County on the edge of the Delta (Solano County is within the Central Valley). Suisun Valley AVA has just a couple of wineries. Although separated from the Napa Valley by the Vaca Mountains, the climate is considered quite similar.

Temecula   California
AVA: 33,000 acres (13,365 ha)
In the South Coast AVA, down towards San Diego. Though it lies amidst quite arid country, the "Rainbow Gap" in the mountains allows some cool air to be sucked through and give life to the vineyards. The area has a housing estate called Rancho California, with related golf courses and retirement homes at 1,400 to 1,600 feet (425–500 m) elevation. Viticulture attracts other buyers. More than a dozen wineries get good business.

Texas Davis Mountains   Texas
AVA: 270,000 acres (109,300 ha)
AVA north of Fort Davis in the west of the state. A handful of wineries have attracted attention for their Sauvignon Blanc and Cabernet Sauvignon.

Texas High Plains   Texas
AVA: 2,000 acres (810 ha)
Cooler part of Texas to the north in the Panhandle, considered the most consistent in terms of quality within the state. Cabernet Sauvignon and Chardonnay rule in terms of quality and quantity.

Texas Hill Country   Texas
AVA: 9.6 million acres (3.9 million ha)

The largest single-state AVA in the U.S., which includes 22 counties and two more AVAs within its borders, Bell Mountain and Fredericksburg. Despite the size of the area, less than 1,000 acres (405 ha) are under vine. Produces ripe, soft styles of wine including those with quite a high percentage of Chenin Blanc and a clone of Muscat.

Umpqua Valley   Oregon
AVA: 768,000 acres (311,000 ha)
South of the Willamette Valley AVA below the city of Eugene, Umpqua Valley has almost 600 acres (245 ha) and a dozen winemakers. A good spread of varieties, with Riesling especially well regarded.

Virginia's Eastern Shore   Virginia
AVA: 436,480 acres (176,650 ha)
Not a lot of vineyards in this large AVA in the Delmarva Peninsula, but it is influenced helpfully by Chesapeake Bay. Virginia's Eastern Shore AVA has a good following for Chardonnay in particular, but a lot still to develop amidst growing local interest in viticulture and winemaking.

Walla Walla Valley   Oregon and Washington
AVA: 178,560 acres (72,300 ha)
Part of the valley in the Columbia River AVA between Oregon and Washington. Walla Walla Valley AVA is sheltered by the Cascade Range, a good winemaking climate for mainstream varieties; even Cabernet will ripen in well-run vineyards.

Warren Hills   New Jersey
AVA: 144,640 acres (58,500 ha)
In the northwest of the state, this AVA includes a handful of wineries mainly growing hybrids, but there are increasing experiments with *vinifera*.

West Elks   Colorado
AVA: 48,000 acres (19,440 ha)
Colorado has about 650 acres (265 ha) under vine and about 12 percent of this is in West Elks, a new (2001) AVA in Colorado's very elevated vineyards. Chardonnay and Merlot predominate.

Western Connecticut Highlands   Connecticut
AVA: 1.01 million acres (408,000 ha)
Inland from Long Island Sound, this is a large AVA with small vineyard holdings not demanding of attention.

Wild Horse Valley   California
AVA: 3,300 acres (1,335 ha)
Part of the California Delta. Separated from the Napa Valley by the Vaca

Mountains, Wild Horse Valley AVA is considered similar in climate. Part of this AVA overlaps Solano County Green Valley.

Willamette Valley   Oregon
AVA: 3.3 million acres (1.34 million ha)
Popular AVA with well-scattered vineyards, highly regarded for its Pinot Noir, which takes up almost 40 percent of the vineyards, although some critics suggest this is not the regional strength. Pinot Gris from Willamette Valley is doing well.

Willow Creek   California
AVA: 6,000 acres (2,430 ha)
Insignificant AVA in Trinity County, along the Trinity River. Little vineyards and no special claim to fame.

Yadkin Valley   North Carolina
AVA: 1.4 million acres (573,000 ha)
A new (2003) AVA in northwestern North Carolina, mostly within the Piedmont Triad region. An area with 200 years of winemaking history, today there are 10 wineries and about 400 acres (160 ha) of vineyards.

Yakima Valley   Washington
AVA: 665,600 acres (270,000 ha)
Within the Columbia Valley AVA, this is a valley of the Yakima River, with Athanum Ridge and the Rattlesnake Hills to the north and Tappenish Ridge and Horse Heaven Hills to the south. A good spread of *vinifera* varieties are planted, Merlot being the most favored, with Sémillon also grown in some quantity. A dry area, dependent on irrigation from the Columbia River.

York Mountain   California
AVA: 9,360 acres (3,800 ha)
AVA within the Central Coast catchment, on the western boundary of Paso Robles AVA. Its Pinot Noir and Chardonnay are respected.

Yorkville Highlands   California
AVA: 40,000 acres (16,200 ha)
An AVA within Mendocino, with just a few small vineyards lying between Cloverdale and Anderson Valley.

Yountville   California
AVA: 8,260 acres (3,345 ha)
Cooler region towards the south of the Napa. Its best vineyards are on stony alluvial soils. Merlot and Chardonnay are especially strong, but there is some development of other varieties like Sangiovese and Cabernet Franc. A sparkling wine base is also produced but is usually blended with other AVAs.

CHAPTER 7

Canada

Vintners Quality Alliance (VQA)
Designated Viticultural Area (DVA)

Although small in volume, Canada has a wine industry of considerable interest. The country is famous for its Icewine, but because yields are tiny, relatively small amounts are exported. Four provinces, Nova Scotia, Quebec, British Columbia and Ontario, have wine industries and their vineyards total almost 23,500 acres (9,500 ha) collectively, which are planted with both *labrusca*, *vinifera* and other cool climate hybrid varieties. Two of these provinces, British Columbia and Ontario, contain the majority of the plantings and both provinces have an "appellation of origin" system known as the Vintners Quality Alliance (VQA).

Although it enjoys warm summers, the stark winters and the length of the cold season present Canada with its own set of challenges. Vineyards tend to be established near lakes and oceans to minimize some of the effects of the cold. Within such restraints, however, Ontario can enjoy a climate similar to Burgundy. In some years it is even warmer over summer, and wines of interest are increasing in this province. There is much development ahead.

Building on the cool winter factor has led to the development of Icewine. This is made from grapes naturally frozen on the vine, which reduces the water and intensifies the sugar and flavors. Made from grapes picked as late as the new year (sometimes as late as February), Icewine is making a big Canadian statement.

In 2001, a ruling allowed Canada's sweet wines (Icewine) into the European Union, an exemption that some other countries have not been given. Canada is said to produce the largest quantity of Icewine in the world, helped by its prolonged patches of frosty nights during the winter. It is not uncommon for Icewine grapes to be picked in the early hours of the morning at 17°F (–8°C) and colder. The frozen water in the juice thus allows a few drops of nectar to come out and give concentrated flavors with plenty of residual sweetness and high acidity, creating a perfect equilibrium and balance.

Canada is also working hard with varieties like Chardonnay, Riesling and Pinot Noir. Some need bottle age to balance, settle and meld components. Shortness in summer warmth may not help ripeness levels every year, but when everything works some lovely wines are produced.

To promote identifiable quality, the Vintners Quality Alliance (VQA) began in Ontario in 1988 and then in British Columbia in 1990. Nova Scotia and Quebec have yet to join. This form of appellation system is essentially based on defining areas that the grapes must come from, similar to the AVAs of the United States. The focus is on "where" rather than "from what" and "how much" but at least regulations, systems and controls are in place.

Designated Viticultural Areas (DVAs)

At present the VQA recognizes a total of seven DVAs in the following two provinces of Canada:

Ontario: Niagara Peninsula, Pelee Island, Lake Erie North Shore.
British Columbia: Okanagan Valley, Similkameen Valley, Fraser Valley, Vancouver Island.

The provinces of Nova Scotia, a total of 250 acres (100 ha), and Quebec, a total of 500 acres (200 ha), have yet to join this system. In addition to restricting the area the grapes must come from, there are some further restrictions on what qualifies as a DVA:

- Wines must be made from within the delimited area specified, and must be from approved varieties (Chardonnay, Riesling, Pinot Noir and hybrids, such as, Vidal Blanc, Marechal Foch and Baco Noir).

- The sugar-level of the grapes at picking time must reach a specified minimum for each variety in each DVA.

- The varietal minimum is 85 percent of the grape(s) named on the label and must show the character of that variety. So a wine labeled Chardonnay, for example, must be made from at least 85 percent Chardonnay.

- 85 percent of grapes must be from the vintage named on the label.

- Wines labeled as "Estate Bottled" must be made entirely (100 percent) from vineyards owned or controlled by the winery in a DVA and the winery must be in the same DVA as the vineyards.

- If a vineyard name is used on the label, the vineyard must be within a DVA and 100 percent of the grapes must come from that vineyard.

- Minimum sugar levels at picking must be reached for wines labeled "Estate Bottled" or named with a designated vineyard.

- Wines must be certified by a tasting panel (and laboratory analysis is carried out if required) before they can carry the VQA nomenclature.

- 100 percent of the grapes used must have been grown in Ontario or in British Columbia.

Icewine

Canadian Icewine (a registered brand) also fits into the VQA system, again only within British Columbia and Ontario to date. The requirements for Icewine are as follows:

- All Icewine growers and winemakers must be registered and available to be monitored in their procedures and audited in their records.

- The grapes must be harvested "naturally frozen on the vine" at a minimum sugar level of 35 Brix; the juice must be at least 32 Brix after pressing.

- No picking is allowed before November 15.

- The temperature must be 17°F (–8°C) before picking can commence.

- No sugar can be added; all sugar must come naturally in the grape juice.

- No tank-freezing is allowed; the Icewine must be "made" by vineyard frosts.

- The finished wine must have a residual sugar of at least 125 grams per liter.

- Full records must be kept and available for audit.

Most Icewine comes from Riesling or Vidal grapes. However, there has been a recent trend towards using some Pinot Blanc, Chenin Blanc, Gewürztraminer and even some red grapes (Cabernet Franc), varieties late in ripening and with some durability, so that they can be left on the vine long after normal harvest times. Their skins are thick enough not to rot before the freezing temperatures cut in. In 1999 this occurred on January 18, 2000, while the 2001 harvest in some vineyards was not picked until the first week of March 2002. It's a risky business, as the fruit can be greatly damaged long before the right picking conditions occur. Birds and animals attracted to high-sugar grapes are just one risk, and netting is extensively used. Weather, of course, is another risk, and grapes for Icewine may be picked before Christmas or as late as March. In between times, nasty weather can wipe out the entire lot while the grower is waiting for the right frost.

Provinces and Designated Viticultural Areas (DVAs) of Canada

Fraser Valley
British Columbia
DVA
Close to the U.S. border, east of Vancouver on the flood plain where the Fraser River meets the Pacific Ocean via the Strait of Georgia. Although home to a major winery drawing grapes from elsewhere, Fraser Valley has only about 60 acres (25 ha) of plantings so this wine is not widely seen.

Lake Erie North Shore
Ontario
DVA
DVA in the southwest part of Ontario on the northern side of Lake Erie; across the border, the banks of this same lake are home to an extensive American AVA. This is a difficult DVA in which to grow grapes; while the lake helps moderate conditions through the ripening season, it freezes over in winter and can wipe out vineyards unless growers take precautions in advance. Some vineyards cover their vines with earth for several months to insulate them from the cold, uncovering them when the worst of the frosts are over. Such a measure requires wider row spacing in the vineyard to allow mechanization of this process. The fine wines produced from the right years' harvests makes this extra work worthwhile.

Niagara Peninsula
Ontario
DVA
With Lake Ontario on the north side, and the Niagara River with its famous Falls to the east on the U.S. border, Niagara Peninsula DVA carries the weight of the Canadian wine industry. About 75 percent of volume comes from here and it is home to most of Ontario's wineries. Affected climatically by the Niagara Escarpment, which protects it against winds, and Lake Ontario, which tempers the coolness, Niagara Peninsula survives some difficult inland conditions and carries with it much of the reputation and image of Canada's wine industry.

Okanagan Valley
British Columbia
DVA
A valley 100 miles (160 km) long with some 3,000 acres (1,200 ha) under vine in the south of the province close to the U.S. border. This is a major region in British Columbia, with more than 90 percent of the province's production. Lake Okanagan helps dramatically in tempering the conditions of this DVA, which has quite wide day/night temperatures during the ripening period, a factor that can help quality considerably when other conditions are right. Almost all grape varieties are *vinifera*; there is Chardonnay, and German hybrids like Bacchus especially, and some red grapes including Pinot

Noir are on the "serious trial" list. It's worth remembering that not too far south in Washington State, Pinot Noir has done very well.

Pelee Island   **Ontario**
DVA
Covers about 600 acres (250 ha) of vineyards on an island in Lake Erie, a one-vineyard, one winery DVA. In the cool, and sometimes very cold, conditions the vintage is late, even by Canadian standards. Pelee Island's winery is known for crisp, fresh wines, but is looking to increase depth and intensity to add body and interest.

Province of British Columbia
This province, which includes the DVAs of Okanagan Valley, Fraser Valley, Similkameen Valley and Vancouver Island, lies at the western edge of Canada on the Pacific Ocean, a great distance from the closest winemaking province, Ontario (and much closer to the U.S.'s Washington state). The majority of production (more than 90 percent) is in the Okanagan DVA. All wines labeled as "British Columbia" must be made 100 percent from grapes grown in the province.

Province of Nova Scotia
Island province on the east coast of Canada in the Atlantic Ocean, almost mirroring in size and position Vancouver Island on the west coast in the Pacific, although Nova Scotia is a couple of degrees latitude further south. Just 325 acres (132 ha) of vineyard. A mix of varieties including *vitis vinifera*, *vinifera* hybrids and some old Russian ones spread the styles of wine available.

Province of Ontario
This province includes the DVAs of Lake Erie North Shore, Niagara Peninsula and Pelee Island. About 80 percent of Canada's grapes are grown in Ontario; Riesling and Chardonnay are well regarded in good years, along with the Icewine. The red *vinifera* varieties, however, seem poised to enter the picture, with Ontario's Burgundy-like climate encouraging Pinot Noir plantings especially. All wines labeled as "Ontario" must be 100 percent from the province.

Province of Quebec
On the east of Canada, Quebec has almost 500 acres (200 ha) mostly in non-*vinifera* varieties (Seyval Blanc dominates the plantings) in a cluster of vineyards. There are about 30 wineries around the town of Dunham, 50 miles (80 km) southwest of Montreal tucked into the border with the U.S., a valley with a cottage industry and only one semi-commercial producer. Because of the tax structure, most wines are sold at the cellar door, and tourists play a major role in absorbing the quantities.

Similkameen Valley   *British Columbia*
DVA
West of the Okanagan Valley, this small DVA of barely 100 acres (40 ha) planted with almost entirely *vinifera* lies along the Similkameen River, and includes only a couple of wineries.

Vancouver Island   *British Columbia*
DVA
Large island off the Pacific Coast. The southern tip lies off the U.S. coast; but the majority of the island runs north past Vancouver, separated from the mainland by a series of straits. The vineyards are on the more sheltered, eastern side of the island but there are barely 70 acres (30 ha) under vine, planted in a wide spectrum of grape varieties from Pinot Noir to German hybrids.

CHAPTER 8

New Zealand

New Zealand is the evolving boutique wine country of the world. Over the 1990s, this island nation became more attractive to wine drinkers internationally despite its small volume. The entire country produced just 90 million liters in 2002 after its biggest-ever harvest to date. In 2003, New Zealand produced just 60 million liters despite increasingly productive vineyards. When the price is spread over volume, its wines are on average the most highly priced on the London market. Yet there are no "high ceiling" wines in terms of price – New Zealand has no Grange, no Lafite, no Supertuscan nor Atlas Peak.

New Zealand's wine industry was reborn in 1970 in a shift from fortified wine to table wine, and revitalized in 1986 with a Government-paid vine-pull scheme. In 2004 the average vineyard is barely six years old.

New Zealand is tiny and idiosyncratic. With almost 50,000 acres (20,000 ha) now under vine, and some still coming into production, New Zealand's whole vineyard is the size of Alsace, half that of Champagne, one-third of Rioja, one-twelfth of Bordeaux and one-thirteenth of Australia. The 120,000-tonne crop from 2002 was a record, yet grapes are still being planted. Sauvignon Blanc rules exports, Chardonnay is the most-planted variety, and Merlot and the Cabernets are perhaps the most promising as an international style. Pinot Noir attracts the most attention and Syrah is the most undiscovered, while "new" varieties like Viognier and Pinot Gris continue to do well and expand in plantings. But as an indication of how critical the climate can be, despite new plantings, the 2003 crop was down 45 percent because of frost damage.

The national vineyard is planted with 12,500 acres (5,000 ha) of Chardonnay and 17,000 acres (6,800 ha) of Sauvignon Blanc. Then follows some 8,000 acres (3,200 ha) of Bordeuax red varieties, while the

8,250 acres (3,300 ha) of Pinot Noir – a rising star for New Zealand – is divided between the sparkling wine (which has its own story) and the often-delicious red.

New Zealand is different than Australia. Not only is it much smaller, its climate is also cooler. While Australia has more economies of scale, and land near water sources is generally cheaper, New Zealand vineyards are small and expensive. Where Australia offers volume at the right price as well as serious, premium wines, New Zealand wine tends to have a higher average price. In wine styles, Australia's warm climate yields hearty, easy-drinking reds, and lots of straightforward but good Chardonnay; New Zealand's cooler climate means grapes are slower to ripen and picking is later, producing a style with more acidity which is slower to open up and not as giving. New Zealand is more vintage-variable than Australia and it has been said that it has more in common with France on the other side of the world than with its neighbor.

Like Australia, there is much to settle with regard to wine law before New Zealand can meet the needs and requirements of the target markets of the EU, the United States and Asia. Because Australia and New Zealand as neighbors have a free trade agreement, wines from each country can flow into the other at will, with no impositions other than local wine taxes. Australia provides New Zealand's supermarkets with affordable quaffers, while a greater proportion of New Zealand production is exported at a higher price.

Label Requirements

New Zealand has no appellation system like Europe, only a legislative framework for a system like Australia's Geographical Indicators (GI) system or the United States' AVA system. However, there is a Geographic Indicators Act, which the wine industry, through its formal body the Winegrowers of New Zealand, plans to implement when necessary, in line with negotiations with other countries and the World Trade Organization.

There are also labeling requirements, closely in line with Australia, as the two countries strive to harmonize their food and drug regulations. One of these is the number of "standard drinks" in each bottle or container. The base for one "standard drink" is a bottle (355 ml) of 4% alcohol beer. This converts to eight standard drinks in a 750-ml bottle of wine at 13.5% alcohol. In other words, the amount of alcohol in that bottle of wine is the same as in eight bottles (355 ml) of 4% alcohol beer. This is now a mandatory requirement to be shown on labels of all drinks.

Varietal minimum: New Zealand regulations require a minimum of 85 percent of the variety named on the label of exported wines. Named blends must be listed in descending order of proportions. A vintage minimum of 95 percent is required when the vintage is shown.

As of 2003, there are now also requirements to show allergens, anything added to the wine that may cause a physical reaction in some people. Some winemakers have been hesitant about this, and there is a need for greater clarification about what must be shown on the label.

New Zealand's Wine Regions

Auckland

South of Warkworth township, down to the Bombay Hills south of Auckland. This region includes the long-established wineries of Kumeu and Henderson west of Auckland, most also drawing grapes from regions to the south. The region also includes the growing and prestigious Waiheke Island area in Auckland's harbor, though not every winery on the island is keeping up the standard. There is also an evolving area known as Matakana, 80 miles (60 km) north of Auckland, and there is a new subregion south of Auckland, around Clevedon, Papakura and Pukekohe, where passionate wine growers with small-scale holdings are producing varied wines ranging from Italian-style reds to intense Bordeaux reds. As a viticultural region Auckland is tiny by global standards, and most of its wineries are drawing grapes from other areas in New Zealand.

Canterbury

The main city of the Canterbury region is Christchurch. A 25-mile (40-km) radius around the city gives us one subregion of Canterbury, although this subregion is crammed with varied mesoclimates. It's cool territory though, and from the inland West-Melton on the highway west towards the mountains, around southern Christchurch and Banks Peninsula, and out to Akaroa on the coast is a collection of locations battling, but doing very well in good years, with Pinot Noir and Chardonnay. There are also some good growers further south, as far as the city of Timaru, where it is even cooler and more risky.

Waipara: The other important Canterbury subregion. Separate to but still very much part of Canterbury, Waipara is almost ready to stand on its own as a wine region. Waipara and Amberley, two towns within 6 miles (10 km) of each other and 45 minutes drive north of Christchurch, have a growing reputation for some sound wines, especially those based on Pinot Noir, but other varieties as well. This is a young region, with lots still to settle, and vineyards yet to age. It has excellent promise.

Central Otago

This most recent star of New Zealand viticulture is inland, a region two-thirds of the way down the South Island. Dominated by mountains of the Southern Alps, the Central Otago wine region is centered around Queenstown, where the airport is, yet encompasses the towns and subregions of Bannockburn, Alexandra, Cromwell and Wanaka. Two-thirds of the plantings are Pinot Noir, and this is the current focus, though the average age of Pinot Noir vineyards is barely six years. There is a lot of potential here, and much work is required to substantiate what has already been done, but already the region is producing some exciting wines.

Gisborne
The third largest wine region in New Zealand, situated on the east coast half way up the North Island. Gisborne is easily written off as a volume wine provider, yet it has the dynamics to surpass that image with the right vineyard site and good vine management. Fertile soils tend to encourage larger yields, but Gisborne has provided some surprises: Chardonnay and Gewürztraminer can work well here when cropped low. Red wine generally has not been strong.

Hawke's Bay
Hawke's Bay is serious wine country located around the cities of Napier and Hastings on the east coast of the North Island, south of Gisborne. There are dynamics here still to be unleashed. Red Bordeaux varieties are the key players here, developing into a new regional strength. Syrah is strong and positive, with young vines and big potential. Chardonnay is making a statement for those willing to be patient and allow three or four years' bottle age after vintage. In the wings, Pinot Noir and Riesling seem to be overlooked, while Viognier and Pinot Gris await their time in the spotlight. There is still a lot to happen here and plantings continue.

Worth noting as label identities within Hawke's Bay are the two following "appellations," although such formal groupings have no legal status other than their own incorporation:

Gimblett Gravels: Soil-based, a defined area of 2,100 acres (850 ha) of old gravelly riverbeds just south of Hastings; most of this is already under vine. Conforming grapes from member wineries are able to carry this title, and a plain brown logo-sticker. Potential for Chardonnay, Syrah, Merlot, Cabernet Sauvignon and Franc has been established, and the identity is growing as a subregion of Hawke's Bay.

Ngatarawa Triangle: Perhaps better known as the "Red Metal Triangle," this is adjacent to the Gimblett Gravels subregion, and the red metal soil is preferred by some as strong territory, for Merlot-high reds in particular. The triangle is based on three major roads – State Highway 50, Ngatarawa Road and Maraekakaho Road. So far, the wineries drawing from this subregion have not incorporated in the way the Gimblett Gravels wineries have done, but this may occur later.

Marlborough
At the top of the South Island, Marlborough is the largest (and fastest growing) New Zealand wine region. The area has a high proportion of Sauvignon Blanc plantings, which seem to suit the breezy sea air between the Tasman Sea and the Pacific, and such conditions can ripen Chardonnay as well. Riesling, Pinot Noir and sparkling wine all have their stake in the future. Marlborough is still finding an identity, an image for itself, but is very much on the rise.

Marlborough contains the following subregions, but it is fair to note sub-regional blends are quite common.

Awatere Valley: About 20 miles (30 km) south of Blenheim. For a long time this was cheaper land because of the distance from town, but now serious blocks suited to viticulture are being snapped up at higher prices. A touch cooler and slower to ripen than Wairau Valley, Awatere Valley seems to suit Sauvignon Blanc, and with the grapes coming in a week later it also helps winery flow at vintage time.

Waihopai Valley: A bit further out, this is almost a tributary valley to the Wairau Valley with the Montana Brancott Vineyard nearby.

Wairau Valley: The mainstream block 10 minutes' drive from Blenheim airport, especially focused on the Rapaura Road and adjacent blocks.

Nelson
To the west of Marlborough, Nelson has an equal claim for its Sauvignon Blanc, but has much less planted. Nelson is a smaller region demanding interest over varieties like Chardonnay and Pinot Noir. This is mixed territory, a collective of areas, soils and climates, and is finding its way through its own subdistricts and its own evolution. Some great wines have emerged from Nelson and more will follow.

Northland
Covers the area north of Warkworth township (40 miles/60 km north of Auckland) to the top of the North Island. A small viticultural region of about 100 acres (40 ha), with enthusiastic participants keen to use the warm-temperate climate. Some highlights.

Waikato
Stretches from south of the Bombay Hills below Auckland, down to Taupo and across to Tauranga. The region around Te Kauwhata once appeared more promising than it is today, but some strong moves are continuing here. Waikato is a tiny region, even by New Zealand standards, and it has not yet attracted much attention.

Wellington-Wairarapa
South of Hawke's Bay, running down to the base of the North Island, lies the province of Wellington, a region that stretches north of New Zealand's capital city of the same name. The wider region includes the province of Wairarapa – which demands vinous attention in itself – and an area of vines on the west coast from Paraparaumu up to Marton, small plantings but with the potential to evolve as a subregional statement.

The main Wellington region wine statement comes from Wairarapa province, however, which runs from north of Masterton down to Martinborough (easily confused with the similarly spelt Marlborough, a separate region at the top of the South Island). Martinborough has a diverse range of wines, from Pinot Noir to Sauvignon Blanc, Riesling to Cabernet and Merlot, and all seem to do well. Martinborough wine demands a premium price and long-term attention. Other Wairarapa subregions are also on the rise, with young, enthusiastic wine growers working young vineyards; so there is much still to happen in this province.

CHAPTER 9

Australia

Geographical Indications (GI)

A vibrant country with about 390,000 acres (160,000 ha) under vine, Australia has made a huge impression on the wine world since 1985 and planted far and wide as a result, while at the same time countries in Europe like Italy, France and Spain have pulled up vineyards at an even faster rate. There were 450,000 tonnes of Syrah crushed in Australia in 2002 alongside 105,000 tonnes of Sémillon, 250,000 tonnes of Cabernet Sauvignon and the same of Chardonnay. With Riesling and other varieties this all adds up to a growing, complex industry.

Australian regions are mostly warm, and high in heat during ripening; yet cooler sites do exist. Coonawarra is considered a cool region, and it is sometimes a struggle to ripen Cabernet there without giving the wine a green, herbal character; but in the right years, this is not an issue. Victoria runs from nicely warm zones in the northwest of the state like Mildura to very warm parts in the east like Rutherglen, through to cooler zones like the Yarra Valley east of Melbourne and the Mornington Peninsula south of that city. In the Macedon hills in Victoria, Cabernet is picked most years in June, mid-winter in the Southern Hemisphere!

West Australia has its own extremes, like the prestigious and cooler Margaret River, just a three-hour drive away from the Swan Valley, which rates among the world's hottest viticultural climates. Western Australia's abundance doesn't stop there; Albany and Frankland River abound in quality wine, Denmark is fighting for its name and image, while areas like Mount Barker have shown very good quality wines for 20 years.

For many international wine drinkers, Australia's wine base is the state of South Australia, or more especially a strip of land running up the eastern side of the state from Mount Gambier in the bottom right-hand corner of South Australia, and from Coonawarra and Wrattonbully up to the big-volume Riverland districts. Just to the west of this line sit McLaren Vale, Adelaide Hills, Barossa and Clare Valley.

The largest Riverland district is hot and the wine is underrated for quality; the district is able to provide a wonderful *terroir* statement of its own with easy-drinking, well-priced wine that is an ideal accompaniment to a casual lunch or a family dinner.

Clare Valley, at the north of the South Australian wine strip, is legendary for its reds. It is perhaps best known for Cabernet, but Shiraz does very well too. Clare Valley also has a long history of success with Riesling, and winemakers are now banding together to bottle that variety under screw caps.

South Australia is best known for the Barossa Valley northeast of Adelaide. This district processes much more fruit than it grows, because it is the center for many wine companies that have vineyards further afield. With its proximity to Adelaide, the Barossa Valley enjoys a busy tourist trade and offers suitable hospitality and some decent restaurants to those inclined to relax for a day or two among the wine-oriented towns like Tanunda and Nuriootpa, steeped in history and reflecting the Germanic roots of its settlers.

The Adelaide Hills, spreading in a semi-circle around Adelaide, demand attention for their cooler zones and ambitious commitment. To the south, McLaren Vale shows some magnificent old vines, and grapes like Mourvèdre and Grenache link with those from 80-year-old Shiraz vines to provide their own statement, in a wine once considered cheap and quaffable that is now a national treasure. Also to the south, within half a day's drive from Adelaide, lies Padthaway, Coonawarra and other coastal and inland regions; these are collectively known as the Limestone Coast, but each region claims its own style.

Coonawarra, McLaren Vale, Barossa Valley and Clare Valley may have their own identities, with a lesser profile for Adelaide Hills and Padthaway, but much wine is also made under a collective belief that the brand is greater than the area. This strip of South Australia, 375 miles (600 km) from Coonawarra to Clare Valley, carries the great blenders of all time. The great Penfolds Grange Shiraz, retailing for about the same price as a first-growth Bordeaux red, may be South-Australia based, using grapes from Coonawarra to Clare, but in some years it may be assembled with a proportion of grapes from Western Australia and/or New South Wales, using whatever it takes to provide the required style, handle specified oak, and mature to be both good-drinking and long-lived.

Blending is detailed here to underscore the point that in Australia the finished product is important, unlike most European styles where the land, the territory, is more important. In Europe, the emphasis is on "the wine of my land" and wine drinkers are encouraged to try "this Gèvrey-Chambertin"or "this Chateau XYZ." But in Australia Penfolds Grange Shiraz is assembled from grapes grown in several different climates and *terroirs* to make a statement and provide a similar quality level to a European wine but in a different way. Each year the assemblage will almost certainly be different than the last.

Neither method is right or wrong; winemakers just do things differently on different sides of the world. To the Australian winemaker, there's no point in a single vineyard wine if it can be enhanced by adding some wine from somewhere else. There are some single-vineyard wines of course, perhaps one of the most treasured wines in Penfold's range is the Magill Estate Shiraz. But these are reasonably rare for the larger companies.

However, such an approach does play tricks on Australia's Geographical Indications (GI) system (*refer below*). For example, a $10 riesling from Young gets the status and prestige of a boutique Hilltops GI. Meanwhile, if Australia's top wine, a $200 Penfolds Grange, comes from Western Australian, South Australian and Victorian vineyards, it can only carry a GI of "Australia." Of course when such wider blends are used, no GI is likely to be shown, as it is not compulsory.

Australia's Geographical Indications (GIs)

Under pressure from the European market, and after an agreement with the EU signed in the mid-1990s to protect names, the Australian Wine and Brandy Corporation Act of 1980 (Commonwealth) was amended to establish a Geographical Indications Committee (GIC) and the Register of Protected Names. The GIC, a statutory committee of the Australian Wine and Brandy Corporation, comprises a presiding member, a winemaker and a grape grower representative and is assisted by the Registrar of Protected Names, an employee of the corporation. The winemaker and grape grower representatives are nominated by the national winemaker and grape grower organizations respectively. The function of the GIC is to determine and monitor Australia's Geographical Indications (GIs). The Register of Protected Names contains these Geographical Indications, along with traditional expressions and any other words protected under Australian wine law.

Empowered by the Geographical Indication Act, Geographical Indications are simply vineyard regions by another name. The Australian GI system has similarities with the American Viticultural Area (AVA) system where the boundaries define the area but, unlike Europe, no further restrictions (such as grapes used, minimum alcohol or maximum yield) are placed on the wine in the bottle other than that if a GI is named on the label, 85 percent of it must come from that GI.

The system allows up to three GIs to be quoted upon a wine label. There is a hierarchy here, as GIs can be multistate blends (as in South Eastern Australia), zones, regions and subregions.

A **zone** GI is a definition of an area of land based on geography, on political map boundaries "that may reasonably be regarded as a zone."

For example, "between this hill, that railway line and that road," or "west side of River X between A and B," and similar geographic references. There is no requirement that the GIC, when approving a zone as a GI, need consider anything viticultural. Even a complete state of Australia can be a zone GI as a geographical statement.

A **region** GI, however, requires "measurable" homogeneity or similarity of grape growing attributes within its boundaries and "measurable discreteness or difference in those same attributes from adjoining areas." Conditions for grape growing within a region must be similar; to use a simple example, there cannot be a hot-climate part and a cold-climate part of a region.

A **subregion** GI must show "substantial" homogeneity or similarity of grape growing attributes within its boundaries and "substantial discreteness or difference in those same attributes from adjoining areas." These smaller areas essentially require a single *terroir* in the area planted with vines. The requirement is for "substantial similarity within and discreteness without." So far there are only a handful of subregions approved, High Eden, Lenswood, Piccadilly Valley, Broke Fordwich, Nagambie Lakes, Swan Valley, Albany, Frankland River, Mount Barker, Porongurup and Denmark. Other applications are being worked through.

This hierarchical system means, of course, that there are GIs within GIs, just as in France AOC Pauillac is within AOC Haut-Médoc, which is within AOC Bordeaux; or in the United States, Rutherford AVA is within the Napa Valley AVA, which is within California. Thus in Australia we have Mount Barker GI as a subregion within Great Southern GI, which is a region within the zone of South West Australia GI.

In practical terms, it is the regions and subregions that have the strongest wine image. Rutherglen GI means something to wine people, while the zone of North East Victoria carries little image. Geelong GI is another example; it sits in a zone (Port Phillip) that includes Mornington Peninsula, Yarra Valley, Sunbury and Macedon Ranges, all with "measurable distinct wine-grape growing attributes" (substantially different area-strengths and picking dates).

Many of the zones have rather clinical names: Northern Slopes, South Coast, Central Western Australia, North West Victoria and so on. In these instances, if wines were blended from regions within such zones, it seems unlikely that the marketing people would choose the zone name to be a strong factor on the label. If the wine was made from a blend derived from a number of regions within a zone and 85 percent was not from a single region, then they would need to either quote up to three regions in descending order of importance or quote a zone that did comply with the blending requirements. However, there is no requirement to use the smallest qualifying GI.

The GI system is somewhat voluntary. The rules, such as they are, require 85 percent of fruit to have come from the named GI but they don't require that a GI be specified on every label. However, when the GI *is* used on the label (front and back labels are considered equally) then the rules cut in. So if a wine's label stated "Happy Magpie Shiraz, Product of Australia," GI rules need not apply. But if the back label refers to Happy Magpie coming from "fruit grown in the Barossa," this triggers the GI law. A protected name has now been used and GI conditions must be adhered to.

There are a small number of zones that could benefit from collective marketing: Limestone Coast, for example, has a great set of regions that could be promoted to tourists under Limestone Coast GI. The Hunter Valley Zone similarly has not sought to have Upper and Lower zones but uses one collective, and promotable, zone.

The list that starts on the following page seeks to provide an understanding of the regional structure of the GI system. Some broad notes on style have been given as well, but the larger GIs (zones) have no style while the GIs within (regions and subregions) may have much more of an image. A simple yet illuminative example is Padthaway. There is as much vineyard land in Padthaway as in the whole of New Zealand, but few wineries! There are Padthaway wines labeled as such, but far more Padthaway wine is blended with wine from other GIs and becomes "Limestone Coast" or "South Eastern Australia."

Label Requirements

As well as GI requirements when a GI is used on the label, there are also labeling requirements that are now closely in line with those of New Zealand, as the two countries strive to harmonize food and drug regulations. One of these is the number of "standard drinks" in each bottle or container. The base for one "standard drink" is a bottle (355 ml) of 4% alcohol beer. This converts to eight standard drinks in a 750-ml bottle of wine at 13.5% alcohol. In other words, the amount of alcohol in that bottle of wine is the same as in eight bottles (355 ml) of 4% alcohol beer. This is now a mandatory requirement to be shown on labels of all drinks.

Varietal minimum: Australian regulations require a minimum of 85 percent of the named varieties when such names are given on the label. Named blends must be listed in descending order of proportions. A vintage minimum of 85 percent is required when the year is shown.

As of 2003, there are also requirements to show allergens – anything added to the wine that may cause a physical reaction in some people. This requirement has left some winemakers hesitant, and greater clarification is needed on what constitutes an allergen.

Australia's Geographical Indications

Adelaide   **South Australia**
GI: Super Zone
Termed the Super Zone by the Wine and Brandy Corporation, this GI includes some GIs hundreds of miles apart. Regional GIs included in this Super Zone are: Langhorne Creek, Currency Creek, Mount Lofty Ranges, Fleurieu, Southern Fleurieu, Kangaroo Island, McLaren Vale, Adelaide Hills, Piccadilly Valley, Lenswood, Adelaide Plains, Barossa, Barossa Valley, Eden Valley, High Eden and Clare Valley. Many and varied *terroir*, many climates, vines, grapes and blends, almost a "last resort" GI (although this Super Zone is also within the South Eastern Australia GI).

Adelaide Hills   **South Australia**
GI: Region within Mount Lofty Ranges
Within the Adelaide Super Zone. A cool, elevated region running from east of Elizabeth down through the east of Adelaide and right down south of McLaren Vale towards (but not quite as far as) Sellick's Beach on the coast. Adelaide Hills is establishing a strong record for fine white wines especially. Within Adelaide Hills are the GIs of Piccadilly Valley and Lenswood.

Adelaide Plains   **South Australia**
GI: Region within Mount Lofty Ranges
Within the Adelaide Super Zone and the Mount Lofty Ranges GI. North of Adelaide, a neighbor of the Barossa Valley GI; west of Wasleys, Roseworthy, Gawler and Elizabeth through to the coast, including Angle Vale and Virginia, and south to Port Adelaide. It has some very distinguished vineyards in its territory. Not a big identity on its own but Adelaide Plains has some very fine wines and contributes grapes to many more.

Albany   **West Australia**
GI: Subregion within Great Southern
Albany is based around the coastal town of that name, with Mount Barker and Porongurup GIs to the north and Denmark GI to the west. Lots of quality wine has come from Albany over the past 20 years and the steady emergence of a typicity – a bold, positively fruited style – is strengthening this.

Alpine Valleys   **Victoria**
GI: Region within North East Victoria
Near Rutherglen and Beechworth, Alpine Valleys surrounds the towns of Myrtlefield and Bright towards the New South Wales border. Building an image as a new identity.

Barossa   **South Australia**
GI: Zone
Within the Adelaide Super Zone and including the GIs of Barossa Valley, Eden
Valley and High Eden. From Gawler (neighboring on the Adelaide Plains GI)
southeast to Mount Pleasant and almost as far north as Kapunda, Barossa ex-
tends the Barossa Valley somewhat and risks being confused with it. Whereas
the Barossa Valley GI "floor" has some hot zones, the Eden Valley and High
Eden GIs are regarded as cool. All three are "Barossa."

Barossa Valley   **South Australia**
GI: Region within Barossa
Within the Adelaide Super Zone. Barossa Valley north of Adelaide runs from
Williamstown in the south almost as far as Kapunda in the north, including
the areas around Lyndoch, Tanunda, Nuriootpa, Grenock and Stockwell.
(Not included is the cooler, more elevated Eden Valley GI to the east.)
     The famous Barossa Valley is warm, hot in some parts. It has a strong
proportion of old vines in its territory, giving magnificent red wines with
class, depth, intensity and finesse when well-handled. Like the Hunter Valley
in New South Wales or the Napa in California there is also a tourist factor
in the Barossa Valley. Many, but not all wineries draw grapes from outside
the Barossa Valley as well. It's a region with notoriety and influence. A true
Barossa Valley wine is part of a long legend in South Australia.

Beechworth   **Victoria**
GI: Region within North East Victoria
With Rutherglen nearby, Beechworth sits up near the New South Wales border and offers a cheerful style of wine. Wines under Beechworth nomenclature are seldom seen, but that will change and Beechwood should be more
evident in the future. This region is strong in a Rhônish-style of Shiraz, and
plantings of other Rhône grapes (Viognier, Roussanne) are increasing. About
400 acres (165 ha) are under vine.

Bendigo   **Victoria**
GI: Region within Central Victoria
A cool climate GI, Bendigo offers some classy wines with elegance and
charm in the right year. Thought of as pinot noir and sparkling wine territory,
Bendigo is going through its own evolution experimenting with a range of
grapes and styles.

Big Rivers   **New South Wales**
GI: Zone
Big Rivers is a big and broad GI from Broken Hill and Parkes in the north,
the state boundary with South Australia to the west and the Murray River
to the south, across to where the Murrumbidgee River feeds the Murray; it
therefore includes the wine towns of Griffith, Yenda and Albury, near the

state border with Victoria. It takes in Perricoota and Riverina GIs and the New South Wales parts of Murray Darling and Swan Hill GIs. A practical region that does not carry any image greater than the component GIs.

A lot of the vineyards within Big Rivers are irrigated using waters from the Darling, Lachlan, Murrumbidgee and Murray rivers that give this GI its name.

Broke Fordwich   *New South Wales*
GI: Subregion within Hunter
Including the towns of Broke and Bulge in the Lower Hunter, this is a relatively small GI adjacent to what may become Pokolbin GI in the future. Quite a few wineries here, but most also draw grapes from outside the area.

Blackwood Valley   *Western Australia*
GI: Region within South West Australia
Based around Bridgetown and Boyup Brook, south of the Geographe GI. The Blackwood River flows through the center of the region. Not a big vineyard area but growing in size and attracting increasing interest.

Canberra District   *New South Wales*
GI: Region within Southern New South Wales
This region lies just outside the Capital Territory border surrounding Canberra. (Capital Territory is to Canberra what D.C. is to Washington in the United States, a defined circle around the city to give the capital city some independence from the surrounding state.) As such, it is surprising that there is land for viticulture. Yet, outside the Capital Territory border in the Yass Valley around Murrumbateman and on the shores of Lake George, about 25 wineries do quite well.

Central Victoria   *Victoria*
GI: Zone
Another broad catchment with Goulburn Valley, Nagambie Lakes, Bendigo, Strathbogie Ranges and Heathcote GIs inside. Individual GIs have a stronger identity than the collective.

Central Ranges   *New South Wales*
GI: Zone
Inland to the southwest of the Hunter Valley GI, Central Ranges incorporates Orange, Cowra and Mudgee GIs, each with their own strong identity.

Central Western Australia   *Western Australia*
GI: Zone
From Watheroo down to Mummballup and across to Tembellup in the south, this strip runs inland east of the Perth Hills GI and reaches the northern border of the Great Southern GI. Not extensively planted in vines.

Clare Valley   South Australia
GI: Region within Mount Lofty Ranges
Eighty miles (130 km) north of Adelaide, Clare Valley has very much its own identity and image. The towns of Clare, Auburn and Watervale are included in this GI territory. Best known for Riesling and Cabernet Sauvignon but also very strong in Shiraz. An important and significant South Australian region.

Coonawarra   South Australia
GI: Region within Limestone Coast
Coonawarra lies in the southeast of South Australia, 270 miles (435 km) from Adelaide, 43 miles (70 km) past Padthaway. The tiny town of Coonawarra, the larger town of Penola (within the region) and the city of Mount Gambier (outside the region) lie to the south. As a region Coonawarra is famous for its red *terra rosa* soil over limestone. However, for many years some Coonawarra wine has come from black soil, hence there is ongoing debate over what is the true Coonawarra *terroir*. Both soil types are now included in the GI. The region is moderately cool but ripens Cabernet Sauvignon often enough for this to be the best-known grape of the region. Shiraz, Merlot, Chardonnay and Riesling have all made an impact in quality wine terms as well.

Cowra   New South Wales
GI: Region within Central Ranges
Lying in central-west New South Wales, inland from Sydney and northeast of Riverina, Cowra has been hailed as everything from simply fine wine country to Australia's best Shiraz territory. Cooler than some areas, it's a GI with some enthusiastic viticulturists, although much of its wine is blended with other regions.

Currency Creek   South Australia
GI: Region within Fleurieu
Within the Adelaide Super Zone. On the shores of Lake Alexandrina, neighboring the Langhorne Creek GI to the north, the Currency Creek region surrounds the town of the same name and extends down to Coolwa almost as far as Victor Harbor, with Southern Fleurieu GI to the west. Currency Creek has a growing reputation for red wine.

Denmark   Western Australia
GI: Subregion within Great Southern
Denmark, based around the coastal town of that name, west of Albany GI and southwest of Mount Barker GI, is a thriving vineyard area becoming well known for reds and whites.

Eastern Plains, Inland-North of WA   Western Australia
GI: Zone
A zone covering about 95 percent of Western Australia, yet with barely a

vine inside it! This very large GI shows that a tiny corner in the southwest of this enormous state has all the viticulture. However, if anyone does plant a vineyard in the Great Sandy Desert, there is a GI ready for them; if they do, let's hope the wine is a less clumsy mouthful than its GI name with three compass points!

Eden Valley *South Australia*
GI: Region within Barossa
Within the Adelaide GI Super Zone. Eden Valley GI, in the hills to the east of Barossa Valley, has High Eden GI within its boundaries. Although "valley" implies low land, Eden Valley is an elevated valley on the Mount Lofty Ranges, almost overlooking the Barossa Valley. Eden Valley is cooler and later ripening, making chardonnay and riesling a speciality but also adding a dimension for red wines from this area. Reds tend to be blended with other GIs; whites give Eden Valley its image and status.

Far North *South Australia*
GI: Zone
As the name suggests, this GI covers the northern part of South Australia, above the Mount Lofty Ranges GI and up to the border with Northern Territory, and across to the border with Western Australia. No vineyards exist here, as the heat is generally too great for grapes; but as a GI it neatly covers the remainder of South Australia. This reminds us that GIs can also relate to other horticultural products besides wine. The emerging region of Southern Flinders Ranges (its GI is still being worked through) is included in this zone.

Fleurieu *South Australia*
GI: Zone
Within the Adelaide Super Zone, Fleurieu GI in turn contains several GIs: Kangaroo Island, Langhorne Creek, Currency Creek, McLaren Vale, Southern Fleurieu. These individual regions have more identity and image than Fleurieu, the latter giving a blending option. In recent history, "Fleurieu Peninsula" was a promoted catchall name; but with the advent of GIs, this has dropped away, with Southern Fleurieu GI logically taking the "Peninsula" status. Fleurieu is a great place for a wine-oriented holiday.

Frankland River *Western Australia*
GI: Subregion within Great Southern
Within Great Southern GI, which in turn lies within the South West Australia GI. Frankland River GI covers the area around the town of Frankland, northwest of Mount Barker GI. The town of Rocky Gully is in the south. Frankland River is a highly regarded part of Western Australian wine, especially for cabernet with its own distinctive style.

Geelong   *Victoria*
GI: Region within Port Phillip

One of the most southern mainland regions, this lies southwest of Melbourne on the west side of Port Phillip Bay. A little isolated yet producing well-respected pinot noir in particular, along with a cross section of other wines including sparkling.

Geographe   *Western Australia*
GI: Region within South Western Australia
Coastal region from Preston Beach in the north to Busselton in the south, where Margaret River GI takes over. Geographe runs inland to include the town of Collie. Plantings around Capel especially have become well respected and Geographe has a growing vineyard area, much of it blended with other GIs and thus not carrying its own name.

Gippsland   *Victoria*
GI: Zone

To the east of Central Victoria GI, Gippsland runs along Victoria's southern ocean coast (in fact including Bass Strait through to the South Pacific Ocean), from below Melbourne at Wonthaggi across to Mallacoota where the Australian coast turns north. A surprisingly big GI in terms of plantings, although not widely seen on wine labels as a region.

Goulburn Valley   *Victoria*
GI: Region within Central Victoria
With Nagambie Lakes GI inside, the Goulburn Valley north of Melbourne has a strong identity, thanks to just a couple of wineries who draw most of their fruit from here. A warm region showing some of the finest Victorian wines around.

Grampians   *Victoria*
GI: Region within Western Victoria
Including the Great Western district and the town of Ararat on the western side of Victoria, the Grampians region (named after the mountain range) is home to a cluster of respected wineries. Some wineries, but not all, draw only from local vineyards, which benefit from the tempering influence of the ranges.

Granite Belt   *Queensland*
GI: Region within Queensland
South and east of Brisbane near the New South Wales border. An elevated and frost-prone strip, the region produces difficult conditions for the vine, but lots of effort is going into the growing.

Great Southern — *Western Australia*
GI: Region within South Western Australia
East of the Margaret River GI, Great Southern includes the GIs of Albany, Frankland River, Mount Barker, Denmark and Porongurup. This gives a collective name to some of the most respected vineyards in the state.

Greater Perth — *Western Australia*
GI: Zone
Wider catchment area for the GIs of Perth Hills, Swan District, Swan Valley and Peel. A coastal strip from Green Head north of Perth down past Perth and Rockingham to Coolup and Waroona in the south. On the eastern side runs the Central Western Australia GI. Greater Perth is a hot viticultural region, cooled a little by the Fremantle Doctor wind. The Swan Valley and Gingin wineries are well known for their wines, but many wineries also draw grapes from the southern GIs of the state to blend with local product.

Gundagai — *New South Wales*
GI: Region within Southern New South Wales
Finding the "Road to Gundagai" is a bit of an Australian legend; the region lies between Wagga Wagga and Canberra but includes neither. A region building its own wine image.

Hastings River — *New South Wales*
GI: Region within Northern Rivers
Facing the coast around Port Macquarie, with the Hunter GI to the south and west, Hastings River has relatively small vineyard plantings but is regarded as a region with potential.

Heathcote — *Victoria*
GI: Region within Central Victoria
Adjacent to the Goulburn Valley GI, Heathcote has its wines of success, often made in wineries outside the area. Shiraz is a speciality of the region.

Henty — *Victoria*
GI: Region within Western Victoria
Sharing a border with South Australia near Mount Gambier and Coonawarra, this GI runs inland along the coast of Victoria below Grampians GI and inland up to Horsham and Wedderburn, with Ballarat on the east side. Henty has vineyards with potential but is not yet widely known.

High Eden — *South Australia*
GI: Subregion within Eden Valley
Close to Adelaide and the Barossa, High Eden is an elevated subregion with a strong and growing record of riesling, chardonnay and pinot noir.

Hilltops
New South Wales
GI: Region within Southern New South Wales
Within the Southern New South Wales GI, Hilltops is also known as Young after the town within it, southwest of Sydney. A cool region with some elevation, considered to have a great deal of potential, and winemakers are working hard to develop this.

Hunter
New South Wales
GI: Region within Hunter Valley
Hunter and Hunter Valley GIs have very similar boundaries. Hunter Valley zone boundaries are affixed geographically, while Hunter region is based on "measurable grape growing similarities." But there are few, if any, grapes grown in Hunter GI that are not in Hunter Valley GI. Some more subregional GIs are likely to emerge in the future.

Hunter Valley
New South Wales
GI: Zone
The Hunter River may not be all that magnificent but it does allow two regions quite some distance apart to claim the same name. The Hunter Valley GI combines the Upper Hunter Valley and the Lower Hunter Valley into one region, despite their differences in *terroir*. This is the broad catchall from north of Mudgee up to Quirindi and down to Cessnock. Within its boundaries lies the Hunter GI.

Kangaroo Island
South Australia
GI: Region within Fleurieu
In the Southern Ocean below Adelaide lies Kangaroo Island, once just a sleepy tourist island with beaches full of seals. In the 1990s, however, grapes were planted, and a small but enthusiastic wine industry is now emerging.

King Valley
Victoria
GI: Region within North East Victoria
Although final approval on GI boundaries has yet to occur, King Valley is widely known in Australia for vineyards both in warm sites southeast of Rutherglen and more mountainous, cooler sites. A large region in physical terms, it is a little isolated and still offering moderately inexpensive vineyard land.

Langhorne Creek
South Australia
GI: Region within Fleurieu
Within the Adelaide Super Zone, Langhorne Creek is a long-established grape growing region (but with only a few wineries) on the shores of Lake Alexandrina, down as far as Milang where Currency Creek GI is a neighbor. Drawn on by major companies for its soft, fruity red style, often used to assist some harder reds from elsewhere. Lake Alexandrina is the exit point of

the Murray River before it reaches the Southern Ocean. The lake rises in the spring to provide a natural irrigation source.

Lenswood   *South Australia*
GI: Subregion of Adelaide Hills
A small GI, Lenswood has gathered a following as a cool region with some top class white wines, especially chardonnay and riesling, and with its own style of shiraz.

Limestone Coast   *South Australia*
GI: Zone
South of the Adelaide Super Zone and not included in it, Limestone Coast GI is an umbrella zone that includes the GIs of Coonawarra, Penola, Padthaway, Wrattonbully, Robe and Mount Benson, some of which (Robe and Penola) have yet to finalize exact boundaries. The word "coast" can be misunderstood as the region extends in from the Southern Ocean by some 94 miles (150 km), but the limestone subsoil is common to much of the zone. The Limestone Coast collective is similar to the Adelaide GI to the north; where the GIs within have a stronger image than the broad external GI. This is similar to Margaux in France, which is within Haut-Médoc, which is in turn within Bordeaux. Limestone Coast is a very strong wine district producing many fine and famous wines.

Lower Murray   *South Australia*
GI: Zone
Big production GI with Riverland GI within its borders. The Murray River flows into South Australia after forming the border between Victoria and New South Wales, linking with the Murrumbidgee just before the Murray reaches South Australia. It then fills the vineyards of Riverland, a big production region around Berri, Renmark and Loxton, and turns left to pass through Murray Bridge, then flows into the sea southeast of Adelaide via Lake Alexandrina.

Macedon Ranges   *Victoria*
GI: Region within Port Phillip
Macedon Ranges is in the hills a long way north, hundreds of miles from Port Phillip Bay. Some vineyards here are picked as late as June, but the area has produced many fine wines; some battle acidity when sipped young but are able to unfold with cellaring. Macedon has produced some wines that are delicious after some bottle age.

Margaret River   *Western Australia*
GI: Region within South Western Australia
On the "knob" of land that pushes out into the sea 175 miles (280 km) south of Perth, Margaret River is something of a glamour GI, building a solid repu-

tation for its reds, and for sauvignon blanc and chardonnay. From Busselton, south and west down to Kudardup, it covers most of the "knob." A much cooler region than the Swan and influenced by offshore breezes that come up mid-afternoon, Margaret River continues to produce many fine wines and rates as very prestigious in Australia's industry.

McLaren Vale   South Australia
GI: Region within Fleurieu
Within the Adelaide Super Zone. The Mount Lofty Ranges GI runs almost entirely around the McLaren Vale GI. McLaren Vale is barely an hour's drive south of Adelaide from north of Clarendon down to Sellick's Beach on the coast and inland to include the town of McLaren Vale, across to Willunga and Kangarilla. This famous heartland deserves as much wine attention as Barossa Valley in the north; it's a warm region with cool pockets inside, growing magnificent Shiraz, Mourvèdre and Grenache and doing very well. Cool spots suit Chardonnay and Sauvignon Blanc nicely also.

Mornington Peninsula   Victoria
GI: Region within Port Phillip
Within the Port Phillip GI, Mornington Peninsula sits south of Melbourne with 2,000 acres (810 ha) of vineyard containing almost 50 wineries. A strong collection of Pinot Noir enthusiasts make this variety the center of attention in cheerful competitiveness with the Yarra Valley and New Zealand. Chardonnay and other varieties also do well in the GI's temperate climate.

Mount Barker   Western Australia
GI: Subregion within Great Southern
One of several GIs in the Great Southern GI, in turn part of South West Australia GI. East of the Frankland River GI and including the town of Mount Barker, this is a highly-respected region for fine reds in particular.

Mount Benson   South Australia
GI: Region within Limestone Coast
One of several GIs within the Limestone Coast GI, Mount Benson is on the coast, running south from Kings Camp. Adjacent on the south side is Robe GI. Some vineyards have been planted by large companies seeking to enjoy the coastal quality for blending, while others have been planted by quality-oriented winemakers seeking strong regional wines.

Mount Lofty Ranges   South Australia
GI: Zone
The Mount Lofty Ranges GI is a big, cumbersome block going from the town of Spalding (north of Clare) across to the Lower Murray GI, then down in a big curve west of the Barossa; it then takes in Adelaide Plains, Adelaide Hills, then goes east of McLaren Vale to wind up below McLaren Vale inland from

Sellick's Beach. The Mount Lofty GI thus includes the GIs of Clare Valley, Adelaide Plains, Adelaide Hills, Lenswood and Piccadilly Valley. Mount Lofty Ranges GI has a similarity to the Adelaide Super Zone, but leaves out the Barossa, Eden Valley and McLaren Vale GIs, and does not go quite as far south as the Langhorne Creek, Currency Creek and Kangaroo Island GIs.

Mudgee   *New South Wales*
GI: Region within Central Ranges
Around the town of Mudgee, inland from the Hunter Valley and west of Wellington (which is not included), Mudgee is a warm GI. It is well known, though not quite claiming regional fame, for a sound range of red and white wines that perform very well in the right year.

Murray Darling   *Victoria and New South Wales*
GI: Region within Big Rivers (New South Wales side)
and North West Victoria (Victoria side)
Covering the northeast of Victoria and the southeast of New South Wales, this GI lies on both sides of the Murray River from the South Australian border up past Balranald to the east; the region includes the substantial irrigated area around Mildura and Robinvale. This is high-yielding country, and few wineries try to establish a "quality" image in Australian terms here, but the quality of the wine has been inching up, as it has with wine from Riverina, the next viticultural region on the Murray River as it passes into South Australia. At their best, clean fresh wines and fortifieds make up a very large volume of the Murray Darling wines, and very few drinkers would be able to tell you exactly where the region is, as the name Murray River is unlikely to be a feature on a wine label.

Nagambie Lakes   *Victoria*
GI: Subregion within Goulburn Valley
Nagambie Lakes is a long established region in vineyard terms, and with several wineries drawing grapes from here, the image is sure to rise internationally. Cross-blending reduces the impact of the area; but now that it has been given the recognition of a subregion, Nagambie Lakes GI should be seen more often on labels. To the east is the Strathbogie Ranges GI.

North East Victoria   *Victoria*
GI: Zone
With a northern border of the Murray River across from New South Wales, North East Victoria thrives on a warm ripening climate, within which lie the GIs of Beechworth, Alpine Valleys and Rutherglen. King Valley GI will almost certainly be included when the final boundaries are settled. Rutherglen is well known for its hearty fortified wines and gutsy chardonnay and shiraz; the other GIs are less well-known, mostly cooler in a typical vintage, and all able to add to each other.

North West Victoria   **Victoria**
GI: Zone
Established on geographic grounds rather than viticultural attributes, North West Victoria includes those parts of the Murray Darling and Swan Hill GIs that fall south of the Murray River into Victoria. The North West Victoria GI's western boundary runs down the South Australia border past Bordertown, south to Horsham and diagonally up past Kerang. North West Victoria is a big zone in quantity terms, a GI recognized more by the trade than as a name on labels.

Northern Rivers   **New South Wales**
GI: Zone
Many rivers flow into the Tasman Sea from the Great Dividing Range, giving this name to the Northern Rivers coastal zone. It runs north of Newcastle and the Hunter GI, up past Port Macquarie and Coffs Harbour up to Coolangatta. Within the southern part of this zone, Hastings River has its own GI around Port Macquarie.

Northern Slopes   **New South Wales**
GI: Zone
Runs from Dubbo at the southwest point up to the Great Dividing Range as its eastern border, including Tamworth and Glen Innes, and up to the Queensland border. Northern Slopes is a semi-outback zone without much vineyard land.

Orange   **New South Wales**
GI: Region within Central Ranges
Small city almost three hours drive inland northwest of Sydney attracting growing viticultural interest. Plantings have increased fivefold in the last decade. Some seasonal risks (frost and rain) exist in Orange and the varietal strengths have yet to be fully revealed, but expect Shiraz, Cabernet and Merlot to play a major role, with some whites. New region with a growing image.

Padthaway   **South Australia**
GI: Region within Limestone Coast
A long strip of vineyards 45 miles (70 km) south of Adelaide on the highway to Coonawarra. A relatively new region by Australian terms (most plantings are from 1970 on) with strengths in Shiraz and Chardonnay, but other varieties have fairly consistent success as well.
    Only two or three wineries, but the tens of thousands of tons of grapes provide wines for many labels, some recognizing the GI, others blended with other regions.

Peel   *Western Australia*
GI: Region within Greater Perth and Central Western Australia
Within the Greater Perth GI, Peel is an L-shaped GI south of the city of Perth
running from Rockingham down the coast to Preston Beach (the north border of the Geographe GI) and inland to the neighboring Central Western
Australia GI. Peel has some very respected wineries within its boundaries. As
with so much of Western Australia, the GI wines are often blended, so Peel
doesn't always get the credit.

Penola   *South Australia*
GI: Region within Limestone Coast
Borders for Penola GI have been up in the air as northern neighbor
Coonawarra GI dithered over its own definitions. Penola is a small but ac-
tive town, surrounded by some vineyards that have been loosely referred
to as "Coonawarra" until the Geographical Indications law shut that door.
Definitions are still to be settled here.

Perricoota   *New South Wales*
GI: Region within Big Rivers
A little further inland from Riverina, the Deniboota Irrigation District draws
Murray River water for irrigation in the small Perricoota region, which extends north of Moama and Echuca up to Barmah in the east and Woomboola
in the northwest. A handful of wineries are building a name here, but much
of the grape supply goes into blends elsewhere.

Perth Hills   *Western Australia*
GI: Region within Greater Perth
Within the Greater Perth GI, Perth Hills is a small GI in the Darling Ranges,
18 miles (30 km) east of Perth, 500–1300 feet (150–410 m) above sea-level.
A small number of vineyards and wineries, most of them quite recent, seek
to give Perth Hills an identity.

Piccadilly Valley   *South Australia*
GI: Subregion within Adelaide Hills
Down the Eastern Highway, southeast from Adelaide, Piccadilly Valley be-
gins at the town of Stirling and reaches north to Summertown, including
Piccadilly. Not big as a vineyard area, but like Eden Valley, winemakers use
the cooler climate to build strong styles of riesling and chardonnay.

Port Phillip   *Victoria*
GI: Zone
Named after the bay to the south of Melbourne, Port Phillip GI is a huge
catchall running up past Melbourne to the hills of Macedon. Included are the
GIs of Mornington Peninsula, Yarra Valley, Sunbury and Macedon Ranges.

Porongurup   Western Australia
GI: Subregion within Great Southern
Within the Great Southern GI, which is in turn within the South West Australia GI, Porongurup is the easterly neighbor of the Mount Barker GI. With the Pongorurup Ranges on the skyline and the Kalgan River on the west boundary, this is a small region with growing significance. Whites exceed reds in volume. A well-established wine festival is held here in March of each year.

Pyrenees   Victoria
GI: Region within Western Victoria
The Pyrenees Ranges in Victoria provide challenges to winemaking ranging from cold nights to kangaroos! A mix of vineyards from boutique size to quite large have yet to establish a strong regional name, partly because of cross-blending between GIs, but the quality of the region is recognized and being built on.

Riverina   New South Wales
GI: Region within Big Rivers
Around the town of Griffith in southern New South Wales, the Riverina GI (also known as the Murrumbidgee Irrigation Area) lies beside a river, which provides water for many types of horticulture from rice to large plantings of vineyards. Struggling to escape the "irrigated vineyard" image, Riverina produces a wide range of wines and styles from magnificent sweet whites to soft user-friendly reds at low prices. This is a great example of the effects of *terroir* – the conditions produce a widely appealing and well-priced wine.

Riverland   South Australia
GI: Region within Lower Murray
Using water from the Murray River, large vineyards around the towns of Renmark, Berri and Loxton provide a steady supply of bulk wine for boxed wine and low-priced bottles. The Riverland GI is an important region; it may rank lower in prestige because of irrigation and high yields, yet it still satisfies thousands of wine drinkers!

Robe   South Australia
GI: Region within Limestone Coast
Border definitions of this GI are still to be finalized. On the coast of the Southern Ocean, below Mount Benson GI, Robe holds a fascination for winemakers seeking to produce quality wines. Motivated initially by the region's "undiscovered" status and lower land prices, these winemakers have been quick to develop what can be fine, individualistic styles from around Robe. A young area, but some keen winemakers and large companies are working with a spread of grapes and sites. Organic vineyards are also found in the region.

Rutherglen   *Victoria*
GI: Region within North East Victoria
Rutherglen GI is situated near the Murray River, which forms the border
between New South Wales and Victoria. The 1850s gold rush created a market for wine in the area, and the first vines were planted here in 1851. This
historic region has been making local fortified reds and whites, including
tokay and muscat, for close to 150 years and there is also a strong industry
in shiraz and chardonnay. With its mix of wineries from old and rustic to
modern and tourist-friendly, Rutherglen is an Australian treasure.

Shoalhaven Coast   *New South Wales*
GI: Region within South Coast
Within the South Coast GI, Shoalhaven Coast below Sydney runs from near
the coastal town of Kiama down to Durras and Bateman's Bay, including the
towns of Nowra, Mollymook and Ulladulla. This GI is barely known to wine
drinkers outside the area, although grapes have been grown here since the
1820s. Whites predominate.

South Burnett   *Queensland*
GI: Region within Queensland
North of Brisbane and a little inland, this region is working hard on its wines
amidst a difficult climate. Some local and tourist following, but little international impact as yet. Tiny volumes.

South Coast   *New South Wales*
GI: Zone
From near Singleton and Cessnock in the Hunter GI north of Sydney, South
Coast is a narrow strip down the coast as far as the Victorian border. Two
regional GIs are within, Southern Highlands and Shoalhaven Coast. There is
currently an application lodged for another "Sydney" GI within this South
Coast GI zone.

South Eastern Australia
GI: Inter-state Zone
South Eastern Australia includes the wine growing regions of Queensland, all
of New South Wales, Victoria and Tasmania states, plus all of the wine-producing districts of South Australia, collectively about 95 percent of Australian
wine-producing regions. A very large catchall that reflects no specific *terroir*, South Eastern Australia GI covers an area greater than 10 countries of
Europe, from the extremes of cool Tasmania to the heat of McLaren Vale and
hotter parts of Barossa right through to the Granite Hills of Victoria, which
picks its grapes in June, while the Hunter finishes vintage by mid-February.
Something of a formality, the existence of this GI means that with the exception of those produced in Western Australia, other wines can have an
umbrella GI to use when they do not fit into any of the smaller GIs.

Southern Fleurieu   **South Australia**
GI: Region within Fleurieu
Within the Adelaide Super Zone. Out on a limb, Southern Fleurieu GI is a little off the beaten wine track, on a peninsula below McLaren Vale and Mount
Lofty Ranges, pointing southwest towards Kangaroo Island. No vineyard
areas have made a big impression thus far, but the closeness to the sea and
the fine wines made in the surrounding regions suggest discoveries may lie
ahead.

Southern Flinders Ranges   **South Australia**
GI: Proposed region within the Far North Zone
GI status is yet to be formalized but is not far away. As to its geographical
boundaries, the name says it all.

Southern Highlands   **New South Wales**
GI: Region within South Coast
Within the South Coast GI, but this region does not have a coastal boundary. Southern Highlands, centered around the towns of Mittagong and Moss
Vale, between Sydney and Canberra, is building an image and reputation for
its white wines, but the strong tourist industry ensures the wines are mostly
enjoyed locally and not a lot goes outside the region.

Southern New South Wales   **New South Wales**
GI: Zone
Broad GI that includes the GIs of Hilltops, Canberra District, Tumbarumba
and Gundagai. Being a zone, it is defined on political and geographic lines,
not on vineyard attributes.

South West Australia   **Western Australia**
GI: Zone
South West Australia GI starts south of Perth and includes the GIs of Margaret
River, Great Southern, Albany, Frankland River, Porongurup, Blackwood
Valley and Geographe. As with so many Australian zone GIs, only limited
use of this name seems likely when the individual GIs within have a stronger
image than the collective. However, use of this broad GI is an option for
blended wines.

Strathbogie Ranges   **Victoria**
GI: Region within Central Victoria
Within Central Victoria GI, Strathbogie Ranges GI covers the area around the
town of Strathbogie with Violet Town and Euro to the north, and reaches
almost as far as Seymour to the southwest. With a mix of soils and elevation
from 500 to 2,000 feet (150–650 m), the region offers a very diverse style.
Mostly whites.

Sunbury   *Victoria*
GI: Region within Port Phillip
Northwest of Melbourne, north of Werribee, across to Bacchus Marsh and including Melton and Sunbury towns, Sunbury is a very historic region whose wine beginnings go back to the 1850s gold rush, but it has only a few wineries. A 100-year-old Sunbury wine buried in an old building opened perfectly recently! Sunbury is a cool region and life is not easy for viticulturists here, but the right site and variety can work well. Chardonnay is the most planted variety.

Swan Hill   *Victoria and New South Wales*
GI: Region within Big Rivers (New South Wales side)
and North West Victoria (Victoria side)
Stretching from North Victoria, well to the east of Rutherglen, and across into New South Wales, Swan Hill GI is a warm region with quite substantial plantings, though much of the grape harvest is sold to wineries in other areas.

Swan District   *Western Australia*
GI: Region within Greater Perth
Just to the north of Perth, this is one of Australia's warmest regions, making a wide range of styles, including fortifieds. Proximity to the city helps sales. Many wineries here also blend, drawing grapes from southern regions within the state. The proposed new GI of Swan Valley, whose boundaries are still being defined, will almost certainly lie within Swan District.

Swan Valley   *Western Australia*
GI: Proposed subregion within Swan District
Confirmation of this proposed subregion as a GI is expected in 2004. Swan Valley will incorporate the wines from local vineyards.

The Peninsulas   *South Australia*
GI: Zone
This zone west of Mount Lofty Ranges GI covers the Yorke Peninsula (down to Stenhouse Bay) and the Eyre Peninsula (down to Port Lincoln) with the Spencer Gulf between them. Not yet a big part of South Australian winemaking, but has potential to develop quality wine.

Tumbarumba   *New South Wales*
GI: Region within Southern New South Wales
A GI around the town of the same name, Tumbarumba sits on an elevated site with red volcanic soil and is given some significance by a couple of major companies' vineyards, but much of its grapes are blended. More development in image and style is expected in the future.

West Australian South East Coastal   *Western Australia*
GI: Zone
Carrying one of Western Australia's more cumbersome titles, this GI starts to the east of Albany GI and runs around the coast of Western Australia towards South Australia, past Esperance, facing the Southern Ocean. Despite its size this GI does not have a big vineyard area.

Western Victoria   *Victoria*
GI: Zone
Literally the west of Victoria with the GIs of Grampians, Henty and Pyrenees inside. Lots of premium wines are made from grapes grown here, though few are identified by this broad GI name.

Western Plains   *New South Wales*
GI: Zone
Something of an outback GI without a lot of vineyards at this stage. The inland territory runs on the west of Broken Hill up the South Australian border to the Queensland border, then east along the Queensland border almost to the town of Goondiwindi, then south to Dubbo and Forbes and west across to Broken Hill. There's not much in that block that encourages viticulture, and plantings are tiny.

Wrattonbully   *South Australia*
GI: Region within Limestone Coast
Wrattonbully GI takes the territory north of Coonawarra and east of Padthaway, over to the little town of Wrattonbully and the more northern city of Naracoorte. There are not many wineries here, just two or three, and the growing quantities of grapes planted here go further afield to be absorbed into bigger blends in GIs like Limestone Coast and South Eastern Australia. Nevertheless, this GI has the qualities required to produce excellent wine and will almost certainly gain recognition as a quality region under its own name.

Yarra Valley   *Victoria*
GI: Region within Port Phillip
The Yarra Valley sits about 30 miles (50 km) east of Melbourne, a highly rated if scattered collection of large and small vineyards, best known for Pinot Noir and Chardonnay grapes but other varieties also do equally well. Several wineries have restaurants and being so close to Melbourne gives it tourist appeal, although it seems to be less recognized by tourists than the Barossa (near Adelaide) and the Hunter (near Sydney).

CHAPTER 10

Argentina

Argentina's wine makes its own statement, rooted in the use of "old" white varieties along with experimentation to test out new clones, new varieties, new trellising and cleaner, New World winemaking. Although a greater investment is perhaps needed, Argentinian dedication and fervor enables the wines to do pretty well.

Separated from Chile by the Andes, which add both beauty and drama to the vineyards, Argentina is on the rise. The hot, dry vineyards, sheltered by the high mountains, make dams and irrigation a necessary part of vineyard life but, when irrigation is well managed, this climate gives Argentinean viticulturists many advantages.

Argentina has about 545,000 acres (220,000 hectares) under vine, spread through 10 regions in a north-south strip on the western side of the country. This strip of Argentina's vineyards is far closer as the crow flies to Chile's capital Santiago than to Argentina's capital Buenos Aires on the Atlantic coast – but, again, the crow would need to be able to fly just as long to scale the steep spine of the Andes!

All 10 of Argentina's wine regions are evolving as the country moves from producing and consuming (20 gallons/90 liters per capita) of simple quaffing wine to making an important contribution to the international wine market, earning some real money for Argentina's economy in the process.

The wine industry is based in a narrow corridor down the west side of the country near the Andes, running roughly from 25 degrees south latitude near the Tropic of Capricorn and the Bolivian border down to 40 degrees south latitude in Patagonia, with the city of Mendoza somewhere near its center. Few vineyards are below 1,000 feet (300 m) above sea-level and some are well over 5,000 feet (1,500 m). The sunshine is therefore intense, the rainfall low and during the ripening season, the nights are much colder than the days.

Criolla (two different clones, one known as Pais in Chile) and the pink-skinned Cereza dominate the white plantings; these contribute little to quality wine, but their role is now less important as "new" or more internationally acceptable grape varieties come in to play. Chardonnay, Muscat and Pedro Ximénez are all being experimented with and styles developed.

Bonarda from northern Italy heads the red varieties, followed by Malbec. Some lovely old vineyards of Malbec (which would have been warmly welcomed today) were pulled out in the 1970s and early 1980s but there remains about 25,000 acres (10,000 ha) in production. However, innovation is the word here, and in wine districts that stretch over large areas and subregions with many different soils and climates, trials and development of all types of viticulture from clones and trellises to new varieties are continuing.

In labeling terms, common law prevails. The National Institute of Vitiviniculture (INV) has about 1,500 winemakers registered with it. The regions are apparent enough but a formal system of definition and control is not yet in place. Four smaller subzones (three in Mendoza, one in Le Rioja) have their own *"denominación de origen"* system, but this must be considered voluntary for now.

A 1999 law gives provision for greater labeling requirements and quality inference. This law has been met with much controversy and is not properly implemented in terms of compliance routine, policing, penalties for breaches and other issues. Much is needed to resolve this including the willingness of the winemakers to work with a law some see as unnecessary.

Under the law there are three levels of quality: Indicación de Procedencia (IP) for table wines containing at least 80 percent of grapes from within the IP region; Indicación Geográfica (IG) for higher quality wines gown, vinified and bottled in a designated area; and DOC for top quality wines.

Argentina's Wine Regions

Cafayate   *Region: 510 miles (825 km) north of Mendoza City*
Within the Salta province, Cafayate, at between about 4,500 and 5,100 feet (1,400–1,600 m) elevation, has 3,700 acres (1,500 ha) of vineyard, but does not have as much claim to fame as some provinces to the south. Cafayate produces lots of torrontés, chardonnay, malbec and cabernet as great value-for-money wines.

Catamarca   *Region: 400 miles (650 km) north of Mendoza City*
This region north of La Rioja has 17 wineries in warm, northern, elevated conditions. Yet despite the number of wineries, vineyards are scarce. The wineries also draw from other regions.

Jujuy   *Region: 820 miles (1,325 km) north of Mendoza City*
The most northern of Argentina's wine provinces, around the Tropic of Capricorn. Quite tiny for its quantity of grapes and not widely known for its wines.

La Pampa   *Region: 370 miles (600 km) south of Mendoza City*
Small wine region in two parcels on the Colorado River, a little to the north of the Rio Negro. La Pampa ("The Pampas" means treeless plains) is a huge desert region with just a few vineyards.

La Rioja   *Region: 280 miles (450 km) north of Mendoza City*
La Rioja has about 40 wineries and 17,300 acres (7,000 ha) of vineyard in hot and usually arid surroundings. The most planted grape variety is Torrontés Riojana, a white grape whose origin cannot be traced with certainty. Barbera, Merlot, Malbec and some Cabernet Sauvignon also ripen well in the warm conditions. Within La Rioja, Chilecito, a town of 35,000 people (not to be confused with Chilecito in Mendoza's Uco Valley), is home to the cooperative that handles much of La Rioja wine in seven separate wineries. Some growers in La Rioja have tried to establish their own voluntary *denominación de origen* system – "Valles de Famatina-Torrontés Riojano" – to build on the strength of this grape and region, but this system is unofficial and not widely promoted.

Mendoza   *Region: Around Mendoza City*
Two-thirds of Argentina's wine comes from Mendoza, the largest of Argentina's wine regions by far, covering about 360,000 acres (145,000 ha). This region is divided into five "official" subregions, although these groupings are more practical than official, and many wineries own vineyards or buy grapes from more than one of these subregions.

East Mendoza: Just south of the High Zone of the Mendoza River, East Mendoza is one of the big-volume subareas in Argentina. On something of a plain, about 150,000 acres (60,700 ha) of vineyards irrigated by the Tunuyán River enjoy generally warm conditions, running as high as 2,500 feet (750 m) above sea level.

High Zone of the Mendoza River: The *Zona Alta de Río Mendoza* is a very important fine wine-producing area. There are some 75,000 acres (30,000 ha) of vineyards and about 360 wineries. Located at 33° south latitude, 3,500 to 5,400 feet (1,060–1,650 m) high on the foothills of the Andes, it is irrigated by the Mendoza River. The climate is temperate and arid; rains, cloudiness and humidity are limited and winds are moderate. While snow is occasional even in cold winters, there is plenty of it in the high mountains and thus the region is irrigated by rivers of melted snows. Quality wine is the focus of many producers. The soils are a direct result of the mountain rocks cracking. The subsoil is stony and covered with a thin layer of fine material: sand, lime or clay. This type of soil is rich in calcareous matter but lacks organic material, and sometimes the rock reaches the superficial level. Under these conditions vines cannot grow vigorously and are therefore excellent for making quality wines. Two areas within this zone, Maipú and Luján de Cuyo, have tried to establish their own unofficial *denominación de origen* system, but it is not widely promoted.

North Mendoza: A low altitude area – 1,900 to 2,250 feet (600–700 m) above sea level – and irrigated by the Mendoza River. The soils are deep, with a slight slope. Average temperatures are 25°C (75°F) in the warmest month and 7°C (45°F) in the coldest.

South Mendoza: Around San Rafael, this subregion is well south of the city of Mendoza but still in Mendoza province. French, Swiss and Italian influences over the years have affected the culture, and it is said that if one speaks Italian, one can live here without knowing Spanish. Wine is less important than tourism these days but obviously the two overlap. Lots of Malbec and lots of enthusiasm, although the spring frost remains a demotivating factor for those entering grape growing. Some growers within San Rafael have established an unofficial *denominación de origen* system, but it is not widely promoted.

Valle de Uco (Uco Valley): Between 3,000 and 4,000 feet (900–1,250 m) and a little cooler than the rest of the subregion. The sloping nature of the vineyards in this valley makes traditional trench irrigation mostly impossible here. There are only a couple of wineries, but lots of big Argentine names have vineyards scattered around the subregion.

Río Negro   ***Region: 520 miles (840 km) south of Mendoza City***
The name of this region, which lies south of Mendoza City in Patagonia, means "Black River." There are 13,600 acres (5,500 ha) under vine here and about 40 wineries. The region gets very cold in winter. A dam on the Neuquen River, above the point at which it becomes Río Negro, provides a long, fertile valley. This is fruit-growing territory and table grapes are also

grown here, but commentators rate its potential highly for an expansion of wine varieties like Pinot Noir and Pinot Gris.

Salta   *Region: 470 miles (750 km) north of Mendoza City*
Just below Jujuy, around the city of Salta, Salta province includes Cafayate Valley, 102 miles (164 km) south of the city. The names Salta and Cafayate have become somewhat interchangeable when referring to this region. However, there are also Salta vineyards in the Calchaquíes Valley, northeast of Cafayate around the towns of San Carlos and Molinos.

San Juan   *Region: 105 miles (170 km) north of Mendoza City*
San Juan province, around the city of the same name, produces about 20 percent of Argentina's wine from 123,000 acres (50,000 ha) of vineyard, with about 300 wineries. Slightly hotter than Mendoza, San Juan's significant factor is its more than 1,250 miles (2,000 km) of irrigation channels. Within San Juan are three main valleys fed by the San Juan River: Ullum, Tulum and Zonda. All three grow wine grapes. Jachal is a further subarea in the north of the province while El Perdenal west of the Media Agua at around 4,500 feet (1,350 m) above sea level is another region seen as having great wine potential. San Juan produces lots of wine, a high percentage regarded as clean and plain; its quality is inhibited by high yields.

Tucumán   *Region: 400 miles (650 km) north of Mendoza City*
Small vineyard area northeast of Catamarca, with some of the most elevated vineyards in Argentina, and indeed the world. No wineries are on record; the grapes are taken to other provinces.

CHAPTER 11

Chile

Denominación de Origen (DO)

Chile is another of the New World's rising stars. Thriving on the challenge of the world market, it is also enjoying the economy of lower wages than many wine countries (leading to lower grape prices and lower packaging costs), and abundant growing conditions. A wide selection of grapes does well here, including the Bordeaux varieties and in particular a much-acclaimed "old" Bordeaux variety called Carmenère.

Yet Sauvignon Blanc succeeds also, and exports of the wine from this grape do well. Chile exports hundreds of thousands of liters to New Zealand, the new international Mecca of sauvignon blanc; the Chilean wine supplies the lower-priced domestic market in that country, while exports of New Zealand's own sauvignon blanc attract higher prices around the world.

A grape known locally as Pais (the "Mission" variety in California and Mexico) has been the most-planted in Chile but as it is now being substantially uprooted, plantings of Cabernet Sauvignon are steadily surpassing it.

Chile was able to take advantage of a New World wave in the 1990s when international wine drinkers began to be attracted to bright, clean wines and those from Chile came at very good prices for value. Wineries invested in new and better equipment, vineyard yields were managed to produce better quality wine, and the time and mood is now right to build on this initial success.

While there is a DO appellation system in place, with various levels, Chilean producers on the world market are still faced with getting "Chile" known, rather than its subregions, zones and specialist "areas." That will come with time, they say.

Labeling

Chile labels are ruled by a *Denominación de Origen* (DO) appellation system administered under Chilean law and related regulations. The DO name on the label defines the smallest of the defined areas for which the wine qualifies. The largest unit is a "region," of which there are five. Within a region there may be "subregions" and within these there may be "zones" or *zonas*, which in turn may encompass one or several "areas."

The area is the smallest viticultural unit allowed to carry a DO statement on the label, as long as 85 percent of the wine in the bottle comes from that area. If grapes are drawn from two or more areas within the same zone then the zone name may carry the DO descriptor. If grapes are drawn from more than one zone within a subregion or from outside specific zones within that subregion, then the subregion name may carry the DO. And thus if grapes are drawn from two or more subregions within same region, or from grapes drawn outside a subregion within the region, the regional name becomes the DO.

This has some similarities in regional terms with Bordeaux (the region), Haut-Médoc (the subregion) and Margaux (the zone), with an extra link (area) within the zone. However, in Chile some subregions have no zones and sometimes one or no areas.

Generally speaking, Chile's areas are undermarketed. Indeed, the surrounding zone or subregion is often used on the label because it is better known. This may change with time.

For wines sold on Chile's domestic market, the varietal minimum requirement, or minimum percentage of the grape variety or varieties named on the label that the wine must contain, is 75 percent; but for exported wine, the varietal minimum requirement must be in line with the importing country. Thus most exports carry a varietal minimum requirement of 85 percent of the variety or varieties named on the label.

The regulations are policed by the *Servicio Agricola Ganadero* (SAG), a department within the Ministry of Agriculture. In turn, the SAG has a group of certified, controlling private bodies that do the physical inspections and the audits of records. Wineries are required to have a full audit trail of all wines from vineyard, right through to sale, including production, any blending, and/or any wines bought in. The Internal Revenue Service also plays its part through their control on goods transported within Chile and their requirements for Bills of Lading, which must show source, variety and vintage traceable back to the winery records.

Appellations of Chile (DOs)

The system provides for five regions within which lie subregions. Subregions may contain zones and/or areas. In the listing that follows, the areas are not given as a separate entry, but are shown under the listings for the wider zones or subregions.

Aconcagua   *Region: Northern Chile*
DO
Includes the area of Marga Marga.
Bisected by the Aconcagua River, the Aconcagua region contains the subregions of Valle de Aconcagua, Valle de Casablanca and Valle de San Antonio. The interior of Aconcagua is Chile's hottest and driest region, while the coastal subregion of the Casablanca Valley is markedly cooler. The fact that Cabernet is the best known variety from Aconcagua highlights the warmth of the region. The region's name comes from the Andes highest peak, some 23,000 feet (7,000 m) high, tall enough to be seen from Santiago. A wide variety of plantings recently have provided for a spread of styles, with Chardonnay attracting attention in the cooler parts.

Atacama   *Region: Northern Chile*
DO
Between Caldera and Huasco at 27 to 29 degrees south latitude, Atacama region is outside the unofficial international "wine climate zone," which begins at 30 degrees. But with the Pacific Ocean on the west side, and the hills and the Andes on the east, Atacama retains its role of being an "extreme" wine region – although vineyards are not a key to the region's economic success as they are mostly producing table grapes rather than wine grapes. Inside Atacama are the subregions of Valle de Copiapo and Valle de Huasco.

Casablanca
DO
Refer **Valle de Casablanca.**

Central Valley
DO
Refer **Valle Central.**

Colchagua
DO
Refer **Valle de Colchagua.**

Coquimbo   *Region: South of Atacama*
DO
Within this coastal region are three subregions: Valle del Elqui, Valle del

Limari and Valle del Choapa. The low rainfall necessitates a practical irrigation system of dams and canals. Fertile soils and a high number of sunshine
hours produce bountiful crops. The wine quality is not highly recognized
here but many devoted producers are working hard to raise its image. Most
vineyards supply grapes for the production of pisco, a distilled "firewater"
made from Moscatel grapes.

Maule
DO
Refer **Valle del Maule.**

Rapel
DO
Refer **Valle del Rapel.**

Région del Sur
DO   **Region: Southern Chile**

Technically Chile's largest vineyard region, although the area within it
in which grapes are grown is quite small. The official designation reads
"… extends as far south in the Southern Hemisphere as vines can be sus-
tained." There are three subregions: Valle de Itata, Valle de Bío-Bío and Valle
del Malleco.

Valle Central
DO   **Region: South-Central Chile**

Beginning just north of Santiago and running down to where Région del Sur
takes over, Valle Central carries by far the greatest weight of Chile's industry.
The valley is between the coastal range and the Andes and thus contains
hills, flat lands and mountain sides all planted with vineyards. Subregions in
Valle Central are Valle del Maipo (widely known simply as Maipo), Valle del
Rapel, Valle del Curico and Valle del Maule.

Valle de Apalta
Pending DO   **Subregion within Colchagua**

This is a pending DO at the time of writing, and is already a very highly regarded, sloping vineyard DO for red wines.

Valle de Aconcagua
DO   **Subregion within Aconcagua**

Includes the area of Panquehue.
An interior valley to the north of Chile's vineyard regions, and the country's
hottest (and, most years, probably the windiest) growing region. The fact
that Cabernet is the best known variety here highlights the warmth of the
region. The name comes from the Andes' highest peak, some 23,000 feet
(7,000 m) high, tall enough to be seen from Santiago.

Valle del Bío-Bío
DO
Zone within Région del Sur

Includes the areas of Mulchen and Yumbel.

Southerly vineyards (at 37 degrees south latitude) with both red and white grapes that tend to be ordinary (much of the plantings are in the simple Pais variety), but the potential for development with more internationally popular varieties is well documented. Gewürztraminer and Chardonnay in particular can do well. About 70,000 acres (28,350 ha) are under vine. Without the protection of a high coastal range like that enjoyed by Maipo and Rapel in the north, Bío-Bío has harsher conditions, a little more rainfall and a few less sunshine hours. But well-managed vineyards are capable of being quality achievers.

Valle del Cachapoal
DO
Zone within Valle del Rapel

Includes the areas of Peumo, Rancagua, Rengo and Requinoa.

Mostly a red-wine zone, warmer in temperatures than Maule to the south yet elevated, with vineyards mostly above 2,000 feet (610 m). Well known for Cabernet, but other varieties including Pinot Noir are on the rise both in volume and in their claim for attention.

Valle de Casablanca
DO
Subregion within Aconcagua

Cooler coastal vineyards open to the ocean near Valpariso, where fogs and spring frosts are part of the territory. Elevated Chardonnay plantings can gain from the longer, slower ripening season.

Valle de Colchagua
DO
Zone within Valle Central

Includes the areas of Palmilla, Peralillo, San Fernando, Chimbarongo, Lolol, Marchigue, Nancagua and Santa Cruz.

Its close proximity to Santiago and natural tourist routes involving wine, cycling and mountaineering all help the industry here. Quite elevated, and although warm it can be windy. Rated wetter than the Maipo to the north. Red wines dominate.

Valle del Choapa
DO
Subregion within Coquimbo

Includes the areas of Illapel and Salamanca.

A valley around the Choapa River, this subregion is well known for the production of grapes for pisco.

Valle del Claro
DO
Zone within Valle Central

Includes areas of Pencahue, San Clemente, San Rafael and Talca.

Valle de Copiapo   ***Subregion within Atacama***
DO
Situated well north, around 27 degrees south latitude, this is a difficult sub-
region for wine, and the region is not big in vineyard area.

Valle de Curico   ***Subregion within Valle Central***
DO
Almost an extension of the Valle del Rapel, separated by the Teno River and
a chain of hills. Almost 25,000 acres (10,000 ha) here, including the zones of
Valle de Teno and Valle del Lontue where, most years, Chardonnay and Pinot
Noir work just a little better than Cabernet Sauvignon and Merlot.

Valle del Elqui   ***Subregion within Coquimbo***
DO
Includes the areas of Paiguano and Vicuna.
Part of the catchment area for making pisco, a distilled "firewater" made
from Moscatel grapes in particular. However, some of the vineyards have
planted wine grapes and the area is building a reputation accordingly.

Valle de Huasco   ***Subregion within Atacama***
DO
Situated well north, around 28 degrees south latitude, this is a difficult sub-
region for wine and not big in vineyard area.

Valle del Itata   ***Zone within Région del Sur***
DO
Includes the areas of Chillan, Coelemu, Portezuelo and Quillon.
Wind-beaten, hilly and remote, and exposed to the Pacific, with frost and
rains a continual bother for grape growing. Grapes are grown on the sides
of the Itata River, Chardonnay and Cabernet doing well in some vineyards
when the vintage conditions work out.

Valle de Leyda   ***Zone within Valle de San Antonio***
DO
Highly regarded area that is still being discovered by wine drinkers, but rates
as one of the potentially great Chilean hot spots of the future for white wines
and Pinot Noir.

Valle del Limari   ***Subregion of Coquimbo***
DO
Includes the areas of Monte Patria, Ovalle, Punitaqui and Rio Hurtado.
One of the most northerly wine regions in Chile, situated 25 miles (40
km) inland from the Pacific Ocean and about 250 miles (400 km) above
Santiago. The Limari Valley lies slightly south of the dry Atacama Desert and
is reputed to be home to the first vineyard in Chile around 1548. The *terroir*

is difficult and there is not a lot of vineyard area, but the region is rising in status.

Valle del Loncomilla   Zone within Valle Central
DO
Includes the areas of Linares, Parral, San Javier and Villa Alegre.
Loncomilla region, which has a river of the same name, is building towards steady development of its wine. A strong cooperative winery works in the region.

Valle del Lontue   Zone within Valle Central
DO
Includes the areas of Molina and Sagrada Familia.
The valley of the Lontue River is being helped by the efforts of some wine producers to become better known for their vineyards. Known for crisp, fresh whites, but also red varietals.

Valle del Maipo   Subregion of Valle Central
DO
Includes areas of Alhue, Buin, Isla de Maipo, Maria Pinto, Melipilla, Pirque, Puente Alto, Santiago and Talagante.
Named after the Maipo River, this is the best known of Chile's vineyard territories for quality red wine. Situated just south of Santiago, Maipo comprises about 13,000 acres (5,300 ha) of vineyard. More reds (Cabernet Sauvignon especially, followed by Merlot) than whites are planted here, but Chardonnay and Sauvignon have also added to the region's reputation. Maipo has a mix of hilly and flatter vineyards, the hills nicely infertile and therefore well-suited to viticulture. The area of Isla de Maipo is a small village in the Maipo Valley. Once an island, a hundred years ago as the Maipo River separated and re-joined further on, one side of the river is now dry after many earthquakes, droughts and volcanoes; it has been planted with vineyards and is gaining notoriety. Alhue is a hilly area in the southwestern part of the Maipo Valley, an area with lots of new plantings of a wide cross section of grapes, mostly red, from Carmenère and Cabernet to Syrah. Buin is going though a process of evolution as some bigger wine companies are turning their attention on this area with large plantings and quality wine in mind.

Valle del Malleco   Zone within Région del Sur
DO
Includes the area of Traiguen.
Rainy area in the southern stretches of Chile's wine lands. There are few people around this region and local industry is centered on wheat and forestry, but viticulture is rising slowly.

Valle del Maule   Subregion of Valle Central
DO
Includes the zones of Valle del Claro, Valle del Loncomilla and Valle del Tutuven.
Well south of Santiago, with the coastal ranges to the east and the Andes to the west, more than 45,000 acres (18,200 ha) of vineyards have been planted here. Within Valle del Maule are three zones, each having viticultural areas within them. With an almost Mediterranean climate, volcanic soils and a high winter rainfall, this is actually a cooler territory than wine areas to the north. Reds here are generally regarded as better than whites, but this sub-region is well respected for most of its wines.

Valle del Rapel   Subregion within Valle Central
DO
Includes Valle del Cachapoal and Valle de Colchagua.
Reds predominate in Rapel and there are more plantings of Cabernet Sauvignon than other varieties, although Sauvignon Blanc has a bountiful presence also. About 22,000 acres (9,000 ha) are under vine. It is warmer here than in Valle de Maule over the southern border, and lots of companies, including larger and foreign enterprises, are keen to exploit the subregion's potential.

Valle de San Antonio   Subregion within Aconcagua
DO
Not to be confused with a Texan city of the same name, Chile's San Antonio includes Valle del Leyda, highly regarded as a potentially great vineyard area for white wines and Pinot Noir.

Valle de Teno   Zone within Valle Central
DO
Includes areas of Rauco and Romeral.
The Teno runs from the Andes west into the Pacific. The Teno Valley is red wine country, with Cabernet, Merlot and Carmenère especially, but also with some Chardonnay.

Valle del Tutuven   Zone within Valle Central
DO
Includes the area of Cauquenes.
In this dramatic countryside shaped by historic natural forces from volcano eruptions to earthquakes, some wines of great style have been seen, and the image of this zone is beginning to grow.

CHAPTER 12

South Africa

Wine of Origin (WO)

The winds of change through South Africa have yet to stop blowing, and the country is emerging once again as a major international force, catching up on a decade in the wilderness after trade sanctions were lifted in 1993. That period left the wine industry struggling, with barrels and tanks full of wine left too long unbottled because of lack of demand, and winemakers out of the loop in terms of the ongoing international winemaking evolution.

There are still criticisms from within South Africa that wine regions and winemakers have not yet caught up, but have coasted on international interest rather than competed in a changing market. But everything is still changing in South Africa – infrastructure, policies, marketing, growth targets, subsidies, grape varieties, clones and rootstocks.

Big companies and institutions, once interrelated to a point that might be considered unhealthy in some countries, have started to restructure away from their incestuous weaving of ownership; but this has taken time, the politics of change slowing the process.

The Kooperatieve Wijnbouwers Vereniging (KWV), once a grower cooperative with broad powers to control the industry and prices, has now been restructured and refocused. The industry trading pattern has been loosened and is now more competitive. More small vineyards are establishing their own brand and reputation rather than depending on cooperatives.

The varietal mix is evolving also. From a base of around 30 percent Chenin Blanc (known locally as "Steen"), a much wider range of varieties and styles is appearing with more modern fruit statements and more in line with *terroir* considerations. There is a sustainable viticulture scheme also, with voluntary membership, to link safety, viability, longevity of the vineyards and consideration for the full environment.

Almost 300,000 acres (120,000 ha) of vineyard (including a substantial proportion for dried fruit and distillation) are situated largely in the Western Cape, the major geographical unit to the southwest of South Africa. Western Cape, with the Atlantic to the west and the Indian Ocean to the south around the Cape of Good Hope, has its share of maritime influence. Only small pockets of vines are found elsewhere in the country, but a "Northern Cape" is also recognized.

Playing their part in the *terroir* are the stark rocky ranges and mountains around and to the north of Cape Town, sometimes sheltering vineyards and sometimes shortening the amount of direct sunlight as the sun disappears as early as 4 p.m. behind some ranges. The country is warm and different, a vinous study in itself. In districts like Paarl, there are several mesoclimates, and soil types that give variety to styles and grape strengths. The barren country well to the north of Cape Town can contain a cross section of soil fertility, warmth and moisture that gives a range of environments for the grape.

Now that it has been accepted as a wine country of note, South Africa will blossom and flower. The industry has to find new markets, however, reestablishing some brands and introducing many new ones under the new industry structure. Much still needs to be done; the industry knows this and is undertaking widespread changes from the vineyard through to winemaking and international marketing.

Wine of Origin System

In 1973 the South African Wine and Spirit Board introduced a Wine of Origin Scheme, classifying wine by origin, vintage and variety. This is voluntary – wines don't have to be submitted to the tests, audits, tastings and examination, but if they do, and pass, they earn the right to the Wine of Origin (WO) seal, which guarantees the wine is 100 percent from the named area and 75 percent (exports 85 percent) from the vintage and the grape variety stated. The system was slow to find acceptance among winemakers; but with exports growing, such a marque boosts business and acceptance is increasing.

The system of physical tests – alcohol, sulfur, acid and sugar levels, plus a tasting to reject faulty wines – gives more of an authentication of contents and a safeguard against major defects than a seal of quality. The taste test by approved tasters is regarded seriously, with appeals available for wineries whose product has not been accepted as typical of the area and the grape variety or varieties that label it.

The label of successful wines carries the statement "Wine of Origin" followed by the name of the Estate, Ward, District or Region it qualified under. A sticker is also applied to the bottle capsule of approved WO wines.

By "origin" the Wine of Origin specifies as follows:

Estate: One or more vineyards, the winemaking carried out on the site of one of the specified vineyards.

Ward: A defined growing area with several vineyards (like Constantia). Some "wards" fit within a "district" but some stand alone.

District: A wider, specifically defined area of vineyards.

Region: A defined group of districts, allowing blending of wines from two or more districts.

South Africa's Wine Regions, Districts and Wards

Note: Some wards are listed below only with a reference to their "parent" district or region. For details of style in these wards refer to the parent area, as no significant style difference from the parent area has yet evolved or been noticed. Many of these wards are new vineyard areas, trying to establish identities or perhaps making the first steps towards establishing their own image separate from the parent district or region.

Aan-de-Doorns   *Ward within Worcester District*
WO

Agterkliphoogte   *Ward within Robertson District*
WO

Bamboes Bay   *Ward within Olifants River Region*
WO

Boberg   *Region*
WO
The Boberg region includes the Paarl district and a portion of Tulbagh, and Boberg may only be used for the marketing of fortified dessert wines.

Boesmansrivier   *Ward within Robertson District*
WO

Bonnievale   *Ward within Robertson District*
WO

Bottelary   *Ward within Stellenbosch District*
WO

Breede River Valley   *Region*
WO
Within Breede River Valley are the three districts of Robertson, Worcester and Swellendam. The Breede River flows into the Atlantic between Witsand and Infanta on the south coast of the Cape. Before reaching the sea, it provides water for a thirsty agricultural industry, which includes the vine. Breede River has historically produced volume rather than class; but in specific instances, strong recent efforts are being made to produce wines with class and stature. These will be more likely to carry one of the three district names above, or the names of wards within them.

Buffeljags   ***Ward within Swellendam District***
WO

Calitzdorp   ***District within Klein Karoo Region***
WO
The town of Calitzdorp overlooks the lush wine- and fruit-producing Gamka River valley. Within the hot and dry Klein Karoo region, Calitzdorp's vineyard owners see similarities in climate (and to a lesser degree soil) with Portugal's Douro Valley, the home of port. Thus the locals have sought to strengthen their production of this style of wine, to the acclaim of markets at home and abroad.

Cape Point   ***District within Coastal Region***
WO
The Cape Point district stretches down south of Cape Town towards Cape of Good Hope, on the western side of the Cape Peninsula ranges with the Constantia vineyards on the opposite side. Planted more with red varieties than white, this is a new yet already highly-regarded wine district on the rise.

Cederberg   ***Ward – not in any District or Region***
WO
In the northwest Cape, this is a small ward with a bigger future than its past. The Cederberg mountain range attracts tourists, with its crystal clear pools, ancient rock drawings and anthropological history. The rainfall from the Cederberg ranges flows into the Olifants River. The well-elevated vineyard area is small but has recently impressed with red varieties (Cabernet Sauvignon, Shiraz and Pinotage) in what had been thought of as white wine country.

Ceres   ***Ward – not in any District or Region***
WO
Approached from Cape Town through Wellington, Ceres falls just outside the Breede River and Coastal regions. Ceres was established in 1849 after the completion of Mitchell's Pass. The temperatures are extreme, and winter brings the heaviest snowfalls in the Cape; yet the fertile soils have made the area the most important deciduous fruit-growing district in South Africa. Grapes are relatively minor as a Ceres appellation.

Coastal Region   ***Region***
WO
A broad catchall region that includes the districts of Cape Point, Tygerberg, Paarl, Stellenbosch, Swartland and part of Tulbagh, and the ward of Constantia. It runs right down the Cape Peninsula to Cape of Good Hope, thus including much of the quality districts of South Africa's industry.

Constantia   **Ward within Coastal Region**
WO
One of the first-planted vineyard areas in South Africa, Constantia lies south of Cape Town, almost behind Table Mountain. It is a small area, cooled by southeasterly winds from False Bay. Mostly white grapes are here in five vineyards; Sauvignon Blanc dominates. Highly regarded.

Devon Valley   **Ward within Stellenbosch District**
WO

Douglas   **District – not within any Region**
WO
These vineyards in Northern Cape Province (to the north of Western Cape) produce big volumes of quaffing wine and a lot of dried grape products.

Durbanville   **Ward within Tygerberg District**
WO
With a long wine history, Durbanville is on the point of change from being a bulk wine provider to a more premium area, using the rolling hills and cooling summer mists at night to full advantage. Roughly equal in reds (Merlot dominates) and whites (Sauvignon Blanc dominates), but plantings continue.

Eilandia   **Ward within Robertson District**
WO

Elgin   **Ward in Overberg District**
WO
East of Cape Town among the orchards, this elevated site within Overberg does well with Sauvignon Blanc and Pinot Noir. Relatively young territory, with lots still to evolve.

Elim   **Ward – not in any District or Region**
WO
Another new area for the vine, southeast of Cape Town on the coast near Cape Agulhas, Africa's southernmost point. Regarded by critics as very promising, but so far small and still to be proven over time.

Franschhoek   **Ward within Paarl District**
WO
This was historically the "French sector," a fact that is still reflected in the winery and township names. A small area producing some wonderful wines. There are about 30 wineries within the territory, not all of which limit themselves to local grapes.

Goudini   ***Ward within Worcester District***
WO

Groenekloof   ***Ward within Swartland District***
WO

Hartswater   ***Ward – not in any District or Region***
WO
Located in the very heart of Northern Cape province, to the north of Western Cape province which produces the main bulk of South African wine. Hartswater is newly recognized as a ward and is building its own reputation.

Herbertsdale   ***Ward – not in any District or Region***
WO
Almost 350 miles (550 km) directly east of Cape Town before the city of George, Herbertsdale falls just south of the Klein Karoo region. Though a little off the beaten track, it gets a share of the wine visitors from the northern region. Only a handful of wineries.

Hoopsrivier   ***Ward within Robertson District***
WO

Jonkershoek Valley   ***Ward within Stellenbosch District***
WO

Klaasvoogds   ***Ward within Robertson District***
WO

Klein Karoo   ***Region***
WO
Within this region are the district of Calitzdorp and the wards of Montagu and Tradouw.
    Klein ("little") Karoo is in fact a large WO in terms of area but does not produce a big volume of wine. The region is an inland strip running east-west, almost in parallel with South Africa's southern coastline. Hot and dry, it is ideal for ostrich farming but something of a challenge for quality vineyards. Best known for fortified wines.

Koekenaap   ***Ward within Lutzville Valley***
WO

Le Chasseur   ***Ward within Robertson District***
WO

Lower Orange   **Ward – not in any District or Region**
WO
Like the Olifants River Region, this is a ward well north of Cape Town producing bulk wine from high yields. The Northern Cape is a province almost
three times the size of Western Cape, the province which houses the premium wine regions. The Orange River flows through it until finally forming a
border with the south of Namibia. It's hot country with big volume vineyards
of mostly white wines (reds are increasing) to supply quaffing-level quality at
a good price. However, where the river nears the Atlantic is something of a
"green" zone and agriculture does well in these conditions.

Lutzville Valley   **District within Olifants River Region**
WO
On the banks of the Olifants River, this generous wine region spreads around
Lutzville, which only became a town in the 1960s after the irrigation of the
valley was complete. There is lots of volume in these fertile conditions, the
locals declared that it has quality and raised the status of Lutzville Valley to
district level on that basis. Mostly whites are grown here, Chenin Blanc,
Chardonnay, Colombard and Semillon, plus Cabernet Sauvignon and
Pinotage.

Malmesbury   **Ward within Swartland District**
WO
The main town of the Swartland region, Malmesbury gives identity to the
vineyards around it. This is largely wheat country, but wine is building momentum.

McGregor   **Ward within Robertson District**
WO

Montagu   **Ward within Klein Karoo Region**
WO

Nuy   **Ward within Worcester District**
WO

Olifants River Region   **Region**
WO
A bulk wine area, Olifants River Region lies well north of Cape Town in a strip
about 120 miles (200 km) long, stretching up to 55 miles (90 km) inland
from the Atlantic Ocean. This regions has huge yields; about 10 percent of
the national harvest comes from Olifants River and Lower Orange, which
contain just 4 percent of the national vineyard. The district of Lutzville and
the wards of Spruitdrift, Koekenaap, Piekenierskloof, Bamboes Bay and
Vredendal are within Olifants River Region.

Overberg   *District – not in any Region*
WO

To the east of Stellenbosch and with a large part of the southern coastline, Overberg is a sizable district in land area, but wine grapes are relatively unimportant. Includes the wards of Walker Bay and Elgin.

Papegaaiberg   *Ward within Stellenbosch District*
WO

Paarl   *District within Coastal Region*
WO

"Pearl" in Afrikaans, Paarl sits about 30 miles (50 km) northeast of Cape Town. Close to Stellenbosch and a little larger, Paarl is important for quality wine and has some strong export brands. With a mix of soils and climates, a wide range of grapes and styles do well here, including botrytis-affected wine and fortifieds. Ownership changes and a shuffling of major wineries were still underway in 2003, with the intention of building on the area's qualities and strengths. Fortifieds may use the Boberg regional name. Within Paarl sit the wards of Franschhoek, Wellington and part of Simonsberg.

Piekenierskloof   *Ward within Olifants River Region*
WO

Prince Albert Valley   *Ward – not in any District or Region*
WO

Prince Albert lies 375 miles (600 km) northeast of Cape Town and a little above and outside the region of Klein Karoo, northeast of Oudtshoorn. Prince Albert is both a town and a valley at the foot of the Swartberg mountains. Pretty and popular, the town of Prince Albert sits near the Swartberg Pass through the mountains. Prince Albert ward is a remote but rising star for wine based on a fertile valley, some water and a handful of energetic growers.

Riebeekberg   *Ward within Swartland District*
WO

Rietrivier FS   *Ward – not in any District or Region*
WO

FS stands for Free State, what used to be called Orange Free State, a very hot and difficult vineyard area. But with the help of the Reed River (Rietrivier), a little wine is made along with a table grape and dried fruit industry.

Robertson   *District within Breede River Valley Region*
WO

This district is hot, dry and heavily irrigated, and produces mainly white wines. It makes up 10 percent of the national vineyard and has 25 wineries. Within Robertson District are the wards of McGregor, Vinkrivier, Eilanida, Boesmanrivier, Agterkliphoogte, Le Chasseur, Hoopsrivier, Klaasvoogds and Bonnievale. Much volume is produced, but Chardonnay has a following, along with brandy and sparkling wine. About a quarter of vineyards grow red grapes.

Ruiterbosch   Ward – not in any District or Region
WO
Previously known as Mossel Bay, this ward sits 250 miles (400 km) east of Cape Town near the famous Garden Route. South Africa's most southern WO, it faces onto the Indian Ocean. The main winery, a cooperative, is about 25 miles (40 km) inland from Mossel Bay. A ward of simple wine, mostly white, but working to develop quality.

Scherpenheuvel   Ward within Worcester District
WO

Simonsberg   Wards within Paarl and Stellenbosch Districts
On its own, Simonsberg is a vineyard area rather than a WO, falling partly in Paarl and partly in Stellenbosch districts. The respective names of these wards are hyphenated to Simonsberg (e.g., Simonsberg-Paarl) to form the WO. Vineyards are well-regarded for both their reds and their whites.
Refer **Paarl** and **Stellenbosch**.

Slanghoek   Ward within Worcester District
WO

Spruitdrift   Ward within Olifants River Region
WO

Stellenbosch   District within Coastal Region
WO
Stellenbosch lies 30 miles (50 km) from Cape Town, and is the home of many of the leading wines from a spread of soils and climates. A university town, it includes a viticulture and wine campus. This is an important and significant district in terms of quality and quantity, doing well with Bordeaux varieties and blends along with Shiraz, Pinotage and Chardonnay. Within Stellenbosch are the wards of Jonkershoek Valley, Papegaaiberg, Bottelary, Devon Valley and Simonsberg-Stellenbosch which is shared with Paarl.
Refer **Simonsberg**.

Stormsvlei   Ward within Swellendam District
WO

Swartberg   Ward – not in any District or Region
WO
Near Prince Albert town, this ward lies 375 miles (600 km) northeast of Cape Town, a little above and outside the region of Klein Karoo, northeast of Oudtshoorn. The Swartberg ("black mountain") Mountains and the Swartberg Pass that runs through them generate considerable tourist interest. Only small quantities of wine are produced.

Swartland   District within Coastal Region
WO
Just 40 minutes north of Cape Town, partly towards the Atlantic but moving inland from Darling near the west coast down to the Olifants Mountain at Porterville in the east, Swartland is a large area where wheat is almost more important than grapes! But through the district are pockets of vineyards which add up to more than 10 percent of South Africa's vineyards. The feeling is that with care, quality wine can be produced here – and work is proceeding in that direction. Swartland is known for big bold wines and fortifieds from the past, but lighter, elegant styles now being encouraged. The wards of Riebeekberg, Malmesbury and Groenekloof are within Swartland, the latter more coastal and cooled by the Atlantic.

Swellendam   District within Breede River Valley Region
Swellendam is east of Cape Town and southwest of Worcester, around Highway N2. Within Swellendam are the wards of Buffeljags (means "buffalo hunt," but the area is best known for water activities) and Stormsvlei.

Tradouw   Ward within Klein Karoo Region
WO

Tygerberg   District within Coastal Region
WO
The Tygerberg Hills near Stellenbosch received recent recognition as a district in a reshuffle of the region. Tygerberg has some highly respected vineyards and wineries but is a new and largely undiscovered name that has emerged from this reshuffle. It includes the ward of Durbanville, which is building its own reputation.

Tulbagh   District within Coastal Region
WO
About 90 miles (150 km) northeast of Cape Town, this is a district on the edge of the mountains adjacent to Swartland, further inland with the Winterhoek Mountains on three sides of it. A district with a long and colorful history, Tulbagh has some smaller wineries (around 20 including a cooperative) pursuing quality. Amidst orchards and fields of wheat, not a big quantity of wine is produced. Fortified wines may use the Boberg regional name.

Vinkrivier
WO   ***Ward within Robertson District***

Vredendal
WO   ***Ward within Olifants River Region***

Walker Bay
WO   ***Ward in Overberg District***
Southeast of Cape Town, this district surrounds the coastal town of
Hermanus, towards Elgin. An area of brave people who have established
a scattering of new wineries with small but in-demand quantities. Among
them are some joint ventures with French producers, whose first wines with
Pinot Noir and Chardonnay have looked very promising.

Wellington
WO   ***Ward within Paarl District***
Wellington, 45 minutes from Cape Town and known to rugby enthusiasts as
the "heart of Boland," offers tasty, robust, mainly red wines. This is a well-
respected vineyard area, although much is blended into wider appellations
rather than sold as "Wellington."

Worcester   ***District within Breede River Valley Region***
WO
Worcester District, further east inland from Paarl and Stellenbosch, is warm
and fertile. Nineteen cooperatives produce about 25 percent of South
Africa's total wine production from less than 20 percent of its vineyards.
Predominantly whites are planted here. It is also the most important brandy
producing area in South Africa. Small quantities of bottled wine within
the district are making a statement and considered good value. Within
Worcester are the wards of Nuy, Goudini, Slanghoek, Scherpenheuvel and
Aan-de-Doorns.

Bibliography

Wine Label Language has been a huge research job using a wide range of resources, of both fact and opinion. I have had enormous help from the following books and extend a warm thanks to the authors who have been able to provide a link, an overview, a confirmation, sometimes a little salt and pepper!

Cass, Bruce. *The Oxford Companion to the Wines of North America*. New York: Oxford University Press, 2000.

Clarke, Oz. *Oz Clarke's Wine Atlas*. London: Little Brown, 1996.

Coates, Clive. *An Encyclopedia of Wines and Domaines of France*. London: Cassell & Co., 2000.

Dominé, André. *Wine*. Konemann, 2001.

Johnson, Hugh. *The World Atlas of Wine*. London: Mitchell Beazley, 1997.

Mayson, Richard. *The Wines and Vineyards of Portugal*. London: Mitchell Beazley, 2003.

Radford, John. *The New Spain*. London: Mitchell Beazley, 1998.

Robinson, Jancis. *The Oxford Concise Wine Companion*. Oxford: Oxford University Press, 2001.

Saunders, Peter. *A Guide to New Zealand Wine 2004, 24th edition*. Auckland: Clarity Publishing & Consulting, 2004.

Young, Alan. *Wine Routes of Argentina*. San Francisco: International Wine Academy, 1998.

Young, Alan. *Wine Routes of Penedes & Catalonia*. San Francisco: International Wine Academy, 1999.

For More Information:

Clarity Publishing & Consulting
P O Box 9527
Newmarket
Auckland, New Zealand

International Wine Academy
38 Portola Drive
San Fransisco, CA 94131
USA